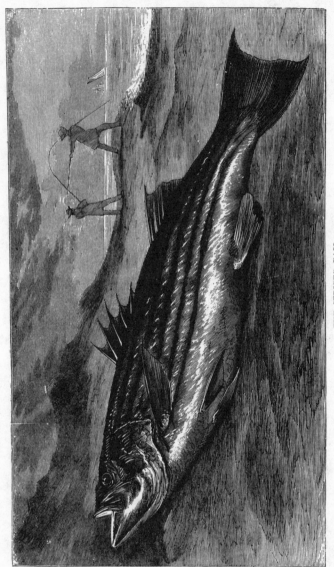

THE STRIPED BASS.
From a Painting by J. B. Stearns.

FISHING
IN
AMERICAN WATERS

Genio C. Scott

WITH NUMEROUS ILLUSTRATIONS

CASTLE BOOKS

TO

THE AMERICAN ASSOCIATIONS

FOR THE PROTECTION OF

FISH, GAME, AND BIRDS OF SONG,

THIS BOOK IS RESPECTFULLY

DEDICATED

BY

THE AUTHOR.

PREFACE.

As it might not be deemed kind in me to inflict upon the reader my thousand reasons for writing and illustrating this book with pencil sketches copied from life, I will therefore merely state that my experience of many years in the practice of the gentle art, which has led me through so many scenes of beauty and loveliness, has made me wish that all the world might learn the enjoyment conferred by the practice of angling.

I have endeavored to portray the recreations of the angler in America, with his implements and his game; adding a small tribute to the temperate and industrious class of men who follow for a livelihood the hazardous business of fishing on the broad seas.

An outline of the progress of fish-culture in Europe and America is also given, with pencil sketches illustrative of the art of hatching and rearing fishes, including stairs and fish-passes for enabling fishes to surmount mill-dams and falls.

The fishes of our coast and estuaries, and the peculiar methods adopted for their capture, form not only a sealed book to Europeans, but to those anglers in America also who confine their recreations to fresh-water attractions. Each game fish affords a distinct interest, with peculiarities worth studying.

My sketches may lack artistic finish, but possess the merit of correct outline; and in the words of Raphael, " The outline is the picture." The reader may be assured that fishing, whether for recreation or gain, entices its votaries to unexplored sources of revenue and pleasure.

I am under compliment to the following gentlemen:

Francis Francis, of "The Field," author of "Fish-culture," and "A Book on Angling," has contributed valuable suggestions, which I am pleased to acknowledge.

Isaac M'Lellan. To this accomplished poet I am indebted for contributing original verses to head my descriptions of several among our most important fishes.

Thomas Tod Stoddart, whose "Angler's Companion" has afforded me both information and pleasure.

Emile Blanchard, Member of the Institute and Professor of Natural History, Paris.

James Rennie, M.A., Professor of Zoology, King's College, London.

Walter Brackett, Artist, Boston, contributed the Brook Trout and Whitefish.

J. B. Stearns, Brooklyn, E. D. Frontispiece of a Striped Bass, photographed from a picture painted by him.

Seth Green, Mumford, N. Y. Fish-culture.

Stephen H. Ainsworth, West Bloomfield, N. Y. Natural Spawning Race.

Middleton, Carman, & Co., Fulton Market. Statistics of Fishes.

Gilbert Comstock, Fulton Market — wholesale department. Fisheries Statistics.

Andrew Clerk & Co., Maiden Lane. Samples of superior Flies and Split Bamboo Rods.

Pritchard Brothers, Fulton Street. Artificial Flies and fine Bass-reel.

Mr. M'Bride, Mumford, N. Y. Fine Trout-flies and Stained Gut Lines.

John Shields, Brookline, Mass. Specimens of excellent Trout-flies.

CONTENTS.

PART I.

COAST AND ESTUARY FISHING WITH ROD AND LINE.

CHAPTER I.

PART II.

FRESH-WATER FISHING WITH FLY AND BAIT.

CHAPTER I.

1*

PART III.

COMMERCIAL FISHERIES.

CHAPTER I.

PART VI.

SOUTHERN FISHES, AND HOW ANGLED FOR.

CHAPTER I.

PART VII.

MISCELLANEOUS FISHES, AND HOW TO TAKE THEM.

CHAPTER I.

MISCELLANEOUS FISHES.

APPENDIX.

LIST OF ILLUSTRATIONS.

Part First.

---✠---

ON COAST AND ESTUARY FISHING

WITH

ROD AND LINE.

FISHING IN AMERICAN WATERS.

CHAPTER I.
GENERAL CHARACTERIZATION OF FISHES.
SECTION FIRST.

ON seriously contemplating the immensity of the waters and their innumerable inhabitants, it is not difficult to realize the importance of these branches of material and animal nature, and I shall consider myself fortunate if able to present reasons sufficient to induce the employment of an amount of time at all commensurate with the proper division of labor between land and water for the purposes of health, wealth, and recreation.

Not only has a larger portion of this terraqueous ball been bequeathed to fish-kind than to mankind, but "its first families" were also more richly endowed by Providence in beauty of form and of coloring. There was a period when all the inhabitants of this planet were fishes, previously to the sublime moment when "GOD said 'Let the dry land appear.'" The ancients thought that the illimitable beauties of the waters were reflected in the heavens; hence they gave to the constellations the names of fishes. Thus, prior to the time of

B

Galileo, when the earth was believed to be a great flat plain, the celestial expanse was divided by them into the northern and southern constellations, the most important of which were named after their favorite fishes. Out of the legends connecting these fishes with heathen divinities there have been evolved and handed down to us, revised and improved, the signs of the zodiac, indicated in almanacs by the figure of a man, which signs are still reverently consulted by both sailor and angler; and the latter is never confident or hopeful of great success unless the sign be above the loins. Whether or no this be a superstition bequeathed by the ancients I have not bestowed much time in examining, but plead guilty to the weakness of individual faith, and feel confident of good sport only when the sign is in the head, stomach, or bowels, but never when it is in the legs or feet.

Man, from his inferior share of the earth's surface, to which little space he appears confined without a fin to dive or a wing to soar, contemplates with pleasure the scintillating heavens; while the sublime roar of the ocean, its breakers beating the shores into fragments with its billowy battalions in close lines, and in storms booming like thunder, penetrate his soul with awe and reverence at the power manifested, to which, in comparison, his own is nothing.

But it is not my intention to estimate the power of the waters, or their value for bathing or manufacturing purposes. My object is to show the reader the attractions of angling, and to convince him that wherever commensurate efforts have been made, the waters have yielded greater profits to his toil or skill than the land. I strongly advocate the maintenance of a large maritime power. As a means of wealth, the experience of the British Isles—isolated, and comparatively insignificant on the map of the world as they are— proves that nothing is too exalted to be hoped for by a liberal maritime power. But it is the wealth of the waters in the riches of their inhabitants to which I would chiefly invite attention. As to the intelligence of fishes, comparatively little is known; but I feel assured that they would rank higher in the " scale of entities" than the fourth class of *vertebrate* animals, accorded them by Cuvier, did all men of thought and science appreciate and pursue fishing.

Fishing, as a term, is general; while angling is a special kind of fishing. The word angling is supposed to have been derived from the bend of the hook, forming an .angle; but the origin or antiquity of the term is comparatively unimportant now. It is sufficient to know that the art of angling " requires as much enthusiasm as poetry, as much patience as mathematics, and as much caution as housebreaking."

That field-sports were among the earliest and most respectable pastimes of the ancients, we have abundant evidence from their poets and philosophers, such as Aristotle, Plato, Cicero, and Horace; and that angling was practiced " with much success and love of the sport is evident from the Halieutics of Oppian, the only Greek poem now extant on this subject;". but we learn from Athenæus that several other writers had written treatises or poems upon fishing some centuries before the Christian era.

"Fishing was a favorite pastime of the Egyptian gentleman, both in the Nile and in the spacious ' sluices, or ponds for fish,'* constructed within his grounds, where they were fed for the table, and where he amused himself by angling,† and the dexterous use of the *bident*, a two-pronged spear for striking two fish at a time. These favorite occupations were not confined to young persons, nor thought unworthy of men of serious habits; and an Egyptian of rank, and of a certain age, is frequently represented in the sculptures catching fish in a canal or lake, with the line, or spearing them as they glided past the bank. Sometimes the angler posted himself in a shady spot by the water's edge, and, having ordered his servants to spread a mat upon the ground, sat upon it as he threw his line; and some, with higher notions of comfort, used a chair, as ' stout gentlemen' now do in punts. The rod

* Isaiah xix., 10.   † Isaiah xix., 8.

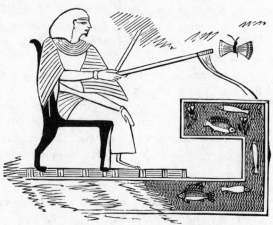

An Egyptian gentleman fishing.

was short, and apparently of one piece; the line usually single, though instances occur of a double line, each with its
own hook, which was of bronze.   In all cases they adopted a
ground bait, as is still the custom in Egypt, without any
float; and though several winged insects are represented in
the paintings hovering over the water, it does not appear
that they ever put them to the hook, and still less that they
had devised any method similar to our artificial-fly fishing,
which is still as unknown to the unsophisticated modern
Egyptians as to their fish."

Prime kinds of fishes are, and have for some years been, in
the cities of this country, expensive articles of diet.   It was
so in Athens; and the following poem, quoted by Athenæus
from "The Purple" of Xenarchus (Yonge's translation), is presented for the benefit of those who retail stale fish from stands
along the streets:

> "Poets are nonsense; for they never say
>   A single thing that's new.   But all they do
>   Is to clothe old ideas in language new;
>   Turning the same things o'er and o'er again,
>   And upside down.   But as to fishmongers,
>   They're an inventive race, and yield to none

In shameless conduct. For as modern laws
Forbid them now to water their stale fish,
Some fellow, hated by the gods, beholding
His fish quite dry, picks with his mates a quarrel,
And blows are interchanged. Then when one thinks
He's had enough, he falls and seems to faint,
And lies like any corpse among his baskets.
Some one calls out for water; and his partner
Catches a pail, and throws it o'er his friend
So as to sprinkle all his fish, and make
The world believe them newly caught and fresh."

In regard to propagating fishes, the experiments of the ancients amounted to little more than robbing the nests of herbivorous fishes, and planting the eggs in other waters; but the moderns have, within the past thirty years, invented successful theories for studying the habits of fishes at their aqueous homes, in rapid streams, or placid lakes, and deep down into the depths of old ocean. As these will be explained in this work under their appropriate titles of ancient and modern fish culture, I merely allude to them in passing as having— through their developments of the habits of fishes—opened up a subject so attractive as to have induced anglers and men of science to study more assiduously and minutely these creatures of elegant forms, whose colors vie with the rainbow, and reflect the hues of every precious stone. See their scintillant scales, their metallic rays, and colors more beautiful than are given to birds of most favored plumage! What satin sheen, aurora borealis, or heavenly sunset can vie with the prismatic colors of the living trout or the dying dolphin? What gold so finely burnished as the spots on the Spanish mackerel? or what shade of carmine so brilliant as the spots on a samlet? What so transcendently lustrous and beautiful as a fresh-run salmon?

The Spanish mackerel, salmon, and bonetta combine to form the models for the speed and beauty of our ships. Even as far back as the Revolutionary War, one of our ships was named "Bonetta." In symmetry of form and beautiful coloring, fishes stand at the head of animal creation.

SECTION SECOND.

PREREQUISITES FOR FISHING.

In order to pursue with success any branch of fishing, a knowledge of both the senses and habits of fishes is essential. Angling is one of the most ancient methods of fishing, as proven by the centre-draught hook exhumed at Thebes and at Pompeii. The hook used in China, when that realm was first discovered by the Christians, was quite similar in bend, and all of the ancient models left nothing to desire but a barb, which is the only improvement made in the shape of the common fish-hook within three thousand years. And it is worthy of remark, that the bend of the ancient hook is so like the best hooks of the present day—eminently the O'Shaughnessy and the American Kinsey, the latter known as the Pennsylvania hook—that some suspect ours to be a copy of the ancient bend, with the addition of an Aberdeen barb. Our age, however, has surpassed all others in artificial disguises to lure the finny tribes, and take the conceit out of them a thousand-fold faster than ever could the ancients.

The habits of fishes to be fished for, whether by angling or any other means, should be carefully studied. So also should their food.

> "Fish have their various characters defined,
> Not more by color than by mind."

They have their times to eat and their choice of food. Thus the trout will take ground bait or minnows as substantial food, but for his *dessert* he prefers rising to the surface for flies. That most fresh-water fishes fast previous to important rain-storms I think has become settled by the experience of old anglers. Their appetite appears to be improved by a shower. Most fishes seem to scent the approach of a shower, and know by instinct that, with the *debris* carried down by a rise in the stream, they will find a variety of food from which to select. Pike generally bite eagerly when it rains; and both trout and salmon will rise to the fly most readily during a fall of snow or rain. Indeed, a snow-storm seems to improve the appetite of some fishes; and rains which do not render the stream too turbid, but give to the water a slightly-darkened tint, do not injure it for even fishing with the fly.

It is a commonly received opinion that angling is not as good as usual during easterly winds; but this is only true when the winds cause the tides to rise so high on our coast that fishes change their feeding-grounds. Fly-fishing for both salmon and trout are, in some waters, best during an east wind. A really windy day is not good for fly-fishing. The gentle, balmy breeze, which merely produces a catspaw ripple on the surface, and carries the cast of flies out, so as to leave part of the merit for their graceful and snow-flake fall to the angler and the rod, under " a sun of mild but not too bright a beam," form a few of the conditions which give fly-fishing its peculiar zest. The prejudice against an east wind with the American angler on the Atlantic slope near the coast is probably caused by the fact that an east wind so raises the tides along the shores, and sets it back in the estuaries and creeks, as to cover shoals and islets of eel-grass. This gives fishes a wider range to forage and prospect over shallow and weedy places for shrimp, shedder and soft-shell crabs, instead of remaining in the tideway to watch for bait carried along by the current.

To converse intelligibly about fishes, it is necessary to know the names of their fins, for these give the means of locomotion; and though this work is not intended as a school-book, or to be especially scientific, yet, as all retailers of fish-stories should know enough of a fish to name its fins, I present on the following page the form of a fish, with the names of them.

The propulsive power of a fish is its tail or caudal fin. The pectorals and ventrals assist a little in speed, but more especially in turning and diving, while the anal and dorsals serve as centre-boards to a ship, to prevent leeway and being easily capsized. Of rapid swimmers in the American waters,

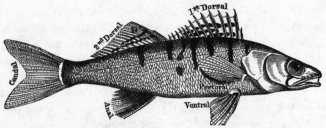

the sword-fish, Spanish mackerel, and the salmon are considered the swiftest of the forked-tails; but the salmon has not, strictly speaking, a forked tail; it is more properly crescent-shaped. Of square-tails, the brook trout, squeteague, and Southern estuary trout are the swiftest swimmers.

SECTION THIRD.

GENERAL HABITS AND SENSES OF FISHES.

Generally speaking, the principal habits and instincts of a majority of the finny armies consist in eating and protecting themselves from being eaten. The fact that over two thirds of the surface of the globe is covered by the sea, and that large parts of continents are covered by lakes, traversed by rivers, and occupied by marshes, proves the impossibility for man to have scanned with perspicacious eye the principal marked peculiarities of a majority of the families which dwell deep down in the bosom of old ocean, however industrious he may have been in such research.

Though the Chinese had understood fish culture many centuries, yet we date our practical knowledge of this art from A.D. 1837, when Mr. Shaw, of Scotland, expounded the theory in Blackwood under the head of "*The transmutation of salmon,*" and M. Gehen, of the Vosges, in France, began to cultivate fish by artificial propagation. We now know that the difference in the species of fishes is no greater than is the diversity of their habits. Some are solitary, and others gregarious; some great wanderers, others restricted within narrow limits; some are surface-feeders, like the mackerel families, others bottom fish, like the flounders and the flat-fish family ; some prefer a sandy bottom, as the kingfish, others a rocky, as the striped bass; and yet others rejoice in mud, as the eels and catfish, with the rest of the silurus family. Some fish prefer salt water, others fresh, and yet others brackish; while eels prefer to spawn in salt water and fatten in fresh, as palpably as do salmon pursue the opposite by feeding in salt water and spawning in fresh. Thus salmon, shad, and striped bass prefer to feed in salt water, spawn in fresh, and dally in brackish waters. Some fishes keep near shore, others in deep water and far from land. Bottom fishes are usually sluggish, while surface swimmers are generally active. Some lose their vitality as soon as they are landed, others live a long time out of water, and dart revengeful glances at their captors. Some can creep like the eel, others climb trees like the *anabas scandens.*

I may also state my conviction that a whale is a fish, and that the porpoise is also a fish, though members of this *genus* travel in pairs, suckle their young, of which they usually have but one at a birth, which the parent mammals guard with jealous care, making it swim between them; and if the calf is harpooned, the mother always yields her life an easy prey to the same weapon. The dudong, one of the most intelligent of mammal fishes, is the Malays' emblem of constancy in affection; and as it is said to cry when wounded by the harpoon and brought on deck, they catch the tears and bottle them as a charm, supposing that the application of a single drop will render a wife constant for life.

The black porpoise and the puffing porpus are great consumers of estuary fishes. They should not only be hunted and harpooned, but small cannon loaded with grape or canister should be so planted as to project their contents into the shoals which attempt to forage near bassing grounds. Porpoises watch mouths of rivers for salmon, and they are supposed to be the principal cause of depopulating many of the Irish rivers of that royal fish.

Either a reward should be offered by each state for every porpoise killed in its waters, or gentlemen who compose sporting clubs for taking the game fishes of our coast and estuaries should adopt a plan for capturing and driving them away. The porpoise is one of the most profitable fishes for capture, as its oil is the finest possible, and used exclusively by watchmakers.

SECTION FOURTH.

ON VISION IN FISHES.

The brain and nerves proceeding therefrom, *a, a, b, b.* The lobes of the brain in five ranks, *c, c.* The nerves of the eye, *d, d.* The nerves of smell, branching off into divergent filaments upon the nostrils, *e, e.*

That certain senses are bestowed on all animals, intellectual as well as instinctive, is too self-evident to the man of science and the angler to require proof. These animals need both, more than do those which dwell on land, to avoid being devoured, and to aid them in capturing and devouring other fishes; for their fortifications are often insecure, and they are obliged to leave them frequently, and always to commit slaughter, or to swallow minor species whole.

In order, therefore, to render this work practical, it is hardly necessary that I should dwell upon principles of science farther than to show by the nature and habits of fishes the motives by which they are actuated, which appear to be, in the main, efforts to eat and prevent themselves from being eaten. These efforts, carefully studied, will assist the angler, and the fisher with nets and other devices. Fishes are generally taken by the angler while they are foraging for food. When salmon or trout rise to feed, they may always be taken with a well-made artificial fly, presented to them gently and artistically.

The form of the eyes of almost all fishes proves them to be near-sighted. All animals with very convex eyes quickly detect the slightest motion, but lack the power to discriminate form. Hence a deer, with its full lustrous eye, will approach any still form to within a few feet of it, but at the first movement it bounds away like the wind. In addition to the eyes of fishes being convex, the density of the water—as a medium through which they see—rather shortens than extends vision. "The vision must also be farther limited from the eye being covered with the common skin of the head to protect the eyeball; and as they have no eyelids, of course the eyes never close; and, whether sleeping or waking, their vision must be indistinct." White, of Selborne, states that eyes of fishes are immovable; but it is known that those of the silver and gold fishes in glass cases turn in their sockets as occasion requires, and that, while they take little notice of a lighted candle, they will dart and appear much terrified if their glass house is touched. As fishes have no eyelids, it is difficult to discern the difference between their sleeping and waking hours. That they do not always sleep in the night is proven by the many instances when trout have been taken by rising to the artificial white miller in total darkness. M. de Blainville attributes the greatest distinctness of vision to migratory fishes, because he states their eyes are the largest; but, instead of that being so, the cod is about the only migratory fish which has larger eyes than the general run of river fishes, while those with eyes of moderate size, such as the *genus Perca* and those of the *Salmo genus*, give indications of better sight than most sea fishes. Anglers of great experience and acknowledged judgment select baits, whether live minnows, or such artificial lures as flies, squids, etc., which contrast strongly with the water and the color of the clouds. What angler does not know that a shiner is the best bait to spin for trout on a dark day?

The sight of fishes is too imperfect to enable them to decide between friends and enemies. A shadow cast upon the water ,whether by a ship, seal, otter, or an angler, frightens them. Sir Humphry Davy illustrates the truth of this theory by the anecdote that some man, while walking up Bond Street from one of the club-houses with an illustrious personage, laid a wager that he would see more cats than the prince in his walk, and that the latter might take which side of the street he liked. When they arrived at the end the prince had not seen one, while the other had counted thirteen. The explanation was that the prince had selected the shady side of the street, while the other person chose the sunny side, knowing that cats prefer sunshine. Sir Humphry, in his " Salmonia," gives the following advice to students at angling: " You have been, naturally enough, fishing with your backs to the sun, which, not being very high, has thrown the shadows of yourselves and your rods on the water, and you have alarmed the fish whenever you have thrown a fly. You see I have fished with my face toward the sun, and, though inconvenienced by the light, have given no alarm."

James Rennie, M.A., states that indistinctness in the vision of fishes proves the fallacy of the routine angler, who fancies the fishes are so well versed in colors and forms of particular flies as to refuse other sorts in some seasons and on particular days, and even at different periods of the same day. " Nothing can be more preposterous than such a notion, universal though it be among the most experienced anglers; yet this theory is founded on natural philosophy, but the result is to be accounted for on an entirely different principle."

Daniell states " there is no evidence of any fishes seeing a considerable distance, and the conduct of many of them, that are deceived by different baits prepared in imitation of their food, gives room to suspect that objects are not very distinctly perceived by them, even when near."

Light seems peculiarly attractive to fishes, as proven by their surrounding a diving-bell with a light in it. Walter Scott, in his Guy Mannering, describes the plan adopted in Scotland for attracting fishes by grates of living coal, or torches carried by the fishermen as they wade shallow streams for the purpose of spearing. When a fish is thus discovered, it remains fascinated by the glare of light, seldom makes an effort to escape, and is easily speared. This is one of the many devices by which the Indians and vagrant whites kill the salmon and trout while on their spawning-beds, both in Maine and in the dominion of Canada.

The Chinese catch fish by employing two narrow boats, with a board painted white and varnished nailed to them, so as to slope outward and almost touch the water, and so as to reflect the light of the moon. Toward these boats the fish dart, and, falling on them, are caught with ease.

From the *pretended* imitations of baits and flies for capturing fishes may be logically deduced the fact that fish are near-sighted, and do not perceive with great distinctness any minute object, however near to them. The most successful artificial baits to troll with for the fishes of our lakes and rivers are thus arranged: a pair of hooks disguised by a few gaudy feathers—bright red and white being the most successful colors—and at the shank of the hook is placed a piece of silver, brass, or copper, of oval or diamond shape, so arranged as to revolve rapidly, and appear as little like any thing living in or out of the water as possible. What is known as the common "spoon," made with swivels, and a shoulder on the shank of the hook, so as to revolve rapidly by drawing it through the water, is frequently a more captivating lure than a live fish. In trolling for bluefish, a piece of lead or bone five inches long forms a more successful lure than the sea-shiner which is its principal sustenance; and a piece of pearl, five inches long by half an inch in diameter, either round or oval, is the most attractive troll for Spanish mackerel; while a plain piece of red flannel, attached to a

piece of lead and drawn quickly through the water, is often
the only bait used by heavers and haulers for bluefish, who
fish for a livelihood.

Of artificial flies, I know that gaudy colors are generally
preferred by the black bass, while the red ibis is one of the
most attractive lures for trout in the waters of Long Island,
and in many streams and lakes remote from the sea-board.
Of course the red ibis fly does not imitate any winged insect
seen on the waters of the State of New York. Its adoption
resulted from the frequent rises of trout to the red float while
fishing with bait. I scarcely suppose a critic will be found
willing to risk his reputation, however slender, upon insisting
that a red float is the imitation of some water-fly. Anglers
generally regarded these trout-leaps at the float as a whimsi-
cal caprice of theirs while on a spree. Not so, however, with
Judge Philo T. Ruggles and Mr. Finn, two among the best
fly-fishers in the state. They concluded to test the fancy of
trout by offering them a red fly. Accordingly, Mr. Finn
bought a red ibis of a taxidermist, and employed a fly-tyer
to make it into flies. The result was a success; and the fly-
tyer, who was presented with all of them but a couple of
dozen, actually made money enough by the sale of them to
set himself up in the fishing-tackle business. Early in the
season this is the most killing fly on Long Island, though perhaps not for large fish, which generally prefer the fly made

THE ARTIFICIAL DRAGON-FLY.

of a claret body, brown mallard wing, and tail of the top-knot from the golden pheasant; or the blue professor, with blue silk body and dark gray wings.

With the following remarks from a clever writer on angling in the Encyclopædia Britannica, and a few comments on them, I shall dismiss the subject of the *vision in fishes:*

"It may be asked upon what principle of imitative art the different varieties of salmon-fly can be supposed to bear the most distant resemblance to any species of dragon-fly, to imitate which we are frequently told that they are intended?"

The reader will please compare the artificial dragon-fly with a true copy of a natural one on the following plate of natural salmon and trout flies:

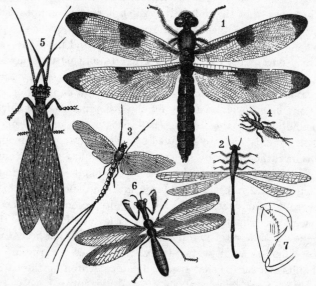

AMERICAN NERVE-WINGED INSECTS, *natural size.* 1. Common Dragon-fly.   2. The Agrion Dragon-fly.   3. Day-fly, or May-fly.   4. Grub or *larva* of the same.   5. Horned Corydalis.   6. A Mantispan.   7. The magnified claw of the Mantispan.

Of the dissimilarity of the artificial lures to the natural ones, the same may be generally said and prove true, whether for salmon, trout, maskinongé, pickerel, black bass, bluefish, Spanish mackerel, and all other surface feeders. Besides, the pretended imitations are used several months earlier in the year than nature produces their originals; thus, while the finest salmon-fishing in Europe is during the spring months, the dragon-fly is a summer insect, and rarely makes its appearance until June.

If artificial flies have no resemblance to natural ones, "how much more unlike must they be when, instead of being swept down by the current, as a real one would be, the artificial fly is seen crossing and recrossing every stream and torrent with the agility of an otter and the strength of an alligator? Now, as it is demonstrable that the artificial fly generally used for salmon bears no resemblance, except in size, to any living one; that the only tribe which it may be supposed to represent does not exist in the winged state during the period when the imitation is most generally and most successfully used; and if they did, their habits and natural powers totally prevent them from being at any time seen under such circumstances as would give a color to the supposition of the one being even mistaken for the other, may we not fairly conclude that, in this instance at least, the fish proceed upon other grounds, and are deceived by an appearance of life and motion rather than by a specific resemblance to any thing which they had previously been in the habit of capturing? What natural insect do the large flies and spoons at which sea trout, lake trout, black bass, etc., bite, resemble? These, as well as salmon, frequently take the lure far within the bounds of salt-water mark, and yet materialists know that no such thing as a salt-water fly exists. Indeed, no true insect inhabits the sea. What species are represented by the palmer, or by three fourths of the dressed flies in use? An artificial fly can, at the best, be considered only as the representative of a natural one which has been drowned, as it is impossible to imitate the dancing or hovering flight of the insect over the surface of the stream, and, even with that restricted idea of its resemblance to nature, the likeness must be scarcely perceptible, owing to the difference of motion and the great variety of directions in which the angler draws his flies, according to the nature and locality of the current and the prevailing direction of the wind."

The sight of fishes is like that of all animals with round and convex eyes. If the angler will stand quite still in the water, fish will not fear to congregate about him, or to flap his legs with their fins; but with his slightest motion they dart to their hiding-places. The convexity of the eye produces short-sightedness in man as well as in quadrupeds, birds, and fishes. The round eye is inferior to the almond-shaped for distinguishing form : thus round-eyed animals and fishes mistake a man for an inanimate object, and, from their shortness of vision, approach him without fear. These general and specific reasons convince me that fishes are short-sighted, and that, while quick to detect action, they are slow to distinguish form.

SECTION FIFTH.

ON TASTE IN FISHES.

The sense of taste in both birds and fishes, which subsist on similar food, is less acute than in other animals, a circumstance strongly indicated by the hard, gristly texture of the tongue when it exists, which it may scarcely be said to do in all fishes, though it is very distinct in the *Cyprinidæ*, and rather less so in the *genus Salmo*.

Dr. Rennie states that numerous experiments made by him on birds whose food consists of small fruit and insects, which they swallow without breaking, leads him to conclude that they choose some and reject others, not by taste, but by touch, probably aided by smell; and he adds, "I have no doubt it is the same with fishes; at least it is obvious, from their so generally swallowing their food without chewing or bruising it, that, even if they possessed acute taste, it could not aid them in the discrimination."

C

The large tongue in the carp may have been providentially furnished to give it a more acute taste for preventing it from being poisoned by eating water hemlock, or other deleterious plants, as it is known to feed on water-plants. That all fish are not thus provided with taste sufficiently acute to enable them to reject what is poisonous, appears from the practice of poachers in poisoning fish by pulverizing and making a paste of fisher's berries, or *Cocculus indicus*, which they form into balls about the size of peas and cast into the water. Fish greedily swallow these, and, becoming intoxicated or palsied thereby, float to the surface of the water and are easily caught, or soon die. Chub and dace are ready victims to this device, as are also the black bass, Oswego, yellow, white, rock, and all the varieties of lake and river bass. It is always dangerous to purchase fish out of season any where; but residents of cities should be especially careful who they purchase from, and the safest houses are those which deal largely with fishing firms of established reputation.

Teeth of fishes appear destined more especially for laying hold and detaining their prey than for chewing. With this view they are bent inward, like tenter-hooks, so that fishes, howsoever small and slippery, are forced back into the gullet, and their escape or return prevented. It is no doubt with the same design that the throats of many fish are studded with what M. Bory St. Vincent terms a pavement of teeth. Such fishes as have teeth thus placed far back on the palate and upper part of the throat, while in their jaws they have none, are termed by anglers "leather-mouthed," but technically *malacostomata*.

Anglers of the British Isles reckon among the principal of leather-mouthed fishes the minnow, gudgeon, roach, loach, bleak, chub, daces, barbel, bream, rud, tench, carp, and other minor fishes. The salmon and the pike have teeth in the jaws and in all parts of the mouth, and the perch in all parts of the mouth except the tongue. The sturgeon and sucker, again, have no teeth whatever.

The division of anglers' fishes into such as are and such as
are not leather-mouthed may be important to the young angler, as different management is required in playing each.
Old anglers considered such fishes leather-mouthed as have
their teeth in the throat. Hooks seldom part their hold from
the mouths of such fishes, which are not generally regarded
as gamy, though good sport for ladies and youth. But the
contrary is the case with the striped bass, squeteague, pickerel, maskinongé, perch, and most game fishes which are
white-meated. These have a bony mouth, and not much
flesh or skin to hold a hook; therefore you are never sure
of landing these fish unless you play them so lightly as not
to permit them a foot of slack line, except, perchance, they
have gorged the hook.

That water-grasses and some other plants are partly the
food of leather-mouthed fishes, especially of the carp *genus*,
is unquestionable; and in the Orient herbivorous fishes are
considered the most delicate and highly prized. But when
they feed on liver, brewers' grains, boiled barley, split peas,
and the like, they probably mistake these for the eggs or cocoons of water animals, inasmuch as they could not procure a
supply of these except by rare accident. That some fish may
feed on the seeds of such plants as are scattered about the
water is not improbable, and it may have been from observ-
ing this that it is recommended by Lebault and Debraw, after removing the fish to let fish-ponds dry, to sow them with
oats or other grain, and, when it is ripe, to let the water
again into the pond, and bring back the fish to feed. Bowlker
remarks that carp will eat barley, wheat, or oaten bread,
while tench and perch will not touch it. Of course perch
prefer meats to vegetable diet; but as the tench differs with
the carp upon vegetable diet, both being vegetarians, it
proves that fishes have discriminative tastes.

Most leather-mouthed fishes like both vegetable and animal diet, and the carp is said to devour young eels, frog-
spawn, fish-roe, and young fishes, including its own species,

as well as water insects, which are the staple food of every
kind of fish from the minnow to the salmon; every thing that
lives and moves being swallowed without—so far as has been
found—any discrimination of species or much nicety of selection.

SECTION SIXTH.

ON SMELL IN FISHES.

Smelling in land animals is immediately connected with
breathing, and we can not easily conceive how smell is produced except by a current of air, in which odoriferous particles are diffused, passing through a moistened channel, as was
so admirably described by Schneider two hundred years ago;
but in fishes which do not breathe, smell can not be thus produced, though there can be no doubt of their being endowed
with this sense.   Water, indeed, is as good a medium for dif-
fusing odors as air, and there is the less necessity for a current of this being produced through the nostrils, as fish move
about so constantly through the water.   Their nostrils, therefore, are generally large, but imperforate backward; that is,
they do not communicate with the throat; but in some fishes,
such as rays and sharks, the nostril opens by a considerable
space into the mouth, and through this a current of water
may probably run.   M. Dumeril and the Rev. W. B. Daniell
think that, from the structure of the nostril and the want of
an aerial medium for odors, fishes can not smell at all, and
that their nostrils perform a function similar to taste; but to
a late professor of zoology in King's College, London, this
supposition appears improbable.   From all that I have discovered, I feel confident that a majority of anglers and men
of science believe that smell in fishes is quite palpable.   Smelling substances for enticing fish to the hook are recommended
by too many honorable names to leave a shadow of doubt
upon the subject.   Walton, for example, recommends numerous strong-smelling pastes for attracting fish to the bait, stating that " old Oliver Henley, now with God, a noted fisher

both for trout and salmon," contended in favor of acuteness
in the smell of fishes. In an old volume on "The Secrets of
Angling," by J. Davors, published in 1813, I find the following:

> "To bless thy bait and make the fish to bite,
> Lo! here's a means, if thou canst hit it right:
> Take gum of life, well beat and laid to soak
> In oil well drawn of ivy which kills the oak.
> Fish where thou wilt, thou shalt have sport thy fill;
> When others fail, thou shalt be sure to kill."

M. Chars, who was apothecary to Louis XIV., composed a
perfume which attracted all kinds of fresh-water fishes by the
use of cat's fat, heron's grease, the best asafœtida, Egyptian
mummy finely powdered, aniseed, camphor, galbanum, Venice turpentine, and civet. These he made into the consist-
ence of thin ointment by means of oil of lavender, of aniseed,
and camomile, which may be preserved for a year or two if
kept where the air is excluded. The bait and about eight
inches of line are directed to be anointed with this to attract
fish.

Of the numerous scented baits recommended, Walton wrote
in favor of petroleum, and Daniell suggested that tar is most
attractive in the composition of a scented ointment for bait.
But the most fascinating of such pastes for fresh-water fishes is
that composed of the roe of salmon; and I should be opposed
to its use if millions of salmon-eggs were not annually wasted
along most of the salmon rivers; and it is to be hoped that,
by the means of science, some successful theory may soon be
adopted for turning this seed into the waters to restock them,
for it is morally revolting to an angler to contemplate the
great loss by the depletion of the waters from the waste of
ova. While the wholesale waste continues, those who desire
to make bait from the roe of fishes should sprinkle it with
salt, and then put it down in a pot in alternate layers with
wool. Rev. W. B. Daniell advised the taking of a pound of
roe in September, and, after boiling it fifteen minutes, beat it
in a mortar until sufficiently mixed with an ounce of salt and

an ounce of saltpetre, the membrane in which the spawn is contained being carefully picked out; it is then packed in jars and covered closely; in that way it will keep good for many months.

It is suggested that roe of other fishes would do as well as that of salmon—such as herrings, because the smell, which seems the chief attraction, is quite similar. A paste made in the same way from shelled shrimps is also attractive. Mussels and putrid meat attract eels, obviously in consequence of their odor.

Independently of these and all other ascertained facts respecting smell in fishes, the anatomy of the head proves that the nerves of smell are large, and thus establish conclusively the fact that fishes are gifted with the sense of smell.

SECTION SEVENTH.

ON HEARING IN FISHES.

Fishes hear. Of this I feel quite sure, without the story of Amphion and the Dolphins, or of the auld Scottish harper Glenkindie, who—as related in verse—"harped a fish out o' the sa't water."

Ælian tells us that the chad is allured by the sound of castanets, and in Germany they take these fishes with nets to which bows of wood hung with little bells are attached in such manner as to chime in harmony when the nets are moved. These fish, it is stated, will not attempt to escape while the bells continue to ring. On the Continent of Europe people are in the habit of calling the gold fishes, as well as other fishes in ponds, to be fed at the sound of a bell.

Professor Bradley states that in Rotterdam, at a preserve of carps owned by Mr. Eden, he saw them fed. "The gentleman having filled his pocket with spinach-seed, conducted me to the side of the moat, where we stood mute for some time, the better to convince me that the fish would not come until called. At length he called in his usual way, and immediately the fish gathered together from all parts of the pond in such numbers that there was scarcely room for them to lie by one another, and then he threw some spinach-seed among them, which they devoured very greedily. This satisfied me that fishes have the sense of hearing." Sir Walter Rogers, an English gentleman, had a pond of pikes which members of his household called together at pleasure; and as carnivorous fishes are more wild and untamable than are those which feed on herbs, it offers the most palpable proof that fishes hear.

M. Lebault advises fish culturists not to permit shooting about the ponds for wild-fowl, etc., as it frightens, injures, and destroys the fish. This opinion is also entertained by celebrated physiologists; and John Hunter, who describes the ear of fishes—always, he says, important—as consisting of a gristly substance, very hard and firm in parts, and in some species crusted over with a thin plate of bone, so as not to permit it to collapse. The ear of fishes he also remarked to possess the singular peculiarity of increasing with the size of the individual, whereas in quadrupeds it is nearly as large in the young as in the full-grown animal.

"When in Portugal," said Dr. Hunter, "in 1762, I observed in a nobleman's garden near Lisbon a small fish-pond full of different kinds of fishes. Its bottom was level with the ground, and was made by forming a bank all round, with a shrubbery close to it. While lying on the bank seeing the fish, I desired a gentleman who was my companion to go behind the shrubs (that there be no reflection from the flash) and fire his gun. The moment the report was made the fish seemed universally affected, for they vanished immediately, raising, as it were, a cloud of mud from the bottom. In about five minutes afterward they began to appear and swim about as before."

The discussions of Dr. Munro, Geoffroi, Comparetti, Scarpa, Weber, and De Blainville, may be referred to, as their works fully settle the question in favor of hearing in fishes. Weber discovered a communication between the ear in fishes and the swim-bladder, the air contained in which is probably affected by sound; and De Blainville expresses his astonishment at the magnitude of their nerves of hearing.

It is superfluous to multiply examples of fishes coming when called by a whistle or a bell. I have frequently called them to me by whistling for them at various fountains and ponds in France, where the chief of the Fisheries Commission, M. Coste, is stated not only to contend that all fishes hear, but that some of them talk! From all the evidence *pro* and *con*, I am convinced that fishes possess the sense of hearing.

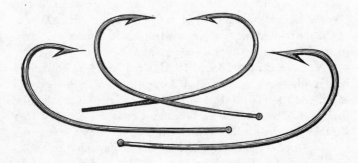

CHAPTER II.

FECUNDITY OF FISHES.

FIRST. Mammalia, including whales, porpoises, and all fishes which bring forth alive and suckle their young, whether herbivorous or carnivorous, seldom have more than one or two young at a birth, which sailors term calves.

Second. The families of which the salmon and trout are the heads are called by naturalists the *genus Salmo*. These fishes have the palpable mark of an adipose second dorsal fin; their meat is of a tint between mallow and pink, and they are regarded by anglers and epicures as the highest game and most luxurious fishes of the oviparous class, or those fishes which replenish their species by laying eggs, which are vivified by the milt of the male, and then, after a time, the eggs hatch in the water. This process is common to all egg-laying fishes; but, while eggs of the *salmo genus* require from three to four months to hatch, those of the *clupea genus* hatch in as many days. Seth Green hatched shad artificially on the Connecticut River within forty hours from the time the ova and milt fell into the hatching-boxes in the stream—being the main current of the river—and not in boxes so placed as that a stream should run through or over them, but anchored so as to float in the current of the river, submerging a sufficient portion of them for keeping the eggs covered with water to a sufficient depth. A salmon is supposed to lay a thousand eggs for every pound the mother fish weighs, consequently they average from ten to thirty thousand for each pair.

Third. Included in this class are all the oviparous tribes but those of the *genus Salmo*. The number of eggs in the roe of some of these fishes is so great as to appear almost incredible. While the carp and the sturgeon produce from half a million to a million and a half, the celebrated Dutch naturalist Leuwenhoeck reckoned that the codfish contains over nine millions of eggs. This estimate was based upon weighing accurately a small part of the roe and counting the eggs, then weighing the remainder, and estimating the whole from the part counted. Without doubt the fecundity of all the food-fishes of the sea is beyond human estimate; so that, if all the spawn should be fructified by the male fishes, the vast body of fishes would, within a few years, become too great for the waters to contain.

SECTION SECOND.

VORACITY OF FISHES.

The innumerable shoals of young fishes constitute the chief part of the food for larger ones, and even those full grown often meet in fierce combat, when the one which has the widest throat comes off victorious by swallowing his opponent. Fish, being cold-blooded animals, are not susceptible to an acute sense of pain; thus it does not hurt an eel much to be skinned, and a shark has been observed to seek prey for some time after he was split open and entirely eviscerated. The prettiest and most playful of fishes, almost domesticated in private ponds, do not fail occasionally to devour such members of their own family as venture near enough. Sir William Jardine states that "the lake trout are very rapacious, and, after attaining the weight of three or four pounds, feed almost exclusively on small fish, not sparing even their own young."

This being true of the finny tribes generally, how malapropos is the sympathy extended for them by good souls who do not understand the savage character of the objects of their solicitude. Such was the poet Dr. Walcott, author of the following verses:

"Why flyest thou away with fear?
Trust me, there's naught of danger near:
        I have no wicked hook,
All covered with a smarting bait,
Alas! to tempt thee to thy fate,
        And drag thee from the brook.
Oh harmless tenant of the flood,
I do not wish to spill thy blood;
        For nature unto thee
Perchance has given a tender wife,
And children dear, to charm thy life,
        As she hath done to me.
Enjoy thy stream, oh harmless fish,
And when an angler, for his dish,
        Through gluttony's vile sin
Attempts—a wretch—to pull thee *out*,
God give thee strength, oh gentle trout,
        To pull the rascal *in!*"

Instances are common of fishes following a hooked one, and, while it is being played by the angler, biting pieces out of it, and sometimes swallowing it, so that both are landed. It may be readily inferred from this that small fish form attractive bait. Fish evince no mercy for any living thing which inhabits the waters, and most of the angler's fishes feed readily on their own broods. As fish are generally attracted by the sight or smell of blood, red feathers, burnt wool, and scarlet braid, etc., are found to fascinate them when attached to trolls; especially is this proven to be the case in trolling for bluefish, black bass, and maskinongé.

I therefore conclude that, as the principal food of all fishes consists of animals and animalculæ, with water-insects, and the spawn deposited in the waters, these last seeming to form the dainties most eagerly sought by them, so the unlimited voracity of fishes, which has no counterpart in any other branch of animal creation, may be one of the means wisely ordered to check an excessive multiplication; and that their extraordinary fecundity is probably a provision of nature for supplying an adequate amount of food, upon the same principle that land insects are so greatly multiplied probably for supplying food to birds.

SECTION THIRD.

TIMES OF FEEDING AND HAUNTS OF FISHES.

Most fish are said to be night-feeders, yet all of them feed more or less in daytime. Like spiders, all of which feed in the night, and are tempted to come abroad when the weather is so cloudy as to resemble twilight, so also the fishes, with this farther peculiarity, that a turbid state of the water from recent rains may so dim the light that they will bite when the sun shines brightly.

When the weather is bright and the water clear, most fishes keep their places of retirement, some among reeds and other water-plants, some under banks or ledges of rock, lurking in deeper and deeper water as the weather becomes warmer, so that the feeding-level for lake trout, which is often from four to eight feet in early spring, is found from fifty to a hundred feet below the surface in July and August. River fishes seek the shade of overhanging trees; some under stones; some squatting close to the ground over springs, sand, or in the sludge at the bottom of the water. In different waters, however, there are peculiarities of currents, eddies, and pools that fish are fond of haunting, concerning which no practical rule of general utility can be laid down. Waters, to be most successfully fished, must be first understood by fishing them.

STRENGTH AND PROPULSIVE POWER.

The true indication of a fish's strength is found in the shape of its head and shoulders back to the first dorsal fin, while its speed or propulsive power is shown by its shape from the front of the second dorsal and anal fins to the end of the tail, and the shape of this caudal continuation. Of the forked-tail, it has already been remarked that the swordfish and salmon are supposed to be the most rapid swimmers, while of the square-tails the brook trout and squeteague are supposed to propel with the greatest velocity. Among fishes

which unite the greatest velocity with the greatest degree of
strength must be reckoned the whale; for, struck with a harpoon or spear with a line attached, the leviathan of the waters
darts down into the deep with such velocity that if the line
were to entangle it would either be broken or the boat would
be capsized.   Upon the act of striking a whale, therefore, one
man is stationed to give his whole attention to the line running off clear, while another is employed to pour water continually on the wood over which the line runs, to prevent ig-
nition by friction.   The angler knows that the sheepshead
has this power of diving with the velocity of lightning; so
have all fishes which are swift and wide compared to their
length.   In diving or darting upward, the swim-bladder is a
great assistance, as it is found to be compressed while the
fish is at the bottom, and expanded when the fish is on the
surface of the water.   Probably the salmon and the bluefish
unite the greatest amount of muscular strength to the greatest power of propulsion.   Other fishes of our coast, such as
the Spanish mackerel, bonetta, cerus, and the horse mackerel,
add to the muscularity of the salmon and bluefish the propulsive power of the swordfish and the dolphin.   The pectorals,
ventrals, and anal fins assist the fish in maintaining its balance or level position of body.   In experimenting upon the
use of fins, Professor Borelli, of Naples, ascertained that after
clipping off the pectoral, ventral, and anal fins of fishes, all
their motions became unsteady, and they reeled from right to
left, and up and down, in such irregular manner as to prove
that they were left at the mercy of their voracious neighbors
of the deep.

CHAPTER III.

COAST AND ESTUARY FISHES.

As the fishes of the Atlantic coast of North America, including those of the estuaries and tidal waters which debouch along our coast, are more numerous, and include a greater variety for both the angler and the commercial fisherman than do the finny tribes of the coasts of any other country, and as nearly every American angler of a tidal river regards the striped bass as the fish of fishes *par excellence* to be angled for, I trust that I shall be pardoned for placing this beauty first on the list, and showing some of the artistic ways for taking him.

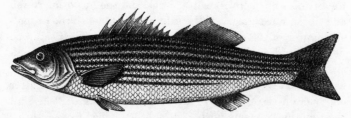

THE STRIPED BASS.

This fish, so beautiful and gamesome, is peculiar to the tidal waters and estuaries of the rivers which empty on the coast of the Atlantic from Portland to Norfolk. The striped bass is known farther north and south, but it exists in the most perfect state in the rivers and along the coast between the points named. It affords good sport with light tackle when its weight is but half a pound; and it tries both the metal and skill of an angler after it rises to the ponderous importance of ten pounds, though it is said to attain to the

weight of nearly a hundred.   I have captured but one which
weighed over forty pounds, although I have angled for them
every season for the past thirty years.   It is great game
when weighing any where from ten to thirty pounds.   In
muscular power the striped bass equals the salmon, but it
lacks the caudal power for leaping, which is so palpable in
the form of a salmon, back of its adipose fin, including its
crescent-shaped tail.

This fish is known south of New Jersey as the rockfish;
but as no two ichthyologists agree upon a classical name for
the fish, it had probably best be called the name by which it
is known where the greatest numbers are taken, and there it
is known only as the STRIPED BASS; and as there is no other
fish which at all resembles it, there is no chance of mistake.
It approximates the *Perca genus*, the front dorsal fin being
composed of seven spinous or spiked rays, and having two
nearly concealed spines.   Its scales are rather large, and of
metallic lustre; gill-covers serrated and edges sharp.   The
color of the back is a blending of black, blue, and green, lighting to bluish-gray at the sides, and to a satin white belly.
The longitudinal stripes are usually seven or eight in number,
and are like narrow black braids, sparkling with silver or
diamonds and emerald.   Its symmetry, marks, and satin sheen
render it one of the most picturesque and interesting fishes in
the world, independent of its great game, generous play, and
luxury as a dinner fish.

The striped bass is eminently domestic in his habits.   He
is not given to wandering or vagrancy.   He is generally to
be found at home and in good condition.   The female deposits her eggs in fresh and brackish waters, but never in the
sea.   In November the bass shoal and congregate in brackish
water-ponds, or back waters of tidal rivers, or in the bays and
bayous of rivers which have an outlet to the sea, after which
time it will not take bait until the following spring, after
having spawned and returned to active waters.   The ponds
formed by the back water of the Seconnet River were, a few

winters since, so full of striped bass that the fish were discovered by their dorsal fins in the ice, where they had been frozen by too close packing. The ice was cut, and hundreds of cart-loads were pitched out with forks and taken to market.

Striped bass will live and increase when confined to fresh water, but its shape then becomes changed, and instead of its symmetry and lustre when having access to both fresh and salt waters, it becomes more chubbed, and its colors less scintillant. This I discovered in those I took in the upper part of Lake Ontario, and it corroborates the opinion which I have heard expressed by other anglers and fish-culturists.

These fish delight in rocky shoals, among which they flap their tails and rub their scales as they prospect for *crustacea*, of which shedder and soft-shell crabs they consider great delicacies. Their great power and swiftness enable them to forage with impunity for disabled menhaden, spearing, shrimp, crabs, shedder lobsters, etc., among the breakers, as they lash and lave the rocky shores of our coast; and it is at such times, when the sea is agitated, that casting for them from the rocks with rod, and reel, and menhaden bait, that the sport is rendered more pleasingly exciting and attractive than angling for any other game fish.

The angler pursues many methods for capturing this beauty of the estuary, the chief of which are still-baiting from an anchored boat along the edge of the tide, trolling with live squid (small cuttle-fish), and casting with menhaden bait—but without sinker—into the surf of a rocky beach, along the shores and islands from New York to Martha's Vineyard.

SECTION SECOND.

ANGLING FOR STRIPED BASS.

In order that the reader may proximately realize the character of the striped bass as a game fish, I propose taking him with me on several excursions after the lustrous beauty. And, first, we will try him in the vicinity of New York. The weather and tide are favorable, and the moon is right for giving fish an excellent appetite and great activity. Fishes in waters near the ocean bite best in the first quarter of the moon, while those which are up rivers and creeks, near fresh water, bite best at full tides, and immediately after a "nor'-easter," when the wind, having backed round by the south has settled in the northwest. You may prove these facts without going a dozen miles from the metropolis; and I have always noticed that it is better fishing in " the Kills" and at the hedges of Newark Bay, as well as at those in the lower part of the Bay of New York, when the tide is low, while the fishing at King's Bridge and Spuyten Duyvel is best at very high tides. The only exception to this rule is applicable to reefs and low rocky shoals, where bass forage most during high tides.

As we are to try the bass to-morrow, suppose we make a day of it? Well, that being agreed to, we will first try Harlem River, or the creek at King's Bridge. Being an angler, you of course know that the baits here are confined to shrimp early in spring and late in autumn; to soft-shell and shedder crab in the summer and until the middle of October; after which soft-shell clam for the English Neighborhood Bridge, and shrimp, with an occasional shedder lobster, serve as baits in the vicinity of New York, except for trolling in Hell Gate, where we use squid; and for fishing in the surf at Newport, and along the coast generally, the menhaden is preferred. Shad roe is frequently recommended for bass bait. I once tried it at Saybrook, near the mouth of the Connecticut River, where the bass were said to bite it unconditionally; but, though I stood on the platform and fished from it, I did not capture a single fish. It was not because the bass did not like the bait, but rather that the great depth of water and strength of tide obliged me to fish with a heavy tracing sinker, and the fish stole my bait before it settled on the bottom, because I was not prepared with the means of porous muslin wherein to tie the bait over the hook. I have never

D

tried the bait since, and though it is very attractive, it is unpleasant to use. The thousands of barrels of shad cured
there every shad season, when the roe is thrown into the
river, attracts myriads of striped bass every May and June,
causing a regret that Seth Green could not use the roe of
this delicious esculent for restocking the river as he does at
Holyoke.

Of course tackle is of the utmost importance. As we are
to angle for small bass, with crab and shrimp bait, we will
rig light, and as represented by the following engraving :

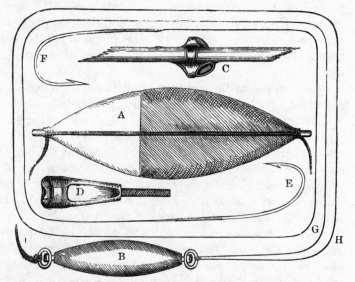

TACKLE FOR TAKING SMALL BASS.

A. Solid Cork-float. B. Swivel Sinker. C. Piece of the top of Rod, showing the
double guides ; on one side bell-metal, and the other agate. D. Agate or Carnelian tip to screw into the top of the rod. E. Upper Hook, rigged a foot above the other hook for shrimp. F. Lower Hook, for baiting with shedder crab. G, H. Single-
gut Leader. I. Line ; of either linen twisted or silk braided ; very small, no larger
than for trout, but from 300 to 400 feet in length.

The reel should be a multiplier, without any stop, check,
or drag ; it should be of brass, German silver, or bell-metal,
run on steel or agate pivots, and with a balance crank.

The rod for this style of fishing should be from 9 to 11

feet long, bearing in mind that a short, stiff rod is the best
to cast with, but not so good to play a fish with light run-
ning-tackle. Of course the size of float and weight of sinker
will be changed to suit the waters and the tides.

> "See that all things be right,
> For 'twould be a spite
> To want tools when a man goes a-fishing."—COTTON.

You perceive that I have selected one hook with an
O'Shaughnessy bend (E), and the other (F) an Aberdeen.

Well, brother angler, a night of sound sleep, and our incomparable breakfast at the Astor, with our drive over the
Bloomingdale Road this beautiful morning, has so enlivened
me to a sense of the beautiful that I feel assured we shall
have good sport to-day, and enjoy it. This is King's Bridge,
the name of the most spicy and succulent oyster that ever
graced the *cuisine* of a Dorlon. Our horse will be well cared
for at this hotel, for the host—an admirable caterer—appre-
ciates anglers.

We will first see what sport there is to be had at the east
bridge, where we will joint our rods, and rig sinkers and floats
according to the movement of the tide. I perceive that the
tide is just on the turn to flood. Rig light for half an hour,
and then change to heavier sinker and larger float. I like
bridge fishing, for, after making a cast, you may humor your
line so as to lead the bait in the most angling manner from
current to current; and then, in striking at a bite forty yards
off, there is so much sport in playing your fish until you get
him into the slack water formed by the piers of the bridge;
and, being from 8 to 10 feet above the water, you generally
fasten the fish at the first bite. Strike! You've hooked him!
There! give him play, but feel his weight, and make him contend for every foot of line you give him, or he will take the
whole without exhausting himself, and you will lose him.
Do not permit him to run back on you, for that is a favorite
dodge of these striped sides to get slack line, and enable them
to dislodge the hook. Keep your rod up nearly perpendicu-

lar, giving him the benefit of its spring, for he is bony-mouth-
ed, though the teeth in his upper jaw are too small and short
to bite or even chafe off a silk-worm gut snell. Keep your
fish out of the swiftest of the tide, and, after playing him until he succumbs from exhaustion, land him on the shore, for
he is too heavy to lift upon the bridge. Well done! Now
bait quickly and cast for another. You perceive that at the
foot of the rapid tide the bass lie in wait for bait, for our
floats dip at that place. But the fish move away from there
after the tide gets running its full strength, and an hour is all
of first-rate fishing we may expect in one tide, therefore it is
necessary to be active in baiting and expert at casting and
playing a fish, always using shrimp on the upper hook and
shedder on the lower one, when you use two baits at a time
in this style of fishing. Now, as the tide has become too
swift for float-fishing, just step into this boat, and we will row
down to the first island in the creek, seventy-five rods beyond
the west bridge, and try Spuyten Duyvel Creek. The fish
are smaller here, but they bite more generously. I took 174
here in one day, and yet Judge Brevoort, my companion,
beat me by one fish. See! one on each hook at every cast!
Say you not that angling for small bass with light tackle
forms a pleasing excitement? Well, having fished out the
tide, suppose we return to the hotel and take our vehicle for
home? This place is accessible by public conveyances over
several routes, but as it is only eleven miles from the City
Hall, I prefer to drive out. We have taken between thirty
and forty bass which scale from half a pound to a pound
each—only three two-pound fish and one three-pounder; and
this may be regarded as an average morning's sport.

SECTION THIRD.

TROLLING IN HELL GATE.

You doubtless perceived, brother angler, that the sport
which we yesterday enjoyed at King's Bridge might be
practiced and greatly relished by ladies. Many ladies of

New York and its suburbs are experts at casting a fly for trout or a bait for bass; and, in my opinion, they lend one of the principal charms to ruralizing. I do not like the pent-up, hide-bound, cynical geniuses of the Diogenes quality, nor yet of those bachelors whose rectangular apartments each side of a hall in our hotels are not inappropriately consider-ed by some as stalls for the stray oxen of society. I agree with Brother Lathy that

"No scenes more suited are to themes of love,
  Than whilst on rivers' banks you fish and rove;
  T' instruct the fair the happy lover tries,
  And, grateful, she rewards him with her eyes.
  No longer, then, our angling sports disdain,
  Since Venus sprung from Ocean poets feign,
  Rising all beauteous from the briny main:
  As, of our grief, do thou partake our pleasure—
  Our life, our heart, our soul, our earthly treasure!"

When you decide to troll for a day over the tumultuously-seething and hissing waters of Hell Gate, where an oarsman must know the tides and shoals to keep his boat right side up, you will require heavier tackle, and will therefore select them from the plate of "implements for angling in lakes, bays, rivers," etc., on the following page.

Select a rod from 8 to 9 feet long, like A, B, C, in the en-graving. Let it taper regularly and be rather heavy. The butt and second joint should be made of ash, and the top of lancewood. Bell-metal top and guides are best for mount-ing a trolling-rod, while agate or carnelian are best for the purpose of casting a long distance, as the friction is less on jewels than on metals. The guides for all kinds of bass angling should be large enough to pass a knot in the line through them. In ringing rods for salmon and trout, the rings should be diminished in size from butt to tip, as the rods taper; but such is not the case with bass guides, all of which should be equal in size and shape, and polished for the line to run smoothly. Large guides are a modern invention. About ten years ago I was fishing at West Island—that par-

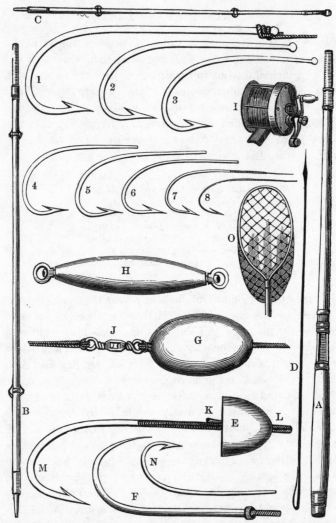

A, B, C. Butt, middle joint, and top of a Brass Rod. D. Baiting Needle. E. Sinker for trolling with squid. F. Gaff for large bass, four inches across the bend. G. Oval Tracing Sinker, with hole through centre. H. Swivel Sinker. I. Pivot multiplying Reel, with balance crank. J. Brass Swivel, for fishing on the bottom with tracing sinker. K. Wedge, to fasten trolling sinker E for the different lengths of squid. L. Loop above sinker E, to which the line is attached; length optional. M. Heavy Hook for trolling. N. Kingfish Hook; small, strong, well tempered, Sproat's bend. O. Scap-net for catching shrimp, or, with larger meshes, a landing-net. No. 1. Shank-bended Hook, with line fastened by three half hitches to angle for, or cast into the surf for large striped bass. 2 and 3. Smaller sizes, for casting menhaden bait, or still-baiting with heavy tracing sinker. 4. Kinsey bend, or Pennsylvania Hook. 5. O'Shaughnessy bend. 6. Sproat's bend. 7 and 8. Kendal Hooks.

adise of the bass angler—when one morning I was awakened from my early slumbers by the loud calls of Mosier, my gaffer, who had tried a cast with one of my rods from the Table Rock, and, in casting, had thrown a knot in the line about thirty feet from the reel; and, as the guides were too small to pass the knot, Mosier, to prevent the fish from getting slack line, ran back as the fish came toward shore, and ran forward when the fish carried off too much line, calling lustily for me as he ran backward and forward in great excitement. I finally relieved him of the rod in due time, and he gaffed the bass, which weighed twenty-two pounds. Since then I have all guides made large enough to pass a small pea. Double guides are best, unless you have Pritchard's patent guides, which turn on a fixed metallic band. It is always best to disjoint a rod when done fishing for the day, and then change the sides of the two upper joints every day, as it prevents the rod from warping or setting.

The reel, like I, should carry 600 feet of hawser-laid linen line, of from twelve to fifteen threads, thus rendering it about the size of a fine salmon line; but the line should be free from any oily composition, and a dip in dye to give it a greenish shade is beneficial. Never, by any chance, use a check reel for coast or estuary fishing. Depend on the pressure of your thumb for checking the fish, and wear knitted thumb-stalls.

Hooks like M, with taper shank and loop of linen line, the same size as that on the reel, extending six inches beyond the end of the shank. Place your squid along the hook so that the extreme bend of the hook will be opposite its eyes, when slide up sinker on loop E' toward L until the sinker is even with the other end of the squid. By this process your tackle will fit your squid. Then fasten E to its place by K; hook the squid back of its mouth, running the point forward, and turning it down so as to bring the point out between the eyes; attach loop L to the baiting-needle; draw the sinker up through the ink-sack, or body, and attach the loop to the end of the reel-line, and you will be ready to commence trolling.

Those who employ a man to row and gaff the fish would do well to direct him to squid half a dozen hooks before start- ing, and lay them aside in the boat under some wet rock-weed before leaving shore. If you have ever been trolling—as I have—when large bass were biting generously, you will real- ize the force of this advice. It is unpleasant to be trolling in rough waters, and, when a bass strikes the back of your hook and takes your bait without fastening, to be obliged to stop and squid a hook before proceeding.

Now for the fray! Our boats are made by Hughes, fellow- apprentice of George Steers; and with Sile Wright and Sandy Gibson as guides and gaffers, we shall be sculled over all the favorite trolling grounds from the ferry below to the Drowned Marsh above Ward's Island. Our first move will be toward Tide Rock, swinging Big and Little Mill Rocks on the way; then we shall glide over the Hen and Chickens, swing Holt's Rock on the Hog's Back, round Nigger Point, and, stopping at John Hilliker's to rest, enjoy a piece of incomparable apple- pie and a glass of milk served by two charming ladies. While indulging these ruminations one day, as my friend was swing- ing* Holt's Rock, he hooked a large bass and played it all the way round the east end of Ward's Island to Chowder Eddy, where, on landing, it weighed twenty pounds.

The sketch on the opposite page represents my friend as the bass first rose and laid its course.

I was not so fortunate as my friend; for, as my squid was struck by a large bass, Sile said he heard the rod crack; but the fish made such a long, vigorous run, that I scarcely real- ized what he said, and, after turning the fish and reeling him in gradually, he broke water with a leap, clearing the surface, and revealing a forty-pounder. While turning and bringing him toward the boat for the third time, he darted down and

---

* Swinging a rock is done by the oarsman holding the boat sixty feet from the rock and swinging it so that the troll will move about the rock on all sides and play as if alive. This art is possessed in great perfection by Hell Gate oarsmen.

FISH AND TIDE IRRESISTIBLE.

snapped the middle joint of my rod in two, when I threw the broken rod down at my feet and took hold of the line; the fish made but feeble resistance, and I towed him alongside the boat and shouted to Sile for the gaff, but he had thoughtlessly placed it in the other boat. I then endeavored to put my hand in his mouth, and, while in the act, the fish turned over, breaking the hook and bleeding profusely as he settled off into the tide, leaving us astonished and almost desperate. On examination, I learned that a flaw in the hook had been the cause of our loss of the fish; but had we rowed ashore and towed the fish after the rod broke, we should probably have landed him. I have never since been caught trolling or angling for large bass without a gaff and tried hooks; and as the gaff is an implement of such high importance, I have given the shape and description in another part of this book; but the one shaped like F among the "implements," and from 3 to $4\frac{1}{2}$ inches across the bend from point to shank, made with a screw to fit into the gaff handle, leaves little to be desired. In using it, drop it below the fish, point upward, and as it is raised to the fish, the fish settles against it, and a simple jerk impales it. Do not strike a fish with the gaff; insert the gaff gently beneath, and it will be hooked with the utmost ease.

Well, with broken rod and tangled line, I ordered Sile to row away from the scene of our misfortune. I found my friend at Hammock Rocks, his fish laid out in state on rock-grass, and he mutely bending over it with a face radiant with pleasurable satisfaction at his achievement. Trolling, to him, was a new-born pleasure, and his first capture a trophy of which a slayer of lions might be justly proud. It would be superfluous to add, we drank to the study for a Stearns or a Bracket as it lay shining on the pallet of sea-grass. Sandy commiserated Sile's misfortune at losing the large bass. In the centre of a radius containing the most picturesque landscape near the metropolis, we rested, wondered, and admired.

> " The skies their fairest canvas spread
>   When the angler goes a-trolling;
>   Relenting clouds float overhead,
>   And tears and smiles alternate shed,
>   When the angler goes a-trolling."—STODDART.

Having toasted the health and appetite of bass in that neighborhood in a glass of sherry, and replaced the broken joint of my rod with a sound one, we again seated ourselves in our boats, and commenced trolling the Little Gate, the Kills, and all about Randall's and Ward's Islands, and, after the usual alternatives of hopes, fears, and moments of ecstasy, we finished up a mess of seven bass between us, the largest nearly thirty, and the smallest four pounds in weight.

Well, having given you a taste of the sport on the waters bounding Manhattan Island on the north and east, let us anchor our boat near the lower hedges of New York Bay, and learn how different bottom fishing with a tracing sinker is from both trolling and angling with a float.

SECTION FOURTH.

STILL-BAITING FOR BASS.

Use a stiffish rod, like A, B, C on the page of implements. It should be from eight to nine feet in length. The Japan

bamboo pole, being a rod without joints, of the same length, and mounted the same, with top and guides of agate or carnelian; multiplying reel like I, which shall carry from four to six hundred feet of fine linen or silk line. Linen is the best for bottom fishing, but it should be made of the finest and strongest flax or hemp. You may use a double-gut leader, three fourths of a yard long, or make a leader from your line, which I prefer when bottom fishing for bass ranging from three pounds upward; then one hook only is used. Use a tracing sinker in the form of a long roll or cylinder of lead, three fourths of an inch in diameter, with a hole for the line longitudinal, cutting off the weight required for a sinker; or let it be an oval form, as represented by G, with a swivel to stop it at the top end of the leader, like J. The swivel should be brass; all swivels for use in salt water should be brass, for steel is soon corroded. Thrust your line through the sinker, and attach the end of your line to a swivel, and your leader to the other end of the swivel. This leader may be either linen or double gut of the silk-worm. If the latter, the hook will require tying or winding on with waxed thread; if the former, the hook should be headed like a pin, and the line fastened to it by three half hitches, as if for fishing with menhaden bait. Shedder or soft-shell crab is preferred for bait; but, if it can not be procured, use shedder lobster.

Now, having finished our rig, we will cast our anchor here, about a hundred feet above the hedge, and fish toward it until the tide turns, when we will anchor about as far the other side of the hedge. These hedges were made to lead shad into channels, across which nets were spread, as you perceive by the spaces left in the different rows of hedges. I always anchor my boat so as to cast at an edge of an opening, or channel, through the hedges. Our boat is not so near as to alarm the fish, while a gentle cast of seventy-five feet reaches them. Make your cast, and let your sinker settle naturally, so that your line be straight, when you will feel the slightest nibble, though bass generally grab the bait and dash away, and, if they feel the hook, continue going until they become exhausted, when they rise to the surface, which is called "breaking water." In this act they inhale a little open air oxygen, which renders them so gay and sportive as to be almost unmanageable. You should therefore always wear thumbstalls or cots on the thumb, a neglect of which has caused numerous thumbs to be blistered by the friction of the line when endeavoring to snub a striped-sided racer, or a bluefish, which intrudes as a guerrilla, and, with its steel jaws, chops up your tackle and occupies the post with impunity; and if perchance you hook a bass, he is sure to liberate it in the endeavor to get the bait, by biting the line off before the mouth of the bass. Gimp snells are as straw to their saw-set teeth, and nothing but piano wire has yet been found strong enough to resist their bite.

There, sir! When you jerk at a bite like that, reel in the slack you have caused, and let your sinker settle so as to keep your line straight. Well done! That fish is game. I will reel up, or he will cross my line, and, by becoming entangled, you may lose your fish. After all, he is not so large as to require a gaff. It is best to have both a gaff and large scap-net in the boat for such fishing.

Our sport bids fair to-day. We have already taken a dozen bass, besides a few squeteague and blackfish, and the

tide is not yet full; but perhaps we had better use the last
of the flood tide to help us up to the light-house on Bergen Point Reef, for the best time there is just after the tide
has turned ebb, when I never failed of an hour's brisk sport.
Let's, therefore, up with our killick and man the sculls, which,
with the tide, will carry us there in twenty minutes.

Well, brother angler, our good arms, assisted by the tide,
have enabled us to arrive in time for me to cast anchor on
this, my favorite ground. The tide is just high-water slack.
Our landmarks are right. Let go the anchor. Be seated
and ready, but do not cast until the boat toles by a decided
ebb of the tide. In the mean time suppose we lunch? Now,
as we enjoy these broiled squab, buttered biscuit, and a modicum of claret to moisten them, we will feast our eyes upon
the captivating scenery. Comparatively few understand the
pleasures of boat fishing. It is removed from the dust and
hurry-scurry of *terra firma*. Our position enables us to sur-
vey several shores and the employments of busy life. What
can be more lovely on a mild autumn day than scenes like
these from a boat? We are near enough to the metropolis
to hear its noises subdued into a musical monotone. That
mountain which you perceive at the head of Newark Bay—
of which we are at the foot—is Snake Hill, at the confluence
of the waters of the Passaic and the Hackensack, which empty at each prong of the fork formed by the head of this
bay. To the south a few miles you perceive a large city,
which is Newark. The spires of a town still farther south
are over Elizabethtown, while two miles south from us is
Elizabethport. On the Staten Island shore, at the east of us,
are New Brighton, Factoryville, Port Richmond, and a series
of buildings and gardens, as a part of the periphery of Staten
Island. Directly in front of us is Bergen Point, being a garden charmingly dotted with dwellings of picturesque architecture. Do not these scenes present subjects for contemplation sufficiently enchanting to pay the artist for a visit without any sporting accessory? Many innocent persons wonder

how a man can "waste" an occasional day "at the stupid
sport of angling." These persons do not even know that the
modern angler is as widely different from the ancient dream-
er portrayed by good old Izaak Walton as are percussion
caps and locomotives from flint-locks and post-coaches.

The tide here appears to take longer to make a decided
turn than at any place known by me. We will shed a few
crabs, as the boat toles nearly right. Notice the landmarks:
the dock at Bergen Point is in range with the steeple at New
Brighton; the south side of the Light-house ranges with the
high chimney on Staten Island shore. These ranges form the
angle where our boat rests, a hundred yards west of the
Light-house, and within casting distance of the submerged
rocks, seven to the left and five to the right, at the stern of
our boat.

Now for commencing. Cast a trifle to the left, and let
your sinker fall just above the seven rocks, and I will cast
slightly to the right of the stern, toward the five rocks.
There! I told you so! You can not sink your bait before
you have a bite. Well, this is sport! Each of us is either
playing a bass, landing him, or casting. Under these conditions, it will depend on the activity in baiting, and dexterity
in playing and landing our fishes, for deciding which will take
the greatest number. It is true that they are not large—from
a pound to two pounds generally, with a three-pounder sometimes, and a semi-occasional five-pounder; but it is rare sport,
for all that. The tide becomes more swift, and our fish are
harder to play. Deftly and gingerly are the words, while not
a moment is to be lost. I have angled here and taken bass
throughout the ebb tide; but if I take from fifteen to twenty-five in an hour, I generally become fatigued, and rest the
pool for some one else.

You know George Wilkes, of the SPIRIT? Well, he and I
were once still-baiting here, and, as we were about to leave,
after taking between thirty and forty bass, our line on which
the fish were strung, and fastened to the thole-pin for keeping

the fish alive in the water, parted as we were in the act of lifting the fish into the boat, and we lost nearly all of them. The same circumstance happened here while angling with George Austin, Esq. Such luck is aggravating to a common man, but an angler soon learns that effects follow causes. If you prefer to keep your mess alive, either tow a fish-car at the stern of your row-boat for placing them in, or deposit them in a net fastened to a thole-pin, or purchase the new invention of a string made of raw-hide by Andrew Clerk & Co.

It is time for us to reel up and count our mess, for we have tide enough left to float us to New Brighton, where we hired the boat in the morning. Your count says twenty-seven fish. Well, that is an average take. We will unjoint our rods, place them in their cases, take up anchor, and you may light a regalia, while we enjoy the enlivening scenes along Kill Van Kull on our row to the landing. This is the bewitching time for driving along the cornice road of Staten Island; and that couple which you now see in a buggy opposite us think that driving a fast horse on a dusty road is famous sport. See the cavalcade of roadsters stirring up the dust! Coaches with liveried drivers and footmen are not rare, and the outriders will come next. But we are at New Brighton, our fish are basketed, and our boat returned. We will now step on board the steam ferry-boat for New York, which stops here every fifteen minutes.

Our sail across the Bay of New York to the Battery, you perceive, is a continuation of the enlivening local and aquatic views which have blessed our eyes throughout the day.

We must part now with a shake of the hand. Your steam-ship is to leave at noon to-morrow, and the engagements of which I spoke to you may prevent me from bidding you *bon voyage* on the deck of the vessel which is to convey you to home and happiness in one of the British Isles. May the blessings which usually accompany true sportsmen be with you; and when thinking of this land of long rivers and broad lands, I trust that you will not forget the slight taste of sport which you have experienced in the immediate vicinity of New York, but that it will prove a foretaste of a whole season to be hereafter enjoyed in angling and trolling for the game fishes of our coast and estuaries.

SECTION FIFTH.

CASTING BAIT FOR STRIPED BASS.

Casting menhaden bait for striped bass from the rocky shores of the bays, estuaries, and islands along the Atlantic coast constitutes the highest branch of American angling. It is indeed questionable—when considering all the elements which contribute toward the sum total of sport in angling— whether this method of striped bass fishing is not superior to fly-fishing for salmon, and if so, it outranks any angling in the world. The method is eminently American, and characteristic of the modern angler by its energy of style, and the exercise and activity necessary to success.

REELS for this kind of fishing have taxed the ingenuity of the best fishing-tackle makers in the Union. The balance crank should be designed with the greatest nicety of proportions, to prevent a momentum hard to check with the thumb, and still the crank should not be so short as to be difficult in reeling. The crank should also be placed so far back and low on the end of the reel as not to endanger the fingers of the angler by a sudden strike of a heavy fish, for a bass does not, like the salmon, stop to study the cause of a pain in the jaw, but straightway makes a run without hesitation. The best materials for reels are supposed to be German silver, brass, or bell-metal. The wheels should run on jewels, and be so covered with an inner case as to protect them from salt water. The reel should not be too long; the one represented on the plate of bassing implements indicates the shape. It should be a triple multiplier, without check or drag, and large enough to carry from two to three hundred yards of fine linen line.

LINES should either be of linen or hemp, hawser-laid, or of

braided silk.　The latter is the easiest to cast, but not so
good to fasten a fish by a strike, because of its elasticity,
while a linen one will respond at a hundred yards to the
slightest strike.　A linen line, formed of from twelve to
eighteen strands, and strong enough to sustain a dead weight

E

of thirty pounds, should be stained to the color of the water, when it forms the best line possible for this kind of fishing, and it should not be larger than a salmon line. The buoyancy of the water, strength of tide, and dash of the surf, render a very strong line indispensable for large bass. Still, as the fish is as gamy as a salmon, and full as cunning, the line must be fine and the rig very clean, or he will select every piece of chum thrown to him, and refuse the one with a hook in it; or if by chance—when feeding on chum—he takes a piece with a hook in it, he rejects it instantly, and before the angler has time to strike, probably distinguishing the difference by the weight of the hook. The most successful way to angle for them is to rig so clean that they will grab the bait like hungry dogs, and dash away for more, or to keep it away from other fishes.

ROD.—Should be from seven to eight feet six inches in length. The two lower joints of ash, and the upper one of lancewood, mounted as indicated by A, B, C, with silver, bell-metal, or brass. Some prefer a Japan bamboo pole, because of its strength and lightness; several gentlemen of the Pasque Island, Cuttyhunk, and West Island clubs are among those, and as these clubs include many of our amateur experts at this elegant kind of fishing, their opinions claim attention. My own opinion is, that a highly-finished, well-balanced, three-jointed rod is the best for use, and of course most convenient for carrying on fishing excursions. Some anglers have jointed bassing-rods made exclusively from split bamboo, weighing less than a pound, including their silver and jewel mountings; the objects attained being lightness, strength, beauty, and just elasticity enough for casting and playing a fish. The sockets and shoulders of the joints of all rods for coast and estuary fishing should be lined and covered with the same metal used for the bands and guide-frames. Double guides, one side lined with jewels and the other made of bell-metal, and a jeweled top, form a good mounting, the shoulders being covered with the same metal as the bands. It is neither artistic nor in good taste to cover the rod several inches with bright metal for attaching the reel. Whether double guides or patent ones are preferred, carnelian or agate make good lining and tip. The tip should be formed with a screw to fit several top joints. German silver, brass, bell-metal, or any other metal, hard and still malleable enough, and which will not oxydize in a saline atmosphere, form good mountings. A solid butt, without elaborate and heavy mountings to hold a reel, is preferable. If the line does not run on jewels, bell-metal is the next best material, except it be the aluminum—a light metal of new invention in combination and manner of manufacture—which is lighter than any other metal, and is said never to oxydize. Our fishing-tackle manufacturers are making trout-reels of it, and, to judge from appearance and recommendation, I should decide that it is the best metal ever employed for reels and mountings of fishing-rods.

As no sinker is used for assistance in casting menhaden bait, and as the striped bass are extremely knowing, the necessity for a clean rig, and nothing to check the impetus of the bait, make up *desiderata* never to be lightly regarded by the bass angler.

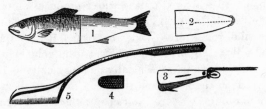

BAITS, CHUM-SPOON, AND THUMB-STALL.

No. 1. The menhaden—*Alosa menhaden*—a species of herring used for bait, and showing the mark, back of which a bait is taken on each side.

No. 2. Bait cut from No. 1, the knife being drawn through the flesh side at dotted line, but not so deep as to part the skin, but to facilitate folding like 3.

No. 3. Bait folded at dotted line and baited on shank-headed hook, with a half hitch of the line cast round the end of bait to prevent it from slipping down and filling the bend of the hook. Some anglers cast one half hitch around the bait just below the head of the hook, and another round the top of the bait; it forms a more compact bait, and better shape to cast; but bluefishes are more likely to cut the line off than when the bait is secured by one half hitch above the hook, as represented.

No. 4. A thumb-stall, knitted from heavy double and twisted woolen yarn, to be worn on each thumb, to prevent the friction of the line in checking the too swift revolving of the reel.

No. 5. Chum-spoon for throwing minced fish with. After taking a bait from each side of the menhaden between the first dorsal and the tail, which is done by first scaling the part from which the bait is taken, then chop fine the remainder of the fish, head and all, with a hatchet or bait-knife, and use the spoon to cast it out on the pool to be fished. The spoon is about a foot long. This chopped-up fish is called "chum," and casting it out is called "chumming," which is continued until the debris of half a dozen menhaden so scattered on the water produces an oily surface, or "slick," as the gaffers call it, extending sometimes half a mile from shore. When bass smell it they approach it, and follow the oily surface toward the point where the chum was thrown in, occasionally finding small bits of menhaden, which the angler on the rocks may see them break water to obtain. Nearer and nearer the bass approach in the path of chum until they arrive within casting distance. The chum should be chopped very fine; some persons cast in the head of a menhaden whole; this is bad practice, for it not only invites sharks and bluefish, but bass feed on it when they might otherwise take the baited hook.

SECTION SIXTH.

A DAY WITH THE DOCTOR.—ANGLING AT THE BASSING CLUBS.

Well, doctor, having arrived at West Island, which is owned by an association of gentlemen who have formed themselves into a club for the incomparable enjoyment of angling for striped bass, they will of course assign us stands to fish from to-morrow. It is the practice here for all members to draw at night for the choice of stands to fish from the next day.

Doctor. A gentleman just handed me a card containing a "number," and "outside the Hopper," marked on it.

S. I perceive by the card that the outside of the Hopper is assigned to us. Well, of course that is owing to the composition of the club; the members have given us their best stands. That is a feature of all the bassing clubs; and besides, William C. Barrett, Esq., is president of this institution, and he is a sportsman possessed of the most discriminative sense of true hospitality. On the morrow we will try to do honor to their estimate of us.

D. Gentlemen, as Mr. S. and myself are somewhat fatigued, and would prefer to retire early, will you have the goodness to join us in a parting glass for the night?

All join; and we retire with a sense of good-will toward all mankind, and indulge school-boy hopes of the morrow.

> "While others are brawling, let anglers agree,
> And in concord the goblet replenish;
> 'Twill cost not a care so long as we share
> The cups of content and of concord."

Our dreams were rose-tinted; but the pleasurable anticipations of the morrow's exploits caused us to awake early, and I sounded the doctor before daylight.

S. Hallo, doctor! Mosier, who is to be our gaffer, rapped at my door and said it was four o'clock.

D. Well, sir, I have been up an hour, and down on the piazza trying to joint my rod, but I can not get a light, and "daylight don't appear."

S. Bravo! I'll be with you in a minute.

D. The sea fog sets in chilly; what say you to a cocktail and a cracker?

S. Oh! Do you know where we are?

D. Certainly; we are near Plymouth Rock, the blarney-stone of America.

S. Tush! I will accompany you, and we will take a sto-machic and a cracker; but do not—for appearance sake—call drinks by their ordinary names in this "land of steady habits," where it is unlawful to taste diffusible stimulants.

D. For medicine?

S. Of course not, if prescribed by a physician!

D. It was upon that hypothesis I ventured the invitation. I brought my diploma with me, and, as a doctor, I prescribe the potion.

S. Ahem! you are right; I feel that your prescription is a good antarthritic. And now we will hie to the Hopper Rocks, take our stands, joint our rods, and be ready by the time Mosier gets the fish chummed in. Mosier calls up the bass here just as a farmer brings his chickens to feed. Let us prepare; but there is no use to make a cast before sunrise.

Mosier. I've throwed in the chum of six fish, an them scups an cachockset comes up an takes it just for all the world as if they was game! an I hain't seen nothin of no bass yet.

S. That is right, doctor! you have jointed your rod perfectly; every joint should be driven home. Now, in fasten-ing the hook to your line, cast two half hitches with the end of your line over the shank, just below the head; then turn up the end of the line, and cast a half hitch over it and the shank, and turn the hook round in the tie thus formed to see· that it revolves easily—cut off any superfluous end of line. See how Mosier chops up the chum, and where he throws it; and just where he throws the chum, cast your baited hook.

Mosier, bait the doctor's hook. I see luminous rays from the God of Day, and he will make a splendid appearance in ten minutes. Now, doctor, reel up your line, so that the bait will be within a yard of the top of your rod, and make a cast to the whirl which you see was made by a bass. Your reel overruns? That is unfortunate. You should keep your thumb on the reel, and check it as the bait drops on the water. Mosier, bait my hook; I have put on a medium-sized hook with a headed shank, and I am going in for the fish refused by the doctor.

Mosier. Mr. S., jist cast along there in Snecker's Gap, for they are reether sassy there on the young flood.

S. Well, Mosier, here goes for a forty-pounder!

Mosier. There! I told you so; I knew that feller wanted breakfast, an I guess he's got enough to last him.

D. Mr. Mosier, as I have succeeded in getting my line out of snarl, shall I cast now?

Mosier. Not quite yet, I guess, for there's no knowin where that critter will yet lead Mr. S.

D. Well, I will take a seat on the rock here, and look at the play. Ugh! that wave wet me all over. Is it not dangerous to remain here?

Mosier. No, sir; ony keep a look-out for them ninth waves; don't git down toward a gulch, but watch where the waves throw the most water when they break, for it allers depends on the course of wind.

D. I see your philosophy is correct, Mr. Mosier, and I have now got a dry seat. Mr. Mosier, do you think that fish will ever be landed? He has run nearly all the line off the reel already.

Mosier. I can't say; there's no counting on them chaps till they are landed, if so be you fish with a pole; but if I had him on my hand-line, I'd make him come humming, and show no quarters.

S. Mosier, keep my line away from the rocks with your gaff, for he seems bent on rounding the Hopper Rock, and

its corners may cut or chafe and part my line. There! he
has tacked again; be ready to gaff him, if I get him near
enough, before he makes another run.

Mosier. I see his mate a keeping alongside of him all the
time; she's 'bout as big as the hooked one. I mean to gaff
that one first. How like tarnation the feller fights, an tries
to whip out the hook with his tail; that shows he's gitting
tired. When they curl themselves up on the top of the water so that you can't budge 'em, you had better be careful
not to hold so hard as to let 'em break the line with their tail,
nor cut it off with their back fin; nor so loose as to let him
git slack line to unhook, or knock the hook out of his jaw
with his tail. There! see him straighten out! He has made
his last fight, and got whipped! His mate has gone. 'Twas
no use for her to stay an try to help him any longer, for she
knows he's dead. Now, with the heave and haul of the tide,
there is more danger of breaking the line an losing him than
if he was alive; but here he comes, an here goes the gaff—a
forty-pounder at least!

S. Well done, Mosier! Struck just in time, for the hook
has let go.

Mosier. Jist so; I hain't no confidence in them hooks with
the barb curling out so that you can not git it into the flesh.
The Kinsey point an Sproat bend, or the O'Shaughnessy with
the Kinsey point, are the best.

D. Well, my preconceived notions of bass-fishing have all
been cast wide. When you first hooked the bass, I thought
I could take a seat and be a quiet looker-on at the play; but
I have been so excited by alternate hopes, fears, doubts, and
surprises, that I want you to pardon me for getting into your
way several times. The truth is, it astonishes me to see the
fish on *terra firma.* I thought him lost a dozen times; and I
can not now fully realize how it is possible to play successfully so large a fish, and one so game, in such boisterous
water, with such slender tackle. I am really afraid to try to
make a cast, for I expect if I get a strike that I shall either
break my rod, or the fish will part my line.

S. Hoot! doctor, don't be too modest; a man who has shot wolves in the Black Forest, and killed salmon in the Dee and Moisie, is not easily demoralized by a striped bass.

Mosier. Yes, doctor, you jist make a cast out into the Rifle Pit, and do it right away, for I see by their whirls that they are hungry.

S. See that your thumb-stalls are well on, and that your line is clear. Now reel up so that your bait is within two feet of the tip of your rod, and when you cast, hold your thumb gently on the reel-line, and as the bait touches the water, press your thumb on the line to check the reel at once, and prevent the reel from overrunning.

D. Well, here goes for a second trial.

S. Very fair cast; far enough for bass at this stage of tide.

D. Ye—ye—es, I see it is, but then I shall not be able to save him—I know I can not, for he runs and pulls so like a reindeer that I can not check him. There! my thumb-stall is loose, and I feel that my reel is not tight. He's gone! I knew I couldn't save him.

S. Don't be so excited, doctor; keep cool, and reel in your slack line; he is only studying a new dodge or making a new tack.

Mosier. He breaks water; I seen him; he's a scrouger!

S. There, doctor, you perceive he has hove to for a lunar, and to discover how to tack; there! he is now laying his course for Newport; reel as fast as you can, and, if necessary, run back to prevent him from getting slack line.

D. This last turn and the dash of spray nearly capsized me. Why, he plays as strong as he did when he was first hooked.

S. How long do you suppose you have played him?

D. Nearly an hour, and he seems to grow stronger and stronger.

S. It is not yet fifteen minutes since you hooked him; bear up, keep cool, and keep your line clear on the reel, and be prepared for his fight. They do not appear to be in a mood for sulking this morning; sometimes they settle behind rocks, and butt the hook against them to spring it out.

Mosier. Don't you hold him a leetle too taut?

D. I don't know; but I can not play him easier, for when I give him an inch, he takes a rod!

S. He will soon stop for his final fight. See! he is preparing. Now ease the line a trifle, and trust to the chance of his being well hooked.

D. He's gone, I know he is! Just see the fellow throw himself like Pat McAroon in a street-fight. There, he's off! No, he is not; what's to be done?

S. Reel up gently; he is dead; that is, he has fought until he has fainted. Gingerly, doctor; reel with the incoming surf, and slacken with the ebb—there!

Mosier. He is a game one, and will weigh over twenty pounds. They're allays hifalorum in them Rifle Pits! Gentlemen, the breakfast horns has been blowin a good while.

D. I am wilted. These rocks are rough to run about on and play a fish, when every now and then Neptune drenches one with spray. I had long heard that striped bass were game, but all that I ever heard or read did not prepare me for such encounters as I have seen and realized this morning. I am not now surprised that Americans consider this the head of game fishes. The accessories of fishing for it, the scenes where it is taken, together with the *modus operandi* of its capture by artistic means, render the sport the most exciting that I know of under the head of angling. I shall certainly prescribe something to steady my nerves. *Eh bien!* To breakfast is the order; and as we have taken two grand bass, *ne quid nimis*, we will even leave off fishing while they are feeding, which, for the vulgar object of ourselves feeding, is, with a real angler, an unpardonable offense against the æsthetics of sport. But, though belonging to the refined confraternity of anglers, our excuse is that we are rigged with human necessities.

As the breakfast-table is the morning's trysting-place for

the members of the club, where they recount their exploits over their tea and coffee, with broiled bluefish, striped bass, and scopogue, or with broiled chicken and beefsteak, the tender of congratulations to my friend for his success, and the stories of successful takes by some, and of parting tackle with others, acted as charming opiates to witch away the time; and when we rose from table we saw our yacht hove-to, and the sails flapping an invitation for us to step on board. With great reluctance and regret we parted from the members of the West Island Club, and the most attractive five-acre island in America.

The sail to Cuttyhunk was remarkably interesting, presenting views of the picturesque landscape, alternating with villas and foliage on Massachusetts shore, and the group of Elizabeth Islands and Martha's Vineyard, with No Man's Land peering above the waves far out in the ocean. We arrived before lunch-time, and, having examined the trout preserve, the black bass and white perch ponds, and taken each a couple of striped bass from that incomparable stand, " Bass Rock," we adjourned to dinner, where we were regaled with choice viands, wines, and the recital of angling exploits by the members of the club, who are justly celebrated as amateur experts with rod and reel.

After dinner we shook hands as an *au revoir, mais pas adieu,* and ran over to Pugne Island, to drop in upon John Anderson, Esq., and learn from him what charms he could see in his little island home of a hundred acres to induce a millionaire of his industrious proclivities and habits—without a knowledge or taste for field-sports or yachting—to shut himself out thus from the enjoyments of the greatest and most social city in the Union—his birth-place, where he has, by enterprise, accumulated a fortune, and possesses one of the finest residences in the metropolis. He informed us that the charming climate, with the constant feast to his eyes in scenery, made up of the main land and the islands, with the ever-changing aspect of the sea, filled his soul with rap-

ture, and made his cup of happiness full to overflowing.
With a promise to visit him before taking final leave of
Vineyard Sound, we steered for Pasque Island, only six miles
distant.

Here we found a club-house with appointments calculated
to render not only the members of the club and their families
comfortable, but all such guests as members of the association think proper to extend invitations to. The island includes more than a thousand acres, which the club has divided into two farms, erected commodious buildings, including
club-house, ice-house, stabling, etc. The club has also vegetable and flower gardens, sail-boats and row-boats, and the
river, which sets back a mile into the island, is stocked with
a hundred thousand menhaden as bait for the use of the club.
This is the *ne plus ultra* of a place for angling, being separate by a strait half a mile wide from Norshon, which is
nine miles in length by two miles wide, fifteen miles from the
main land, and stocked with all the English and Scotch game
birds and most of their game animals, including also several
hundred American deer, prairie-fowl, etc. It also contains a
large pond well stocked with black bass, besides several perch
ponds; the latter is not regarded as a very valuable accessory to any piece of real estate, for perch fishing is not considered sport in America. I mean the common yellow perch
with barred sides; but the white perch, like those of Cuttyhunk, offer good sport to ladies and children, and are a very
good pan-fish, ranging in size from three ounces to three
pounds.

We remained at Pasque Island several days, most of the
time angling for striped bass, but occasionally, on a dark
day, spending it in a cruise after swordfish, which we took
with the harpoon. Other days we rowed a little boat out a
hundred rods from shore, when we put down killick and still-
baited for squeteague, weighing from five to fifteen pounds
each. Then, again, if the bluefish came in such shoals as to
turn our strait into a state of commotion resembling soap-

suds, we rigged to the end of our bass-line about two feet of piano wire, on which we wound a hook with copper wire. Then we anchored on the edge of the tide, and cast out a hook baited without much care, and the moment afterward we were saluted by a jerk and a summersault a yard clear of the surface, and a short, vigorous fight to bring the blue-fish to gaff. An hour of energetic sport, and twenty bluefish of from eight to twelve pounds each, generally satisfied us; and though the fish challenged us by menacing leaps to continue the contest, we preferred to retire—however ignominious it might appear to them—and recuperate for another time.

It was hard to part from those charming scenes and the healthful recreation. The doctor decided to return home to England, arrange his business, come back, and spend his life at Pasque Island. But how to leave those captivating aquatic scenes, ranging from simple loveliness to grandeur, and sometimes rising to sublimity? What scene can be more refreshing and exalting than an expansive view of the mighty waves, dotted here and there with such beautiful islands as those in the Vineyard Sound? The Elizabeth Islands offer the condiments of existence to season the dry hurry-scurry and commonplaceism of the business world on the main lands of America; and they will, before many years, be numbered with the watering-places of the world *par excellence*. While aquatic birds skim the waves, and the gulls are screaming, dipping, and darting over a shoal of bluefish or menhaden, vessels outward and homeward bound are always passing, for it includes in its range of view the packets and steamers for England, and the steam and sailing crafts between New York and Boston. We have here the foreground and perspective worthy the pencil of *Claude de Lorraine*, while the background is formed of the granite shores of Massachusetts, with its improvements so varied and important as to give surety of an intelligent and industrious population. Who would not delight to angle here?

"Eternal ocean! old majestic sea!
　Ever I love from shore to shore to look on thee,
　And sometimes on thy billowy back to ride,
　And sometimes o'er thy summer breast to glide;
　But let me *live* on land, where rivers run;
　Where shady trees may screen me from the sun;
　Where I may feel, serene, the fragrant air;
　Where, whatever toil or wearying pains I bear,
　Those eyes which look away all human ill
　May shed on me their still, sweet, constant light,
　And the hearts I love may, day and night,
　Be found beside me, safe and clustering still."

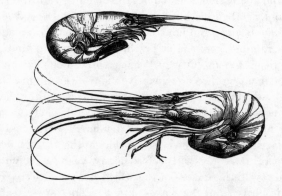

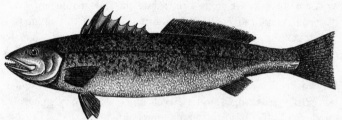

WEAKFISH, OR SQUETEAGUE.—*Labrus Squeteague.*—Storer.

CHAPTER IV.

WEAKFISH, OR SQUETEAGUE.

THIS fish is considered the second in interest by the angler of the coast and estuaries of our Eastern and Middle States. It never visits fresh water, and either spawns along the sea-shores, or on deep middle-grounds of estuaries or bayous, the latter being small bays and back-sets of tide waters. It is probably a family of the *Clupea genus,* one of the marked characteristics of which is that it contains roe in different stages of approximate maturity, though this fish differs by continuing to spawn at different times from the last of March until the first of November. It is, therefore, quite probable that the squeteague visits our shores to spawn, and that it remains during the spawning season; and if it be true that the time of their stay is regulated by the duration of their spawning season, then we may reasonably suppose that they spawn along the term of time between March and November, though the best time to angle for the squeteague is from the first of June until October. From the middle of June until September the tidal parts of rivers from Chesapeake Bay to Vineyard Sound actually teem with them. I have taken with light bassing-tackle, comprised of a nine-foot jointed rod, a reel carrying a hundred yards of fine linen line, a swivel sinker, single-gut leader, hooks snelled on single gut, like those represented on the plate for taking small striped bass, medium-sized cork float, and shrimp bait, on many occasions,

a pair a minute for some time; but the fish would not *scale*
over half a pound each. Shoals of them rise to the surface
like mackerel, at full tide, and take bait as fast as it can be
cast to them; but after they sink it is useless to angle longer
for them. Then you will generally hear a croaking sound in
the water all round your boat, which indicates their presence;
but while croaking they will seldom bite. They generally
croak for half a minute after being landed.

At full tide slack I once rowed out from the Bath Hotel,
where I was passing the summer, nearly to the mouth of Coney Island Creek, where I took eighty-four squeteague within
forty minutes. They averaged about three quarters of a
pound. This was in July. At every cast I hooked a pair,
and fished as expertly as possible until a shoal of porpoises
approached, when the squeteague settled, or sank, and quit
biting.

This is a white-meated fish, the meat rather mealy when
small; but after it scales ten pounds it becomes as flaky as
a salmon, and resembles one very much, except in its being
a square-tail. It is an excellent pan-fish if cooked when first
caught, being free from the flavor of any foreign substance;
but it soon deteriorates, and its juices become absorbed. In
point of delicacy of flavor, many epicures prefer it to either
the striped bass or bluefish. Its eyes being oval, it is supposed to possess the strongest sight of any estuary fish. Although it has no teeth on the tongue or in the throat, its jaws
are armed with pretty strong and sharp ones, which are set
so far apart as to prevent it from biting off a gut snell. Its
mouth is very bony, and the meat being tender, it is therefore liable to unhook easily by the hook tearing a large orifice, or not taking sufficient depth of hold. I therefore recommend a hook of fine wire, well tempered, and of large bend.
The rushing bite of a squeteague is precisely like that of a
brook trout, but its play is of shorter duration, and it sooner
yields to fatigue.

The shape of the squeteague is represented by the engraving, and its colors are gray, masculated on the back and down to the middle of the sides with clouded spots of darker shade, and all terminating in a gold-colored belly, pectoral, ventral, and anal fins. The dorsals and tail are clouded like the back. The first dorsal is composed of spiked rays, and the second soft.

In angling for large squeteague about the Elizabeth Islands and in the Vineyard Sound, heavy combination tracing sinkers are used, and the shank-headed bass-hook, baited with menhaden, is preferred. There they are taken by still-baiting from a boat anchored from thirty to fifty rods from shore, in from fifteen to twenty feet water. The squeteague is one of the swiftest fishes of the square-tails, and its ready and dashing bite, and short fight, render angling for it with light bass-tackle as exciting as for almost any other fish of our estuaries. For the very small fish shrimp is the best bait; for the yellow-fins shedder crab is the best; but for those of the large and rounded form of the salmon, the menhaden bait is generally preferred.

It is almost superfluous to state that angling in the tideways with success requires that attention be paid to the stages of the tide. In general, squeteague bite best on the second half of the flood tide, but there are places where they bite best on the ebb. If outside the mouth of a river, the first of the flood is best, while well up the estuary they begin biting when the tide is half up, and continue until half ebb.

Though feeding-ground for squeteague is in deeper water than is chosen by striped bass, yet they generally forage along the bank of the channel. I have frequently anchored my boat so that, angling with the tide, I was sure to take nothing but striped bass, but by casting to the right or left, outside the bank, within three rods of the boat, I would take nothing but squeteague, and an occasional blackfish or tautog.

In a commercial point of view the squeteague is important. The runs of shad up our rivers cease about the first week in June, when the squeteague become numerous in our bays and

F

the estuaries of the larger rivers. Great quantities are then taken in seines, pounds, and set-nets, which supply the marble stands of the markets lately vacated by the shad. The squeteague at this time divides interest with the early run of blue-fish, and about the middle of June the sheepshead visit us, when the variety includes also tautog and black bass, with the bonetta, cero, and the incomparable Spanish mackerel. These do not include any of the fresh-water fishes, of which the black bass is very numerous in June.

SECTION SECOND.

SOUTHERN SEA TROUT.

From Delaware Bay all along the Southern coast, and in the estuaries of rivers which debouch into a bay or arm of the Atlantic, this fish is taken in great numbers with nets and angling tackle, and is known as the "sea trout." Both its habits and play are so much like those of the squeteague, or weakfish, that anglers along the coast of New Jersey term it the spotted weakfish, to distinguish it from the other, which they call the mottled weakfish; but the inhabitants of the coast from Delaware to Florida know it only as the "sea trout," or "spotted silversides."

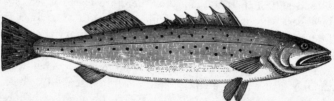

SOUTHERN SEA TROUT.—" *Otolithus regalis.*"

The body of the sea trout is more round, and it is smaller from the tail to the second dorsal and anal fins than the weakfish or squeteague. Its meat is also firmer, and the flakes closer and more compact, while its silver-gray back and sides are of a bluish tint, which shines like burnished steel, and its belly and the lower fins are white, without a yellow tinge.

It is also sprinkled all over, including its dorsal fins and tail, with jet black dots about the size of a pea.

Professor Mitchill, in writing of the squeteague, states: "A beautiful variety of this fish is sometimes seen with the following characters, to wit: *Spotted squeteague—[Lab. Sq. maculatus].* There are black, well-defined spots among the specks over the back and sides, and checkering the caudal and second dorsal fins. The pectoral fins are rather small; ventral and anal fins not yellow, but brownish. The parts thus variegated with spots have a pretty appearance." Without doubt, the professor alluded to the Southern sea trout; and as it shoals with the squeteague, and only visits the shores of New Jersey occasionally and in small numbers, he did not see proper to distinguish it by other than a peculiarly marked variety of the squeteague; whereas it differs more palpably from the squeteague than do some families of the mackerel tribes, eminently the Spanish mackerel and the cero, which differ only in the color of their spots, the first being gold color, and the latter black.

The sea trout is superior to the squeteague as a table-fish; its scales are about the same size, but firmer, brighter, and not so viscid. As a game fish, it is fully equal to the squeteague, as free a biter, and as readily netted. Both fishes are summer spawners, laying from 175,000 to 700,000 eggs.

The sea trout appears along the coast and estuaries of the Southern States nearly all the year round, but takes the hook most freely from June until December. It is taken of all sizes between a pound and fifteen pounds' weight, and if there is a difference in game between this fish and the squeteague, it is in favor of the sea trout, which is a heavier fish of its size, and rather more elaborately rigged with fins. It should be angled for in the same manner and with the same tackle used for taking squeteague; and shedder crab is its weakness. But as all the shores and estuaries of the South are alive with crabs, as well as other *crustacea*, baits are easily obtained for striped bass, trout, golden mullet, hogfish, grunters, sheepshead, and several other species of anglers' fishes, all of which are much more numerous than they are in the latitude of New York. Fishes for the troll are also very numerous along the coost of the Southern States; such, for example, as the Spanish mackerel, bonetta, or *bonito*, pompineau, redfish, cero, and bluefish; and while gunners extend their sporting tours as far south as the Floridas, and west to the Rocky Mountains, anglers seem contented with trouting in spring, visiting Canada for salmon in summer, and casting the hook baited with menhaden for bass in the surf along the rocky shores of the Atlantic in the autumn. But it would be well worth while to make an angling tour southward in autumn; and such as may desire to extend the sporting season would do well to take a trip to Washington, and angle for striped bass below the falls of the Potomac; thence to Norfolk, for meeting the Spanish mackerel, striped bass, sea trout, and hogfish—a great delicacy—and other fishes of the coast. If the sportsman be a relative of Nimrod, he may close the season's sport along the coast of North Carolina by shooting wild geese, and the numerous varieties of duck which congregate there in myriads.

SECTION THIRD.

SHEEPSHEAD.

At mouth of river, or where deep
O'er mussel-beds the bay tides sweep,
The bulky sheepshead loves to hie
When summer suns ride hot and dry ;
And there, for hours, in anchor'd boat,
Hopeful, the patient anglers float,
Only too happy if a score
Of dainty fish enrich their store.

The sheepshead is one of the most interesting on the list of anglers' fishes. It is a dinner-fish, and by many termed the American turbot, because it frequently figures at aldermanic dinners. It is really a delicious fish when either boiled, or stuffed and baked. It usually makes its appearance in our bays and estuaries about the first of June, and remains until

the middle of September; but it does not visit streams above
the estuary, and is found in greatest numbers along the mus-
sel shoals or beds, and around old wrecks in the bays. When
it first makes its appearance in our waters it is thin and
lean, but it soon increases in plumpness and succulence, so
that from an average weight of four pounds early in June,
it increases to nine pounds by the middle of August. Its
maximum weight is twenty pounds, but the runs along the
coasts of Long Island and New Jersey, where they are confess-
edly in best condition and flavor, seldom range higher than
from ten to fifteen pounds. Its mouth is paved throughout
the roof and lower jaw with square teeth of flat surface, like
eight-inch square mosaic, but rather larger at the outer edge
of the jaw, where its even teeth resemble those of a sheep,
from which it is supposed its name is derived. But the teeth
are not sharp, and there is space between them for a fish-line
to play, so that it seldom parts a line, or even a single gut
snell, while mussels and clams are instantly crushed to pow-
der by its powerful jaws.

SHEEPSHEAD.—*Sparus ovis.*—De Kay.

Its scales are large, and surpass in brilliancy the highest
metallic polish; they are about half an inch in diameter, hard,
and radiate from concentric lines, lapping so as to form a defense on the back and sides against a blunt-pointed gaff.

The crescent-shaped bands on each side are sometimes quite
black on the back, and lighten gradually to a dark gray tint
near the belly.   The color of the fish is neutral-tinted on the
back, which lightens gradually to the lateral line, below which
it is like white *chene* silk.   The spiked dorsal fin is followed
by a second of soft rays.   The upper ray of the pectoral fin
is spiked.   Its eyes are large, and almost beam with intelligence.   The cheeks are often tinged with a pinky glow; and
when first raised from the water, and lying exhausted and mo-
tionless in the landing-net, it is one of the most beautiful and
happy-looking objects ever raised above the sparkling wave.

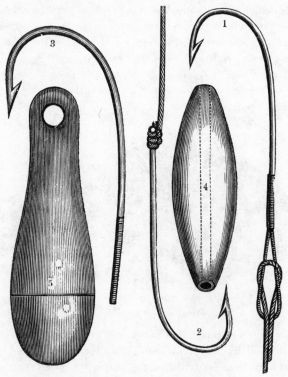

HOOKS AND SINKERS FOR SHEEPSHEAD.

As the play of the sheepshead yields a new sensation to the amateur who for the first time indulges the penchant of angling for this dinner luxury, and as the *modus operandi* of its capture is somewhat peculiar, the opposite sketch is given to indicate the forms and sizes of the hooks and sinkers used by anglers with rod and reel, and by members of the hand-line committee.

No. 1. Hook of the Sproat bend, small but strong, of finest tempered steel, and the short point and barb sharpened like a fine knife-blade, not round and needle-pointed like those for striped bass and squeteague. There is a fine gimp-wire loop wound to the shank with fine waxed sewing silk or fine linen thread. I recommend waxed linen thread when snells are wound to hooks for any of the respectable sized game fishes of our estuaries; for fresh water, silk is preferable.

No. 2. Shank-headed hook, with the line fastened below the head by two or three half hitches, the same as for use in fishing for large striped bass. In fastening the line to the hook, cast the two half hitches around below the head, then turn up the end of the line and cast another half hitch over the shank and the end of line, filling the space to the head. Then draw the hitch tight, cut off the end of line even with the head of hook, and turn the hook in the tie until it turns easily, and you have the best possible hook-rigging. The hook should be made of finest tempered steel, and the point very sharp, or it will be either turned or broken in the mosaic pavement of the mouth before it slides to the rim of the jaw, and by the turn of the fish fastens the hook in the lip or corner of the mouth.

No. 3. This is the size of hook for hand-line fishing, at which a large business is done during July and August, and sometimes throughout September. There is a greater number caught by the hand-line than by sweep-nets or seines, the only other methods of taking them for market. The Virginia bend, like 3, with knife-blade edges of barb and point, is preferred; and the fine but strong linen leader, or twisted or braided hair leader a yard long, is armed with a hook at each end, one to be baited with a whole soft-shell clam by inserting the hook between the shells, and the other with the clam taken out of the shell.

No. 4. Tracing sinker of lead, with a hole through the centre longitudinally. All sinkers should be of lead, as one of the most ponderous metals. At the upper end of the leader—which is the same material as the line—three fourths of a yard above hook No. 1, the leader should be tied to a brass swivel, and, after running the end of the line through the sinker, the end of the line should be tied to the upper end of the swivel, to prevent the sinker from falling too near the hook, and still to permit the line to play freely through it when it rests on a mussel-bed at the bottom, so that the angler may feel the slightest nibble. This is also a marked point in still-baiting on the bottom for striped bass and squeteague.

No. 5. Sinker for hand-line fishing. Tie the end of line to the sinker though the hole in the end. About ten or twelve inches above the sinker, tie to the main line a leader with a hook like No. 3 at each end. The leader should be nearly a yard long, and if made of hair it will be lighter and play easier than if of linen; and when the sinker lies on the bed of mussels where sheepshead feed, it is well to have the leader so light that the hooks will be moved about by the tide. One hook should be about a foot from the main line, and the other two feet. When thus rigged, and you have cast as far as you can astern of your anchored boat, take up all your slack line and your heavy sinker, which will permit you to draw the line straight without moving it, and this will enable even a member of the hand-line-committee to feel the slightest bite.

I am thus particular in describing the rig for hand-line fishing because many good anglers consider the electric dips and dives of a " head" too quick for a line to render before breaking a rod. I do not appreciate a repugnance to a rod because a fish plays rapidly and with powerful demonstration. The angler should use a heavy rod, about nine feet in length, and, like the ordinary bass rod, the two lower joints should be of ash, and the top of lancewood, or the whole rod should be of Japan bamboo. I rather favor a bamboo rod for sheepshead fishing. The angler should use the heaviest make of a steel pivot bass reel, large enough to carry six hundred feet of line, though there will probably never be more than half that length carried off the reel; but the fish doubles and turns so rapidly that a large drum, or much line on a reel, is necessary to wind the line in quickly and prevent the fish from getting slack line, and to give him time to disgorge or break the hook.

To the angler who has never fished for sheepshead I would say, "You have a rare treat in store, so enjoy it the first opportunity." If a resident of New York, you will find Canarsie, or the "Old Mill," near East New York, the most convenient places to take sail-boat from, and bait is generally plenty at either place. Sail down the channel above the inlet toward Near Rockaway; about a mile below Remsen's Hotel, feel by sounding for a mussel-bed: they are numerous for a mile along shore, about 200 yards from it. When found, cast anchor far enough away, so that when the boat toles round by the tide toward the feeding-ground, the cast required for dropping your sinker on it will be about fifty feet. The water should be about seven feet deep at low tide, and it rises there from four to six feet. The best tide to fish is during high and low tides, when the water is slack, and until it runs at the rate of five miles the hour, or one hour after it begins to run; for when the tide runs at its full strength, sheepshead seek some still-water ground, and wait for a moderate motion of the waters. During the intermission I am in the habit of taking up anchor and trolling for bluefish, or of seeking some feeding-ground up a bayou, or some sunken vessel, where I angle for sea bass, squeteague, striped bass,

blackfish, and an occasional sheepshead, until the tide again
serves on the mussel-beds, which generally border the main
channel.

At the right times of tide, the locations of the mussel-beds
are plainly indicated by a fleet of from twenty to fifty small
sail-boats of hand-line fishermen. Many of them are farmers
who reside near the shore of Jamaica Bay, and employ the
interregnum between hay and grass to unite pleasure and
profit by earning from three to ten dollars a day at fishing
for sheepshead. There is always ready sale for the fish at a
price nearly equal to that obtained for salmon.

Having grouped the implements—except the necessary one
of a large landing-net, of heavy brass rim and large meshes
of strong twine—suppose we drive down seven miles to Canarsie, and go out from there to try the "head" for one turn
of tide?

Crossing the ferry from New York, our drive from Brooklyn lies through a labyrinth of flower and vegetable gardens,
forming a landscape dotted here and there with *chateaux*
whose surroundings prove the *ménage* to have been designed
with a view to uniting comfort with elegance. .Those old
oaks, cherry-trees, and black walnuts, together with the ser-
pentine windings of a couple of trout brooks, are the only
marks left of that antiquity which antedates our Revolutionary War for Independence; but the gardens, lawns, fruit-
trees, and margins of flowers, forming the landscape into a
picture of beauty, and loading the air with perfume, demand
that the senses of smell and sight shall do their duty.

*   *   *   *   *   *   *

Yes, judge, we are already at Canarsie, and I do not wonder at your surprise that in less than one hour we should
have left urban blocks of brick and marble, and been wafted,
as it were, through seven miles of flowers, to be set down on
the margin of the sea, with all its aquatic views breaking
upon us like a startling pun or paradox. Be pleased to step
upon the piazza of the hotel and take a look seaward, while

our host orders Captain Abrams to bring his yacht along the
dock.   It was amusing, when I first inaugurated rod-fishing
for sheepshead, to perceive the members of the hand-line-committee cast furtive glances at me as they winked knowingly
to one another, as much as to say, "All's fish as comes to our
net, and a greenhorn is as good as any, if he pays." The clam-
rakers and crab-catchers, whose small sail and row boats dot
the shores and shoals of Jamaica Bay as they saunter about
barefooted and clad in a red shirt and rolled-up trowsers, also
believed that anglers for sheepshead with rod and reel were
monomaniacs; and though they freely took my money for
bait, they frankly advised me to use a hand-line for "head."
This want of faith, however, lasted no longer than did the
gibes and sneers of the shad-fishermen at Holyoke when Seth
Green stated that he could hatch a million of shad a day, and
within a week he hatched six times that number daily.   So
the members of the hand-line-committee and bait-catchers
soon became not only civil, but vied with each other in sec-
onding my wishes by taking pains to procure me peculiar
baits, etc., concluding finally that angling with a rod and reel
may be as respectable as fishing with a hand-line.

SECTION FOURTH.

ANGLING FOR SHEEPSHEAD.

The saline air is invigorating, and a slight haze protects us
from an unwelcome glare of the sun.   The gulls scream as
they dip and sweep over shoals of young herring and menhaden.   Members of the hand-line-committee are out in full
force, and sixty clinker-built and copper-fastened tiny sail-
boats, with poles lowered and sails wrapped round them, are
anchored along the banks of mussel-beds, intent on baiting
with clams, and casting their heavy sinkers—catchung! ca-
lung!   Our captain rounds our craft to as if he intended to
swamp half a dozen tiny craft; but all is serene and the anchor cast, when the captain falls to opening shedder crab and
soft-shell clams, and throwing the shells overboard at the bow

of the boat, so that the tide will carry them astern and attract the fish.

With the sail lowered over the centre of the stern and lashed, the judge takes his stand on one side of it and myself on the other, when each with a single-rigged hook, as before stated, and well baited with shedder crab, make our first cast.

"Judge, permit me to advise that when your sinker touches the water you do not slack your line or permit any to run from the reel, but let it sink naturally, and the tide will keep your line straight, so that you will be able to distinguish the faintest nibble after it settles on the bottom. If you do not get a bite in a minute, jerk—as if you intend to hook a fish—and reel in a yard or two of the slack caused by the jerk, and then let the sinker settle as at first. Keep striking and reeling a few feet every minute until you have effectually fished over all the ground from where you cast to the boat. Then reel all the way up and repair damage to bait, and cast again. I have cast and reeled in for hours, sometimes without getting a single bite from a 'head,' and in such cases my friends resorted to segars and other expedients to prevent them from becoming discouraged; and if they saw the hand-line men catch a few and string them to a cord fastened to the thole-pins, leaving the fish in the water to keep them alive, they would forthwith order our captain to bargain for a few at a dollar each. But, before we or they discontinued fishing, we would take the greatest number of any craft in the bay, and frequently more than we knew how to dispose of. But the tide slackens, and 'head' will begin to bite very soon. Keep your line clear on the reel, and straight from the tip of your rod to the sinker." "There! I've hooked one!" "His shooting up to the top of the water is no sign of weakness, for you perceive that I can not prevent him from diving to the bottom quicker than he came up. Captain, man the landing-net, and be ready and careful, for he is a fifteen-pounder! There, he is off again; you perceive that I can turn him and bring him to the surface, but as soon as he smells the upper air he turns quicker than thought, and, unless I yield him line, he will either part it or break my rod. The sheepshead is what Lord Dundreary said of a certain bird, 'werry wobust.' You are right, judge, he is beautiful; but do not count him until he is in the landing-net. There! stand out of the way of his dorsal and pectoral spikes; I always wear boots when angling for sheepshead or trolling for bluefish."

"Ho! judge, you have hooked a good one. Good! Play him gently and gingerly."

"He'll not let me! I expect to lose him. There, that's the third time I have brought him to the surface, only to see him take more line and get farther from the boat at every turn. By the powers, there! Captain, how much will he weigh?"

"I guess summut near on to ten pound."

"What! You don't mean to say he'll not scale more than ten pounds?"

"Yes, sir; maybe et's summut bigger."

I check the interesting colloquy by stating that I think our fishes are about the same size, but that the one I have just hooked is larger than either. The judge then sees that it is best to employ all his time at fishing while the biting continues. As I land the second one, I remark:

"Judge, you perceive there is no mistaking the bite of a sheepshead; his bite informs you that he is in earnest."

"Precisely so. His bite is like that of no other fish. It is as spasmodic as a bluefish and as powerful as an alligator, and he gives, also, an indescribable premonition, informing you that a powerful fish is examining your bait. There! he's gone!"

"Well, judge, please examine your hook. The point is broken off. The only safe place to hook a 'head' is in the lip, or at the angle covering the mandibles. I took thirteen here one day, and played a greater number which I lost. Our fishing-tackle kings should inspire greater confidence and better temper by giving us finer tempered hooks."

The captain counts eleven as our take. Moderate, but enough. Suppose we reel up? Captain, head the craft homeward. Let's unjoint our rods, put them in their cases, and enjoy the sail. To our left is the lower bay of New York, the fortifications and shore of New Jersey. To our right is Rockaway, and the great South Bay. Those birds in the weeds are yellow-leg snipe, and those on the sand-bars are summer snipe, of numerous varieties. The gulls seem to be at war, for they sally from the islets and descend on spearing and shoals of small fry as if they were storming a fortification.

Our horse is ready, and our fish are stowed under the carriage seat. We will try to drive home before sundown.

There are many places along our shores better than Jamaica Bay, where we fished to-day, for sheepshead. The hand-line-committee make it pay at Fire Island, and there are many superior feeding-places in the South Bay. About the wreck of the Black Warrior, near the Narrows, is celebrated for great numbers of them. In truth, our whole coast south of Long Island is rendered inviting by this delicious fish.

Late in autumn the sheepshead are numerous along the shores of Virginia and the Carolinas, but they are not so good any where else as within the latitude of the State of New York. The sheepshead of our northern chain of lakes is an inferior fish, and should not be confounded with our coast and estuary delicacy.

Along the shores of New Jersey sheepshead are numerous from May until October:

> Where inlet of the Barnegat
>   Opes to the boiling surf its gate,
> When the young flood-tide washes in
>   Limpet and crab, a luring bait,
> Then, where the affluent current pours
>   The deepest o'er its mussel floors,
> The greedy sheepshead hidden lie
> To seize whatever may float by.
> And there, in dancing boat that swings
>   At anchor in the floating tides,
> The angler line and plummet flings,
>   And takes the robber where he hides.

SECTION FIFTH.

THE KINGFISH.

By many anglers this fish is regarded as the best water-game of the estuaries. It is justly entitled to be considered one of the best food and anglers' fishes of the waves which wash the shores from Sandy Hook to New York City. Its small and hard mouth is bordered with a gristly rim, peculiarly adapted to holding a small hook. In the waters about the city this fish is not numerous, nor are the members of the limited shoals of large size, running only from a half to two pounds each off Communipaw, Kill Von Kull, and Newark Bay; but at the south end of Staten Island, in Amboy Bay, and where it merges into the lower Bay of New York, near Freeport, and in Jamaica Bay, near Barren Island, they sometimes run as heavy as five pounds. All along the South Bay and the New Jersey shore and inlets this delectable fish is taken in greater or less numbers in fykes, seines, pounds, and with the hand-line, while they yield tithe to sportsmen with rod and reel.

THE KINGFISH.—*Sceœna Nebulosa.*—Mitchill.

The meat of the kingfish laminates in flakes of very close texture. It is a very heavy fish for its size. Though eminently a breakfast fish, yet for a chowder the epicure prefers it to sea bass or cod, the acknowledged chowder fishes. The

color of the fish is gray, with irregular marks nearly black.
It is covered with fine, rigid scales, which extend over the
head. The first dorsal is spinous, and all the other fins are
soft-rayed. The fish possesses great propulsive power, as indicated by its fins, so that a three-pounder at the remote end
of a line, with delicate bass rod, generally induces the novice
to believe the strength, speed, and endurance of the fish un-
der-estimated. "Gently, but firmly," are the words in playing a kingfish, which some denominate "barb," because a
short adipose barb shoots out beneath its lower jaw; but it
bears no resemblance to the barbel family. It spawns in
spring-time, as most white-meated fishes do; and, though
rather solitary in its habits, it remains in our estuaries and
small bays along the coast from May until November. August and September are the best months to angle for it; and
as the tackle required should be adapted to its size of mouth
and great propulsive power, the following cut may assist the
angler who would enjoy the sport of taking the fish, which—
for his inches—is eminently the king of game fishes.

The rod is the common three-jointed bass-rod, from eight
to ten feet in length. Pivot, multiplying reel of German silver or brass, large enough to carry from four to six hundred
feet of fine linen line.

The play of a kingfish is peculiar, though like the striped
bass he takes the bait without hesitation and starts away,
and when he feels the prick of the hook, accelerates his speed,
swimming low, and making a very long and strong run. If
you have never taken one you will be puzzled with his invet-
erate persistence in keeping down and running deep, and
your surprise will not be diminished when he finally breaks
water a hundred yards from the boat; and you will wonder,
after landing a fish which has taken you nearly half an hour
to kill, that it weighs scarcely three pounds. The vital spark
of the kingfish is very brilliant, and he is very tenacious of it;
but, once landed, he exhibits a vanquished look, and his or-
ange-colored eyes and scaly head turn downward, as if both

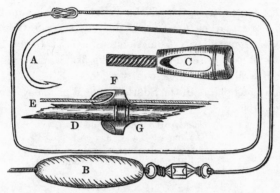

KINGFISH TACKLE.

A. Strong hook, but small; either the Virginia or Sproat's bend, made of finely tempered cast-steel, and needle-pointed: a short bend and low point is required, because the mouth is very small; and a hook of large wire in proportion to the size of the bend is necessary, because of the great strength of the fish. B. Tracing sinker: the size should be graduated to the strength of the tide, hence the combination sinker is the best, because its ponderosity may be increased or diminished without untying the line. C. German silver tip, mounted with carnelian or agate, to screw into duplicate tops of lancewood: regular size. D. Part of a lancewood top, showing its size, double guide, and line. E. Line, showing how it passes through a jewel-mounted guide. F. Guide, of German silver, bell-metal, or aluminum. G. Bell-metal guide, attached by the same ring which fastens the carnelian. H. Brass swivel, to one end of which the line is attached, and to the other the leader, which is three fourths of a yard in length, and the snell to which the hook is wound is looped to the leader: both leader and snell (or snood) are double silkworm gut.

fatigued and ashamed; not like the striped bass and sheepshead, who look happy, and seem to say, "Mr. Angler, I guess you had your metal tried in playing me;" or like a traveler just arrived from Europe, assuming an air of importance, as if condescending to visit America just to see for himself what the Yankees are like. But, though the kingfish looks like a deck-passenger after a long voyage, the angler is sure of one point in his favor, and the cook, as well as the epicure, will be fully assured of another.

The kingfish shoals on a clean sandy bottom, feeds on *crustacea*, and prefers shrimp, shedder, and soft-shell crabs and lobsters. Anchor off Barren Island to the north of the edge of the channel, and expect sport. Anchor east of Chesnequack Creek, on the border of the channel between there and Freeport, and in August and September you can not fail of ob-

taining rapturous sport.   Take your bait with you from a
New York market, for fear of delay.   Caving Channel, a
sandy bottom tideway from Communipaw to Jersey City, is
said to be a favorite run for small kingfish, where good sport
is often realized on the first of the flood.   Kingfish feed also
at numerous places in the South Bay, and all along the coast
of New Jersey.

> To anglers who dwell near the coast,
>   The kingfish is a peculiar joy ;
> And among all the scaly host,
>   This they choose as their favorite toy.

SECTION SIXTH.

THE HOGFISH.

This fish is very numerous on the Bahama banks and along
the coast of the Southern States, visiting in the spring, which
is its spawning season, as far north as the mouth of the Chesapeake Bay.   It is white-meated and very juicy, requiring no
butter or lard in cooking, and its peculiar flavor is very rich
and creamy, being the best table-fish among anglers' fishes of
the South.   It ranges in weight from five to fifteen pounds.
Its scales are rather large, except on the head, where they are

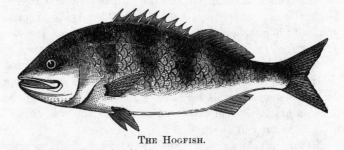

THE HOGFISH.

very small.   The first dorsal is spinous-rayed, and all the
rays of the other fins are soft.   It is marked similar to the
perch, with rays or bars of a darker shade than the rest of the
fish, which is a reddish-brown.   This fish is angled for by
still-baiting with shedder or soft-shell crab, and with shank-

headed hooks, like those for taking large bass.   As its scales
are very tenacious, some cooks recommend skinning it as the
New Englanders do tautog and yellow perch.   It is an excellent fish when stuffed and baked, but it is rather adipose for
boiling.

Apropos of scaling fish: First, lave them in vinegar, and
the most tenacious scales will be easily removed.

THE GRUNTER.

This is a silver-sided fish with gray back and white belly.
The fish is very plump, round, and fat, without any foreign
taste.   It usually weighs from two to five pounds, and is
juicy enough to fry without butter.   It is one of the best
breakfast fishes of the shores and estuaries, and usually shoals
with the squeteague, and utters several grunts after being
landed.   It is angled for the same as the squeteague.   Its
fins are all soft-rayed, and it is leather-mouthed; medium
sized scales cover the body.   In speaking of a frying fish, I
believe in the epicurean theory of never frying a fish which
weighs over half a pound; and that boiling, broiling, baking,
and chowdering are the only true ways to cook fish, except
the primitive ones of rolling them in buttered paper and roasting them in hot embers, or threading them on a birch toast-
ing-fork, with a slice of pork, and roasting them before a
camp-fire.   The grunter is a great delicacy, and very good
game for the sportsman with rod and reel.

THE GRUNTER.

THE GOLDEN MULLET.

This is eminently a fish of the coast and inlets of the Carolinas, though in summer it is taken in considerable numbers as far north as the coast and estuaries of New Jersey. Its mouth is very small and toothless, so that a person might be led to suppose that it lived on *animalcula* did it not bite so ravenously. In size, the golden mullet range from half a pound to a pound, and they are so fat that cooks say " they fry themselves." I know of no fish possessing in an equal degree the rich, sweet juiciness of the golden mullet. It is always distinguishable by from two to four jet spots above the tail. The color of the back is brown, sides golden, belly white, meat a cream color. Its scales are small and soft, fins soft-rayed. The body is masculated in dark shades like the squeteague, and the tail is straight across the end.

THE GOLDEN MULLET.

The golden mullet affords exciting sport to the young angler with very light bass and perch tackle. The rod should either be four-jointed and ten feet long, or a plain bamboo pole, mounted with guides and reel-rings. The reel may be small, but large enough to carry a hundred yards of fine linen line, because the angler sometimes hooks squeteague, grunters, striped bass, and kingfish while angling for the smaller delicacy. The golden mullet affects shrimp bait, but will sometimes take mussels and soft clams. The hook must be small—single leaders are preferred—and a swivel and float afford the prettiest sport, with two hooks, as rigged for small striped bass. The golden mullet seldom ventures far above the estuaries of rivers, and it should not be disgraced by confounding it with the numerous family of mullets of the *Mugil genus.*

THE WHITE PERCH.

This fish is found at the meeting of salt and fresh waters all along the coast from Cape Cod to the Carolinas, and, though similar in essential marks, it differs in shade and symmetry either according to its food or the waters it inhabits. It is a little fish at best, ranging all the way from three ounces to three pounds. Of course you throw the small ones back if you do not hook them in the gills. The back is neutral-tinted, sides a silvery lustre, and belly white. The first dorsal is spinous, and the others soft-rayed, except the first anal. The head is small, and, with its silver-plated gill-covers, small mouth, and little teeth, looks pretty, bites freely, and resists the angler merrily. This fish is peculiarly adapted for the sport of juveniles. It is a pan-fish, white-meated, flat, easily scaled, and quite a delicacy in November, for it is one of our latest biting fishes. Angle for it with light bass-tackle, and it is generally to be found near where a creek of fresh water empties into salt water, or in brackish waters over springs which bubble up from the bottom of a pond or river. A white perch which weighs but a pound affords sport with light tackle, and, when weighing three pounds, it plays very vigorously.

THE WHITE PERCH.

THE SMELT.

This is a small, delicate fish, supposed by some to belong to the salmon tribe, though it is not nearly so much like it as is a shiner like a shad.   It is almost translucent, and from five to eight inches in length; its meat is soft, white, and sweet, with no bones but the spine and ribs, which are so small and tender that they are eaten with the precious morsel of a fish when fried hard in olive oil, or rolled in flour and fried in butter so as to be crisp.   Its scales are imperceptible, but the skin, traced in small diamond lines, is like the canvas skin of the trout of Long Lake.   It is ash-colored on the back, with white sides and belly.   This is a favorite bait for trout or salmon, and an excellent sample for a spinning bait.   As affording sport, the smelt is no mean game.   Late

THE SMELT.—*Osmerus Eperlanus.*—Yarrell.

in the autumn, when ice begins to border the streams, the angler rigs a long perch-rod with a small multiplying reel, and a fine line rigged with half a dozen small trout or minnow hooks on short snells fastened to the main line, six inches apart, and baited with pieces of shrimp or bits of clam, and resorts in boat up small tidal streams, anchors and angles for them during the flood tide, when it is not uncommon to take from a fourth to half a dozen of these pearly beauties at a time, as fast as he can bait his hooks and cast them near the boat.   There is nothing prettier than these gems dangling and shining at the end of the line, when they emit the odor of fresh cucumbers.   On the approach of winter, anglers of all ages are seen on the bridges and along the saline streams of the coast, from Delaware Bay to the eastern boundary of Maine ; and as an article of commerce, thousands are sold in

the New York markets, the average retail price being twenty
cents a pound.   The smelt is eminently the winter sport for
the angler, succeeding the white perch in small tidal creeks.
This fish will also take the fly when sunk to their feeding
level near the bottom.

> When twinkling icicles depend
> From woods that with the bright freight bend,
> When salty stream and open sound
> With adamantine ice are bound,
> Then o'er the solid frozen stream
> The tents of the smelt-fishers gleam ;
> Each opes with axe the crystal floor,
> Then patient watches at the door.

THE SPEARING, OR SILVERSIDES.

This is the same order of abdominales as the smelt and
caplin, shoals with them, and is eminently a bait for the salmon and striped bass.   Late in October, in a tideway, bait
with this fish for striped bass.   On Pelham Bridge, anglers
are seen letting the line carry out with the strong tide this
shiny bait, or casting with float, light swivel sinker, and this
bait, which—where the most rapid current slackens toward
an eddy—attracts the leap of a striped, satin-sided beauty,
forcing the blood to the ends of the digits of the angler.   The
·upper part of the head is rather flat, and the tiny gill rays
are six in number, and the side-belt shines like silver.

" *Color.*—Pale olive-green above the lateral line ; opercles
and sides silvery ; obscure traces just below the lateral line

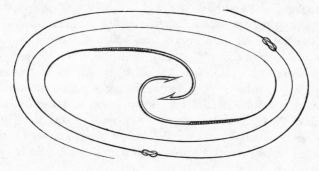

THE SPEARING, OR SILVERSIDES.—*Genus Atherina.*

of a broad satin-like band, extending the whole length of the body; the place of the ribs indicates lustrous stripes, which disappear shortly after death; upper part of the opercles, near the nape, dark green; caudal dark at the base, and with an obscure marginal band; dorsal caudal fins light green; pectorals, ventrals, and anal light colored, tinged faintly with bluish; irides silvery; bones of the head sub-diaphanous."

The foregoing quotation is from De Kay's description of the *smelt;* but he inadvertently described a *spearing.* I am not surprised at that, for they shoal together, and even Dr. Clerk, an angler and a scholar, did not know the difference until I casually pointed it out to him.

> When in the autumn's latest time,
>   And first the streams run icy cold,
> In Indian summer's crimson prime,
>   When forest trees are touched with gold,
> Then take the silvery fish that gleam
> Along the eddies of the stream.

THE CAPLIN.

This is the tiny, translucent fish, of from three to six inches in length, which shoals in great abundance on the shores of Newfoundland and Labrador, and is chiefly used as bait for cod. It will be seen that this fish belongs to the same order as the smelt and spearing, the chief difference consisting in its double anal fin. All codfish fleets employ a sloop, two row-boats, and a set of hands with caplin nets, to keep them supplied with bait. It is an interesting sight to witness a city of boats distributed over many miles of water in the Gulf of St. Lawrence, or about Newfoundland, and the bait-tenders hauling seines over shoals and about islands where the tiny caplin resort for protection from the cod. So, it ap-

pears, Great Nature has wisely ordained that big fishes shall
eat the little ones, and, to compensate for this consumption,
fishes naturally increase many hundred fold faster than land
animals, as before observed.

I have presented these three great baits—the smelt, spearing, and caplin—for the angler's information, for I have been
acquainted with many anglers who could not name the different fishes when taken together in great masses. Shoals
o. these fishes are followed by salmon, codfish, and by the
larger fishes of prey, such as the horse mackerel, cero, and
bonetta, over which hover flocks of gulls, and ever and anon
the latter swoop and shriek as they pick up the debris floating on the surface left by the monsters as they follow and
feed on the shoals of these tender delicacies.

THE CAPLIN.—*Mallotus villosus.*

All the estuaries of rivers and shores of the St. Lawrence
teem with the caplin, and sometimes with the smelt also, and
occasionally with all these three shoaling together. They
form the staple food of the silver trout of the estuaries. All
these fishes spawn in the spring, and, therefore, I am surprised that they should be supposed to belong to any branch
of the *Salmo genus.*

SECTION SEVENTH.

THE SEA BASS.

Where low the level Jersey shore
Spreads out its ribb'd and sandy floor,
At break of day the fishers launch
The little skiff, so swift and stanch,
Spread the white sail, forsake the strand,
To dare the ocean miles from land.
Full well by shoremarks they may know
Where reefs of weeds are hidden low;

There, anchor'd at the dawn of day,
They rob the marine banks of prey.

The sea bass is not strictly a vegetarian, though it visits
vegetable banks to spawn and feast upon the numerous small
crustacea which hide amongst sea-weed. It occupies a respectable place in the culinary calendar, and is preferred to
cod for a chowder. It is eminently a coast fish, and seldom
ventures far above the estuaries, bays, and back-waters, or
bayous. The sea bass, porgee, and tautog banks along the
coast of New Jersey form one of the attractions of Long
Branch, and they are a real blessing to the members of the
hand-line-committee, who realize in them a cheap relaxation
from business and the lassitude caused by too constant work
in a city during the heat of summer.

THE SEA BASS.

Several excursion steamers run every alternate day to the
Fishing Banks, where they make a day's excursion for half a
dollar, and whence often on the evening of the same day each
passenger returns with three dollars worth of sea bass. A
large business is done throughout the summer and autumn
in the capture and sale of sea bass.

The meat of the sea bass laminates in compact flakes, not
so soft and watery as the cod, but more succulent and delicate in taste. This fish usually runs from three to twelve
pounds, and is what angler's term a bottom-feeding fish, consequently not an especial favorite with the disciples of rod

and reel. Its feeding-grounds extend along the coast from Delaware to Maine, wherever the sea-weed grows from beds of mussels. This fish, like many herbivorous fishes of the Orient, lays its eggs, and they are vivified on the weeds and among the shells of the bottom. This process continues from May until August, and the shoals remain on the banks until most of their annual progeny leave the shell, when they all resort to deeper waters to winter.

It is a ravenous fish to bite, and seldom breaks water until ready for the landing-net. Unlike the tautog, its mouth is large and leathery, easy to hook, and tenacious to hold. Its color is a bluish, and sometimes a greenish black, lightened a trifle at the lower parts of the sides and belly. Its scales are about a quarter of an inch in diameter, and its dorsal fins— while spinous—are not very hard; the other fins are soft-rayed, except the front ray of the anal.

The sea bass is a boiler, but epicures regard it as superior in a chowder. Chowder clubs use no fish but sea bass. Little Neck clams improve the chowder, and, as I was for some time secretary of the Latourette Chowder Club, and superintended a combination of the gustatory elements, I will here describe a simple chowder for anglers. A common iron pot, of globular shape, is best to make a chowder in. Slice, as thin as possible, enough salt pork to cover the bottom and sides of the pot, to prevent the chowder from burning. Then cover the pork with a layer of quartered onions, which have been previously parboiled fifteen minutes; then cover the onions with a layer of fish cut in two-inch-square pieces; then cover the fish with a layer of tomatoes; then a layer of sea-biscuit; then a layer of clams; then a layer of onions, and continue the layers in the rotation described until the pot is filled. Season each layer with salt, and a mixture of red and black peppers, together with such other condiments as desired. Cover the pot, and let it stew or boil an hour; then pour upon it from a pint to a quart of Chateau Margaux, or good Bordeaux claret, and let it simmer half an hour longer.

Chowder should remain over the fire nearly two hours. This chowder has the merit of being simple, and—to a hungry sportsman—it is palatable, though not so epicurean as the chowder made by the late Daniel Webster, the receipt for which is given on another page.

Chowder-parties and clam-bakes are American institutions, and they are indulged in annually in July and August throughout the whole length of the coasts of New York and New England.

In a commercial point of view, the sea bass ranks with the tautog, and next to the cod, being consumed annually to the number of millions.

For capture with rod and reel the common striped bass-tackle is used. I have taken hundreds of small ones in a day while angling for sheepshead. They take with equal voracity shrimp, clam, and shedder crab. A shoal of a single pair of fish number probably five thousand which attain to the weight of half a pound and over; not more, because ground-sharks and other marine carnivora thin their ranks when fingerlings. Their feeding-time is during the lull of the waters, between the turn of the tides, when they yield themselves willing victims to the angler's captivating art. They weigh from half a pound to five pounds, and some shoals run from eight to fifteen pounds. As one of our common food fishes, it is a shade more respectable than most of those which have by quality and *status* been consigned to the hand-line multitude.

THE PORGEE.

This fish runs from a quarter to three pounds in weight, and unites with the blackfish (tautog) and bergall (cachogset) to form the guerrilla army of thieves for robbing bait when the angler, with hooks too large for its mouth, is fishing for larger game. Its mouth is armed with pin-point teeth like those of the perch, and while it can not bite in two a single gut snell or thin linen line, is most dexterous in robbing bass hooks, or mauling and mutilating the bait. It is a greedy little shiny sinner, which is both herbivorous and carnivorous, foraging on both fish and vegetable diets, and shoaling with the *omnium gatherum* of bottom fish, which make their summer habitations among the weedy banks called by their name all along the coast from Maine to Georgia, from three to six miles from shore, purveying every where from their homes, into all the estuaries and tidal back-sets, for provender. The porgee is one of the most numerous of coast fishes, and as greedy as it is plenty. Dr. Brown, in his Anglers' Guide, states that the steam-boat which runs daily to the porgee banks in summer returns with many thousand por-

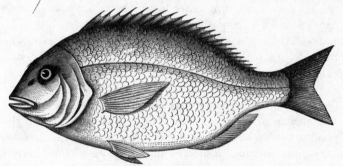

THE PORGEE.—*Pogrus Argyrops.*

gees, besides the sea bass and tautog, averaging from six to ten thousand as their daily catch with the hand-line. To the mechanics and clerks of the metropolis these daily excursions in midsummer to the fishing-banks are great blessings; for, besides the inflation of the lungs with bracing sea-air, the change of scene, and the exercise out of doors, they bring back more than an adequate compensation for the pittance expended for the day's recreation. There can not be too many boats engaged in making fishing-bank excursions, provided the boats are sound and well managed. In general, the captains of excursion steamers are well acquainted with the topography of the banks, and know where to order the heaving of the anchor for good fishing. The charge for passage includes hand-line tackle·and bait, so that a man may start in the morning empty-handed, and be landed at home the same evening with a large mess of fish.

The porgee is a pan-fish of sweet and delicate flavor when first caught, but its juices soon become absorbed, and, with the loss of its juiciness, becomes nearly tasteless. While casting along the coast for striped bass, anglers frequently hook these nimble shiners, and the guides always draw them at once and place them in moss between a cleft of rocks for their own eating, preferring them to the striped bass.

The porgee is supposed to spawn on the weedy banks with the sea bass and tautog early in spring, when the last year's hatch leave for estuaries, purveying to the head of tide-waters. In angling for this fish perch tackle is used. The rod is from ten to eleven feet in length, multiplying reel carrying a hundred yards of fine linen or silk line, cork float, and swivel sinker, single-gut leader and snells, with minnow hooks. Taking them is pretty sport for ladies and children. Use shrimp or clam bait, and let the bait nearly cover the point of the hook; and where they are numerous—as they are throughout summer in nearly all tidal waters in and above the estuaries—the angler will pair them nearly every time he baits his hooks. The fashion is becoming more and more prevalent along the tidal waters of the Atlantic coast, where they are shut in from the heaving and throbbing of the sea, for whole families to take a seat in a row-boat toward evening, and row out to some favorite ground not far from shore, but at a sufficient distance to enjoy different landscape views of both shores, and there to anchor the boat and angle for porgees, with an occasional sea bass, squeteague, and black-fish. Rocking in a boat over the running tide is great food to vitality, and the evening scenes from the water, with the pleasing exercise of angling, are blessings to be thankful for.

SECTION EIGHTH.

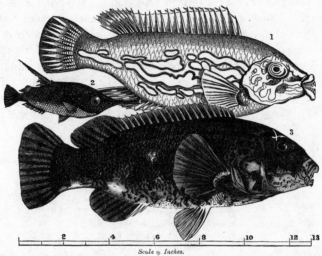

Scale of Inches.

1. Blue-striped Wrasse, *Labrus mixtus.* 2. Trumpet-fish, Sea-snipe, or Bellows-fish, *Centriscus scolopax.* 3. American Tautog, *Tautoga Americana.*

The family of the wrasses, or rockfish, includes our common bergalls, the New York tautog or common blackfish, and those fancy-colored species known as " old wives of the sea." Of the latter there are several varieties, such as the *red* old wife, the *blue* old wife, and the *yellow* old wife, which are so named in accordance with their prevailing colors. The thick pouting lips of the fish of this family are their most striking characteristic. The wrasses were known to the poet Oppian, who describes the beds of sea-weed as their favorite places of resort :

> " And there thick beds of mossy verdure grew—
> Sea-grass, and spreading wrack are seen : below,
> Gay rainbow-fish, and sable wrasse resort."

The foregoing is an extract from Willson's Fifth Reader, and forms a part of the " Glimpse of Ichthyology" which this work includes.

THE TAUTOG.

This fish (Fig. 3) is termed *tautog* along the coast of New England, and is equally well known as *blackfish* along the shores of Long Island and New Jersey, south of which it is not numerous, nor is it north of the Vineyard Sound, though it has greatly increased along Cape Cod within the past fifteen years.

> Wherever kelp and sea-weed cling
> To ramparts form'd of rugged rocks,
> The tautog finds a dwelling-place,
> Deep down in waters at their base;
> Or where a passing boat hath met
> Its fate along the rocky shore,
> And, with its broken ribs and keel,
> Lies rotting on the ocean floor—
> There, where the clinging shell and weed
> Gather, and barnacles abound,
> The blackfish, seeking out their feed,
> In numbers by the hook are found.

The tautog is one of the largest family of fishes which inhabit the waters along the coast from Vineyard Sound to Delaware Bay. Urchins along shores begin fishing by taking cachogset, kunners, and bergalls—all of the diminutive carnivora or bait-robbers—and if, in their efforts, they succeed in capturing a tautog, the lucky urchin who thus succeeds to the first step of fishing thereafter scrapes money together to purchase a regular hand-line and two tautog hooks, with a heavy sinker. He then rigs a hand-line *en regle*, and considers himself a juvenile member of the "hand-line-committee," not to be entitled to full membership until he can earn by fishing a miniature scow large enough to float two youngsters of from seven to ten years of age. Then, with a stone for anchor, they scull from clump to reef of rocks near the shores of our tidal estuaries and small bays, and once in a while add to their catches of blackfish a weakfish, or even a striped bass! This achievement affords the barefooted regiment a week's discussion, and forthwith the lucky urchin becomes the *arbiter* in all piscatorial disputes, as well as the counselor in all arrangements of fishing-tackle, until some other boy takes a larger fish.

But the blackfish, or tautog, is not to be disdained by the disciple of rod and reel. Though he is eminently a commercial fish, yet a tide-runner of his family which weighs from eight to twelve pounds makes such dips and runs as try both the angler and his tackle. A somewhat celebrated senator of Rhode Island (now the Chinese embassador) used annually to spend several summer weeks in fishing for tautog with an artistically-rigged hand-line. He sculled his boat to the edge of the tide, on the bank between a rapid current and nearly slack water, and near an islet or reef of rocks in the Seconnet River, where the water is about fifteen feet deep; anchored his punt firmly, standing up in the stern, and cast some seventy-five feet of line, armed with two hooks about two feet above the sinker, and baited with clam. In this way I have known him to take one hundred pounds of tautog in one hour.

At the mouth of the Seconnet River there are numerous pounds, built of stone, or staked out with netting, for the purpose of catching tautog, porgee — or scapogue, as the large ones are called—and numerous minor bottom fry. Recently a salmon was caught in one of these infamous traps, and, if it is seriously contemplated to restore salmon to our deserted rivers, the first step should be to take up all nets fastened to stakes in the rivers and along the coast.

Tautog are eaten while fresh. Neither the tautog or any other fish of the estuaries which is angled for are cured by salt or refrigeration. They are, as it were, hand-to-mouth fishes. Both the tautog and sea bass are kept alive many days, and sometimes weeks, in fish-cars anchored in water suited to their growth. The blackfish is next to the shad in affording the greatest amount of estuary fish to our markets. Its meat is watery, and the scales are so firmly set that some persons invariably lave them in vinegar before scaling. In

H

New England they generally skin the tautog, as an easier process than scaling, and consider it a culinary delicacy when properly cooked, of which there are three methods, *i. e.*, broiling, frying, and stewing. Before frying the fish, score him across each side an inch apart, as you would any breakfast pan-fish. Fry some salt pork to a crisp; take out the pork, and, while the fat is so hot as to be next to blazing, roll your fish in a mixture of rye and corn meal, and place it in the sparkling hot fat, and let it brown. Turn it twice, and dredge it each time with flour, so that its crust will become an eighth of an inch thick. After broiling, and while piping hot, baist it with butter, salt it, and give it a simple dash of red pepper, which stimulates without inflaming the stomach, and the slightest dash of black as a bouquet, though it does inflame the stomach without stimulating or assisting digestion.

The following receipt by an editor of *quelque chose de goût* is worth remembering:

"Now, fair ruler of the destinies of dinner (for if thou beest a man I have no sympathies toward thee), smoke-compelling Betty, or Mary, or whatever else may be the happy appellative in which not only thou, but all of us rejoice, thou hast before thee one of the most delicately absorbent substances in nature, imbibing flavor from every thing which surrounds it, whether of adverse or of propitious tendency; subject, as Warren Hastings said of the tenure of the British possessions in India, alike 'to the touch of chance or the breath of opinion.'

"Thou hast it, my choice Mary! The small, deep stewpan—with its thin cullender or strainer, on which the fish is to be lowered to the bottom, that it may, when stewed into soft delight, be gently raised again without injuring its integrity of form—glows with brightness in front of thee! Thy vigorous arm of mottled red, thy round wrist, and small, compact fingers, grasp the sharp-pointed knife with which to satisfy thyself that not one scale remains around the head, the fins, the tail.

"Now tail and fins are nicely shortened in their termination, not hacked off. A little salt is thrown over the fish, merely to *harden* and *not salt* it, and it lies two hours for this purpose. It is then scored, that it may not break when it swells, and browned well upon the gridiron, from which it is carefully taken up, and laid to repose upon a bed of nicely-peeled and very fresh mushrooms, daintily spread over the strainer.

"While the fish was hardening, Mary has had a communication from up stairs. An extra bottle of the Chateau of twenty-five had been unavailingly opened the day before to tempt a total abstinence friend who had arrived from the country. Good part of it remains, and at this moment it is decanted into the stew-pan; the freighted strainer descends into the wine, and the fish, entirely immersed in the amethystine element, regrets no more its loss of life, of liberty, and youth. A white onion or two is sliced into rings, that fall as decorations over him; a few berries of pepper thrown in; six cloves; two blades of mace; an eschalot, if you think proper; and Cayenne or not, according to your taste. The stew-pan is then covered, and a careful, slow, epicurean simmer completes the work."

During winter the blackfish hibernates under rocks in the bays and estuaries, as proven by the vent entirely closing and a thin film growing over the mouth. In the spring they appear with the dogwood blossom and the chestnut leaves.

> "When chestnut leaves are as big as thumb-nail,
> Then bite blackfish without fail;
> But when chestnut leaves are as long as a span,
> Then catch blackfish if you can."

In angling for the tautog, use a heavy bass rod, heavy tracing sinker like that for sheepshead, but hooks of the Virginia bend and short nib. Swivel sinkers are preferred by some. Let the point of hook be very sharp. Sometimes striped bass, sea bass, squeteague, grunters, and sheepshead feed with the tautog. It is necessary, therefore, to rig with as large a

hook as will answer for small striped bass and squeteague,
and one strong enough for tautog, or one rather larger than
the common blackfish hook.   Let your leader be part of your
line, say three fourths of a yard long, and attached to a brass
swivel; run the line through the tracing sinker, and attach
it to the upper end of the swivel.   Bait with shrimp, shedder
crab or shedder lobster, fiddler, soft or hard shell clam, or the
sand-worm dug along the sandy shore at low tide.

The tautog bites like the sheepshead, but with less power.
You feel the premonition, but when he dashes aside the pull
is weaker than that of a sheepshead.   I mean now a tide-run-
ning tautog of from three to eight pounds, which feeds on the
edge of swift water, has a white nose, and is fair game.   The
tautog which feeds close to the base of the rocks is an adept
at getting hooks or sinkers fastened in the clefts, for so soon
as he bites he darts under or between the rocks, leaving the
angler thankful if the fish will liberate the hook or sinker as
the price of his freedom.   The bite of a small blackfish of
from one fourth of a pound to a pound is like that of a roach
or sunfish, but large ones bite with energy, and play so as to
afford sport.   All the fishes angled for along the coast, except
the striped bass and bluefish, are usually landed with a net.
The color of the tautog is bluish-black, with a lighter shade
under the belly and lower mandible.   The mouth is furnished with very small teeth.   The engraving is a perfect counterpart of the fish in appearance.

THE FLOUNDER.—*Pleuronectes Flesus.*

The flounder is an important estuary fish for boys and hand-
line fishers, though it is not appreciated very highly by rod
fishermen.   It is one of the latest fishes angled for in autumn
when the icicles begin to form, and it is the first fish that
bites in the spring.   It is to be found in the estuaries and up
the rivers as far as salt water runs; also in our bays.   It is
a fish of the temperate zone, and, from its great numbers in
spring in all the inlets from the Atlantic, is a profitable fish,

and a great blessing to the poor. Though generally caught with a hand-line, many are taken in set-nets and fykes. With light perch tackle, small hooks, and clam bait, it furnishes sport to the disciple of rod and reel who does not fish for trout, and has no fishing in the vicinity of New York until the striped bass awaken to a feeding sense, which is usually from the first to the twentieth of May, toward the head of tide water.

SECTION NINTH.

THE BLUEFISH.

Professor Mitchill has given to this fish, which affords more sport with the troll than any other, the classical name of *Temnodon Saltator,* the first from *temno,* to cut in pieces, probably indicating its sharp teeth; and the last signifying a pantomime dancer, doubtless with reference to its leaping or skipping; but, as if these names were not sufficiently descriptive, he adds those of *Scomber Plumbeus,* or leaden mackerel.

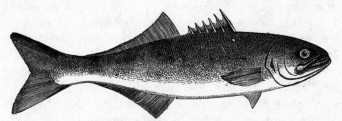

THE BLUEFISH.—*Temnodon Saltator.*—Mitchill.

The bluefish is known along the coast of New England as the horse mackerel, but that is a different fish, and grows to the weight of a thousand pounds, and sometimes more, while the bluefish seldom attains to twenty, though I have heard of thirty-pounders. The color from the back to the almost imperceptible lateral line is a leaden blue, whence it gradually lightens to a white belly. The first dorsal fin is spinous —very sharp and strong, while the second and anal are approximately rigid, being fixed and translucent; the rays, though not spinous, remain standing even after life is extinct. These fins are like sails always set, or like a centre-board above as well as in the keel. The body, head, and fins for half an inch are covered with infinitesimal scales. The jaws are very strong, and the gill-covers like three plates of steel. The jaws are armed with a row of strong, closely-set, sharp teeth, which will cut a cord of one fourth of an inch in diameter in two as smoothly as it could be done with a knife, for they are sharp-edged, and those of each jaw are like sawteeth which match perfectly; therefore beware of fingers in dislodging a hook from its powerful jaws.

The young bluefish, which are hatched in quiet nooks of bays along the beaches, wag their way like other estuary younglings, without being provided with a bag of provision suspended by the umbilical cord, like the young of the *Salmo genus*, but by instinct they propel their tiny selves to the saline creeks and inlets from the sea, to prevent being devoured by the parents which visit the spawning beds early in June, to subsist on such of their young as have not yet emigrated. The young fish are vulgarly called "snapper" or "snapping mackerel," and are the bright little predacious thieves which steal by small particles the angler's bait before striped bass or squeteague can get a taste of it. In October, having grown to the weight of half a pound each, the shoal reunites preparatory to going into winter quarters, where the Gulf Stream keeps the water at an even temperature; and if perchance they meet gut snells on their way, they bite them in two without effort. During the last fortnight of their sojourn near the shore they purvey for young menhaden and spearing, but keep at a respectful distance from shoals of older fish. This is supposed to be the case with nearly all shoals of coast and estuary fishes, and a shoal is merely the progeny of one pair of fishes, and the hatch of one laying of *ova*. Though in summer they may wander apart for food, yet, warned by an unerring instinct, they reunite in autumn to form an army.

The bluefish returns to our shores after its first voyage a two-pounder, being then one year old; and by autumn these eighteen-months' old fish weigh from three to five pounds each; but only those which weigh from five to fifteen pounds, with a semi-occasional twenty-pounder, are regarded as good sport for the troll. These large ones are seldom taken in pounds or nets, for they can liberate themselves with their teeth from almost any net or pen not made of steel; but the younger shoals evince more prying curiosity, which leads many of them into nets fastened to ground fixtures in sufficient numbers to keep our markets supplied with them from June until November.

But the midsummer bluefish, having recently spawned in our bays, are lean and dry food unless cooked within the same hour they are caught, when they are juicy and tender, but lack the rich succulency of the October shoals. The bluefish taken in autumn is equally good as a broiler, or to bake or souse, so long as it can be kept sweet by the use of ice. This is the case with every branch of the mackerel family; and the bluefish of October, when canned in salt, is preferred by many to the common mackerel. Both the bluefish and mackerel are in best condition from the middle of October until the tenth of November, when they begin to deteriorate and fall away to thinness, probably because the butter-fish and bay-shiners have settled away to hibernate, and the smelt and spearing have moved into brackish waters, leaving the bluefish no alternative but to starve or move farther south, and within the influence of the Gulf Stream.

It is well understood by amateurs and fishermen that the bluefish, like the prawn, visit our bays and estuaries periodically, remaining sometimes only a season, and at other times several years. The present visit of the bluefish has been the longest one known to the oldest inhabitant of Long Island, having lasted twenty years. Every year since its present advent it has become more numerous and larger. In 1850, a ten-pound bluefish was a greater curiosity than is a twenty-

pound one now. Then, shoals of bluefish were rare; now
they are to be met with every where that the angler plies his
gentle art along the Atlantic coast.

In trolling for bluefish, metal squid are supposed to be the
best, though bone, ivory, and pearl are frequently used in a
light breeze for small fish. Large, heavy baits are best for
large bluefish. The following engraving illustrates the
shapes, and they should be made from five to six inches in
length, or they can be purchased of the right weights and
patterns at our best fishing-tackle stores.

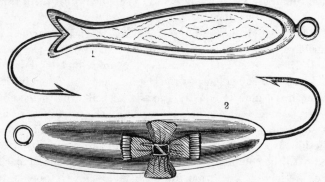

BLUEFISH SQUIDS.

No. 1. Material German silver, with a pearl plate inlaid on
each side. The shank of the hook extends through the
squids, and the trolling-line attaches to the ring by a
double hitch, or to a strip of raw hide—which is better—
that plays freely in the ring. The points of the hooks are
at right angles with the width of the squid.

No. 2. Block tin or Britannia metal, flat on the under side,
and forming three edges, as represented. The loop at the
end of the trolling-line closes at the hole in the end of the
squid by thrusting the loop through and over the end of
the squid. On each side of the middle there is a hole
drilled, in which red webbing or burnt wool braid is inserted, and a knot formed with it as represented, for either
red cloth or blood attract nearly all species of game fish.

The hooks should be very strong, and the points should be filed very sharp: this last piece of advice applies to all hooks for all kinds of fishing, and its importance is not generally appreciated by amateur fishermen.

Trolling-lines of cotton are better than linen lines. They should be hawser-laid, so as not to kink, and be from three eighths to a quarter of an inch in diameter. Although it is well to have them fifty yards in length, yet when the fish are feeding in earnest fifty feet is line enough to let off. Always fasten the end of your line to the boat, and in case you put outriggers, a check line should be attached to each to draw them to the boat or yacht, so as to take hold of them without disturbing the rigger. Lines to outriggers should be so short as to skitter on the surface of the water.

Gloves of heavy woolen yarn should be worn; the line will wear through leather much quicker than through wool, and woolen gloves do not slip, and they are more comfortable to the hands. It is common to double the gloves over the forefinger and on the under side of the little fingers. Buckskin or dogskin, the two best kinds of leather to use when wet, are only a momentary protection, good for nothing as trolling-gloves or thumb-stalls.

THE FLYING FISH.

Trim the white sail; the rising breeze
Blows freshly from the open seas;
It ripples over ocean's breast,
Tips with the foam each billow's crest.
Now cast astern the dripping line,
That cuts and whistles through the brine.

TROLLING FOR BLUEFISH.

ROLLING for bluefish by New York sportsmen is generally done in sail-boats, and the flood tide is best. Therefore, whether we start with sail-boat or yacht from the city, or go to Islip or South Oyster Bay, or to Rockaway or Canarsie to sail from, it is best to sail out to the feeding-grounds during the ebb tide, so as to be sure of no delay after the fish begin to bite; and as the fish approach nearer shore with the rising tide, the sail-boats may be working nearer home, so as not to be obliged to stem a strong ebb tide in returning to port. The best grounds for large bluefish are outside and near the inlets of Fire Island. These inlets are formed by the tides of the Atlantic passing through Fire Island into the South Bay; the principal ones are opposite Islip and South Oyster Bay. But late in the fall the best trolling is off Rockaway and Jamaica Bay, the grounds extending from the Highlands, off the Jersey shore, to some ten miles below the light-ship.

As a sample of the sport, I will recount my last day's experience. My respected friend Gilsten having retired nearly twenty years ago to the charming village of Fort Hamilton, of which he owns the greater part, residing on the border of the trolling-grounds, and in close proximity to the favorite resorts of sheepshead, squeteague, and kingfish, has given his exclusive attention to field-sports for many years, angling and trolling in the waters between New York City and the Narrows until November, when he repairs to his island near the coast of Virginia, and shoots duck and wild geese until the first of January. Being a gentleman of good taste and large experience, as he could not angle in the winter, he has kindly employed his time in designing trolls and stools for fishing and shooting. Well, my friend Gilsten called at my office one evening late last October, and left me two squids, with notice that the bluefish were biting generously in the Lower Bay, and that he would be obliged if I would try his newly-designed models, of which the foregoing samples were copies. I therefore acted promptly upon his generous advice, and called on my angling friend Charles Gaylor and several others, all of whom agreed to meet me promptly next morning at seven o'clock at the yacht moored in Jamaica Bay. Of course none of them came to time; and as Captain Morrison brought the yacht alongside the dock, a haze, perceptible on the waters, was just lifting at the rise of the sun. A generous breeze flapped the sails of the trolling crafts lying-to

awaiting company, but nearly all the trolling fleet had sailed
hours before, and the lowness of the ebb tide warned us not
to delay.   We therefore wore away, passing between Barren
Island and Rockaway Beach, amid shrieks of gulls and flights
of duck, the sun lighting up the beach and the breakers, and
rendering them scintillant as they flashed upon us between
the clouds of fog which at fitful turns enveloped us.   Presently a gentle, fog-subduing warmth, with wind freshening,
made our jolly craft dance along, and all nature appeared de-
lightsome.

> "On the surface ranging, boys,
>   We'll beat from bay to bay;
> Sea and water changing, boys,
>   It's the angler's way:
>   So we troll,
>   One and all,
> And cheerily, cheerily pass the day."—STODDART.

We passed on near the Black Warrior, whose battered
wreck was lifted silently above the waves as a warning to im-
potent man against rashness.   Toward the Narrows and the
light-ship the fleet of trollers were gayly tacking and crossing each other's wakes hither and thither over the bluefish
shoals, so that,

> "Why sure, thought they,
>   The devil's to pay,
> 'Mongst folks above the water."

Soon we joined the merry fleet.   Our trolls had been put
out as we entered the bay, and our outriggers from each side
of the craft, a little aft of midships, consisting of stiff poles
with a line attached to the end of each, and a troll at the other end, but the line so short that the troll skittered on the top
of the waves.   A check line was fastened to the main one,
with its end in the boat, so as to draw the main line in without moving the hoop-pole rod to which it was attached.   In
addition to the two outriggers we had four trolling-lines out,
the ends of which were fastened to the taffrail of the boat.
Captain Morrison took the first fish, a ten-pounder.   "Small,"
said the captain.   Presently a whirl was made at one of my

squids; another dash, and he hooked himself. I took hold to pull him in hand over hand, but the pull was quite enough for me. Before I landed him another was on my other squid, which my helper landed. Now a whopper fastened to my first hook, and I found him difficult to draw in; he weighed nearly twenty pounds, and was as much as I could manage. The prospect was most gay and enlivening, as the fleet consisted of small sail-boats, cat-boats, sloops, schooners, and yachts, over sixty in all, crossing and jibing, while the trollers were tugging and hauling at fish, and all seemed to vie with the jollity of the gulls and the fun of the loons, which kept jabbering, with now and then a scream and hurrah, as if they joined in our sport.

We continued trolling until noon, when the wind died away and we turned our craft homeward. We counted our take, which numbered thirty-six fish, and weighed four hundred and eighty pounds, averaging over thirteen pounds each. Thus ended one of the most interesting, health-giving, and delightful days of the season.

Trolling with sail and row boats in September and October is extensively indulged in by amateurs and professional fishermen who fish for a livelihood along the shores from the east end of Massachusetts to Chesapeake Bay; and as the shoals begin to turn southward in September, the best trolling is in October along Long Island and the Jersey shores, after which the angling is good along the coasts of Maryland and Virginia up to December.

Although the bluefish is sufficiently plucky to take a coarse troll, and few venture to angle for him with ordinary tackle, even with gimp snells, yet, with good bass-tackle and strong hooks, either wound with copper wire on a heavy gimp leader or snell, or with a hook fastened with wire to a piano string, capital sport is found at still-baiting for them from a boat anchored along the edge of tideways in the estuaries and near the shores of bays. The coast of Rhode Island, and

the islands which form the Elizabeth group, are filled with
shoals of them all summer and fall, where they forage for
menhaden and young mackerel; and, anchoring in either of
the straits which separate those islands, we find that the cast
of a menhaden bait is usually met by the generous offers of
half a dozen fish, whose whirls make the tide boil. Were it
not that the electrical jerk of the bite of a large bluefish has
such great power in it as to make the angler sometimes feel
that he too is being fished for, and that its teeth are so sharp
as to make strong and heavy tackle necessary, it would be
considered incomparably the highest game-fish of the American coast.

When estimating the value of anglers' fishes by the play
they give, and the scenes into which the angler is led in
search of each kind, the bluefish must occupy a foremost
rank; and the man who has neither trolled nor still-baited for
this peculiar fish—the best breakfast fish on our coast except
the Spanish mackerel — has two treats in store, which, the
sooner he improves, the earlier he will regret that he had not
tasted before.

SECTION TENTH.

THE SPANISH MACKEREL.

Lovely with all their spangled dyes,
Fairer than flush'd autumnal skies,
With gold-drops all their sides a-glow,
Tinct like the rainbow's prismy bow,
The Spanish mackerel gorgeous roam
The rolling, yeasty world of foam ;
Now glittering o'er the waves they skim,
Now lost in deep abysses swim.

This incomparable breakfast luxury is a comparative stranger to us, and, though never known to venture as far north
as the fortieth degree of latitude until about ten years since,
yet his families are now as numerous on our coast as are those
of most other estuary fishes. He is coy and careful, slow to
make acquaintance, and doubtful of a squid or baited hook.

A select family of the mackerel tribes, he is not yet fully understood by either amateurs or fishermen, and commands a
higher price than salmon in the markets. Apart from being
the greatest beauty that swims, he is undoubtedly the best
fish for the gridiron to be found in the waters of either hemisphere.

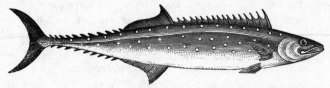

THE SPANISH MACKEREL.

My experience in trolling for the Spanish mackerel off the
inlets of Fire Island has convinced me that the fish is as numerous as the bluefish, more so than the striped bass at certain seasons, and a little farther seaward than either of those
fishes. The striped bass is the fish which ventures nearest
shore; the bluefish feeds in a range farther from shore, and
the Spanish mackerel feeds farther from shore than either,
except the large bluefish at the last of the season. Every
year the shoals of Spanish mackerel become more numerous,
and more are taken, but never in sufficient numbers to reduce
the average price below sixty cents per pound.

The shoals which I saw, when last trolling for them, would
have formed an area of nearly five miles square, and still the
most successful boat did not take more than a dozen in three
days. He will not bite freely at any artificial lure, and
though numbers came near leaping on the deck of our yacht,
they treated our lures with an indifference which savored of
perverseness. " Oh !" thought I, " how I would like to be anchored in a small boat, and still-bait for you with a pearl
squid, a shiner, or a gar-eel !" But the difficulty was that
their favorite feeding-grounds seemed to be just beyond the
verge of anchorage for a row-boat. This fish is eminently
shy of all kinds of nets, and, when a shoal is surrounded by a

shir-net or seine, will point their heads down in the bottom of sand or weeds, and the nets glide over their backs without capturing one. Two intelligent fishermen of the south side of Long Island, men well learned in their trade, and who have for many years followed fishing successfully, concluded that they would turn their exclusive attention to the Spanish mackerel, and, by studying their habits and watching their movements, invent some plan for their capture, and thus enrich themselves. They persevered for three years, trying all sorts of artificial lures, differently constructed nets and fykes, set in different ways, besides employing the Spanish casting-net; but their patience became so exhausted that they relinquished the enterprise, and had learned to look at a shoal leaping so that thousands were above the wave at a time without causing the slightest emotion or sensation of either hope or fear. A few silly fish occasionally stray away from their shoal, and are found in a fyke or pound, and an occasional one hooks himself by indulging a dangerous curiosity; but the genius who will invent a successful method for taking the Spanish mackerel may be as sure of a fortune as the person who owns a goose which lays a large egg of gold every day.

The Spanish mackerel is much more beautiful than the dolphin, even when the latter is dying. Its back and sides, down to the corrugated lateral line, are dark blue, shot with purple and gold; below the line it is pink and gold for a short way, terminating in a white belly. The shaded parts of the body are ornamented with spots of gold, like new gold dollars, to the number of between twenty and thirty. Its scales are imperceptible to the naked eye, but they extend a short way up the fins also. The first dorsal is spinous-rayed, and the first rays of the second dorsal and pectoral are spinous; all the rest are soft, though the tail and anal fins are nearly rigid or set, and do not fall together or close like those of the common mackerel. There is a small adipose fin on each side extending from the tail three inches upward. Its head is a perfect cut-water, carved most artistically, and small in proportion. Its jaws are armed with small, fine teeth, that laugh at silk or linen reel-lines; gills of two rigidly resisting plies; meat white, but neither mealy nor flaky, though of close texture, creamy and peculiarly delicate, of most delicious flavor.

The Spanish mackerel is seldom taken with rod and reel, though small ones of from three to six pounds sometimes venture to taste a baited hook. I have taken two while angling for striped bass with shedder crab bait; but it is eminently a fish for the troll, if captivating trolls can be invented. These fish surround a shoal of gar-eels, butter-fish, shiners, spearing, or young menhaden, when the tiny baits—anxious to escape—rise to the surface, followed by the Spanish mackerel, which may be seen two miles distant, leaping, a thousand at a time, their forked tails conspicuous, and their bodies gleaming like miniature rainbows. The bite of a Spanish mackerel is very different from that of a bluefish. It is not so dashing or strong ; and when hooked, it swims deeper, and does not resist so pertinaciously. In size it ranges from three to fifteen pounds. It is often reported as having been taken of thirty pounds' weight, but this, I think, is an error. The bonetta is very like it in outline, and it is also a comparative stranger along our coast; one of these fish was recently taken in Jamaica Bay which weighed about thirty pounds, and the daily papers noticed it as a large Spanish mackerel; but the bonetta—as a food fish—is vastly inferior.

Both the Spanish mackerel and cero are spring-spawning fishes, and no doubt spawn in our bays, for there are occasionally small ones taken by the angler in June, before the large ones visit our shores, and I argue, therefore, that the small half-pounders are of last year's hatch.

Spanish mackerel and large bluefish shoal together while feeding, and woe be it to any soft-rayed herbivorous beauty that crosses their path. Bluefish and striped bass feed together also, but the bass swims deeper than the bluefish, and generally nearer shore. This is frequently proven while cast-

I

ing for striped bass; for if the cast be made beyond a certain
range, the angler is sure of a bluefish, if any thing.

I have here roughly sketched a part of a shoal of Spanish
mackerel feeding. To troll with hope of success for these

SPANISH MACKEREL FEEDING.

delicacies, employ a light, swift-sailing craft, and rig it with
a long outrigger on each side; for a heavy vessel cleaving a
shoal disperses the live bait on which they are feeding, and
the fright causes the shoal to settle without biting. Frequently have I trolled through a shoal of thousands, with
hundreds in sight all the time, and as the craft passed through
and got far enough from the shoal to tell, I have felt the bite,
and, while drawing the fish in, have commented upon the ease
of detecting the difference between the Spanish mackerel on
my troll from the hard-mouthed bluefish, only to be laughed
at a moment afterward as I landed a bluefish in the boat.
Said I, "This is, of course, a Spanish mackerel; any novice
might distinguish him by his bite; and then he comes in so
gently, but swims low." I can detect by the bite, when still-
baiting, almost any kind of estuary fish; but in trolling any
angler is liable to be deceived.

From the limited experience thus far gained by using

bright metal trolls, not one Spanish mackerel in ten thousand
will pay the least regard to them. Having ascertained that
they feed on several kinds of fishes, the squid-makers have
recently obtained some data to work from, and the following
are the latest and most captivating samples.

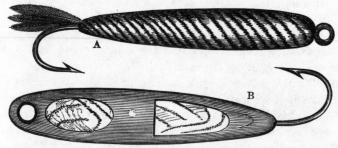

SPANISH MACKEREL SQUIDS.

A. Artificial squid or bait, made of Britannia metal, block tin,
or German silver. The hooks of all trolls should be tinned
or silver-plated. The shank of the hook extends through
the squid, and forms an eye to attach a trolling-line. Feathers extend beyond the bend of the hook to form the tail
of the gar-eel. The form of the squid is tapering, cylindrical, and about five inches long exclusive of the hook. It
should be kept polished as bright as possible, and is a very
taking lure. A tail of red ibis feathers would probably be
the most attractive.

B. Squid as bright as polished silver, inlaid with pieces of
pearl, and intended to represent a sea-shiner, about five
inches long besides the hook. The line is attached by a
hole in the end, and at the other there are several small
feathers from the red ibis. The shape of the body is half
as thick as it is wide, and in order to render it as ponderous as possible for its size, it is best to cast it of lead over
the hook, then plate it with copper, and plate or wash it
with silver. Spanish mackerel do not generally feed on
fish as large as the bluefish bait, and it is therefore impor-

tant to have a small but ponderous bait attached to a fifty-
yard line of the smallest size for trolling. The jaw of the
Spanish mackerel is tender, therefore he plays more gingerly, and does not resist so hard in landing as does the
bluefish; but he should be handled carefully, and prevented from taking slack line, as he unhooks easily.

My opinion is that this fish will yet be taken in great numbers with rod and reel. As they annually become more numerous, they come farther into the estuaries and back-sets
from the bays along the coast, and after they get a taste of
shedder and soft-shell crab, with smelt in abundance, and a
modicum of spearing and shrimp, they will soon make themselves more familiar, and accept the dainties offered on the
angler's hook; and when once fairly converted, he will afford
the angler better sport than the salmon or the striped bass.

SECTION ELEVENTH.

THE BONETTA, OR BONITO.

The bonetta is the beautiful and swift fish after which one
of our war vessels of the Revolution was named. The Spanish name is *bonito*. I prefer the other name because of its
associations. This fish is found in great numbers about the
West India Islands, where it preys on the flying-fish. His
first arrival along our beaches and in our bays was about
eight years ago, and his shoals have increased remarkably
fast ever since his advent. As a table luxury it ranks with
epicures below the striped bass and bluefish, but because of
its comparative rarity it commands a price rather above

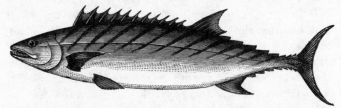

THE BONETTA, OR BONITO.—*Thynnus pelamys.*—Cuvier.

either. The numbers of this fish annually taken about the
approaches to our harbors with the troll and in nets increase,
so that it bids fair to become nearly as numerous as the bluefish. Of the shoals which venture along the shores of beaches
or breakwaters, the fish range in weight from five to fifteen
pounds, while farther south they are said to attain to the
weight of nearly a hundred.

The menhaden of our shores form the leading attraction to
the food-fishes of the troll, and they are so prolific that, if they
can be protected against oily speculators, there will be no
danger of our losing entirely any of the large food-fishes of
the coast.

The bonetta is very beautiful, having a dark greenish-blue
back, which lightens to midsides, and terminates in a satiny
white belly. The diagonal rays are nearly black, and extend
a little below the sinuous lateral line. The first dorsal is
spinous, as are the first rays of the second dorsal and pectoral. The tail is framed by two spinous rays, and never closes.
The anal fin is also rigid. There is an adipose fin about three
inches long from the tail up the lateral line, as on the Spanish
mackerel and cero. The mouth is armed with teeth both
strong and sharp. The tufts of fins from the second dorsal
and anal to the tail add to its superior means of propulsion,
and its shape, being perfectly adapted to cleaving the waters,
prove it to be one of the swiftest fishes of the soundings and
harbor approaches. Its scales are so small as not to be seen
without the aid of glasses. It is usually taken on a large
metal squid in trolling for bluefish, and very few have been
caught in fykes and pounds. It is a very voracious fish, and
generally in good condition and very gamy. It spawns about
June in our bays, but probably earlier in the season farther
south. While angling in company with Alderman Dodge,
last year, in Jamaica Bay, he took one which weighed less
than a pound, on shedder-crab bait; it was one of a shoal
hatched the year previous. Some fishing naturalists state
that it spawns about the islands of the Western Archipelago,

where it is known as the "albicore," and comes to Northern
waters for recuperation. Others suppose it to be the "tunny,"
which follows ships for the crumbs from the table, and attains, off the coast of Spain and in the Mediterranean, the
weight of a thousand pounds. I do not believe the bonetta
to be similar to the tunny, but I know that it is called albicore by some Southern fishermen. The fishes of our coast
and estuaries which I name as belonging to the troll are supposed to be of this hemisphere, and are spine-rayed families
of the mackerel tribes. I am often surprised at the innocence
of intelligent anglers, who do not know a cero from a Spanish
mackerel, nor the latter from a bonetta, or a spearing from a
smelt, and can not distinguish the great Northern pike from
the maskinongé.

SECTION TWELFTH.

THE CERO, CERUS, OR SIERRA.

It is rather a *cereus* matter to ascertain the names of such
fishes as ichthyologists have left out of their catalogues; and
as I make no pretensions of claiming this to be a school-book,
the angler will please scan the illustrations which I made per-
sonally from the fishes of which these are intended to be true
copies.

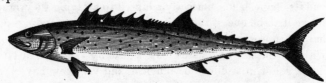

THE CERO, CERUS, OR SIERRA.

The cero is evidently a member of one of the mackerel
tribes, and in esculent quality ranks between the Spanish
mackerel and bonetta. It is a new visitant along the shores
from Virginia to Rhode Island, but it is quite numerous in
the West Indies. It evidently spawns in spring-time; is
white-meated; ranges in weight from four to twelve pounds;
is longer in proportion to its weight than any other of his

mackerel kindred; an individual specimen a yard in length weighs from six to eight pounds only. The cero is of a leaden color on the back and sides; belly and belly-fins white; back and sides sprinkled thickly with black dots nearly the size of peas. The first dorsal is spinous, as are also the first rays of the pectorals and second dorsal; all the others are rigid, but not spinous. The frame of the tail is spinous, but the tail is translucent; it has an adipose fin each side on the lateral line at the tail. Its jaws are armed with serrulated teeth which laugh at any cords softer than copper wire. I believe that none have yet been taken with rod and reel, though they are said to be very ravenous biters and ambitious vaulters, which can leap much higher than a salmon. They are taken in increased numbers annually by persons while trolling with common Britannia metal squids for bluefish. This fish has no apparent scales.

THE HORSE MACKEREL.

HIS monster mackerel is supposed to be a "*thynnus*," as some members of its family weigh nearly a ton; but I may be in error, and the fish may be the head of the mackerel tribes, whose family commands the coast from Nantucket to the Straits of Belle Isle. At Quebec and Gaspe it is called "Bluefish." The name may have been derived from its leaden color, and having a head like the New York bluefish, though its body discloses a few mackerel marks, and its tail is like that of the *bonito*. While in Gaspe I sketched the head and tail of a horse mackerel which had just been harpooned in the Bay of Gaspe by Thomas Morland, Esq. The fish weighed

seven hundred and fifty pounds, was nine feet in length, and
six feet in circumference. The illustration here given is a

THE HORSE MACKEREL.—Genus *Thynnus*.

copy of my sketch of the fish made from still life. As Gaspe
is a great fishing port, the "old salts" would have detected
this fish as a tunny, had it been one. That it is a great delicacy for the table is proven by its marketable value, which
nearly equals, per pound, that of the salmon in the vicinity
where both fishes are taken. It is stated that this fish attains
to the weight of two thousand pounds, but it is very rare to
take one of more than a thousand. This eight-hundred-
pounder towed the boat to which the line of the harpoon
was fastened nearly five miles. They are taken, like the
swordfish, by sailing for them; and when coming on a shoal,
or even a single one, a well-aimed harpoon is sent into the
fish where its head unites to the body, and then the towing-
line is manned carefully, and the fish tows the boat until he
gets fatigued, and, when in a fainting condition, the lance
bleeds him in the gills, and he is towed alongside until his
powerful rigid tail has made its last flap; then he is raised
into the boat, a subject of wonder to the amateur. I think
the horse mackerel one of the links in the chain of fishes
whose head is the tunny, and which rank as follows: Tunny,
horse mackerel, bonetta, bluefish, Spanish mackerel, cero,
winding up with the common mackerel, which—as the bar-
ber said of the baker when asked to shave a coal-heaver—
"is as low as we go."

It will be seen by the conformation of the horse mackerel

that his propulsive power is equal in proportion to that of the bluefish, and so are his teeth. The foot or hand of a man would stand no chance in the jaws of this monster delicacy. Talk of the bad reputation of the *Silurus glanis* of the Danube because portions of human bodies have been found in their stomachs! the horse mackerel would make nothing of chopping up both man and fish. This is not a fish for the troll, or the rod and reel; for it is as strong in proportion to its weight as the bluefish, and it would trouble an angler to kill a thirty-pound bluefish, or even take him in by trolling. But sailing for horse mackerel is rare sport; and I would advise those about New Bedford and Martha's Vineyard, who delight so much in sailing for and harpooning swordfish, to sail down about Nantucket for horse mackerel, where they are comparatively numerous.

To conclude: Having presented the best samples of the coast and estuaries for affording sport by the recreative art of angling, I will postpone for the present the description of those commercial fishes which belong of right to the harpoon, the net, and the hand-line.

> Pale student, who consumes the night
> With learned vigils till the light;
> Merchant, who toils in city street
> Through all the summer's fervid heat;
> All ye tired sons of gold and gain,
> Turn from your weary tasks of pain,
> And haste to wood, and bay, and stream,
> Where health, and joy, and sunshine beam.

Part Second.

---⟨⟩⟨⟩---

FRESH-WATER FISHING

WITH

FLY AND BAIT.

CHAPTER I.

THE POETRY OF ANGLING.

SECTION FIRST.

"The patient angler threads the winding brook,
Tempting the dainty trout with gilded
bait ;
And ever and anon, as fleecy clouds
Pass o'er the sun, the fish voracious
darts
From the cool shadows of some mossy
bank,
Swallows the bait with one convulsive
act,
And learns too late that death was at
the feast ;
While the glad sportsman feels the
sudden jerk,
And plays his victim with extended
line,
Swiftly he darts, and through the glittering rings
The silken line is drawn with ringing
sound,
Till, wearied out with struggling that
but serves
To drive the barbed weapon deeper
still,
He seeks his quiet shelter 'neath the
bank,
And thence in triumph to the shore is
borne,
A prize that well rewards a day of
toil."

THE question has been discussed by hundreds of enlightened minds, from King Leopold to Bill Kromer—from men
highest in the sciences and most exalted in the state, to the
lowest in worldly means and position, as to who can ade-

quately describe the pleasures that surround the angler? The most compendious, truthful, and summary is contained in the poetical exclamation of O. W. Holmes in the following couplet :

> "Oh! what are the treasures we perish to win,
> To the first little minnow we caught with a pin!"

But who can catalogue the pleasures which cluster around the angler's pursuit? He pursues his avocations amid scenes of beauty. "It is he who follows the windings of the silver river, and becomes acquainted with its course. He knows the joyous leaps it takes down the bold cascade, and how it bubbles rejoicingly in its career over the rapids. He knows the solitude of its silent depths, and the brilliancy of its shallows. He is confined to no season. He can salute Nature when she laughs with the budding flowers, and when her breath is the glorious breath of spring. The rustling sedges make music in his ear when the mist has rolled off the surface of the water, or the dew been kissed from the grass by the sun's rays." The lark sings for him, and robin red-breast, with the brown thrush and jolly bobolink, pipe and chirp their mellifluous notes along his path. The gorgeous kingfisher heeds him not, and the meadow-hen seldom moves from her nest as he passes. The storm and the tempest scarcely hinder his sport. He throws the line when ruddy Autumn gilds the western heavens, and the fruit of the year hangs heavy on the bough, or waves in golden abundance on the uplands. Even stern Winter does not forbid him his enjoyment. If he cares to pursue his favorite pastime, he may do so equally when the tall bulrushes, wavy reeds, and chestnuts rattle with December's winds, as when the marsh marigold opens its big yellow eyes on an April day, or the birds of all song, size, and feather congregate along the streams, and teter on the sprays that kiss the ripples, while they chirp and cavort with their mates on yonder side the stream. The autumn trolling season over, the angler begins to think of the springing into life of all nature, when again the frogs begin to croak, the trout to leap, the wild geese to honk, the kine to low, and material nature gushingly bursts forth into new life and loveliness. If he is an ardent sportsman, the whole year is before him. When the trout in spring, the salmon in summer, the striped bass in early autumn, and the trolling for bluefish, Spanish mackerel, cero, and bonetta wind up the falling season, he may hie to the Carolinas and Florida, where the oranges, amid labyrinths of flowers, greet his senses, and there troll for black bass and angle for bream to his heart's content.

"It was always so in the infancy of mankind; the finny tribes were pursued by a primitive people with as much ardor as they are by civilized men at the present time. Savage and cultivated nations equally followed, either as a business or as a pastime, the occupation of capturing fish with a line and hook, with or without a rod. We find its praises celebrated in ancient poetry, and its memory embalmed in holy writ." The rudest appliances of a savage life have been used to aid the angler at his delightful task, and science has not disdained to aid the modern fisherman in his sport. There are tribes who yet fashion fish-hooks out of human jaw-bones, and the Saxons managed to snare fish with hooks formed of flint. Indeed, the Anglo-Saxon race have followed angling with an energy and a zest far beyond any other nation, not excepting the Chinese, whose great perseverance is devoted rather to cultivate fishes than insnare them. We know the inhabitants of the British Isles pursued it as a profitable occupation in remote times, and we have it on the authority of the venerable Bede that the people of Sussex were at one time preserved from famine by being taught by Wilfred to catch fish. Among the earliest printed books is one on fishing, by Dame Juliana Berners or Barnes, prioress of the nunnery of Sopwell, near St. Alban's. This book was printed in 1496. The old lady shows that if sport fails the ambitious angler, his time is not spent in vain, for has he not, "atte the leest, his holsom walke, and merry at his ease, a

swete ayre of the swete sauvoure of the meede flowres, that
makyth him hungry; he hereth the melodyous armony of
fowles; he seeth the young swannes, heerons, ducks, cotes,
and many other fowles with theyr brodes; whyche me sem-
yth better than all the noyse of houndys, the blastes of
hornys, and the scrye of fowlis, that hunters, frunkeners, and
fowlers do make. And," says the good old lady, " if the angler take fysshe, surely their is no man merier than he is in
his spyryte."

Angling, in modern times, is the most refined of all field-
sports. If the angler take a fish, he knows that it is only one
of a spawn of from a thousand to many hundred thousands,
and that all shoals which can, prey on one another. Not only
so, but the old prey on their own offspring; and from the
time when the mother fish appears in the spawning-pools,
there are several milt fish waiting to gorge themselves with
the *ova;* and so, during all stages of fishhood, the larger eat
the lesser ones, and—as cold-blooded animals—they can not
be susceptible to an acute sense of pain. These truths can
not be said in favor of killing a land animal, whose annual
procreative increase never amounts to a tithe of any individual of the oviparous fishes.

The innocence of angling is therefore a feature which has
commended it to the good of all ages. "When bank and
meadow lie starred and enameled with flowers; when the
trill of the song-bird issues from every thorn; when all sounds
and all prospects are joyous and exhilarating, and the cloud
itself, sleeping high in the arch of heaven, is as the honored
presence of some benevolent watcher;" with the soul toned
by the sights, sounds, and exercise into a state of harmony
with all nature, then.the angler realizes that the precious gift
he enjoys is

> " One of the spirits unwithdrawn,
> That, erst the fall, were charged to minister
> To the earth's gladness, and continually,
> Out of their ample and unfailing horns,
> To pre-endow the advancing tracks of men."

Modern improvements in anglers' implements, and recent inventions in lures to captivate by trolling, have rendered the angler of to-day very different from the ancient dreamy fishing philosopher. Especially is the difference from the ancient angler—as portrayed by good Izaak Walton—observable in the United States of America, where an angler is expected to scull a boat with alacrity and pull an oar gracefully, to sail a boat and man a pair of trolling-lines, to brave the ocean's dashing surf and spray, and, clad in sailor's garb of water-proof material, stand on the rocks of the shore and cast menhaden bait for striped bass, and play large fish from a stand where the dashing waves threaten continually to wash him off.

The art of angling has become so rich in variety of implements, so varied in scenes, so replete with all the elements for exercise—as well for the student as for the man of action —as to render it a recreation entirely satisfactory to its disciples, who believe that

> "All pleasures but the angler's bring
> I' th' tail repentance like a sting."

Men of cultivation and natural gentleness of disposition have frequently been known to indulge in the chase, and follow a well-trained dog with pleasure, though they are often known to forego these for angling; but there was never a true angler known to exchange his gentle wand, his quiet rambles among the most charming haunts of nature, for any other means of recreation.

> "Bear lightly on their foreheads, Time!
>   Strew roses on their way;
> The young in heart, however old,
>   That prize the present day.

> "I love to see a man forget
>   His blood is growing cold,
> And leap, or swim, or gather flowers,
>   Oblivious of his gold,
> And mix with children in their sport,
>   Nor think that he is old.

K

"I love to see the man of care
　　Take pleasure in a toy;
I love to see him row or ride,
　　And tread the grass with joy,
Or throw the circling salmon fly
　　As lusty as a boy.

"The road of life is hard enough,
　　Bestrewn with slag and thorn;
I would not mock the simplest joy
　　That made it less forlorn,
But fill its evening path with flowers
　　As fresh as those of morn."

SECTION SECOND.

THE BROOK TROUT.

Where the tangled willowy thickets lave
Their drooping tassels within the wave,
There lies a deep and darkened pool,
Whose waters are crystal clear and cool.
It is fed by many a gurgling fount,
That trickles from upland pasture and mount,
And when the deep shadows fall dense and dim,
The speckled trout delight to swim.

The illustration on the opposite page is a copy of a trout drawn by Walter M. Brackett, Esq., of Boston, as a contribution to this work. Of his gifts and inspirations, it is difficult to decide whether he draws trout best with a fly-rod or a pencil. He is authority for either, and in painting fishes has no superior.

This book—not being especially devoted to ichthyology—could scarcely be improved by giving the *genus* and family of each separate fish of which it treats; but as the heading indicates that the brook trout belongs to the *genus Salmo*, I will add that it is still questionable with some ichthyologists whether the trout is not the head of the *genus*, and the salmon belongs to the *genus Trutta*, or the trout is distinct from the *genus Salmo*. Pliny confounded them, and the different members of the *genus Salmo* were never assigned their position by the aid of science until within the present century.

The scales of the trout are imperceptible to the naked eye;

The Brook Trout.—*Salmo fontinalis.*

all its fins are soft-rayed except the second dorsal, which is
adipose; its caudal fin, or tail, is nearly straight across the
end, contradistinguished from the other families of the *genus,*
including lake trout.   Its meat is generally pinky or salmon-
colored, and of all the shades between pink and white, the
mallow-colored trout is preferred for perfection of *goût.* The
meat laminates in flakes, and, when in best condition, there is
a curd-like leaf of creamy succulency between each flake.
Trout taken in streams which empty into tide-waters are
usually in best condition, because their food consists of smelt,
spearing, shrimp, herring roe, roes of other fishes and their
alevins, in addition to their *desserts* of flies to render them
more delicate, to say nothing of ground bait driven down the
stream by freshets, and from which our Beau Brummels of
the estuary turn aside their beautiful noses.   Streams backed
by saline tides are not often impregnated by the *débris* carried down with the floods or by any foreign substance; hence
New Yorkers regard Long Island trout as the best, while Bos-
tonians consider the Marshfield trout as the *ne plus ultra.*
Though I accord a preference to trout which have access to
tide-waters, those of mountain streams are better than any
pond trout.   Writers upon angling mention many families
of the brook trout; there are doubtless very many, but in the
United States I know of but few.   A marked peculiarity is
observable in the trout of the Umbagog range of lakes and

rivers, in the State of Maine, whose fins are bordered on one side with a ray of pure white; but I know of none which are not definable as *Salmo fontinalis*, differing only in quality and unimportant superficial marks, generally caused by the distinctive properties of the waters which each family in habits. Thus the black-mouthed trout of the swâmpy forest would soon become assimilated to the trout of the saline estuaries were they transported thither. Upon this subject permit me to quote from Thomas Tod Stoddart, a very high authority:

"Of the food and habits of trout I have said comparatively little; nor have I called direct attention to what may be termed the cross-breeds, in contradistinction to the true or original breed peculiar to each stream or lake. * * * * I may notice that the cross-breeds to which I refer are simply those which have their origin in the different varieties of the common trout brought into contact with each other at the breeding season, and do not implicate the questionable produce, or mule breed, arising from any haphazard connection between the *fario* and bull trout, or whitling, a connection altogether discountenanced by nature, and not likely to take place. I may also remark that, although cross varieties may for a season, or term of seasons, rival in number the true breed belonging to this or that stream, and threaten to extinguish it altogether, yet there is no fear or likelihood of such a result, the peculiar nature and qualities of the water, aided by the remaining original stock, always tending to reinstate the breed." This is merely reasserting that the qualities of the *water* and *feed* will govern and regulate the *color* and *quality* of all trout of the same breed, whether *fontinalis* or *fario*.

The speckled beauty known as the brook trout has been an exhaustless theme for pastoral poets of all ages. It has afforded recreation for thousands of years to most of the lovers of nature throughout the temperate zone of the northern hemispheres. The old and young, the learned and ignorant, the poor and rich—all classes, ages, and conditions, have enjoyed the sport of angling for trout. It possibly calls forth more tact and discipline of both mind and body to successfully invent and present the lures most captivating to it than to any other fresh-water fish. Although the brook trout is probably the most numerous of all the game fishes, and sought for by the greatest number of contemplative philosophers, yet it may be angled for with the commonest tackle, and with a willow wand cut by the side of any stream, or it may be fished for with a very elaborate apparatus, and in either case afford genuine sport.

The common trout is the standard sport of the enthusiastic angler. In many countries the trout and salmon are the only varieties of game fishes which interest the angler; and while salmon-fishing may be justly regarded as the highest branch of fresh-water sport, yet it has been justly said by Francis Francis that "a good trout-fisher will easily become an expert at salmon-fishing; but a very respectable practitioner with the salmon-rod will often have all his schooling to do afresh, should he descend to trout-fishing, before he can take rank as a master of the art."

But it is left to the American angler to enjoy those numerous and various resources of sport unknown to the European. Our black bass are nearly as high game as the salmon, while some think the striped bass higher, not to name the other varieties of game for the rod and the troll, which shoal in myriads along our coasts, and in the estuaries of innumerable rivers debouching in salt waters.

After enumerating the fascinations of all other fishes, the mind settles in pleasurable contemplation of the brook trout. His capture is so delicate, and yet so artistic. Even the rustic is taught refinement of address by following a trout stream with his ash wand. Trouting is an abiding and universal source of pleasure to all classes and conditions of men and boys—ay, and of ladies also. It must therefore be invested with a great variety of elements intended to create refined emotions of pleasure to the best minds; and while much of it is due to the incomparable beauty and superior qualities of the fish, yet his habits and attributes command unmixed admiration. "He is an intellectual kind of creature, and has evidently a will of his own. He looks sagacious and intelligent—sedulously avoids thick, troubled, and muddy waters—prefers the clear spring stream—displays an ardent ambition to explore streams to their source—is quick, vigorous, and elegant in his movements—likes to have the exclusive command of the stream—keeps up a rigid system of order and discipline in the little community of which he is a member—exhibits a remarkable degree of nicety and fastidiousness about his food—is comparatively free from vulgar, low, and groveling habits—entices his pursuer into the loveliest scenes of Nature's domains—calls forth from man his utmost ingenuity and skill—and, in a word, in every stage of his existence preserves a dignified demeanor, unattainable by any other living occupant of the streams.

"While these may be styled his social and intellectual qualities, his physical constitution is equally entitled to our respectful consideration. He discloses a prepossessing and fascinating figure, moulded in strict conformity with most refined principles of symmetrical proportion, sparkles in all the gorgeous colors of the rainbow, and occupies a distinguished position in the important science of gastronomy."

Reasons which combine to establish so high an estimate in the regard of anglers are connected with the idea that the amber beauty is gifted with *mind*, for in every thing which claims human attention, mind, real or imaginary, in the object is necessary to attract our serious notice and to secure our lasting esteem.

Once nearly every stream in the Middle, Northern, and Eastern States teemed with both trout and salmon. The salmon have been driven away, and, had not anglers interfered to save the trout, the luxury would now only be known from books and the stories of the oldest inhabitants. As it is, the trout streams have been so depleted and thinned of their most attractive beauty that restocking by artificial means has been found necessary as a last resort.

Before addressing myself to the task of describing the artistic means for capturing this beauty of the brook, it should be known that it is not lawful to take trout in the State of New York by any other means than with the angle in fly and bait fishings. Considering the diminished numbers in our best streams, and the swift-growing density of the population throughout the North, it is a question of importance whether this law should not be adopted by all the states north and east. The inhabitants of the United States are a peculiar people in some things, and in no one element is this more patent than in their running on the last idea, to the disregard of all others. This is eminently so in artificial fish-culture. There are many waters which require protection only to render the increase of trout abundant; but instead of protecting the waters by proper legal enactments, and faithfully carrying them out, some states leave the waters to the mercy of nets and spears. They appropriate sums of money for propagating trout, and while the fish-culturist is hatching trout on the middle of a stream, the mouth is being netted, and the spawning-grounds thinned with the spear. This is "feeding at the spigot and leaking at the bung."

Game-laws should be enacted in each state establishing the fence or close seasons for game fish and game animals, thus protecting them while with young, while hatching, and until they have recovered and fattened sufficiently for the table. The legal season for taking trout in the State of New York is from March until October, leaving six months of the year wherein it is unlawful to take trout by any means. It would be well if the Northern and Eastern States could unite upon a close season, as it would assist to prevent poaching. Although I have no key to fit the humor of the selfish proprietor who would begrudge the laboring man his snatch of pleasure at this universal and favorite pastime, or limit him to

A POACHER.

hours in a day's fishing, where by he might add a real zest in the way of luxurious variety to his every-day fare, yet I would second all efforts to thwart the poacher, who robs the streams of their life and beauty to sell, when these waters are bequeathed to the poor as well as to the rich as a health-giving blessing.

"Bill Blossom was a nice young man,
 And drove the Bury coach;
But bad companions were his bane,
 And egged him on to poach.

"*Once*, going to his usual *haunts*,
 Old Cheshire laid his plots;
He got entrapped by legal *Berks*,
 And lost his life in *Notts*."—HOOD.

The poacher is an unmitigated scamp wherever found. On Long Island he robs the streams by night with fine silken nets, which he conceals in a pocket or in the crown of his hat (if he have one), and, knowing all the by-paths of the island as they meander among the net-work formed of dwarf pine and scrub oak, he approaches a trout stream after midnight. There are usually two poachers in company. They set the net across a narrow place in the stream, and while one attends to it, the other drives in the trout. The meshes of the net are so small that a two-ounce trout can not escape. Before daylight the poachers are back at their wretched homes, and those who wink at the crime purchase the fish, and send them to the New York markets. The fish being in season, no questions are asked. It is difficult to detect poachers on the island, because proprietors of real estate and hotel-keepers are afraid to inform against these desperadoes, lest they should, in revenge, add arson to poaching.

There is not within any settled portion of the United States

another piece of territory where the trout streams are comparatively so numerous and productive as they are throughout Long Island.   It is scarcely possible to travel a mile in
any direction without crossing a trout stream, whether from
Coney Island to Southampton on the south side, or from
Newtown to Greenport on the north side; and when taking
into account the necessity for a kind of recreation which shall
not be too violent for the thousands of debilitated citizens
who are pent up in squares of brick and mortar, and engaged
at sedentary occupations, it is impossible to estimate in dollars the value of a recreation which, while it is sufficiently
free, airy, and attractive to inflate the lungs, jog the biliary
organs, and unbend the mind, is not so difficult to pursue as
to prevent the most delicate in *physique* from enjoying it.
The value of the Long Island trout streams to New York City
is inestimable, for each one of them is approachable by railroad in a few hours.   In a hygienic sense, therefore, they are
above price.   How deep must therefore be the turpitude of
the crime of that vagrant class of vagabonds who recklessly
rob the streams of their life, beauty, and means of recreation
to the overworked citizen who depends on angling instead
of physic for restoring his waning health of body and decreasing vigor of mind !

Streams in New Jersey and Connecticut, and those west
of the Hudson to the Delaware Rivers, and far beyond in both
this state and Pennsylvania, contain trout, and many of them
are well stocked.   Indeed, it would be difficult to find a stream
within a radius of a hundred miles from the city of New
York which has not more or less trout in it.   The paper-mills,
railroads, bleaching-fields, chemicals of acids and gases, lime,
manures, and numerous kinds of manufactories which cast
their choking and poisonous débris and filtrations into the
streams, have not proved sufficient to depopulate them of
their speckled beauties ; and were it not for the poacher, who
stops not at nets, spears, snares of singular device, killing the
trout by liming the streams and poisoning them with *coculus*

indicus, they would still be so numerous as to require nothing toward propagation but protection.   Want of moral rectitude, indolence, and greed make up the modest sum total of a poacher's character; and the sooner the class is forced to work for the state the better, therefore our legislators will please take note of the true penalty for poaching.

SECTION THIRD.

FLY-FISHING FOR TROUT.

> "Thin, o'er the wave, the quivering insects skim,
> And faintly dip their pinions on its brim.
> Winter its power has not yet resigned,
> And yet, I fear, the weather is unkind.
> But there, an answer to that doubt receive—
> A gallant trout!—behold it, and believe."

Here we see the fly-fisher wading a brook while it rains, with shoulders protected by a water-proof cape, and extremities clad in India-rubber boots, with silk rubber attached and extending up to the thighs, thus rendering the toggery light, and so impervious as to keep the shoulders and feet of the angler dry.   The boy with rolled-up trousers represents the ancient angler.   He quietly contemplates and fishes in a drenching rain, taking eels, catfish, and chubs in the pool below the beaver-dam, never dreaming of a trout, when an apparition wading the stream surprises him as the fly-fisher casts his line, armed with artificial flies, quite over his pole, and hooks a trout to his great astonishment.

Fly-fishing is more indolent and elegant than bait-fishing. From the streams on the Styrian Alps, eastward over Hungary, and westward over all the vast empire of intellectual man, wherever the lands are divided by the ornamental tracery of trout streams, even to the mildly sublime Pacific Ocean, fly-fishing is regarded as an elegant accomplishment. To cast a fly gracefully, so that it will fall in the right place like a snow-flake, or light like a winged insect, requires practice.   The beginner should not attempt to cast too long a line.   Let him first try to throw a line as long as his rod, say

FLY-FISHING FOR TROUT.

twelve feet of line; then increase the length as he learns to
cast it, so that it will lie straight on the water, and a trout,
in attempting to taste, will be sure to hook himself, because
there is no slack line. This is important; for if the trout
strikes at a fly on a slack line, he at once becomes disgusted
at so lame an effort to deceive, and the slack-line fisher will
never receive a second visit from him. But if you cast
a straight line, and the trout misses the fly, he will come

again, sometimes as many as four times, before he fastens. It is necessary that the line be so straight that a slight touch will be felt by the angler, and that a responsive jerk at the top of the rod will be sure to fasten the fish. But if the line is slack, and the trout happens to get hooked, he will be likely to disgorge before the angler has time to strike. Do not be in a hurry to lay out more line than you can cast straight from the tip of your rod to your stretcher-fly. Some good fly-fishers prefer to cast a short line, because it is so much easier for them to hook their fish and play him. Especially is this the case when trout are plenty. On Long Island they are educated; but even there do not strain your nerves and muscles to make a wide cast. Experience is the only teacher who will confer the perfection of casting.

So soon as the angler learns to lay out thirty feet of line straight, without a bend from the tip of his rod, he may count himself a fly-fisher; and as he continues to practice for improving in the elegance of his casting, he will naturally acquire the habit, so that fifty or sixty feet casts will be done with perfect ease, grace, and precision. Over-hand and under casts will be his next practice, in order to succeed in wading a stream overhung with willows or alders, or margined with large trees whose wide projecting branches warn the angler to beware lest he cast too high.

Many simple souls suppose angling an indolent pastime; and Johnson's plagiarism from a Greek author of " a stick and a string, with a fool at one end and a worm at the other," helped to fix in the minds of the ignorant the impression which the stolen aphorism was intended to convey. Such vulgar witticisms may please the splenetic; they only disgust liberal-minded men.

A word more about the costume of our model angler. The color of the dress should either be *green*, to blend with the foliage, or *gray*, to harmonize with the shade of the rocks. Wading boots, with rubbered silk extensions, are the lightest and best, except, perhaps, the Scotch wading stockings, of quite recent invention, and imported by our principal fishing-tackle houses. A cape of water-proof silk may be carried in the pocket, and put on as a protection to the shoulders in case of a shower, as it is not too warm and does not impede casting.

Trouting on Long Island is the most artistic angling that I have ever seen practiced, either in Europe or America. The trout there appear to have learned to detect many of the angler's artifices. Fly-fishing is there practiced near the estuaries of streams, where they are influenced by the tides, so that in flood tide the fisher begins below and casts along as the tide makes, as far up the stream as the trout feed; and when the tide turns, the angler fishes along down with the tide and the feeding fish. There being little protection to veil the angler from the tenants of the stream, it is necessary that he keep far back from the bank, which necessitates long casts, and frequently the first intimation which the angler receives of a bite is the gushing and slapping rise of the fish, and the tremulously nervous resistance at the end of his line; then approaches the play and the contest, when light—but finely-constructed—tackle tells. Deftly and gingerly are the words, for Long Island trout are not to be trifled with. The rod should be permitted to do its duty, and the angler be neither impatient nor excited. Anglers who have never visited Long Island are comparatively innocent of the real zest of trouting; for, without being annoyed with stinging and biting flies, the trout are as large and as free from rust or the effects of discolored waters as are those of the estuaries on the coast of Maine or along the Gulf of St. Lawrence. On the island they run from a quarter to three pounds in weight, sometimes more, and are in the highest state of succulent adiposity. The climate is charming, surroundings most inviting, hotels where good cheer greets the sportsman throughout the year. I love Long Island, and venerate its trout streams.

> " Nature hath endless aspects : to the angler
> She doth her beauties and her glories all unfold ;
> A magic light rests upon land and sea,
> And all her brooks are silver, all her sunshine gold."

What angler's heart does not beat more quickly at the joyous announcement of the opening day of the trouting season? He will find, upon asking himself seriously, be he rich or poor, learned or ignorant, that no announcement of any other recreation so thrills his heart. The emotion caused by the school-master when he used to say " boys may go out," or " there will be a vacation until next Monday," is quadrupled and sublimated by the permission given from a higher sphere, as if Heaven said " boys may go out." Go forth from your counting-houses, your mephitic offices, your workshops, for it is the opening day of the trouting season!

> " With Winter's frown let sadness cease,
> And cankering care,
> And o'er the brow sweet smiles of peace
> Wreathe garlands fair ;
> From joyous Nature catch the smile,
> And every weary hour beguile
> From care and pain—
> Join, join with bird and flowing stream
> In shouting forth the rapturous theme,
> 'Tis Spring again,
> 'Tis Spring again!"

Who can forget the angling of old at Oba. Snedicor's? The late Daniel Webster used to be there on the opening day of the trouting season, and so did many of our truly great men. It was there that John Stephens was advised to sail his yacht in the regatta in England, which resulted in his winning the race. But the Snedicor Preserve is now in different hands. A close club of wealthy and intellectual sportsmen own it, and they have rendered it worthy of its name, the " Southside Club."

The light, artistic character of the fly-fisher's tackle proves him a disciple of the fine arts, though translating their spirit into graceful action.

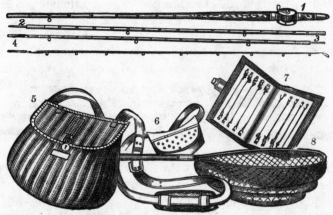

TROUTING TACKLE.

Numbers 1, 2, 3, 4. Split bamboo trout-rod and click reel. The hand-hold above the reel is either velvet or plain wood. This trout-rod is eminently American; joints and rings of German silver, the rings gradually diminishing in size from butt to top. A spliced top joint is to be preferred. 5. Wicker-basket with padlock, and plate for owner's name; sliding shoulder-pad on the strap. 6. Tin bait-box, painted, perforated lid, and waist-belt. The strap is sometimes so made as to connect with the basket-strap, when the box is worn or left off, at the option of the wearer. In case of connecting the bait-strap with the basket-strap, the basket is supported by the left shoulder, and the bait-strap attaches at the waist, so that the right arm is entirely free for casting. 7. Fly-book with leaves of Bristol-board, or other stiff material, to which are attached short ends of elastic, with a hook to attach a loop, and a ring at the other end of the leaf for the hook. This plan of carrying flies without bending the gut was invented by Mr. Hutchinson, of Utica, New York, and the cards may either be attached to the book or laid in as leaves, so that the angler may merely take a single leaf of selected flies, and place it in his pocket-book for a day's fishing. 8. Landing-net. Rim of hollow brass wire. Meshes large and of not too fine twine. Handle formed of two joints which screw together, or made so that the joint connected with the net will slide into the butt. The oval shape of rim is better than the round one.

MODERN SPLICE FOR FLY RODS.

A correspondent of the FIELD (London), January 4, 1868, described the modern splice, and gave it his name of the "Robinson Splice," but since then several contributors claim to have used the same splice many years; and the reason for giving it to my readers is that every angler, when writing upon it, commends it. It is generally used for splices of salmon-rods, but I can not see why it would not be equally useful for splicing the top joint of a trout-rod. The following is the description: "The splice is of the ordinary length, with a small, thin rim, or flat ring of brass at the thick end of each splice; the thin end of each splice fits so tightly into (under) the brass rim or ring at the thick end of the other one that it will not shift in the least degree; a length of waxed glover's or tailor's thread, tied on at your leisure (for all is hard held to your hand by the brass rings), completes the splice."

Numbers 1, 2, 3 present a side view of the splice, and 4, 5 a surface view. Of course the ferrules or rings are fastened firmly on the thick ends of each splice, and splice ends are requisite after unjointing the rod for protecting the thin ends of the splice when thrusting the joints into a case to carry the rod after a day's fishing, or when the angler desires to pack his rod. That is, " corresponding pieces of spliced wood, with brass rings (or ferrules) attached, are made, joined together, carried in the pocket, and when the rod is untied and unjointed they are detached from each other, and attached to the spliced parts of the rod, to save the splices from any accident." This is a precaution necessary for protecting all kinds of splices of rods.

In returning to the general subject, the spring opens earlier on the south side of Long Island than in any other part of the state. This is owing to the island extending so far into the Atlantic that the Gulf Stream mellows the air by its warmth. Radishes, celery, lettuce, and sometimes eschalots, are not uncommon on the 1st of March, while the martin and meadowlark enliven the air, and the robin is not far behind in putting in an appearance to open the full court of Spring ; and as the angler casts from the bank or from a boat, all nature is alive. The island being in the direct route for the passage of wildfowl, the honking of them high in air, and the gunners' intonations on the bay, give a touch of sublimity and grandeur which, when mingling with the sounds of lowing herds and the music of birds, brings heaven and earth together, and in a condition of harmony never dreamed of by the care-worn racer after the rusty dollar.

Persons who have never practiced the angler's gentle art can scarcely appreciate the feelings which well up in the soul of an expert who has studied nature, the habits of trout, and the devices necessary to present lures gracefully for their acceptance. His fly-rod is twelve and a half feet in length, including a telling-top of split bamboo. His reel is a narrow click one, upon which is wound a braided line of silk and hair, which tapers from the middle to each end, and is thirty yards in length. A nine-feet-long casting-line is looped to the end, and with the attractions of a cinnamon fly as a stretcher, a gray professor as the first drop, and a red ibis as the hand-fly, he feels sure that the trout in the first pool will leap for joy at his approach. As he walks over the meadows, sees the birds, hears all nature waking into new life, his very step upon the mead when the grass is beginning to shoot confers a sense of velvety elasticity; and as he nears the stream, sees the cat-tails of the willows dip and play on the margin of the ripple, and the trout rising and leaping after flies so that they cast miniature rainbows over the stream, with cautious step he approaches within casting distance of the pool. He makes a cast, and a large trout meets his fly and fastens. For an instant the angler is transfixed ! The old sensation of rapture returns with the new spring, and as the circulation of his blood quickens, he spontaneously ejaculates, " Well, this is worth living for !"

L

CHAPTER II.

FLY-FISHING ON MASSAPIQUA LAKE.

FLY-FISHING from boats or punts on ponds and lakes forms a most interesting branch of the art of angling. The tackle is fine, and the boat comfortable. When the pond covers not more than fifty acres, the oarsman rows across from side to side without turning the boat, but merely changing his seat and sculls; thus the angler, at the bow when crossing first, is at the stern while returning, and the oarsman continues to cross and recross the water back and forth, with sufficient lee-way to prevent the water being twice fished over. The angler must needs be ambidexterous, for he must change hands every time the water is crossed. On the trout lakes bordering the Adirondacks the boats are very light, and finely constructed of narrow and thin cedar boards, very closely braced

with small ribs; they are clinker built, and about fourteen
feet long and four feet wide, and are intended for one angler
and his guide. The guide has a seat toward the bow, and
the angler takes a seat near the stern, either to troll or fly-
fish. Between the angler and guide is a basket of heavy
splints and thick oaken cover, opening across the middle by
brass hinges. On the bottom of the basket is placed a huge
lump of ice wrapped in a woolen blanket, above which—or
half way up the basket—is a piece of canvas, attached by
strings to the basket, and fitting all round. The guide rows
along the margin of the lake, and when approaching a stream
which falls from the mountain into the lake, turns the stern
toward it and backs the boat to within casting distance, and
when the angler hooks a trout the guide rows out away from
shore, where the fish is played and landed without alarming
the other fish of the pool. The guide draws the fish at once,
throws it into the basket on the canvas above the ice, and
then backs the boat toward the shore for the angler to take
another. This is a deliberate way of angling, by which the
pools at the mouth of every brook are tendered the choice
of a cast of flies, and yield their tithe as pay for their cruel
curiosity.

Lake Massapiqua, at South Oyster Bay, on Long Island, is
probably the best trout preserve in the United States. It is
owned by William Floyd Jones, Esq., who is one of the finest
samples of an American gentleman. The preserve covers
eighty acres, and is fed by a spring-brook which is seven
miles in length, and all of it on Mr. Jones's estate. This gentleman maintains the preserve for his exclusive use and that
of his invited guests, who are the ardent disciples of the angle
and promoters of field-sports. Not only for his fish-preserve
and his system of fish-culture is Mr. Jones pre-eminent,
but as a farmer and horticulturist, a sportsman of first-class
in all its ennobling features, from the winter joy of following
the hounds to the refined and contemplative amusement of
casting the fly, he is worthy of emulation by all who would

so dispose of the bounties with which Providence has favored them as that they shall confer blessings on all classes.

There are several reasons in favor of fly-fishing from a boat over that of wading a stream, or catching casts from streams bordered with foliage. It is out on the water, away from shore, and free from the danger of getting flies fast on the limbs of trees while casting or playing a fish. There is room to play your fish. Your shore views are less restricted. Two anglers, in such case, form the best company possible. The business of the world may be canvassed while excellent sport is enjoyed amid the gushing music and harmony of nature.

SECTION SECOND.

HOW TO FISH A STREAM.

"Where the robin carols loudly—
   Gayly and untroubled sings,
And the lark is poised most proudly
   On his strong, untiring wings,
There may I be found each morning,
   With my rod and reel complete,
Not a speckled beauty scorning
   In the pearly streams I meet.

"Oft I pause to hear the thrushes
   Trilling out their morning song
In those wild and rapturous gushes
   Which to melody belong."
Then mingled is with song of bird,
The monotone of barn-yard herd;
Anon, a flock of geese appears,
Honking to calm each other's fears;
And as I angle the streams along,
All the world seems made of song.

HUS we deftly cast the artificial lure on the margin of the streams, or on the bosom of lake or pond, whipping, whipping, whipping all the day, and playing trout till twilight.

Questions in relation to fishing *up* or *down* a stream should be decided by the condition of the stream and its borders. While casting from the shore, it makes very little difference which way the stream is fished; but in wading, it is best to fish up stream, because it does not roil the water, and there is not so great liability to alarm the fish. In making a cast, it is always best to draw the flies across the current, for then the drop-flies will play clear of the casting-line. This is the opinion of most good fly-fishers. First, cast up stream along the shore, and if the stream be not too wide, cast to the farther shore, drawing your flies across the stream, but not too fast, lest the trout become suspicious. In striking, you can not be too quick when fishing up a stream. Cast first near shore; then a yard or two farther off; next, across the stream. If you get not a rise, take a step or two up the stream and repeat. Continue doing so until a doubt arises as to whether the trout admire your cast; then replace one fly by another of different color from any on your cast. If that does not take after presenting it several times, take it off and try another extreme in color. Keep changing until you hit the fancy of the trout. When you have found the fly that the trout admire, change your other flies (if you fish with three) to those of colors in slight relief to the taking one; that is, put on one a trifle darker and the other a little lighter in shade. Anglers are not so high a remove above the rest of mankind as not to be susceptible to a slight influence from the baser sentiments of humanity; but I have actually seen a man so self-willed as to fish all day without a rise, "because," as he said, "he was determined to bring the trout to his terms."

All kinds of angling call for the exercise of patience; but fly-fishing requires the gift of genius. Do not fish with too long a cast. In fishing a creek up stream, thirty to forty-five feet are quite sufficient. In striking, let it be with sufficient force to fasten the hook in his jaw; but play your fish most gingerly and even tenderly, but not so as to give him slack line, or he will disgorge the hook. One of the principal causes of losing large fish is the being in too great a hurry to land them. If the hook is well fastened, the more delicately your fish is played the better; for snubbing a fish hard at all points wears an orifice in its jaw from which the hook falls by the mere turning of the fish. It is true that the trout has a good mouth to hold a hook, but the hook must first be well fastened to hold, and then the orifice made in hooking should not be worn larger in playing, if possible to avoid it.

SECTION THIRD.

KNOTS, LOOPS, AND DROPS.

While anglers should let every trade live, and buy their tackle in preference to making it, yet with the make of certain parts of tackle every amateur should be familiar. Of course he should know how to tie on a hook, and how to make a loop whose equal bearings would prevent it from chafing or breaking at the loop-knot.

No. 1. Bending on, or tying on a hook. The hook should be tied on stained silk-worm gut, round, clear, and strong; for in playing a fish the tackle generally parts near the hook. Use scarlet silk, well waxed with a drab wax made from tar, like shoemaker's wax, only light-colored. From about half an inch below the end of the shank, make half a dozen turns with the silk to the end of the shank, and place an

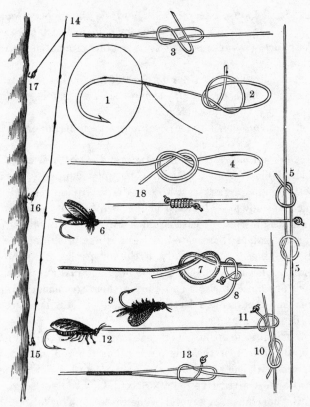

end of soaked gut on the shank, and begin to wind it on at
the end of the shank, winding close, tight, and neat, until
you have wound down to near the end of the gut, or nearly
half the length of the shank, when hold the end of your silk
there and form a loop of the remainder, and cast it three or
four times over the shank as represented; then draw up the
loop by the end of the silk thread, which will leave the end
fastened under those three or four loops cast over the bend
of the hook, thus forming a good finish, so that you may
cut the end of the silk thread close to the tie without danger of its drawing.

No. 2. Snell loop. Soak the gut, and tie the loop as represented. It is the very best tie for a loop, and I have endeavored so to represent it as to enable an amateur to imitate it.

No. 3. A helm-knot, or tiller hitch, useful in sailing a boat or yacht, because the hitch—though secure—is loosened instantly by a jerk at the end.

No. 4. The *common* knot for forming a loop at the end of a silk-worm gut or line.

No. 5, 5. Two half hitches, forming a slide-knot in a casting-line, to slide for holding a drop, and for changing drops at will. Some anglers cast the end twice round instead of once, as shown. The drop hangs well from it, being at a right angle from the casting-line; but with only one hitch of each end, as represented, the gut is apt to slip and part the casting-line, especially if the drops are frequently changed, because, when the knots become drawn very tight, they are hard to slide, and sliding them to change drops weakens them; but I have taken many hundreds of trout on drops so arranged.

No. 6. The first drop, of the correct length. It is the red ibis fly, all formed of the ibis feather but the red silk body, wound with very small gold or silver cord. This is one of the most attractive lures for trout, but it is not so good as the coachman, or several of the professors, for large fish. The tail and hackle at the neck are brown.

No. 7. A knot recommended by many accomplished anglers for connecting lengths of gut to form a casting-line. Some bend the end twice round instead of once, as shown. If only once, the ends should be lashed with waxed silk.

No. 8. Drop, fastened by a half hitch round the casting-line and the end of the gut near the knot. After tying the knot of the casting-line, draw it tight, and cut off one end close, leaving the upper end half an inch long. Lash this end to the line, and cover it with varnish, and loop the end of the drop over it. By this plan the drop will not chafe or

weaken the casting-line. This fastening is recommended
by Mr. Francis, and shellac might form a good covering for
the lashed end.

No. 9. Green trophy-fly. Peacock's wing body and Guinea-
fowl wings.

No. 10. Square tie in a casting-line. After drawing it close,
cut the ends to half an inch long, and lash them with fine
silk, and varnish them.

No. 11. The gut of the drop, soaked, and a knot tied in the
end; it is attached to the casting-line close to the knot by
a half hitch. This is a very secure method and clean rig
for forming a casting-line and fastening a drop, especially
when fishing for large trout of from two to five pounds'
weight; but for fish under two pounds I prefer the rig of
line and drop 5 and 6.

No. 12. Alder-fly—*phryganea*—body of peacock's herl whipped with red silk; wings of gray cock's hackle.

No. 13. Attaching the casting-line to the reel-line. This loop
is quite secure, scarcely any chafing, is small and neat, yet
it may be easily loosened without cutting the knot from
the end of the casting-line. This is recommended when
the reel-line has a loop at the end; but I prefer a loop in
the end of the casting-line, as represented. The fastening
is the same in either case, whether the loop forms the end
of the casting-line or the reel-line. Sometimes a loop is
made in each; but if in one only, I prefer it in the casting-
line, as I consider it the neatest finish.

No. 14. The casting-line, rigged with stretcher and two drop
flies. The object is to show the student how they should
be rigged, so that all may fall at the same time on the water, calculating the natural angle of the casting-line.

No. 15, 16, 17. No. 15 is called the stretcher-fly; 16, the first
drop; 17, the second drop, or hand-fly, being the drop nearest to the angler's hand. The drop for the hand-fly should
be four inches long, while the first drop should be from
two and a half to three inches in length. The knots in the

casting-line show where the lengths of gut are tied—thus, from the stretcher-fly to the first drop are four lengths of gut, and three or four lengths from the first drop to the hand-fly. These distances will be changed to suit taste and the distance of cast. For long casts, the drops should be a yard apart.

No. 18. A tie for uniting lengths of gut, so that they will break at any other part as easily as at the tie. Tie a knot in the end of each length of gut; lap them an inch, and wind them closely between the knots with white waxed silk. This is the best tie for a salmon leader or a trout casting-line. Casting-lines should be made of stained gut, the gut selected so as to taper regularly from the reel-line to the stretcher-fly; and the drops should be of fine, clear, round gut, stained to the shade of the casting-line. It is an indication of very bad taste in a fishing-tackle maker to offer finely-tapered and stained casting-lines and flies tied to coarse gut, and not dyed or shaded to the tint of the casting-line. All should be in harmonious keeping, from the reel-line to the casting-line and drops. For casting from a boat or from the clear margin of a stream, the casting-line should be nine feet in length, or even a foot or two more, only have a care not to make it so long that, with the bend of a twelve-foot rod, you can not reel up sufficiently close to bring your fish within reach of your landing-net. For rough fishing on a stream of bramble margins a casting-line of from six to seven feet in length, and one drop besides the stretcher, may be sufficient. Many anglers dispense with drops, and fish with one fly only on some streams in the interior of Pennsylvania, Maine, New Hampshire, and throughout the region in New York known as the Adirondacks, which is about forty miles square, and one of the greatest fish and game regions in America.

HOW TO STAIN SILK-WORM GUT.

Gut may be stained by leaving it in a strong decoction of

cold coffee or tea twelve hours. Tinging the gut thus does not weaken it or render it less pliable. Logwood and alum form a decoction very commonly in use for staining gut. Lemon-juice and indigo produce a delicate tinge. The outer skins of onions, when steeped, produce a dye which stains a yellow or leather-color without injuring the gut.

Stoddart states that walnut leaves produce a brown dye, which is a good general tinge for all waters; and such materials as stain the gut a neutral tinge, or bluish, are best for clear waters. Steep two handsful of walnut leaves in a quart of water, and when cool, soak the gut in the water two or three hours. The rind of the American black walnut forms as good a dye for general use as can be obtained. A bluish dye is obtained by boiling a handful of the dust or shavings of logwood a quarter of an hour in a quart of water, adding a lump of alum half the size of an almond. Dip the gut in the decoction while it is yet very warm, and allow it to remain half an hour, or until the shade required is obtained. Gut should be entirely dried after staining it, and then it should be thoroughly washed in tepid water, when, after drying it perfectly, it should be rolled in chamois skin, or stretched on a board with the ends fastened to keep it straight. An excellent plan for keeping the gut straight upon which flies are tied is Hutchinson's, before mentioned. The distances between the loops or rings and the hooks should be so graduated as to accommodate different lengths of gut, as illustrated on the page of trouting-tackle, thus enabling the fly-fisher to change his flies or replace one quickly. This plan is excellent for drops, but stretchers would require too long a fly-book for convenience. On going a-trouting, I usually put up a couple of casts, such as I may think will suit the waters which I contemplate fishing. For most waters I rig a stretcher and two drops; and I seldom make a mistake in the selection of flies. In the early spring I employ the cinnamon as the stretcher for one cast, a red ibis as a stretcher for another, and a mallard wing, with claret body, for the third. The

first drop above the cinnamon is an ibis, and the first drop
above the ibis is a cinnamon, and the first drop above the
mallard wing is a cinnamon. The hand-flies are the blue dun
or the cow-dung. The blue professor is also an excellent fly
early in the season, as is also the gray; the yellow is better
in May.

My advice to the angler is to purchase his flies of the best
fly-tyers in New York and Boston, where competition has produced the necessity for employing first-rate materials in all
the departments of fishing-tackle, whether of gut, flies, hooks,
lines, reels, rods, and the coarser paraphernalia of the angler.

TROUT REELS.—The click reel is incomparably the best,
though it is not so good to dry a line on as is the Billinghast
reel, which is formed of brass or German silver wire, and the
line open on all sides to the air. The click reel checks the
line to a certain weight of resistance, to which the angler
soon becomes accustomed, and in giving the fish the butt, he
does it with confidence, because he has ascertained from experience how great a check he puts upon the fish, and the pre-
cise strain caused to his casting-line, which he has regulated
accordingly. This is not the case with a reel whose tension
of drag may be changed several times during one day's sport.
But the best reel for my use is a click reel, with a large perforated barrel or cylinder to reel the line on, and it should
also be perforated at the ends over the cylinder, for drying
the line. The advantage of a large cylinder to reel the line
on when the reel does not multiply is important, because it
shortens the time of reeling. Besides, with a large cylinder,
thirty yards is a sufficient length of line. I once killed a five-
and-a-half-pound trout in a very rapid stream with a nine-
ounce rod and only thirty yards of line. It took me two
hours and twelve minutes to kill the fish, timed by Dr. Bethune, of Boston.

A click multiplier is better for angling with the worm or
minnow, but many bait anglers of the country prefer a small
multiplier without a click or drag. Bell-metal is supposed

to be better than German silver or brass, but alumine, or aluminum, is better than either.

FLY RODS.—Rods made from split bamboo are unquestionably the best in use; but a Robert Welch rod, of ash for the butt and second joint, lancewood for the third, and split bamboo for the fourth or top joint, is the best rod that I have ever owned for general fly-fishing. The split bamboo rod is much lighter, and full as desirable. A fly rod should not be under twelve feet in length, and I had rather have it six inches over, or so made with duplicate top and third joints as to make it either twelve or twelve feet six, though my longest fly rod is only twelve feet and two inches long. I prefer a single action rod to the one of double action or a "kick in the handle," though the latter may send a fly farther, and deliver it more gracefully, but it lacks the snap of the single action to strike. Fly-rods from split bamboo should weigh from seven to ten ounces when mounted; and if from ash, lancewood, and split bamboo, if strictly for single hand, their weights should range from nine to fifteen ounces; and if the latter weight, they should be about twelve and a half feet long. Neither rod should be too withy, but have snap or elasticity enough in the top to hook a fish without yielding enough to permit the sinner to disgorge. One of the pleasures of fly-fishing is to use a rod which will responsively hook a trout without an effort of the angler. The sport consists in delivering a fly neatly on a straight line—seeing the trout rise gushingly to the surface and accept the lure—and playing a trout gracefully. The charm consists in the manner of taking the trout, and the surroundings of a pleasing landscape—the music of birds, the spring-time of general rejuvenation, and the running harmony of intellectual conversation. There is society in trouting, but it does not prevent the soul from basking in all the life and beauty of sound and gayety around.

LANDING NETS.—If for landing in a boat or on shore, a two-jointed handle is the best. If for wading, a short handle, at-

tached to an elastic cord and suspended from the shoulder,
or a double-jointer, in which the second one slides into the
first, and is attached by a loop to a button on the breast, is
the least cumbersome. I have found the hollow wire rims
the best, and brass is the best metal for them. The hollow
rim is light, and it does not rust. As to the round and oval
shapes, they are matters of caprice, and as to the wicker
frames of wood, they are no lighter than hollow brass wire,
while they offer fourfold resistance to the water. The rim
should be large, the meshes large, the twine not too fine, and
the net itself large. A landing-net, large, strong, and light,
is one of the angler's sources of delight.

TROUT BASKET.—Let it be plaited or woven from the thin
outer grain of the willow or osier, very light and large; to
contain ten, fifteen, and twenty pounds of fish are the sizes.
They should be stained inside and painted outside, or by
painting the inside also they are more easily cleaned. Green
is the color preferred. The shape not very deep, with a hole
in the lid, brass hinges, a staple extending up through the lid,
fastened with a padlock. The strap should be of worsted
webbing instead of russet leather, or if of russet leather there
should be a pad attached, with straps to slide on the shoul-
der-strap to the right place. The New York fishing-tackle
dealers have introduced a new gear, by which the weight
rests on both shoulders, and the basket is held more securely,
and is less cumbersome in forest-fishing. The angler's coat
should be made with a strap and button on the shoulder, under which to hold the strap of the trout-basket; and there
should be another strap on the coat at the left side, to prevent the basket-strap from moving, and the basket from
swinging about while climbing over logs and fences. But
the great *desideratum* consists in getting a light and small
basket, which will contain a great many large trout of your
own taking.

BAIT BOX.—Of course bait-boxes and fly-books are articles
to purchase at the fishing-tackle stores; and while there are

numerous theories about fly-books, there can be but few about
bait-boxes. I will therefore state, beware of those three-
story complications. Procure a box as simple as possible in
construction, made to slide on and be supported by the waist-
belt which holds up the wading water-proofs, or the common
leather waist-belt. It should consist of two compartments,
one for worm and the other for minnow, or for grub-worms
and grasshoppers.

CARRYING CASTS OF FLIES.—Instead of winding a casting-
line round the hat, a double band is made to fit the hat and
buckle round over the hat-band, and the casting-line or snelled flies are attached to it and folded in, so as not to expose
them, or render them liable to get loose and dangle about, to
the danger of the face and eyes. The Calcutta or Gibraltar
sporting-hat, illustrated on the plate with the salmon-rod, is
excellently adapted for carrying snelled flies or casts. A
"snelled fly" is a length of silk-worm gut, with a fly at one
end and a loop at the other.

STRAIGHTENING CASTING-LINES.—Hitch the line at one end
either by the hook or a loop, and rub the line with brown
paper between your thumb and finger, and it will take the
turns out of it; or, rub it between India-rubber; but both
these methods tend to chafe the gut more or less, and neither
should be resorted to if you can have time to soak the gut in
tepid water half an hour. I am in the habit of soaking my
casting-line over night in cold water if I intend to fish early
the next morning; and I am accustomed also to selecting the
flies which I think may be necessary, and on the rim of a glass
nearly filled with water I hang the hooks, letting the gut fall
in the glass and soak all night. I do not approve of straightening gut by friction when soaking it is possible.

Thus, with a finely-balanced and finished fly-rod, a click
reel attached to the rod below the hand, a silk and hair
braided line, protected from the effect of water by being
oiled, varnished, or saturated with some oleaginous substance,
braided like a whip-lash to taper each way from the middle,

a stained gut casting-line tapering from the reel-line to the stretcher, a well-selected cast of flies, with drops artistically fastened to the casting-line, and of proper length, a good landing-net and light basket, and I am ready for the fray and to angle all day; for I never yet experienced a day long enough while fishing.

Oh! the varied and mixed emotions of the fly-fisher. How often he is tantalized by false rises, which suddenly inflate him with hope, to collapse as soon by disappointment. Sometimes he misses a well-intended rise of so bold an effort as to render the fish too much alarmed by the sights and sense of the upper air to trust a repetition. Anon he hooks a fine trout, and in playing it the hook parts from the jaw of the fish, leaving to conjecture whether it was really a disgorge or a too tender hold. Thus he continues whipping the water, exercised by various emotions, when a large feeding trout springs above the water, revealing all his beauties of color and proportions, and, taking the fly, he darts away with the power and celerity which prove that he is going to try the strength of the tackle. What interesting moments to the angler! The numerous runs of the fish, his wiles and strategy to escape, are all tried in vain, and he is finally helped out of the wet by means of the landing-net.

The man or boy who has never taken a trout has not really seen one—with angler's eyes. To the angler, a large, healthy trout in full season, just taken, when fish are scarce and bite shy, is the prettiest object in the whole world of beauty.

NATURAL AND ARTIFICIAL TROUT FLIES.

Letter A, the artificial, and B, the natural dun-cut fly (*phryganea*), is a good lure for the month of May. Body of brown bear's hair, mixed with blue and yellow worsted, whipped with green and yellow; brown feather wings, and squirrel's-tail hair for antennæ.

Letter C, the artificial, and D, the natural of the green-tail fly

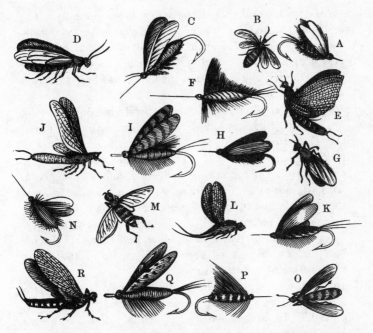

(*phryganea*). This is regarded as a successful fly for April; body dubbed with fur from hare's ear, whipped with gray or green silk, hackle from gray cock, and wings from the prolace of a partridge wing.

Letter E, the natural, and F, the artificial of the prime dun, a fly for March (*ephemera*), and for which month the great dun, dark brown, little red-brown, and the small dark brown are also favorites. They are composed of different shades of mohair, dun and speckled wings, and gray and light brown hackles.

Letter I, the artificial, and J, the natural dun drake, or March brown, or Moorish brown (*ephemera*). Body of hare's-ear fur and yellow worsted, or black wool whipped with red silk; mottled wings, and hackle from the gray cock. Professor Rennie, M. Carroll, and hosts of other authorities, consider this the best March fly.

M

Letter G, the natural, and H, the artificial cow-dung fly. The body of lemon-yellow mohair and a yellow feather, whipped with yellow silk, and the wings of grayish-blue feather of a hen, land-rail, or mallard. This is one of the taking flies for March and April, and the best that I ever saw were tied by Pritchard Bros.

Letter K, the artificial, and L, the natural blue dun or violet fly. Body of light worsted violet, mixed with gray down; the wings from the pale feathers of a starling's wing, whipped with pale yellow silk. The black gnat, early and late bright browns or cinnamons, palm fly, and whirling dun, with the blue dun, dun drake, with palmers, hackles, and the stone fly, are intended for both March and April.

Letter M, the natural, and N, the artificial hawthorn fly. Body of black ostrich herl or black seal's fur, mixed with buff mohair; wings of horn shavings, or of the palest snipe's feather or mallard's wing.

Letter O, the natural, and P, the artificial oak fly. This is a May insect, famous under the names of oak fly, camlet fly, down-hill fly, and canon fly. The body is dubbed with dark brown shining camlet, whipped with very fine green silk, or is made with a bittern's feather, and the wings from the double gray feather of a mallard or of a woodcock.

Letter Q, the natural, and R, the artificial green drake or green May-fly, the common fresh-water fly for May. The body is dubbed with hog's down or light bear's hair, mixed with yellow mohair, whipped with pale floss silk, and a small strip of peacock's herl for the head; the wings from the rayed feathers of the mallard, dyed yellow; the hackle from the bittern's neck, and the tail from the long hairs of the sable or ferret.

The gray drake is similar in form, but different in colors, having the body dubbed with whitish hog's down, mixed with black spaniel's fur or white ostrich herl, whipped with black silk; the wings dark gray mallard; black hackle, with silver twist; whisks of tail from a black cat's whiskers.

COMMENTS.—From the perusal of previous pages addressed to the questions of "senses in fishes," the reader will not be surprised at the difference between *natural* and *artificial* flies. Fishes in general, and indeed all fishes, are generally more readily attracted by the size, color, and action of a lure than by its form. And as a floating lure is better than a sinking one, the fly-tyers prefer such floating hairs as those from hog's ears, seals, bears, the South American fox, otter, etc., while for feathers they prefer those of the mallards, the barred feathers of the wood-duck, and numerous other oil-quilled feathers, including all such as do not lose their lustre by the action of water, and, like the topknot of the golden-pheasant, will shine as brilliantly in the water as above it. It is doubtless true that more care in selecting floating materials, and the adoption of a greater number of oleaginous substances in mounting flies, would be an improvement upon the almost perfect state to which the art of fly-tying has already attained. I prefer a body of silk to one of mohair for the *cinnamon fly*, because silk retains more lustre when wet than does common wool, or even mohair; and so with the *blue professor*, another attractive fly for large trout, the body of which should be wound with lustrous blue silk. The nearest copies of nature that I ever saw in flies are those of gutta-percha, recently imported by Andrew Clerk & Co., who keep the largest assortment of hooks, duffings, feathers, silkworm gut, and all the materials requisite for the angler to be prepared with on a lengthy fishing tour, of any house in America, if not in the world.

Many fly-fishers claim that a different fly is required for every month during the trouting season; but that has not been my experience with trout, nor of the best anglers with whom I have conversed on the subject. I refer not to fledged lures for salmon, as that royal fish is as capricious about flies, and changes its mind as frequently as did the Empress Josephine about bonnets.

Barker, an authority on angling, says:

"A brother of the angle must always be sped
   With three black palmers, and also three red;
   And all made with hackles.   In a cloudy day
   Or in windy weather, angle you may."

He then recommends the May-fly, and states that the hawthorn fly should be small, while the oak fly with brown wings
and the grasshopper should be carefully imitated, concluding
with the following advice:

"Once more, my good brother, I'll speak in thy ear:
   Hog's, red cow's, and bear's wool to float best appear;
   And so doth your fur, if it rightly fall;
   But always remember, make two, and make all."

CHAPTER III.

MIDDLE DAM CAMP.

THIS camp is situated at the head of Rapid River, and at the foot of Mollychunkemunk Lake, being the next lake east of the Umbagog, in a chain of a dozen lakes, in the State of Maine, which head near the mountains separating that state from Canada. Rapid River falls into Umbagog Lake, and as this is a famous trouting region, I give a view of the camp, where the angler luxuriates on brook trout and spruce partridges, and rests from his day's labor on a spring-bed. Trout of nine pounds' weight each have been taken there, though I never took one which scaled much over six pounds. It was here that I met a new experience in the character of trout, and think it worth relating for the benefit of anglers.

While I believe that trout are not generally so discriminating in the selection of artificial flies as to evince acuteness of vision, yet I have experienced that at certain waters, when the streams are low and clear, a copy of the living fly is more or less necessary to success. This is the case at the pool and rapids below the middle dam at the head of Rapid River, and half a mile below Middle Dam Camp, where a large shoal of —apparently educated—trout keep leaping and tumbling so that from fifty to a hundred speckled beauties of from two to five pounds' weight are always in sight. But it used to be said that they would not take an artificial fly; so, school-boy like, the guests at the camp sent every angler, on his arrival, to "try below the dam," as a sell. It pleased them to see a fresh man's face glow at the first sight of those sportive beauties, which acted as if half in coquetry and half in defiance of anglers. I felt thankful when witnessing the self-denying hospitality which prompted several anglers, who were entire strangers to me, to cease angling opposite the camp for the sole purpose of showing me a pool full of very anxious trout. They left after I had tried in vain to coax a favorable notice at one cast of flies. I changed my cast several times, and then rested the pool to allow them to change their minds or whet their appetites, until I devoted in that way about two days, to the amusement of the anglers at the camp, and finally began to think that the stories I had heard about the sagacity of those trout were true. On my return to camp after each trial below the dam, I saw that my brethren of the angle were interested in my efforts by their furtive glances and sly winks at each other as they anxiously inquired what sport I had enjoyed. But all their jokes fell short, for my mind was with the sparkling beauties below the dam. After having exhausted my fly-books of their attractive lures, I concluded to repair to the dam and study the trout. There they were, apparently as jolly as ever, rolling, tumbling, and leaping about the surface of the clear, curling pool. I had not sat long on the dam, and peered into the sparkling eddies below, before I saw a trout rise gracefully and swallow an ash-colored midge which had floated down from the dam. On looking around me, I saw a cloud of drab ephemera, rather larger than musquitoes, swarming over the dry timber

dam, and ever and anon, as one fell on the water, a trout
rose very gracefully and swallowed it, turning quickly down,
and causing a whirl made by his caudal train, which had so
excited me when I first looked upon the pool.   With assiduity I commenced examining my flies in search of an ash
midge.   I soon found a pair, and, placing one on as my stretcher, the first cast I made with it fastened a three-pound trout,
played and landed it.   The next cast I fastened another, but
so slightly that the hook parted from his mouth.   Two or
three more casts assured me that the shoal " smelt a rat;"
and as minks, muskrats, and flies with hooked tails are their
terror, I adjourned to another pool, and did not return to the
dam until nearly night, when I took the conceit out of four
more beauties; but, after playing the fifth nearly half an hour,
he made a rush for the rapids, and went over the *chute*, carrying away my casting - line.   Having captured five, and
played two more trout that day, I felt satisfied.   I had for
years contended that trout might be taken with artificial fly
when in feeding humor, but I had never before found them so
fastidious or discriminative.   Since then, Mr. James Stephens,
of Hoboken, and myself, hired a trout-pond in Connecticut,
and though I fished it three days, and Mr. Stephens three
weeks, yet neither of us succeeded in capturing one with the
fly.   Neither would they take a minnow, while they rose
freely to angle and grub worms, cast, without sinker, as a fly.
On the last day of my visit to the pond I saw the trout rushing furiously after tadpoles; but, as I had not time to remain and try that bait, I probably lost a treat, for I have
since heard that it is the favorite lure for trout in some parts
of the state.   Indeed, the fish-culturists of France propagate
frogs, that the trout may feed on tadpoles.

The angler, on making a lengthy tour for sport, can not
have too great a number or variety of artificial flies.   He can
procure them at the principal fishing-tackle establishments
in New York, where competition has so sharpened invention
and enterprise that the best flies and fly-tiers are imported,

together with the best materials, from wherever on earth they are to be obtained. Or he may be supplied in Boston, Montreal, Quebec, or at Rome, Rochester, or Mumford, New York.

In addition to an extensive assortment of flies, the angler should carry silks, wools, mohair, duffings, and feathers of various colors, gold and silver threads and tinsels, fine hooks, and selected gut, so that he may occasionally extemporize a cast of flies, which, though not so finely tied, may combine size and colors attractive for the finny epicures which show themselves fastidious about putting in an appearance. This course is pursued by many experienced anglers, whom, I may justly add, are great bunglers at tying a fly or properly mounting a hook. Half a dozen lessons from Pritchard Brothers, or from one of the fly-tyers for Andrew Clerk & Co., could scarcely fail of being useful to the student of contemplative philosophy.

SECTION SECOND.

SELECT ARTIFICIAL TROUT-FLIES.

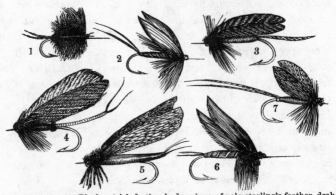

No. 1. Black Gnat.—Black ostrich-feather body, wings of pale starling's feather, drab tail and antennæ. 2. Red Ibis.—Red body, wound with gold or silver cord; brown hackle and tail, red ibis-feather wings. 3. Wilson's Professor.—Yellow gut body, mounted by M'Bride, of Mumford, N. Y.; red ibis tail headed with gold tinsel, brown hackle, gray mallard wing. 4. Stone Fly.—Green drake wing and hackle, drab body and tail. 5. Pritchard's Stone Fly.—Composition body, drab wings, tail, and antennæ. 6. Cinnamon Fly.—Orange body, ash-colored wings, brown hackle and tail. 7. Green Drake.—Silver body, tipped with gold; short black hackle, black head, brown tail; wings and shoulders of green drake feather.

ROUND BEND FLY-HOOKS.

These are Adlington and Hutchinson's superfine warranted cast-steel hooks. They are imported in great numbers by Andrew Clerk & Co., and, whether straight or curbed, are the best fly-hook in use, and infinitely superior to the common Limerick hook.

FISH-HOOK PHILOSOPHY.

Upon the subject of fish-hooks, their important qualities and bearings are applicable to hooks for all fishing purposes. The draft, or pull on a hook, is equally applicable to a hook for fly-fishing or for capturing the largest sharks. It is conceded by hook-makers that the forged hook is the best, whether it be hammered flat, square, or round. The needle-pointed, cast-steel hooks, of round bend, are probably best for mounting with flies for salmon, black bass, or trout, or baiting for striped bass, squeteague, and maskinongé; while for sheepshead, kingfish, and for all fishes which have a small and hard mouth, the Sproat bend is preferable. Of the Kinsey or Pennsylvania hook, the shape is good for small fish, but it gapes so much that a large fish is apt—in sulking and beating its nose against a rock, or rubbing it on the gravel bottom—to spring the hook out. If made of large wire and well tempered, it is good for sheepshead and kingfish, because it is not so long from the bend to the barb as is the Limerick

of the O'Shaughnessy pattern, or the regulation hook for exportation. The Virginia hook, and the Sproat and round
bends of Redditch, are the best that I have seen.

The foregoing cut, representing the samples of two hooks,
was clipped from a recent number of the FIELD, and as it
embodies philosophy founded on experience, I give it, refer-
ring to the cut, as follows :

"Now I have this autumn devoted particular attention to
this subject, *i. e.*, hooks. I have been fishing with Hutchinson's Limerick and Sproat bends (I may remark that I can
not speak too highly of the latter for its prehensile capabili-
ties), and the following is the result. In seven consecutive
days' fishing I hooked thirty-six fish, and of them landed
twenty-seven. I was broken four times. Once my single
gut, with which I always fish, was frayed by a heavy fish
against sharp boulders, and three times the hooks were the
traitors—two were Limericks, and one was a Sproat. Three
out of thirty-six is too large a proportion, and it is very desirable to reduce it. Even in fishing with single gut, the
heaviest fish, if properly handled, barring the circumstances
of snags or boulders, seldom succeed in breaking the line.
But what handling will save a hook ? One *will* go sometimes, and most unaccountably, probably from being fixed so
as to allow the fish to wrench, jerk, or squeeze it. The first
step to a cure is to find the weak point.

"The only Sproat hook which has broken with me went at
the point *a*. I think it is an admirable form of hook, although I tried it first as an experiment this year, with much
prejudice against the looks of it. It is less apt to break than
the Limerick, both from its form, and because the pull, *b*, *c*, is
nearly in the direction of the point, whereas in the other the
line of pull, *d*, *e*, forms an obtuse angle at the point *e*. Of
the thousand and one Limerick hooks which I have seen broken, either against stones or in fish, by far the greater proportion have failed at the point *f*, where—in good hooks to a
less, and in bad to a greater measure—the wire is reduced in

forming the barb. Having determined the weak point, I think it can be merely a mechanical difficulty which prevents that part of the hook being made as strong as the rest, and anglers should insist on manufacturers overcoming it. I obtained some hooks from Messrs. Bernard, of St. James's Passage, which were flat-sided—that is, they were filed to angles, and the section of the wire would be nearly an oblong. They appeared exceptionally strong, but were otherwise objectionable, being over-ironed and over-barbed. I think something might be done by flattening the wire from the beginning of the bend, the shank being left circular for fly-dressing facilities. A section of the wire at the bend would then be elliptical. However, ignorance as to the manufacture, unfortunately, is in the way of my suggesting any thing practical; but if I succeed in drawing attention from anglers and manufacturers to this subject, my object in occupying so much of your space will be fulfilled.   SALMONICEPS.

"[The hooks which 'Salmoniceps' describes as flat and filed at the sides are, we fancy, not filed, but hammered, as they are usually described in the trade as 'forged Limerick tapers.' We have previously expressed a very high opinion of the Sproat bend, which is undoubtedly one of the best, if not the best, salmon hook made.—ED.]"

Having a greater variety of fishes to angle for in America than there are of angler's fishes in Europe, it will be necessary to recur to this subject, for the fish-hook is the foundation of all fishing-tackle; and if it gives way, all the expense of mounting or baiting it, with expense of other tackle and loss of time, besides the chagrin, amounting to mortification and sometimes almost desperation at losing a very large fish, go for worse than nothing. The centre-draft hook of the ancients is quite similar to the hook a, b, c, minus the barb, and it is probably the best form for all large fish.

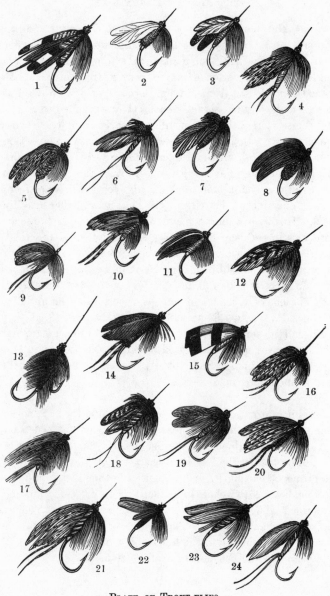

PLATE OF TROUT-FLIES.

No. 1. Red body, wound with gold cord; streamers red, blue legs. 2. Coachman.—White wings, green peacock herl body, brown legs. 3. Drab upper wings, and brown under ditto; cinnamon body and legs. 4. Red body and legs, brown mallard wings. 5. Peacock herl body, Guinea-hen wings, brown hackle. 6. Gold body, orange wings, sandy legs, and gray tail. 7. Silver-drab wings, yellow body, and black legs. 8. Reddish-brown wings and legs, with peacock herl body. 9. Drab wings, brown body, legs, and tail. 10. Brown body, red legs, gray mottle wings and antennæ. 11. June-fly.—Orange wings, brown body and hackle. 12. Red body, brown wings, gray mallard wings. 13. Brown hackle and two hooks. 14. Purple body, wings, legs, gray tail, and green herl at root of tail. 15. Gold body, yellow and black legs, wings white and black bars. 16. Silver body, speckled wings, brown legs. 17. Black hackle over body of orange wound with gold, gray wings, and yellow tail. 18. Brown body wound with gold cord, gray wings, red and black hackle. 19. Green body, red tail, gray legs, and hackle round the neck. 20. Yellow Professor.—Yellowish-gray wings, red tail, golden body, gray antennæ. 21. Gray Professor.—Brown mallard wings, red hackle, gray body wound with gold, yellow legs. 22. Black Gnat.—Black body, legs, hackle; ash wings. 23. Blue Professor.—Body dark blue and gold, legs blue, and drab wings. 24. Body brown South American fox, wound with silver cord; dark brown wings and legs.

SECTION THIRD.

BAIT-FISHING FOR TROUT.

" Hail to the spring-time and the hills!
  Hail to the meadows and the fog!
Hail to the gorges and the rills!
  All hail the trout 'neath yonder log!
      Have good care,
      That's his lair :
      Heigh-ho, hop,
      Flip, flap, flop.

Hail to the shocking old straw hat,
  Second-hand trowsers, coat, and boots,
Box of worms, lively and fat,
  All hail your hook in those old roots!
      Careless man,
      Mad as bran,
      Neither snap,
      Nor flip, flap.

Blessed and calm the smiling morn;
  Birds sing wheresoe'er we roam.
Flowers the fields and woods adorn;
  All hail my line 'midst dancing foam!
      Now look out—
      Silent stand—
      And a trout
      Will kiss my hand.

Hail the graceful silver gleam!
  Lo! a trout, with sudden spring,
Forms a spray-bow o'er the stream,
  And is added to my string.
      Verbum sap,
      Flip, flop, flap. "

The above pastoral was contributed by a clergyman who is as eloquent in the pulpit as he is persuasive along the streams. The disciples were fishermen.

The bait-rod should be a little heavier and longer than the fly-rod. I prefer one not less than fifteen feet in length, formed of four joints, the top one lancewood; and in place of rings, I prefer guides of aluminum. A click multiplier is the best reel. In angling a stream of tangled brush margin, it may be fished without the bottom joint by tying on the reel; and in carrying the rod through brambles, it is best to unjoint, leaving the line and reel on when the distance is only from one trout pool to another, or not more than a mile. The bait-fisher is much more eager in pursuit of his game than is the fly-fisher. He threads his way through thorns and brambles that appear impenetrable to any one but a bait-fisher. He prefers to wade the stream if it be not too deep, but he permits nothing to prevent him from fishing all the pools. He generally prefers to fish down stream, and if he discovers fresh tracks of an angler gone before, he will either endeavor most adroitly to get before him, or he will fish so slow as to let the trout recover from the fright caused from the disturbance of the waters by the angler ahead of him. In the mean time the foremost angler is continually on the alert to see that no one gets before him on the stream; but if he suspects an attempt to outflank him, he pretends to reel up and prepare for home, when in reality he is only putting up his tackle to make a long detour and arrive at the stream at a greater distance below his adversary. The bait-fisher does not—like the fly-fisher—fish all the stream, but knows how to judge where the trout lie in wait for bait. The fly-fisher often takes them from the shallow reefs before they seek their hiding-places, where the bait-fisher finds them. Bait-fishing is, of all field-sports, the parent of more patience and eager perseverance than any other.

CHAPTER IV.

LESSON BY "JOSH BILLINGS."

ANGLERS with bait are a more queer, quaint, peculiar class of sportsmen than are the devotees of the fly, and they include in their class students deeply read in nature and books. If you desire to find an original genius, you will most readily succeed among anglers with bait, who use primitive rods and tackle, and follow the streams solitary and silent, in a meditative mood, enjoying the sights and sounds of nature unmolested by the presence of the less contemplative fly-fisher, or the worshiper of dog and gun. Such a one Josh Billings appears to be, with his coat buttoned on the wrong side, if his writings are any index to the man. His lesson is included in the following original verse:

"Whare the dul stream
Haz fatted tew a pulp
The sooty arth,
Go seek the dark-skinned alder
(A tiny forest),
And from the crowded growth
Selekt a slender wand,

> Tru tapering from base to pinnakel,
> Four yards in length.
> Bee it thy care
> Smoothly the bark tew cleave from awl the pole
> Save near the springy top.
> Thare leave the natiff kivver two feet or more;
> Haply thus the game no fear will hav
> When thwart the brook yu stretch the reed."

Anglers will agree that "Josh" has studied both the rod and the habits of trout, for he describes what a fishing-rod should be for general use in angling along a stream where reels and jointed rods are scarcely ever seen. The favorite baits for such anglers are, 1st, angle-worms, or common earthworms, kept in moss a day to scour, and then sometimes sprinkled with milk to feed them, and still not to darken their color; 2d, the white grub-worm, found in great numbers by splitting decayed logs of soft maple or cherry; 3d, the shiner of the brook; 4th, the grasshopper. The two latter baits are preferred by members of highest rank in the profession; and in lieu of the shiner, when near the coast, they use smelt and spearing with nearly equal success.

THE ARDENT ANGLER.

Our wide acres and free streams are favorable to the cultivation of liberal, poetical, and artistic ideas, and I select the following verse from a poem by a gifted student at painting and the fine art of angling:

> "We break from the tree-groups, a glade deep with grass;
> The white clover's breath loads the sense as we pass.
> A sparkle—a streak—a broad glitter is seen,
> The bright Callikoon through its thickets of green!
> We rush to the banks—its sweet music we hear;
> Its gush, dash, and gurgle all blent to the ear.
> No shadows are drawn by the cloud-covered sun,
> We plunge in the crystal, our sport is begun.
> Our line, where that ripple shoots onward, we throw;
> It sweeps to the foam-spangled eddy below;
> A tremor—a pull—the trout upward is thrown,
> He swings to our basket—the prize is our own!"
>
> ALFRED B. STREET.

The ardent Angler.

I have also seen excellent fly-fishers with such an extemporized rod as Josh Billings recommends. On Pine Creek, in Pennsylvania, anglers who fish for a livelihood use such a rod, and fish with only one clumsily-tied fly. They wade the stream—which is a good plan to avoid meeting rattlesnakes —and to a string tied over the left shoulder and under the left arm they attach their fish, and tow them along as they angle down the stream. On some days they take from thirty to fifty pounds of trout. On Trout Run, a tributary to Lycoming Creek, the best native anglers use a rod formed of two hickory joints lashed together, and a top joint of whalebone lashed on—whole length about nine feet. They fish down stream, wading the middle of the creek where not too deep, and casting right and left some forty feet, under boughs which barely clear the water, bringing out large prismatic beauties at nearly every cast with a single fly of domestic make. They do this where gentlemen amateurs, from all parts of the country, find it extremely difficult to get a rise to their superior flies, though presented with the best make

N

of split bamboo rod, handled by expert anglers. The natives tie on their click reel; and for guides and top, use loops of leather or raw-hide.

Reprenons notre Discours.—Of bait-fishing nothing seems more simple to the uninitiated than to be able successfully to angle with a worm. Mere urchins have succeeded with a rough stick, linen line, and clumsy hook, more clumsily tied on, and covered with a worm, in landing a goodly-sized fish. But this is a mere matter of luck, and it would be absurd to classify the performance among the efforts of scientific bait-anglers.

Entertaining, as I really do, great respect for many bait-fishers of trout, I the more cheerfully present the following opinion from the genial angler and man of genius, Thomas Tod Stoddart, whose " Companion" and "Anglers' Rambles and Songs" have afforded me so much pleasure and instruction:

" It may perhaps startle some, and those no novices in the art, when I declare, and offer moreover to prove, that worm-fishing for trout requires essentially more address and experience, as well as better knowledge of the habits and instincts of the fish, than fly-fishing." He does not refer to the practice followed in brooks and petty streams, nor as pursued after heavy rains in discolored waters, and goes on to say: "My affirmation bears solely on its practice as carried on during the summer months in Scotland, when the waters are clear and low, the skies bright and warm. Then it is, and then only, that it ought to be dignified as sport; and sport it assuredly is, fully as exciting, perhaps more so than angling with the fly or minnow."

As I agree in the method recommended by this teacher, I will give its principal features, and leave with the angler to decide in his course of practice between us. " The rod should approach seventeen feet in length, but light, top pieces somewhat stiff, of lance or hickory."

The common trouting-line of stained silk and hair, tapering

from the middle to each end, as sold by our fishing-tackle men, is the best. The same may be said of the ordinary click reel, though it were better did it multiply. "The casting-line of silk-worm gut should be well tapered, and seven lengths of long single gut, tinged rather than dyed with the ordinary decoction of logwood and alum. The knots should be tied with care, but not whipped with thread—an operation which should be confined solely to the upper joints of the line. They ought to be of picked material, sound, clear, and fine, without flaw or fretting."

Hooks should be of finest steel, needle-pointed, and either the common Aberdeen round bend, Hutchinson's round bend, Sproat's bend, or the Kinsey bend, known as the Pennsylvania trout-hook. "Before attaching the snell or gut, file and break off from a quarter to half an inch of the shank, which is usually too long." This I have found best with hooks for small striped bass, which weigh each from half a pound to three pounds. Tie on the hooks with red silk, well waxed. "Some worm-fishers of celebrity adopt a small projection of gut or bristle, as in the tackle used for the stone fly," etc.

Sinkers should be made of split shot, from all sizes between pigeon and buck shot, according to the tide or current, or by winding sheet-lead round the line a foot or more above the hook. The bait should play under water, be kept moving, and never allowed to sink to the bottom or float on the surface; and when the current is swift, shot should be distributed above the regular sinker on the casting-line.

The best bait-anglers seldom use a float; when they do it is very small, only large enough to float the lightest sinker that will answer for the water. Casts should be regularly made, and the bait kept moving as if it were a fly under water; or if in the current of a stream, should be made to move with the current, as if there were no hook in it. The head of the worm should be broken off, and the hook so baited with the remainder as to leave an inch of the tail free to play naturally.

Of the varieties of angle-worm, that with rings, from five to six inches long, and about the size of a wheat-straw, is the best. Place the lot dug for fishing in cold water a little salted, and leave them in five minutes; then take them out, and place them on a dry board for ten minutes. To farther scour them, place them in swamp-moss which is damp, but not wringing wet; let them remain over night, and next morning go a-fishing.

The grub-worm is best in streams after a shower, because, being white, it shows best in discolored water. But the best bait of all for trout, to my notion, is a live shiner. Large trout will take it in preference to any other bait. As trout do not usually bite freely previous to a shower, it is best to bait-fish in the rain, or just after it has ceased. Fish know by instinct when it is going to rain, and they fast until it begins, because they expect the rain to swell the stream and bring down to them all sorts of delicacies; therefore, as soon as it commences to rain, they take any thing offered which they can swallow.

It is the angler's duty and pleasure to study all the peculiarities of weather, with the habits and haunts of trout, and to practice upon them; for as the bait-fisher does not usually whip all the surface of the water, but selects his places to drop his bait, it is necessary to know on which side of a rock or log it is natural for the trout to lie in wait for bait. The successful bait-angler studies also the condition of the water, and selects his favorite pools, while the fly-fisher looks for a gentle wind that will carry his flies off, and trusts to his skill and good fortune for attracting sport.

Fly-fishing possesses its peculiar advantages. As a means of exercise, it reaches just the degree to brace the muscles, exercise the temper, enliven the spirits, and produce the alternations between hope and despair characterized as sport. It encourages fine address and graceful attitudes, produces earnestness and even enthusiasm, and while the practice in minutiæ is not so close as to pin the mind to earth, every sound of bird or sight of flower is enjoyed by the devotee, and as he casts his eyes aloft and around, the earth appears a paradise, and anglers the only appreciative recipients of its blessings. Hence, from the variety of emotions which entrance the mind of the angler, men of genius and learning, especially those of ideal temperament, such as poets, painters, sculptors, philosophers, and worshipers of nature, become so penetrated with the beauties which surround its pursuit, that the cold, calculating outer world deems them mad upon a trivial subject. But it was owing solely to the pleasures which angling confers that Thomson, Burns, Scott, Hogg, and a host of other acknowledged worthies, succeeded by Prof. Wilson, Wordsworth, King Leopold, Dr. Bethune, and Daniel Webster, eagerly exchanged the gray goose-quill and the fellowship of books for the gently-tapering trout-rod and the music of the rills and cascades, older than the rhythm of Homer, and as attractive as the propositions of Socrates. "Therefore it was that Paley left his meditative home, and Davy his tests and crucibles, Chantrey his moulds, models, and chisel-work—each and all to rejoice and renovate themselves," and to fish up new ideas as with the gentle wand they cast their lines in pleasant places, playing trout in sparkling waters, and enjoying a sportive recreation which ever fills the mind with pure and joyous emotions, tempered by serene philosophy.

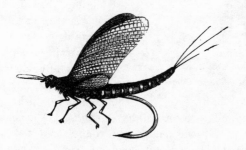

SECTION SECOND.

ANGLING FOR CHILDREN.

"Come when the leaf comes, angle with me,
Come when the bee comes crossing the lea;
Come with the wild flowers,
Come with the mild showers,
Come when the singing bird calleth for thee!"

STODDART.

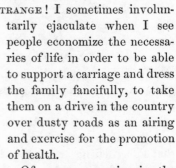

TRANGE! I sometimes involuntarily ejaculate when I see people economize the necessaries of life in order to be able to support a carriage and dress the family fancifully, to take them on a drive in the country over dusty roads as an airing and exercise for the promotion of health.

Of course, exercise in the open air is necessary for the preservation of good health; and a residence in a city where the only breathing-places are its parks, or in the few country places which are remote from waters that offer the recreation of angling, there is an excuse for the next means in the simple catalogue for promoting and preserving health, which is driving or riding on horseback. But in our country of broad acres and free fishings, every parent should teach his children to angle. The sport, which is not laborious, soon renders the young student so ardent in its pursuit that he will get sufficient exercise, while his mind will be rendered logical by the realization of cause and effect, and his whole being will soon become attuned to the harmonies of nature. The pleasurable exercise and anxieties in the practice of angling rest and recuperate the mind, so that children are thereby enabled to commit their school lessons to memory with greater ease, and to understand them more fully.

A small stream to angle in from the shore, or a pond to row out on and anchor the boat to fish from, is a great luxury which a family should not omit the enjoyment of. I have noticed with pleasure that the taste for angling has been increasing annually for the past ten years with our ladies. They begin to delight in fishing excursions and in the harmony of angling. There is, therefore, hope of a large crop of anglers from the rising generation. Twenty years ago there were scarcely a dozen ladies in the metropolis who could scull a boat, but now many ladies ply a pair of sculls very gracefully. With those families settled near the shores of the numerous water approaches to New York, and along Harlem River, the taste is setting in favor of light, buoyant, comfortable, and elegant row-boats; and morning and evening, these boats, laden with joyous families of children, lend an enlivening charm to the scene.

Sometimes papa and mamma take the children a-fishing. Whenever they do, they should supply them with a light bamboo rod, and attach at a joint one third from the top end a very fine silk or linen line; wind it a few times round the rod, and cast two half hitches over the top end; then affix a float according to the depth of the water, so that the bait will sink within six inches of the bottom, and a foot above the hook fasten to the line from one to three split shot. Let the hook be the minnow size, and the bait—a piece of angle-worm dug the day previous, and laid in moss or green grass over night to scour, if for small fresh-water fishes—should merely cover the point of the hook. Never bait with the head of the worm; always break that off and throw it in the water.

Sometimes it is best to take an extra supply of worms, and
cut some of them into small pieces and throw them into the
fishing-pool to attract the fishes to the place where you intend angling.   The liver of any animal is good bait for sunfish, shiners, chubs, dace, etc.   If angling in salt-water for
white perch, smelt, spearing, porgees, and tomcods, use shrimp
for bait; or, if they can not be procured, use either soft or
hard shell clam.   Rig the line with only one hook, and let
papa regulate the whole tackle according to the size of the
fishes to be angled for.

Oh! well do I remember the time when I first essayed to
capture the finny beauties of the brook.   I was about seven
years old, and as my father, who was devoted to educational
pursuits, had found both recreation and consolation in angling, he used sometimes to permit me to accompany him
and carry his strings of trout, and finally rigged me out with
a wand, line, and hook.   The first fish that I caught was a
shiner.   The sensation caused by the bite of the fish, and the
sight of the trembling and shining beauty as I cast it over
my head, and when realizing, by running to my hook and
learning that I had actually caught it, were moments as indescribable as they were ecstatic.   I was anxious to return
home at once and show the trophy to the family, and was
not dissuaded until my larger comrades pointed out the possibility of my taking a long string of such jewels.

After practicing a season with this light tackle, it will be
best to procure regular perch-tackle, and the next season a
reel and trout-rod may be added to the outfit.   Then grasshoppers will be found the favorite bait for trout and young
black bass, and small shiners and white grub-worms will be
found most attractive after a shower for large trout, black
bass, perch, and now and then a sand pickerel, which some of
the fishermen call *dorée*.   The lad will soon learn that the
most rapturous sport is realized along a stream and among
the birds as they chirp and sing while flitting from spray to
spray, for they rightly regard the young angler as a friend,

and so nearly a companion that they vie with each other in melody to charm him on.

After tea both mamma and papa take a seat with the children in the punt, when papa rows out on the pond and anchors the punt, and then baits the hooks and takes off the fish. This is the contemplative philosopher's recreation. It is simple, innocent, and charming.

> "Delicious musings fill the heart, and images of bliss;
> Ah! that all pictures of the past were innocent as this!"

> "Like distant music—heard at even,
>   When the gold light has left the dying day—
>   Which, like some spirit song from heaven,
>   Swells softly, then as softly dies away;
>   Yet dieth not away within the soul,
>   But leaves a soothing influence behind,
>   That oft will in our thoughtful hours control
>   The grosser, worldly cares that crowd the mind—
>   Just so the thoughts of dearest friends will steal
>   Over the pensive soul with fond reflections,
>   And, waking slumbering chords of love, reveal
>   Those hidden ties that bind our best affections;
> And—goodness gracious, bless me!—what a deal
> Of good it does to have such recollections!"—C. Bede.

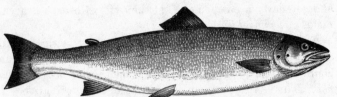

THE SALMON.—*Salmo salar.*

CHAPTER V.

THE SALMON.

THIS is the head of a numerous species, or rather of many families. The body is covered with fine scales; the fins are all soft-rayed except the second dorsal, which is composed of a soft adipose film. It has an air-bladder which extends the whole length of the abdomen.

The *genus Salmo* contains those species, such as the salmon and trout, in which the upper jaw is formed by the superior maxillary bones—the intermaxillaries being small—situated between the maxillaries. Usually these bones descend into the front of the superior maxillaries, and form the upper boundary of the mouth. The maxillaries, palatines, vomer, and even the tongue, are furnished with teeth. The branchiostegous, or gill rays, are about ten in number.

Numerous species of this *genus* are found in the seas of the northern hemisphere, one of the largest of which is the common salmon (*Salmo salar.*—Lin.), a fish too well known, both as to flavor and appearance, to require particular description. Cuvier states that it is found in all the arctic seas, whence it enters the rivers in the spring.

The *Salmo salar*, which the inhabitants of the British Isles appropriately distinguish as both "noble" and "royal," because it is the fish which affords them their highest degree of sport in angling, according to their estimate of the value of field-sports, has been differently esteemed for its esculent qualities at several periods in modern history, though at no time have its gamy qualities been questioned. In the eighteenth century its shoals became so numerous as to make it necessary to guard, by a clause in indentures, against feeding apprentices with it more than two days in each week. This was the case in England and in some of its colonies. But from many of our rivers, which teemed with salmon at the beginning of the present century, this delicious and graceful fish has been driven away; and were it not that—through the efforts of a few angling philosophers—the public has become sufficiently enlightened to see the necessity for the employment of means to restock our salmon rivers, it would be scarcely worth the time and ink necessary to describe the salmon in its varied aspects for the table, for commerce, and as an interesting feature in the recreative sports of the country.

But, thanks to a few public-spirited gentlemen, whose scientific discoveries were derived from experiments instituted at their own expense, the recent reports of the Fisheries Commissioners of New England show that the waters are being restocked with such zeal and alacrity that it will not be more than five years before most of the rivers north of Pennsylvania will be literally repeopled with salmon. The favorable prospects thus extended, when coupled with the generosity of our Northern neighbors, whereby the Dominion permits us to compete equally with its own people in the leasing of Canadian salmon-waters, gives hopeful promise that salmon-fishing with the fly will soon engage the attention of our anglers for striped bass during June and July, and thus add an interesting feature to the sports of the year, without trenching upon the best season for striped-bass angling.

The Highlander who stated that " no man has any right to a hunter's badge who has not killed a red deer, an eagle, a salmon, and a seal," had never been in America, or he would have made some additions to his prerequisites. If it exhilarates and even astonishes to take a salmon in the modest rivers of the British Isles, with gaffers as helpers, who know every cast in a pool, what must the sport be on the large, wild, and rapid rivers of Canada, with no adequate help?

Since we have no other choice, if we would go a salmon-fishing, but to repair either to Scotland, Ireland, or to the Dominion of Canada, and as several rivers in Canada are leased by American anglers, and all sportsmen from the States are liberally and even courteously treated there, I should give a preference to Canadian salmon-waters over those across the Atlantic, even were the fishings offered at the same price; but in the matter of expense, Canada is much the most economical for our anglers. The fish are also much larger on this side on an average, the scenery is more majestic, and the rivers more grand. To spend a summer month on one of the rivers which empty on the north shore of the Gulf of the St. Lawrence is to rest the mind by the most absolute exclusion from the world. When I essayed the ascent of one of the great rivers which empty into the Gulf of St. Lawrence north of the island of Anticosti, the world was tranquil. I rested there free from the news of civilization. For a month I admired the grandeur of the mountains, the majesty of the broad and rapid river, the elegant play of salmon, and the dexterity of the seals; and at night the brilliancy of the northern horizon and gorgeousness of the lunar bow enraptured me. On my return down the river, I was astonished to hear that a great war was in progress between Prussia and Austria, and that the cholera was raging in many places; but I was delightfully surprised to learn that the Atlantic telegraph was in successful operation, though shocked at hearing of the deadlock in Washington and the intention to impeach the President. Neither of these important topics were spoken of when I left New York to visit the wilderness on the north side of the Gulf of St. Lawrence. I therefore advise those who desire to unbend the mind and become perfectly Rip Van Winklefied, to try the rejuvenating effect of salmon-fishing in Canada.

Anglers of the United States who desire to fish a salmon-river in the dominion of Canada should club together and apply for the fluvial parts of rivers. The estuary is usually devoted to net-fishing, but it would be a better plan to apply for a whole river, and then have the estuary netted if preferred, or devote the whole river to fly-fishing. As salmon do not rise to the fly in the tidal parts of rivers, if the river is well stocked, the company might have the tidal part netted with sweep-nets to a certain extent, but gill-nets and other nets fastened to ground fixtures should be avoided. A party of four gentlemen own the lease of the Godbout, and permit no netting. It is contrary to law to fish on Sunday in any part of Canada. The government leases the rivers for a term of nine years, and the rivers unlet on the first day of each year are advertised by the government to be let to the highest bidders. The places of residence of those tendering for fishings are not considered in letting a river, and if a gentleman of the States overbids a Canadian, the river will be declared as his. Rivers are therefore hired by Europeans as well as by Canadians and citizens of the States. Prior to the formation of the Dominion of Canada out of the provinces, the salmon-rivers were under the control of the Minister of Crown Lands; but now they are managed by the Minister of Marine and Fisheries, at present the Hon. Peter Mitchell, to whom all applications should be made for leases of rivers. Rivers are either let in whole or in parts, each part permitting the use of a given number of rods, generally four. The fluvial part of the Moisie, for example, is divided into three fishings, the estuary being hired for fishing with nets. The other two parts accommodate eight rods. Parties, on making application to the Hon. P. Mitchell, at Ottawa, should state what number of rods they desire to accommodate, and on which side of the St. Lawrence they prefer a river. He will then forward the applicants a list of the rivers to be let, with such other information as he may deem necessary for their guidance. After receiving the list of rivers and a note of information, they should apply to some gentleman of the Do-

minion to make the tender for them.   If necessary, on application, I will name a suitable person at the seat of government to whom they may apply with confidence.

The course which I recommend to gentlemen of the States
is pursued by sportsmen of Canada.   The prices for the fluvial parts of rivers are very modest.   I belonged to a party
of four anglers who hired the whole of the fluvial part of a
first-class river for three hundred dollars for a single season.
The leases of fluvial parts of rivers vary from two to six hundred dollars a year for from three to eight rods; and the
price for guides or gaffers is a dollar a day.   Canoes and provisions are cheap there; a first-rate canoe may be purchased
for from twelve to fifteen dollars; and as for desiccated meats
and canned vegetables, with potatoes and eggs, also wines
and diffusible stimulants, they do not cost more than half the
sum demanded for them in the States.   Then, as an economical summer trip of a month or six weeks, the cost is less than
the expense of staying at a watering-place hotel, which is
similar to a city hotel minus its comforts.   If the lovers of
field-sports in the United States can but be induced to try
salmon-fishing, it will not be long before the rivers in the
States will teem with the silver beauties.   I have before me
a score of five weeks' fishing in the Godbout for four rods.
The total count was 279 salmon, weighing 3116 pounds, or the
average weight of each fish 11⅛ pounds.   They did not average the use of more than three rods daily, or more than five
days each week.   I have seen larger takes, but this is a high
score for salmon-fishing in any part of the world.

As I have stated, an application to hire the fluvial or angling part of a salmon-river from the government of the Dominion is to be for the term of nine years, and the prices of
the rivers must necessarily advance as anglers multiply in
numbers and America increases in wealth; for salmon-fishing, on the list of recreations which most deeply interest cultivated men, is esteemed a high art.

SECTION SECOND.

OUTFIT FOR SALMON-FISHING.

1 tent, either a marquee, wall-tent, or a common circular tent.

2 rubber blankets.

2 head-nets.

1 musquito-bar.

1 pair wading trowsers, water-proof and large.

1 water-proof overcoat, large and light.

1 oil-cloth coat and pants, to wear when fishing in the rain.

2 pairs of pegged army shoes for wading.

6   "   heavy woolen half hose.

1 pair of heavy woolen blankets.

1 rubber bag, large size.

1 rubber pillow.

1 pint *aqua ammonia*, for applying to bites of black flies, for preventing the secondary effect of swelling.

1 small case of medicines.

To guard against being bitten by black flies and musquitoes, carry a bottle of castor-oil mixed with a strong tincture of camphor. Some salmon-anglers employ a composition of tar and camphor, which gives them the tawny tint of the Indian, though it is one of the best protections against flies. The black fly is the worst during daytime, while the musquitoes and gnats begin their depredations at sundown and continue until sunrise. Your gaffer should fumigate your tent every night before you retire with a smudge smoke. Both the head-net and musquito-bar should be used every night.

For constant wear, day and night, supply yourself with a pair of woolen gloves extending near to the elbows, worn over the coat sleeve and held up by an elastic strap; or sew a pair of cotton stocking-legs to the wrists of a pair of gloves, either dogskin, buckskin, or close and thick woolen gloves.

A trip to Canada for salmon-fishing would be the gem of the year for all anglers, and even summer excursionists, were it not for the flies; yet they are no worse there than they are in the Adirondacks, nor so bad as they are in the wilds of Maine and New Hampshire.

A fishing-hat like No. 1 is formed of two parts, like 2 and 3, the latter setting on the band of 2 so that the vents will not meet, but the outer ones alternate with the under ones just above the brim. The edge of 3 is tacked down on the brim, which leaves a space between that and the upright part of 2 of half an inch or more, and cover the sewing to the brim with a band. The ventilation of this hat is excellent. The hat is known by name as the Gibraltar hat, while others call it the Calcutta hat. It is usually made of drab felt, and worn as an undress hat by European military officers when doing duty in warm climates. It is unquestionably the best ventilated hat made, except those from India, woven from grass or platted from bamboo; but the felt ones are the best in shape, and lighter than the real Indian hat.

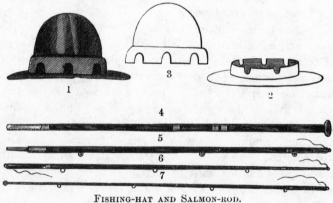

FISHING-HAT AND SALMON-ROD.

2 SALMON RODS.—The salmon-rod of four joints is indicated by Nos. 4, 5, 6, 7. The two upper joints are spliced with a small ring covering the end of each, as directed for the modern splice illustrated on another page. The following explanation I think worthy the attention of fly-fishers:

"Sir,—Not the least pleasure of the angler consists in
looking back upon the summer-time when he 'wandered
dreamily away up among the hills by the side of a tiny beck,
new to the angler, with no sound but the plover or the curlew, or the distant tinkle of the bell-wether; no incumbrance
but a light rod; no bother about what flies will or will not
suit; no tackle beyond a yard of gut and two or three hooks
in a piece of brown paper; a small bag of moss with well-
scoured worms within; a sandwich or cold mutton chop—
the latter for preference—in one pocket, and a flask of the
dew " that shines in the starlight when kings dinna ken in
the other," etc., etc. ; and when autumn, with its bracing air,
succeeded summer, to the wild, excited, yet concentrated
thrill that shot through his frame when he hooked the " lordly salmon," and which lasted till he could say to himself, " It
is my turn now; you shall not have all your own way with
me." '

" Such have been my feelings this cold, stormy winter evening, as I sat over a cosy fire in my easy-chair.   I felt inclined
to good fellowship with all anglers, especially such of them
as have arrived at my time of life, when they naturally look
back to what they have been in preference to what they are
now, but are still fond of the sport when strength and opportunity allow of following it.   For the especial benefit of the
latter, if you and they think it worth accepting, I have turned
to my writing-case to give you the particulars of a light salmon-rod, equally good for worm or salmon fishing, which I
got made at home last year.

" Its weight is 1¼ lb. ; length, 15½ feet; first fish killed
with it, 18 lbs. weight.

" The first week in September this season I hooked and
killed a male fish, 17 lbs., and hooked and killed on successive
days seven fish, aggregate weight nearly 90 lbs., without losing any thing once hooked.   Two or three had the sea-lice
on them—one especially, a 15½-pounder, which for running,
jumping, wheeling round and round in circles, shaking its

head, and lashing the water with its tail, exceeded any thing I ever had on. An old angler who was on the opposite side of the river, and has himself killed above fifty salmon this season, said it was the wildest fish he ever saw.

"Well, not to be prolix, I give you the result of many hours' study in few words, prefacing them with the observation that the rod is as straight and serviceable now as when first made, and has never failed or needed repair.

"For the butt, 5¾ feet of well-seasoned, selected memel, with the fibre of the wood running straight in the direction of the rod; if these conditions are not observed the wood is useless. For the middle piece, 4⅞ feet of selected ash. For top, 4⅞ feet of lancewood. The memel butt is brass-hooped, has good strong brass hoops for the wheel, and is joined to the ash middle-piece with the usual brass ferrule. The lance-wood top and ash middle-piece are joined with a new splice, which is superior to the ferrule joining for its lightness, impossibility of any shifting, and the quickness with which it is put together. This is the 'modern splice for fly-rods,' which is illustrated and described on page 160, under the head of 'Trouting Tackle.'

"There are twenty rings, graduating in size from the butt to the top, including the top ring, which is just large enough to allow the line to run freely. Proper ringing of a rod distributes the weight of a fish equally over it until it comes to the ring on the butt end. The rod graduates from the butt end to the top, is neither stiff nor supple, and throws a long line. The weight of the whole rod will give an idea of the thickness of each piece.

"I wish to draw especial attention to the material of the butt, the ringing, and the new splice. This new form of splice obviates the only objections (loss of time in tying, loosening of splice during use, and the wearing of the ends of the splice) against a spliced rod, and renders it incomparably superior to a ferruled rod."

Francis Francis states that "the best wood is unquestionably greenheart, and next to it hickory ;" adding that they in the British Isles had tried bamboo, and found it a failure. He also thinks that ferruled rods are better than spliced ones for general use, and shows, by comparing their weights, that the ferruled ones are not appreciably heavier. Since Mr. Francis gave an opinion against a bamboo rod, Dr. Clerk, of the firm of Andrew Clerk & Co., has visited Scotland in the salmon season, and carried with him a split bamboo rod made by their house. I have seen the same rod used in Canada, where it was pronounced, by such competent judges as officers of the army, the best they had ever seen in use. The doctor stated that to be the opinion of the anglers and experts in Scotland. This is the fourth season that it has been used, and, though it has played and killed many salmon weighing from twenty-five to thirty-five pounds each, yet it has never started in any part, but appears as good as new. Having seen it used by the side of Castle Connell and Martin Kelly specimens, I frankly confess that the split bamboo is vastly their superior in delivering a fly at a great distance, and retrieving the line; in playing a large fish while the angler is on the shore of a wide, rapid river, and in all the essentials which conduce to elegance and satisfaction in salmon-fishing. The rod is twenty feet long, and not more than three fourths the weight of a greenheart or hickory of the same length. The reel is attached to bands from eighteen inches to two feet above the end of the butt, as easier to hold while racing down a river with a salmon. By the use of a couple of feet below the reel, the angler may place the butt under his left arm, and, with the rod perpendicular, let the rod and reel do their duty, while he runs an unequal race along a rocky shore, tangled with shrubbery and fallen timber. I sincerely believe that the split bamboo is the perfection of a salmon-rod. Its make is a secret, but there is no doubt that the butt and second joint are corked with hickory or some one of our tough woods. The only part of the rod which is bamboo is the outside, composed of the outside and tough part of the bamboo, and wound at intervals of six inches throughout its length with waxed silk lashings. Of course the rings are graduated in number to the length of the rod.

The angler, on visiting Canada for salmon-fishing, should be armed with two rods, or an extra rod besides his bamboo, but should expect to fish with the bamboo. I am partial to a three-jointed rod over a four-jointer; but either of them may be balanced well. I am also in favor of the lower joint being ferruled, and the others fastened with the " modern splice" of bands at each end of the splice. The bamboo rod should be from nineteen to twenty-one feet long. For a second rod, I should recommend one rather stiffer than the bamboo, intended, if necessary, for angling from a boat. It should be from sixteen to nineteen feet long, and the hickory ones made by Martin Kelly, of Dublin, are preferable to any that I have seen except the split bamboo. The Castle Connell rods are rather top-heavy, and approximately double-acting, with a kick in the butt which nearly upsets a person when wading in a three-feet-deep rapid water. Mr. Johnson, of Boston, makes an excellent salmon-rod, and so does Robert Welch, of New York. I suppose that Pritchard Brothers might make a good salmon-rod, as they are old salmon-fishers. An excellent salmon-rod is made with hickory butt, next joint of ash, a third of lancewood, and top of split bamboo; all of the same pattern as a Long Island trout-rod, only heavier and longer. The butt should be ferruled, and the other two joints spliced.

2 CLICK REELS.—Each of these should be large enough to carry a hundred and fifty yards of English salmon-line; that is, a silk, or silk and hair braided line, tapering, and protected by varnish from becoming water-soaked. Good salmon-reels are only to be procured at our best fishing-tackle establishments, and it is worse than love's labor lost to use any other.

1 spare line for the reels.

6 casting-lines of twelve feet in length each, made of stained gut, one fourth three-ply at the upper end, one fourth two-ply next, both twisted, and six feet of single gut. Let the

gut be round, clear, and perfect, and as strong as you can procure.

2 horse-hair casting-lines, from eighty to one hundred feet long each, braided in the form of a whip-lash, and nearly one fourth of an inch in diameter in the centre. Pritchard Brothers make this upper casting-line to perfection. It is light, and its shape greatly assists casting, while it is not so liable to sink and drown as the silk, or silk and hair line, though protected with varnish. This casting-line is a *desideratum* not to be neglected. Before splicing it to your reel-line, cut off from the latter as many yards as you add by the upper casting-line.

6 dozen, or nearly a gross, of assorted salmon-flies, and a quantity of materials to enable you to duplicate the size and color of either; for salmon of different pools in the same river have different tastes, and keep changing so frequently that a Montreal fly of brown mallard wings, claret body, and golden pheasant top-knot for tail, which they curved their velvet tails at yesterday, is the favorite to-day, to be superseded to-morrow, perhaps, by a Tweed fly. When the angler runs nearly out of a favorite fly, he selects a hook of the same size and combines the same colors to mount it with; and though it be not artistically tied, it generally proves successful, for salmon do not scrutinize very closely when they witness the combination of colors which they admire. When yellow is the favorite color, and you have run out of flies of that tint, tie a new fly, or, if in a hurry, add yellow to another fly.

1 hank of round, clear, and heavy silk-worm gut, stained.

GAFF-HOOKS.

A is the salmon-bend gaff, and B the striped bass. The distance across the bend of the first is $2\frac{1}{2}$ inches, and $2\frac{3}{4}$ across the bend of B. The screws are of steel or brass, to fit into a handle six feet long, and composed of two joints. The gaffs should be heavy, and from one fourth to three eighths of an inch in diameter in the heaviest parts.

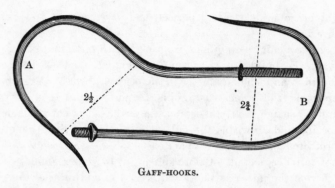

GAFF-HOOKS.

In addition to the foregoing list, do not omit a couple of changes of heavy woolen clothing. At the far north, where it is light enough to read twenty hours of the day, the other hours are cold enough for several blankets and overcoats. For the employment of guides, cook, gaffers, and the purchase of canoes, it is best to employ an agent in Quebec or Gaspe. Mr. Willis Russell, of the St. Louis Hotel, Quebec, always takes great pleasure in advancing the interests of anglers from the States, and, on application, will name or appoint suitable persons and direct them.

Of supplies for subsisting the party, either Quebec or Gaspe are equally advantageous for the south side of the Gulf, but for the north side I should prefer to supply at Quebec.

Smokers will find segars and kinnikinnik, with brier-wood pipes, or a meerschaum, something of a protection against flies. Parties that prefer may charter a schooner at Quebec or Gaspe for five dollars a day, including a navigator and two sailors, who subsist themselves for that sum, the whole expense being only five dollars a day for having a vessel manned at the party's command.

Thus, having studied the subject and made our preparations, we propose starting for Canada or Labrador on a salmon-fishing excursion, and pray the reader to accompany us in spirit while we recall our recollections of one of our trips to Canada.

Having previously expressed the bulk of our outfit to Quebec, the banker and myself started from New York in marching trim, with the few articles here illustrated, to wit: Water-proof satchels—salmon-reel—clearing ring and reel—scap-nets—gaff—trout-basket—leather case containing rods—and a bottle of hartshorn to cure fly-bites.

SECTION THIRD.

DEPARTURE FOR SALMON-FISHING.

The noble Northern rivers that pierce the mountain chain,
Where leap the gleaming salmon in their watery domain,
Invite us to their waters, by the fir-tree shadow'd shore,
Their shoals, and pools, and torrents with fish-rod to explore.

s our party consisted of four gentlemen and two ladies, we concluded to divide routes, three going from Quebec *via* Gaspe to the St. John River, while the banker, his lady, and myself awaited the departure of the government steamer Victoria, and, as it proved, this was an unexpected advantage, for the steamer was employed by government to provision the light-houses along the shores of the Gulf of St. Lawrence and the island of Anticosti, to assist wrecked mariners, and accomplish the double office of charity and police. I was especially thankful for so good an opportunity for seeing the salmon-rivers on the north shores which come rushing and tumbling down every few miles from mountain heights, to swell the tides of the Gulf. It gave me the advantage of conversing with the government agents who superintend the fisheries, some of whom had been employed to supervise the fisheries under the Hudson Bay Company for many years; and all agreed that the Company had greatly depleted the rivers of salmon, and necessitated the exercise of wisdom and care on the part of the government to restock them with a supply as ample as would be required for rendering them profitable, besides supplying the needs of the growing population. I was glad to be thus furnished with *data* for correctly reporting the condition of the salmon-fishery; and in that report to the *Spirit of the Times*, having had no pique or prejudice to gratify, but, on the other hand, entertaining the most lively sense of gratitude for the hospitality with which I was every where greeted, I expressed the wish that their people might become " altogether such as we are, except our bonds."

The week's sojourn at the St. Louis in Quebec was in itself a great treat. The hotel is first class, and intrinsically good. Mr. Russell, its accomplished proprietor, is enterprising, and his guests are as well served as are those of the best hotels in New York, leaving nothing to be desired. The suburbs of Quebec are beautiful, besides being interesting from a historical point of view. In sight of the city are the Falls of Montmorenci, the picturesque islands in the river below the city, Point Levi on the opposite shore, with a broad belt of green foliage and pasture lighted up by country residences, some of which partake—with their surroundings—largely of the ornate. The weather was highly refreshing, and the promenade on the Plaza, with the enlivening music belonging to the military station, made the time pass gayly. I would here state, parenthetically, that Quebec is a beautiful place to remain for a few days on a bridal tour. But the day arrived for our departure on the Victoria. Our passage was very agreeable, and on the morning of the fourth day we were landed at the mouth of the St. John, some six hundred miles from Quebec, and with the hazy outline of the island of Anticosti in sight to the south.

We were rejoiced at finding a hamlet of huts, where resided the cod fishermen of the station, who employed some sixty smacks, and were in full tide of operation, fishing with hand-lines on the banks between the main shore and Anticosti. The salmon-fishers of the estuary also resided there, and were fishing with gill-nets fastened to stakes which were fixed in the bottom of the river, but not technically called stake-nets. Mr. J. Beaulieu, a superintendent or fishery warden, resides also at the mouth of the St. John during the salmon season. The doctor, with the general and his lady, having arrived two days previously, had ascended the river with canoes to the plateau where we designed encamping, twenty-seven miles up the river, and had sent back two canoes and guides for us. While the grocer was preparing our breakfast of fried salmon, with salt pork, bread, butter, and English breakfast tea, I concluded to reconnoitre, and soon found that curiosity called the black fly, who left his mark on my nose. I saw also the salmon-netters land with their boats, containing many salmon which were either headless or showed signs of having been bitten in different parts of the body, and so mutilated by the seals, and perhaps otters and minks, as to be entirely valueless. I therefore concluded that either the seals should be destroyed, or that salmon should not be taken with gill-nets fastened to stationary stakes in the stream, where all water-vermin can feast on the struggling salmon, helplessly fastened in the meshes, from whence many of them, bitten in pieces, necessarily drift down the current to pollute the river, and warn salmon just entering to seek some other spawning-ground.

OUR START UP THE ST. JOHN.

After breakfasting bountifully we repaired to our canoes, where we found our baggage stowed appropriately, and were invited to take seats on the bottom and in the centre of the canoes, our four willing guides manning the bow and stern of each canoe with paddles, iron-pointed setting-poles, and a long rope attached to each bow for towing us up the rapids along the shores, which they call "cordeliering." On the fir-brush flakes, which bordered the shore and covered acres, were strewn codfish to dry, whose fragrant aroma seemed to threaten even the black flies. The water was enlivened by thousands of sea-trout, foraging in every direction and leaping after flies. But we bade the last signs of human abode adieu, and started up the river, through deep mountain gorges of rock, whose summits were sparsely covered with small fir-trees. It was a pleasant morning in June, and we had not gone far before our Canadian guides began to chant, without regard to the time of day, their favorite river music of

AVE MARIA.

son nid d'oi - seau;   A - ve Ma - ri - a! Car voi - ci l'heure

sain-te   La cloche   tin - te,   A - ve Ma - ri - a!

Vous êtes la voile
  Du pauvre marin ;
Vous êtes l'étoile
  Du bon pélerin;
Ave Maria !
Car voici l'heure sainte
La cloche tinte
  Ave Maria !
Vous êtes servante
  Des pauvre blessés ;
Vous êtes l'amante
  Des cœurs délaissés.
  Ave Maria ! &c.

Votre nom si tendre
  Sur un front mortel,
Fait toujours descendre
  La beauté du ciel
Ave Maria !
Car voici l'heure sainte
La cloche tinte
  Ave Maria !
Aussi les Maries
  En chœur gracieux,
A vous réunies
  Montent vers les cieux!
  Ave Maria ! &c.

Having journeyed too far north for the robin and bobolink, the stillness of the scene, whose monotony was only relieved by the dashing currents of a mighty river, the leaps of salmon and sea-trout, and the stealthy movements of the seal, now hiding, and now galloping up a rapid like a race-horse, at every leap throwing itself half out of water, gave us a fair chance for reflection, and to wonder that people could be found willing to settle in that sterile region. But, on inquiry, we found that none had yet ventured, not even an Indian, which furnished me with another evidence of human sagacity, for even bruin's anxious family know better than to settle there in great numbers. We passed a late Hudson-Bay fishing-station, where remain standing their log huts and birch-bark smoke-houses wherein they cured their salmon; but since their charter expired several years since—grace to the salmon—there is not a human soul settled above the mouth, within fifty miles of it.

On our guides rowed, poled, and " cordeliered"—stopping only to eat a mouthful of bread and raw onion—until sundown, which found us seventeen miles on our journey. Here

we halted for the night, saw the canoes unladen and hauled
on shore, a fire quickly made to keep off the flies and enable
us to extemporize a supper with scarcely any vessel to cook
in or eat out of, pitch our tent, etc. While these duties were
going forward, a large salmon, of over 20 lbs. weight, leaped
several feet above the pool in front of our tent, and not thirty feet from shore. As quick as thought was one of our
guides seen skulking along the shrubby margin of the river,
waiting to see the seal which was the cause of the leap of
the salmon. Presently the seal made its appearance in the
middle of the river, and in the strength of the rapid, swimming with its head above water, and looking like a young
negro bathing. It turned its head and looked all around, apparently in surprise, as if scenting danger, while approaching
the shore in response to the plaintive call of the man with
the rifle; but the gunner was too slow on the trigger, and
the seal went on its way rejoicing.

Boughs of fir, for bedding, were cut by the guides and laid
in our tent while we were taking supper. Our first night of
tenting in the wilderness was signalized by pleasant dreams,
and we arose early, made our toilets, and watched the salmon
disport in the rapids while breakfast was being prepared,
and canoes launched and reladen.

After breakfast we started for our camping-ground, ten
miles farther up the river. The whole of this distance may
be properly considered a rapid, and one third the way a very
dangerous one. Salmon were abundant. While many were
leaping above the current in the middle of the river, scores
were seen darting from near the shores where our guides
were tugging along.

All animate nature seemed more than usually active that
morning. The seals were out in force and galloping up the
rapids. Salmon were leaping and splashing, and even the
silver trout were breaking, as if to demonstrate that they too,
though less important, were gay and happy.

While admiring the mountains of rock, sparsely covered

with a very thin apology for a forest, the close thicket of
birch and poplar which bordered the river, and the numerous shoots of a wide river of pellucid waters, in which none
but the highest styles of game-fish found a residence, a duck
shot out from the shore with a little brood of over a dozen
following her. I told Duncan—my guide and gaffer—to
slacken the speed of the canoe. I was interested in this duck
of a mother with a numerous brood. Her anxiety was exciting. For an instant she would turn toward her brood and
urge them with the most impressive gestures to quack-qua-
qua-ka-qua-qua-ka-ka, and then she would turn from them
and swim toward the middle of the river in utmost speed;
but, bethinking herself, she would turn again and find the
little ducks a great way behind. Then she would swim back
toward them, and qua-qua-qua-ka-ka-ka until the little things,
beginning to realize their critical situation, would use their
wings as well as their feet, and make many shell-drake splut-
tering demonstrations, until, by the numerous turns of the
mother, her emphatic quacking calls, and their own exertions,
they gained the opposite shore of the river, and we acceler-
ated our speed. But we had not proceeded far before we
ran against a rock, and broke a hole in the bow of our bark
canoe that made us land and unship cargo. A fire, by the
means of birch bark, which is the most ignitable substance
in the forest, heated some pitch, and with a piece of cotton
cloth six inches square, the hole was patched and pitched so
as to render it water-tight and as good as new. In the mean
time our friends overtook us, and we discussed the " cussed"
hard traveling. My friend was on the point of musically ex-
claiming, " Oh, carry me back!" but we changed it into the
following voluntary:

> " 'Twixt you and I, I almost think
> It's almost time to take a drink,
> For we're all nearly home."

We agreed with him, and, after imbibing a glass of sherry,
once more started to admire the beauties of the water, for

there were none on the land; though, to speak candidly, the
hills were sometimes so low along the river, and the sun and
shade so captivating, that it appeared as if we might find or-
chards and gardens over the first small hill, and I often asked
my friend to run over and bring us some fruits and melons,
but he reluctantly declined, for fear of encountering Mrs.
Bruin and her anxious family. But with stout hearts, and
the brawny arms of our guides, we soon reached our tenting-
ground.

SECTION FOURTH.

THE ENCAMPMENT.

'Twixt the fir-tree skirted ranches,
  Where the Rattling Run doth shine,
We erect our hut of branches,
  Roof of birch bark, wall of pine;
Floor it with the boughs of saplings,
  Fragrant, soft as couch of kings,
Rioting in forest pleasures,
  And the sleep that labor brings.

It was nearly noon when we arrived at our camping-
ground, which is a level piece of bottom-land, covered with
sand and cobble-stones, a mile long, by the river shore, and a
quarter of a mile wide, the base formed by Rattling Run, a
small river emptying into the St. John just below our tents.
It was a very hot day—*hot* is the word for the middle of a
clear, still day, from the 20th of June to the 20th of August,
even in Labrador, where there is frost nearly every night.
There was only one tent pitched; but the lady was superin-
tending the erection of a log cabin, while the gentlemen were
away up the river angling for salmon. The lady sent her
servant—a " contraband" that followed the general from Tennessee—to inform them of our arrival.

I noticed with pleasure that the general's lady had not suffered much from the annoyance of flies.

"Oh no," she replied; " it's perfectly charming here; one
bit me on the eyelid before I knew what to apply for anti-
dote, and it nearly closed it; but now, as soon as I am bitten,

I just touch the bite with ammonia, and it gives me no pain, and never swells. The black flies do not trouble you after dark, and that's a great comfort."

I saw a few signs of defaced beauty, but kept mum. In fact, on looking upon those two ladies, I felt proud of such specimens. One of them had visited most of the courts of Europe, and the other had accompanied her triumphant husband throughout our recent great war. We therefore numbered six in the party, two ladies and four gentlemen; and I am bound to acknowledge that, throughout our month of camp life, hundreds of miles from a post-office, the ladies exemplified the highest degree of spirit and pleasure, with the least appearance of annoyance at any discomfort; and these were the two first white ladies that ever ascended the great St. John River.

Having examined the surroundings, and admired the great contrasts of the heavens with the mountains, and the wide,

rapid, roaring river, with its tributary of Rattling Run, and
while I was beginning to scan the lay of the grounds for deciding where to pitch tents, behold our comrades! They
came fishing along, towing four salmon on the gaff, while
the general played a fifteen-pounder all the way down from
the falls, a mile up the river.

It having become midday, we compared notes and took
dinner. At dinner we discussed the almighty salmon in all
his aspects—from his seclusion in corners of the earth, where
he is protected by flies and an almost impenetrable wilderness, to his high game, and, finally, the epicurean appearance
he lends to the dinner-table. Our dinner consisted of

> *Saumon à la maître d'hôtel.*
> *Saumon frit.*
> *Saumon au gratin.*
> *Jambon brulée.*
> *Les oignons de Bermude.*
> *Biscuit de mer.*
> *Le pain et du beurre.*
> *Du thé et du sucre.*

Having twenty-seven miles of rapids against which to
transport our stores, our potatoes and our claret were left at
the mouth of the river, besides our desiccated meats, soups,
vegetables, and fruits preserved in cans. Even our old Jamaica rum was left, and the only diffusible stimulant was gin
—Holland gin! But, in order that our coffee, milk, and the
numerous luxuries laid in for the campaign should be on
hand for the glorious Fourth of July, we divided our men
and canoes, half to transport our provisions from the mouth
to the camps, and the other half to serve in the way of pad-
dling us to our places for angling, gaffing our salmon, and
pitching our tents, waiting on us, cooking, etc.

The general and the doctor had so excited my friend the
banker and myself with stories of captivating sports, that,
immediately after dinner, we hardly thought of a cigar, but

forthwith commenced splicing our rods. To save me that trouble, as he saw my anxiety, the doctor kindly tendered me the use of a Castle Connell rod, which, he stated, had nearly broken his back and used him up, but he hoped it would behave more generously with me. It was a twenty-foot rod, by which a long cast could be made; but it was so top-heavy, and with a sort of double action, like a "kick in the handle," that it came back on me several times, and made me sit down in the river to cool off; but not on that day.

The doctor accompanied me, to give an idea where I would likely find salmon, and how I had best move my fly so as to render it captivating in that wide and rapid river. I admired the river; the breaks of salmon of from ten to twenty-five pounds each excited me. I soon thanked the doctor, and told him that I believed myself a match for them, when he ignited a cigar, and proceeded onward to where he expected the salmon were waiting for his flies.

Left alone, with the injunction that if I should hook a salmon. to shout for a gaffer to come to my assistance, as Duncan had returned to the mouth of the river for provisions, I again examined my tackle. "It is true," thought I, "these fish average from eight to thirty-eight pounds only, and I have taken a forty-pound striped bass; but my tackle for striped bass was a strong line, while here it is only a single silk-worm gut."

Having intellectually weighed and investigated the theory of the audacious fish in that river of great power and majesty, and so examined that I thought all things were right, I made a cast and let my fly float round from the current to the side. I continued so to cast and drop down stream a step at each cast, about half an hour, when a salmon accepted my lure. The fish did not take the fly as a trout does by rushing at it from beneath, but rose over the fly and took it on going back. He soon convinced me that he was there by a jerk and a leap above water, and out farther into the river where the current

P

was stronger. When he leaped, as he did numerous times, I lowered the top of my rod as if bowing to his mandate. By-and-by he suffered himself to be reeled up quite near me, no doubt because his curiosity prompted him to study the cause of his difficulty, and to try, if possible, to reach its source. In the mean time I was shouting for some man to come and gaff my salmon.

After having scanned " the head and front of the offending," he turned and ran off moderately until he arrived in the swiftest part of the current, and then all I could do would not stop him. I was therefore obliged to follow, and down I started along the stony shore for a quarter of a mile, when I became fatigued; and, as if to spell me, the fish halted and remained until he rested long enough, and then he rose and made a quadrilateral leap, or four leaps in as many directions at the same time. Said I, "My chap, you are some!" "How many lives have you got, anyhow?" thought I. But there was no use of thinking or speculating, for he had mounted his high horse again, and down the river I had to follow. My extemporized gaffer advised me to snub him. I replied that I had, but it was of no use. Presently he halted again, and, drenched with perspiration, I doffed my head fly-net and prepared to do battle in open air. It was not long before he gathered strength again, and started for the middle of the river; but a little harder play coaxed him to change his mind. He then began leaping and cavorting, as if he was only in fun all the time, and had as lief as not come in out of the wet. In a few more turns, the gaffer made a pass at the fish and missed him. The fish then showed great vigor, and acted as if he would never say die; but after several efforts the gaffer brought him up, and he weighed only twelve pounds.

With perspiration rolling down me and not a little fatigued, I started back to where I hooked the salmon and commenced casting for another. It was not long before I hooked him, and without much make-believe he started down the river and I after him. Presently he waited to rest, and then turned and ran up the river. Then he sulked. Next he leaped and dove, swimming rapidly up stream to form a bight in my line. But, finding all his tricky efforts useless, he started with great speed down the river, and I brought him to gaff half a mile below where I had hooked him. He weighed within a pound of as much as the first one.

Again I retraced my steps to the head of the pool, to where a long cast would send the fly beyond a submerged rock in the centre of the current, below which salmon appeared to rest preparatory to ascending a lengthy rapid which carried them to the great pool below the falls. Several times I delivered my fly so as to sweep the current and eddy without a salmon putting in an appearance. I therefore walked along the shore, casting out as far as I could on the rapid stream, and every time the fly floated round to the edge of the eddy at the side I took one step down stream and cast again, so as to fish over all the ground on my side of the river. I had not fished more than a quarter of a mile, when, in response to my feathery invitation, a very large silvery fish sparkled in the air before me! I admired him with intense interest; and, after a short contest, he came up persuasively, seeming to say, "I'll land without the gaff." Thus he played off and on shore, in the air and in the water, until I realized a new sensation, and began to regard him as a charming pet. I saw that he was a very large fresh-run salmon, and much more tractable than either of the two which came to gaff. Presently he slackened speed, and even stopped to rub his nose against a rock, and perhaps try to spring the hook out; but these were merely casual experiments to whet his ingenuity, while on his way back to the sea, to rid himself of hooks and stake-nets. By-and-by, after he had led me about half a mile, sometimes fast and at other times slow, as suited his fancy, making me appear very like, though less artistic, perhaps, than Pat with a shillelah in one hand, his hat placed akimbo, and with his other hand holding a rope fastened to a pig's leg, the pig too large for Pat to control. About that time I did not think of black flies, nor rocks and sore shins. My friend sometimes generously came near shore, and once I thought I saw him throw his tail up, as a sure sign of growing weakness, but it was all sham. He was only studying my tackle, and his means of escape by parting it. He was up near the gaff several times, and eyed the instrument critically, but with a whirl of astonishment akin to anger and disdain, as if in this age of negro suffrage a man so cruel could be found as to fight salmon with so unequal and hideous a weapon. But he curled on the water, and while he touched his nose with the end of his tail, he looked askance for an instant; then he made a prodigious leap down stream, and plunged some ten feet under water and came up five rods above, thus forming a bight in the line, by which he expected to gain slack and extricate himself. But it was all no go. I thought he was mine, and preserved great care lest he should unhook while bringing him to the gaff. He came forward as willing as a pet lamb until within three rods of shore; he then made a turn, and with dips, dives, leaps, and other devices, liberated himself, and took my fly-hook with him. I felt wilted; worse, I was outgeneraled; worse still, I was vanquished. I once more mechanically walked nearly a mile to the foot of the rapid, but I could not cast with hope and confidence, and, as the sun was about setting and the musquitoes began their carnival, I repaired to the tent and to supper, used up, though partially successful.

Thus ended my first afternoon's angling for salmon in Lower Canada.

SECTION FIFTH.

TENTING IN THE WILDERNESS.

Our guides had pitched our tents, and carpeted them with fir-boughs which they clipped from the shrubbery background of the plateau. My bed consisted of two breadths six and a half feet long of canvas, closed by a seam lengthwise up the centre, and hemmed six inches wide at each side

for inserting poles. A log at each end a foot in diameter
served to fasten the poles to, thus forming a canvas bed 6½
feet long, 3 feet wide, and a foot above the carpet or ground
of the tent. If preferred, the foot-log need not be so large as
the head one; only have regard to stretching your bed high
enough to admit the circulation of air under it. The following sketch may help illustrate.

CAMP BED.

The guides had also cut the poles and inserted them in the
hems of the canvas, which I bought and brought with me
from Quebec, and with stretchers across the ends of the canvas, they had fastened my bed to the head and foot logs,
made my bed, and had built a smudge fire in front of my
tent. Oh, how refreshing the aroma of a tent carpeted with
fir-boughs! no one, without experience, can properly appreciate the luxury.

After a social supper, we convened in a circle around the
smudge fire before my tent to discuss the mighty salmon,
and to inform the ladies of the changes in the fashions up to
the day we left, being a week after their departure. Of
course the changes had been considerable, and the gentlemen's forty-eight hours' advance in studying the peculiarities
of the salmon there had entitled them to the honors of Men-
torship. So, after summing up and being summed up, and
the tent smoked out with a smudge fire on a piece of birch
bark, I laid my rubber blanket on the bed, and was soon
dreaming that I had captured the beautiful salmon that I
had played so long, and was being serenaded by all the other milt salmon for ridding them of the dandy of the river.
Being vociferously called on for a speech, it so shocked my
nerves that I awoke, and the light peering in through the interstices of my tent, I forthwith arose for the morning.

"The little landscape round
Was green and woody, and refreshed the eye;
It was a spot which you might aptly call
The Valley of Seclusion."

Bright and beautiful was the weather, and the two birds which charm the mornings of that wilderness wild were piping their mellifluous notes, while the only responses heard were the snores of our guides in a one-sided bark shanty, where they lay on fir-boughs, toasting their feet before a smudge fire. As it appeared to be about seven o'clock, I was surprised to see not a soul moving. I walked a few rods to the river, where I watched admiringly the salmon's leap, but looked in vain for a seal. After having been up nearly an hour, and perceiving that friends and guides were still asleep, I concluded to call up the gaffers and *cuisinier*, or cook. As our cook was perfectly innocent of any language but a *Kanuck patois*, by which tongue potatoes or *pommes de terre* are known as *potack*, of course I found it difficult to make him understand either English or French, and that is an unpardonable fault in a cook.

Well, as they lay snoring, and not one awake, I thought I would see what time it was before arousing them; and on consulting my watch, I learned that it was precisely half past three o'clock! Well, said I, *sotto voce*, this *is* a strange country, and, lest I should disturb my lodging comrades, I reclined outside the tent, and tried to take another nap; but the black flies had also awoke, and began paying their *distresses* to me, much to the sacrifice of an amount of beauty too scant to lose any without an exposure of its want. I remonstrated at the presentation of bills at such an unseasonable hour, but they only shouted the louder, and called together so great a number as to oblige me to decamp. I therefore resorted to Rattling Run to take a bath. While bathing it was all very well, but between undressing and dressing they took me at a disadvantage, and by both musquitoes and black flies I was decidedly worsted. On my return to the tents there were no signs of life but an occasional snore, the noises of hares, porcupines, and squirrels in the grove hard by, and the two songsters singing so merrily as to drown the music of the musquitoes. On examining my watch I learned that it was five o'clock. I therefore determined on arousing the cook and the gaffers. They arose with reluctance, rubbed their eyes, washed their faces and hands in the river, and that was all the toilet-making needed, for they had slept with their boots and shoes on as protection against flies. John, the captain of the gang, because of his superior Milesian intelligence, who could speak equally well bad English and villainous French, informed me that it never had been the custom under Dr. Bluff, of the First Fusileers, or any gentleman who had previously fished that river, to rise before seven, or to commence fishing before nine. Well, then, I replied, we Yankees will teach you a new lesson. But, upon ascertaining that my friends were opposed to rising early, or fishing before breakfast, I yielded; and thenceforward the cook and guides suited their own comfort about rising, and we did not get started for angling until the sun had scorched the toes and dried the whistles of the musquitoes.

But it seemed that the noise caused from mustering the men had awakened the doctor, who crawled out of his tent with modest care for fear of arousing the other two inmates, when he mildly saluted me with "Good morning; how came your eye out?" I replied that my eyes were good enough to perceive that three or four bites from black flies had changed his phiz into a picture of a Chinese monstrosity. "You don't say so!" he ejaculated. "Where?" I pointed to one of his eyes, his bare caput, his face, etc. On examining them, he forthwith applied ammonia to the bites, and bathed mine also with it.

Smudge fires were at once made before our tents and extemporized breakfast-place. Our *cuisinier* was soon engaged at frying pork and Bermuda onions, broiling salmon, making

tea, etc., etc. As we had not tasted potatoes in a week, we
began to long for them. Our table was set, and breakfast
about ready, when the general and the banker made their
appearance with their ladies, and, after mutual salutations,
we all seated ourselves for breakfast. Our plates and dishes
were composed of cast-iron outside and porcelain inside; and,
though nearly as beautiful as sets and dishes of figured china,
they were as durable as iron, and just the kind that should
be adopted for kitchen use in the metropolis. By each plate
a stone about the size of a goose-egg was placed, to use in
cracking our sea-biscuit. Good sea-biscuit is much better
than common bread in the wilderness, and when cracked up
and crumbled into a bowl of tea, or, by being first dipped into
cold water to soften it, is afterward fried in the fat of the
pan after pork and eggs, is excellent, especially in the absence
of potatoes.

I was almost shocked on perceiving that the right eye of
the banker's lady was closed, and a large lump on her left
temple, almost spoiling her beauty; but I did not allude to
it until she mentioned that the flies had somewhat disfig-
ured me, when I asked her how she had rested. She replied,
"Very well; but this morning, while bathing my face, I found
that I had a large lump on the left side of it, and my right
eye felt fatty. I called to my husband, and asked him what
it was. He replied by asking me to shut my left eye and
look at him with my right one, and when I obeyed he said
he was surprised, for my right eye appeared to be entirely
closed. Neither my eye nor my face pain me at all, but the
general's lady has applied ammonia to the bites, and I expect
nothing more serious from them. Hereafter I shall wear my
head-net night and day, and my Esquimaux boots." I com-
plimented her philosophy, and imitated her example by wearing boots every night for a month, though fishing in shoes
and wet trowsers, and, on returning to the tent twice a day,
doffing my wet clothes, and rubbing down with a crash towel, and substituting dry clothes and boots until ready to start

for the river again, when I would doff the dry clothes and replace them by wet wading ones and shoes, with thick woolen
half hose—sometimes two pairs—in a very large pair of shoes.
Wide-soled pegged bottoms are the best. This changing of
dresses was our daily *modus operandi ;* and I waded, bathed,
changed dress, whipped, played salmon, and was bitten by
flies until I reduced my weight more than twenty pounds.
I therefore suggest salmon-angling as the best training that
a person can indulge in whose adiposity preponderates. This
system has the advantage of "Banting on Corpulence," because, while it reduces the amount of fat or adipose matter,
it hardens the muscles, and thus improves the wind and physical power of a man. If a person desires training so as to
endure great fatigue, and render him more active and supple,
I advise him to forthwith apply for a salmon-river; and, after having secured a lease of it for the usual term of nine
years, to send a good, trusty man there next April, and let
him employ a couple of Canadian half-breeds, buy a couple
of bark canoes, to be had for fifteen dollars each, and let your
man build a couple of log huts at the foot of each of the principal rapids or falls, and let him cover them well with birch
bark, and line them throughout with the bark, so as to keep
out the flies. A chimney is quite unnecessary, as a smudge
fire in the middle of the cabin will keep the flies away, if
musquito-netting covers each window or aperture left to admit light. Then I should advise visiting the river as early
as the 15th of June, and angling until the end of July. This
plan will insure a month of good fishing, and no trouble
from the effects of flies worth naming. In fact, it will unbend the mind, invigorate the body, and renew your lease
of life.

Of biting flies, the following, written by the Bishop of
Quebec while on a journey up the Red River, in his "Songs
of the Wilderness," is truthfully expressive:

" Among the plagues on earth which God has sent,
    Of lighter torment is the plague of flies :
Not as of Egypt once the punishment,
    Yet such sometimes as feeble patience tries.
Where wild America in vastness lies,
    There diverse hordes the swamps and woods infest.
Banded or singly, these make man their prize ;
    Quick by their subtle dart is blood expressed
Or tumor raised.   By tiny foe distressed,
    Travelers in forest rude with veil are fain
To arm the face ; men there whose dwellings rest
    Crouch in thick smoke ; like help their cattle gain.*
Oh wise in trials 'great, in troubles small,
    Who know to find mementoes of the Fall."

A MORNING'S EXPERIENCE.

Our two solitary "birdies" were piping the peculiar notes
of the Northern wilderness, the salmon were leaping and
splashing, and I longed to tackle the mate of the silver beauty lost the evening previous.

Having already soaked my casting-line, I shouldered my
heavy and lengthy friend, the Castle Connell rod, and march-
ed up the river about a hundred rods to where a bend in the
shore threw the current out around the eddy rock.   I selected a medium-sized fly with purple body, blue legs, brown
mallard wings, and golden pheasant top-knot for the tail.
Then I commenced casting out toward the middle of the river, and letting the fly float down and around to near the
shore.   About my third cast brought a bite and a leap that
made my heart palpitate with anxiety.   I played him about
half an hour, he once and a while running off about two hundred feet of line, and then coming back as tame and cosy as
possible, until by-and-by his patience became exhausted, and
he thought he would start up the river a hundred miles or so
to the spawning-beds.   He navigated the rapid about twen-

---

* It is asserted as a truth by border settlers that, when burning off a summer fallow, and the smoke no longer protects cattle in contiguous pastures,
that they run lowing to the house to have the fire renewed ; and it is sometimes necessary that they shall stand in dense smoke to enable them to remain still long enough to be milked.

ty rods above, but I turned him, when he went down stream much faster than it was convenient for me to follow; but he stopped to rest where I hooked him, and glad enough was I, for the morning was oppressively warm, and my rest had not been of the most refreshing kind during the previous night. Here I began to call loudly for a gaffer, and presently I saw the doctor's demijohn form approaching with a gaff, and closely following was the general. By the time they arrived my friend had concluded to return to sea, and started; but he soon found a resting-place, and, while playing him here, the general insisted so strongly against playing him too gently that I put a little more stress on the line. The fish rollicked around the pool, and showed his whole size and beauty, when my friends judged that he would weigh over thirty pounds. I thought so too, and played with great care. But the salmon became impatient of restraint, and started. He had not darted more than a hundred feet before the hook sprang back to me, and he went on his way rejoicing, while my friends returned to the tents.

I felt as if I needed a strong glass of lemonade with a stick in it to sustain me; but, being strictly temperate—that morning—I sauntered back to the point above the eddy where I had hooked my recently-departed friend. There I examined the fly and hook with care, and found it *secundum artem*. After becoming sufficiently rested, I made a cast, and at once hooked another salmon about the same size as the one which had just unhooked. On realizing that my fish was on, with a slight jerk I fastened the hook, in order to play him gingerly if he wanted to "gallivant and cavort" some. Two or three times he revealed his enormous size and great symmetry, so that I felt quite sure I had hooked the mate of the first one. This also remained half an hour trying small tricks about the pool, when all at once he dashed away across the current, and, on rising to the surface, I distinctly saw the line wound three times round him. After this he plunged and leaped up, down, and across the river, until he liberated himself, and

took my fly. Well, thought I, salmon of such great size, in
so large and rapid a river, should be fished for with leaders
or casting-lines of double gut all the way. I will return to
tent, and try to rig gut leaders to hold them.

The situation of our *ménage* began to look inviting; and
with the birch bark gathered by our gaffers, and the illustrated papers and magazines, our log cabin and dining-room
were cheerfully ornamented by the ladies, and the *menu* of
our dinner would not have dishonored a metropolitan hotel.
The gaffers' shanty was finished, and the *cuisine* attractively
arranged in order. After dinner, numerous sentiments worthy of the day we were commemorating—it being the glorious Fourth of July — were given, and we made the welkin
ring with shouts and music.

The evening was spent in tying flies, and concluded by examining the lunar bow through the smoke of a camp-fire and
the bottoms of our punch-glasses until the near approach of
midnight, when we retired to fight again the battles of the
day in our dreams, and to mingle in them the faces of be-
loved ones far *awa*.

SECTION SIXTH.

HISTORY AND RUMINATION.

Neither the Greeks nor Romans knew any thing about angling for salmon. The Saxons knew not the real luxury of
angling. A thorough appreciation of angling can only be
known by man civilized. "Catch who catch can" is the
motto by which savages are guided, and the surest means of
killing game is to them the best. Savages kill solely to eat.
They know no better, and lack the genius of the civilized
poacher to invent stake and concealed nets. Civilization enables the true sportsman to adopt suitable means to secure
sport, and as civilized men enjoy a more prosperous condition
than savages, they are not so dependent on the fish or game
they take or kill. Hence the sportsmen of the civilized world
can afford to give the animal pursued some fair-play "law,"

supposing the nature of the prey entitled to it.   But, in the
opinion of an uncivilized people, to allow a quarry or a shoal
the smallest chance of escape would be considered great folly.
To the ignorance and cruelty of the poacher may be attributed the reason for the robbing of salmon-rivers of their life
and beauty.   Existence could not have been so enjoyable to
the angler in either the palmy days of Greece or Rome, or
during any era since, while robbing the rivers of salmon was
pursued, as it is in our day, when science revives sport and
invents generous means for its perpetuity.

*Les travaux sur les Poissons se sont singulierment multi-
plies durant la periode qui s'etend de l'epoque de la mort de
Cuvier au moment actuel.*

Having flown in my cogitations from Greece to Rome, and
from thence to the British Isles and part way back to France,
where I endeavored to think in French, and as if in danger
of being overcome by a fresh swarm of musquitoes, I supposed
myself aroused by their singing, when, to my surprise, on
looking up, it was the doctor at the door of my tent, insisting in stentorian tones that I should get up.   I asked him
the time of night, and he replied that it was beautiful.

There is no use to contend with a doctor, and so I arose,
when, before my tent door, he was complacently seated on a
bench, with a smudge fire and the boiling tea-kettle on one
side, a bowl of loaf-sugar on the other, and a bottle of old
Jamaica before him.   Being already dressed, for I slept with
my overcoat, body-coat, and boots on, between army blankets on an India-rubber one, and yet was generally cold toward morning, I concluded to join the doctor and learn what
new system of philosophy or astronomy he was prepared to
propound.   With looks of amazement, he pointed to the brilliant *aurora borealis* in darts shooting up through the lunar bow like streams of gold and fire through a rainbow!
We viewed it with unstinted admiration until he composed
a hot rum punch.   We then examined the *aurora borealis*
and lunar bow through the bottoms of our glasses, and the

sight was really gorgeous! After three or four similar rep-
etitions, we agreed that we saw the North Pole distinctly,
heading Sir John Franklin's grave, and the bow, spears, and
stars of the *aurora borealis* were merely the flag over Franklin's tomb.

While the doctor was evolving a new theory of mundane
matters, only to be understood by draining a dose of diffusi-
bility, John appeared. He was greatly excited, but breath-
less. So soon as he recovered power of utterance he said,
"Gintlemen, bedad there's a bear just fornent yees! I see'd
him."

"Well, John," we replied, "how did he look?"

"Bedad he was as big as an elephant, and had a tail as
long as meself, and as big around, be gorrah!"

"How long was he?" we inquired.

"Bedad he was as long as I can reach with my two arms."

"What color was he?"

"Be gorrah, to tell the thruth, I couldn't see his color precisely."

"Was he green?"

"No, yer honors, not perzactly. I should say he was more
brownish."

"We supposed so, John; it is a fox."

"No, no, yer honors! Dr. Bluff, of the First Fusileers, said
he'd often see'd bears here, an' I think the beast I seed is
won."

"This was at the shoot, twenty-seven miles farther up the
river," we replied; and just then the halo of the rising sun
began to illuminate the eastern horizon, and teach us to prepare for the fresh-run salmon which had arrived that morning
from their visit to the sea. Having consulted our watches,
and learned, to our surprise, that it was only three o'clock,
and as our gaffers were still asleep, we reluctantly retired to
our tents and to sleep until called to breakfast.

As it was our custom to rest the salmon-pools during the
best part of the day for angling, in order to protect the river

from too great a depletion by our captivating flies, we started to fish our several pools at the time of the forenoon when the salmon seeks the shady side of a rock in the river, and which had perceptibly fallen during the previous night, so that, from its clearness, we could distinctly see numerous salmon lying in pairs beside the rocks. They were very interesting to look at, but it was hard to induce a rise. Presently the general, who had been angling at the falls a mile above, was seen approaching, and doing some pretty tall walking, now in the river and then on the shore, following a salmon as best he could, for the fish seemed determined to return to sea. Down they came, passing us, while the perspiration streamed from the general's face, and he was too busy to return our salutations, but he finally brought the fish to gaff.

In a short time thereafter the doctor was seen coming at the speed of two-forty on his rejoicing way down the river from the falls, led by a large salmon. We soon saw that the salmon was playing the doctor, who, finding that he was losing strength, called lustily for help, which was instantly rendered, and a twenty-four pound salmon was soon played out and landed. The doctor retired to his tent and was not seen again until the next morning, when he said, " It's heavenly to play a generous salmon, but when he turns the tables and plays you, he's worse than the cholera !"

It was the banker's turn next, and, thoroughly aroused and divested of his dignity, down he came, skipping over rocks and through brush at a very rapid rate. Down he came to Rattling Run, and brought his fifth salmon to gaff that day, the largest twenty, and the smallest eleven pounds.

The doctor's serious intent at evoking a reliable theory for the brilliant coruscations near the northern horizon prevented him from risking the play of another salmon until he should quite recover from his last encounter. In the mean time, every fresh contest with a salmon increased my respect for the fish; and I lost so many in proportion to the great number hooked, that I began, when my fly was first taken, to realize an indescribable sensation of nervous hesitancy; and the more gentle he appeared when first hooked, the more I dreaded the fight that I knew must come, sooner or later; for a salmon never surrenders until he faints. As the waters settled until as transparent as ether, the fish became not only more shy, but they gave better play and were harder to exhaust. They bit gingerly and short. I had ample opportunity for testing some theories which had been told me by anglers with great seriousness. One of them is, that "if a salmon rises to your fly and misses it, you should not cast again immediately, because he is sure to settle back before rising. You had better, therefore, light a segar and smoke half of it, or take a glass of sherry, and rest the pool at least fifteen minutes before repeating the cast." This I ascertained to be all bosh. Once, in particular, a salmon took my fly at the fourth cast, though having rose to it at every previous one and missed it, while I repeated my casts with as little suspense as if angling for brook trout. A salmon will return to the fly, if he rose to it in earnest at first, as often as will a trout; but either fish, when pricked by a fly-hook, will refuse to come again until he forgets it. Again it is said that "if you hook a salmon and he parts your tackle, taking your hook and a piece of the gut snell to which it was attached, he will not rise to an artificial fly again that season." This is also a mistake; for the gentleman who owns the "York River," Gaspe, fished with a friend who lost a hook and part of a leader by a salmon one morning last July, and on the evening of that day took the salmon with the hook and gut still in his mouth; and what appears most singular is that he hooked the salmon with the same kind of fly that was then fastened to the jaw of the fish.

SECTION SEVENTH.

JOLLY SPORT ON RATTLING RUN.

"Oh! not in camp or court
Our best delights we find,
But in some loved resort
With water, wood, and wind;
Where nature works,
And beauty lurks,
In all her craft enshrined."

The days were divided into four hours of night, made scintillant by the aurora borealis, and the lunar bow more brilliant than daylight, but cool and hushed, so that no sounds
remained but the rushing waters, the splashing of the royal
salmon, and the piteous cries of seals; three hours of morning, mild and serene, enlivened by the wild music of the birds
of the wilderness and the occasional sounds of animals foraging for breakfast in the mountain forests by which we were
surrounded; fourteen hours of a day, when clear, ranging in
the sun from eighty to ninety degrees Fahrenheit; and three
hours of mild twilight, with light enough to read.

The morning was clear and still; not a zephyr swept
through the gorge by the falls, or came up laden with the
fragrance of codfish from the Gulf. The shrill music of our
two charming birds and an occasional splash of feeding salmon were the only sounds which relieved the monotone of the
clear and rapid river. Our plateau, surrounded by majestic
mountains, steep and rocky, formed a vast amphitheatre.
The river was still falling, and as thin and clear as possible.
Our assembling at breakfast proved that the black flies had
partially desisted from scoring us, and each member of the
party felt relieved of farther danger from that scourge. It
is worthy of remark, that from the almost unbearable annoyance caused by the punishment from black flies on our arrival, we had in one short week become so accustomed to
them that they ceased to elicit our fear or attention.

The morning time to angle for salmon having expired, we

Q

regarded the river as having been protected, and the pools rested long enough, and so mounted our toggery and arranged our flies for the fray. It was the doctor's turn for the upper pool, at the foot of the falls; the general's for the bend to Rattling Run; the banker's included all the opposite of the river, while my sporting-water was Rattling Run, and I had never fished it. My gaffer was wanted elsewhere, and the doctor most generously consented to supply his place. He led the way with gaff on shoulder, marching up to the first pool with an *elan* and energy which meant that he was determined to show me where salmon disported. After walking half a mile through the brush, we emerged opposite a salmon-pool on Rattling Run. The run was about twenty rods wide, with shallow water three quarters of the distance to the opposite bank. The doctor pointed to the pool on the opposite shore, and told me that a salmon made a feint at his fly there two days previously. The water ran swift over a pebbly bed, but it was not much above knee-deep on our side of the pool. I waded to within casting distance of the head of the pool, and commenced casting while moving slowly down the stream, until, having made half a dozen casts, and swept the surface with great care, I delivered my fly just above a rock near the foot of the pool, where a salmon made its appearance and rose to take the fly, but missed it. The next cast delivered the fly beyond and below the rock, in the white-water foam, when the salmon accepted the fly, and fastened good and strong. Instead of turning to the falls just below, he shot up to within a few paces of me. The doctor, seeing his move, ran below the salmon to prevent it from dashing down the chute. For a full half hour while the play lasted, it was so amusing to see the doctor run and flourish the gaff in his endeavor to drive the salmon to the pool above that I could hardly restrain my laughter enough to stand and steady the fish's head occasionally against the current. But the doctor finally conquered, and the fish became so fatigued that the doctor took him out of the wet with his gaff, when it scaled twelve pounds; and, though not large, it is something to play and save a twelve-pound salmon with a single gut in a swift and shallow rapid just above a chute.

We now proceeded to the second pool above, where the doctor seated himself to rest on shore and watch my movements. Here also the run was about twenty rods wide, with the channel along the bank opposite. I therefore waded out so as to cast across the main current, and let my fly sweep round to the eddy, some eighty feet below. I had not made many casts before a salmon deliberately swam up to my fly and examined it, and then, as if suspicious, turned from it like electricity, his turn forming a most exciting whirl. In vain I cast several times more, but the run was too wide to deliver my fly at the farther shore, where was a deep pool from which I might have enticed him. But we gave up the chase and commenced a return, the doctor walking along the shore, and I wading and casting as I went. We had not gone far when I hooked a very elegant salmon. There was a pool on each side of the run, and the salmon took the fly on the farther side. As soon as the fish realized that he was firmly hooked, he came across the run for the pool near us. I stood in the water nearly between the two pools, but rather above them. As the run was very rapid all the way below until it entered the St. John, I requested the doctor to fall below the salmon, and thus prevent the fish from running the chute. The doctor waded below the pool on the left, and as he saw the salmon darting for that pool, he ran below, to prevent the fish from turning down stream after it should learn that it was mistaken in finding protection where it was going to seek it. The salmon came to the near pool, and, finding no assistance, it endeavored to sulk a little, but finally resolved to run the chute, or return to the pool at the farther shore.

After a close contest of an hour's duration, in which the salmon passed twice between the doctor's legs, the fish was brought to gaff, and weighed fifteen pounds. On returning to dinner, we learned that our friends had fished hard for modest results. By the supervisory care of the ladies, the dinner was served in the following order or *menu:*

Vegetable soup.

Boiled salmon and fried trout.

Roast mutton, green peas, and other vegetables.

Claret wine, tea, bread and butter, etc., concluding with a dessert of marmalade and dried fruits.

After dinner we concluded to rest the pools, burn some to-bacco, and tie some flies. When we first began angling, the preference by the salmon seemed to be given to the Montreal fly, or a purple body, brown mallard wings, and tail from the top-knot of the golden pheasant; but within the last two days they would not touch it. Their next favorite was a good imitation of the real salmon fly, body and wings light gray; but after a couple of days more they refused all flies but those with a preponderance of bright yellow and orange, tied on a very small hook. The double-hook flies were the most successful in bringing salmon to gaff, but I never tried them; and it is contended by some that two small hooks fall better, and are more attractive than a single one. Forrest, of Kelso, is the favorite fly-maker with Canadian anglers, and he generally ties on a double hook.

SECTION EIGHTH.

FLY-FISHING BELOW THE FALLS.

"Below the Falls of St. John, from deep crevice stealing,
　　The bright salmon watches his prey,
And when 'mid the white foam some stray fly lies wheeling,
　　Slyly bears—slyly bears it away.

"'Tis thus in this bright world, at joys without measure,
　　Unheeding, we ardently spring,
And forget that oft hid by the plumage of pleasure
　　Lies a hook—lies a hook in the wing."—STODDART.

To a man unaccustomed to the broad, rushing, tumbling torrents which debouch in the Gulf of St. Lawrence from the north, there are many subjects to inspire wonder, and some

few to challenge admiration. The bold mountains of gray
rock, from which a few stinted fir-trees struggle into the
light of day above the fissures and dark gorges, are sombre
to see and sublime to contemplate; and the rivers, tumbling
down frantically in their narrow passage between high walls
of solid masonry, would appear frightful did they not contain
thousands of beautiful salmon and trout, which make their
way with great assiduity to clear themselves of sea-lice by
the action of fresh water, deposit their eggs, and, when warn-

ed by fresh-water parasites, return to sea to recuperate and fatten preparatory to another visit up the river to their spawning-grounds.

One day, while fishing the pool below the falls, I felt a tug, and as my reel spun round whir! whir!! whir!!! I raised my rod to a perpendicular, when—the reel still continuing—I saw three leaps at once, each fish leaping fastened to my fly. Thought I, "If you make three leaps at once there is small chance of saving you," and so it resulted. By the manœuvre, it formed a bight in my line and unhooked.

My captures were very fair that day, and it is a remarkably interesting pool to fish; but the river was so low, and its waters so transparent, that I could count scores of salmon lying in pairs by the rocks, awaiting a rise in the river to help them surmount the chute.

The next morning I fished the same pool from the opposite side of the river, and in response to my second or third cast I hooked a large salmon, which ran out to the middle of the river and took nearly all the line off my reel, when it made a leap about twenty feet up the river, and several feet above the water, and the swiftness of the current made such a bight in my line that its weight parted the single leader, though I dipped the point of the rod as I saw the leap coming. As my line came back I felt despondent at losing such a beautiful fish; but I venture to state that no angler, under the circumstances, could have saved it. Such is salmon-angling. You must use a single gut for the half of your casting-line toward the end, and tie your fly on a single gut, or you will be regarded as a coarse angler, and all your large scores will count you naught as an artist at angling. Here are salmon in a broad, rapid river, large enough to try the strongest striped-bass tackle; and yet they are to be taken on a single gut, and played from half an hour to three hours to bring to gaff. Add to the delicacy of play necessitated from the lightness of tackle the fact, also, that the mouth of a salmon is very tender. These are points to be noted if you would angle for salmon. No one ever hears of a string of salmon, for the very good reason that their bodies are so heavy and gills so tender that they will not sustain their weight.

I put on another fly and cast again. For some time my eyes were not blest with the sight of a rise; but by-and-by a salmon accepted the fly in earnest and fastened. The prick of the hook gave it such a shock that it bounded and leaped three or four times, as quick as thought, several feet above the water. Finding itself still hooked, it came toward me, and I retreated, for fear that too acute an angle of the line and rod might enable it, by a salmon dash, to break the top of my rod. I therefore walked backward, and the salmon followed me until within five feet of the shore. It then turned as quick as lightning, and whir! whir! whir!! went my reel. Another leap showed it to be in the middle of the current, with but little line remaining on my reel, and a reef of rocks rising above the water between me and the salmon. I at once saw that it might extricate itself and take my fly and some of the line; but it misjudged its own situation, and started to leap the falls. By its failure I turned its head shoreward, and brought it within a rod of me, when it took fright again and started down the river. After checking and turning it, back it came to me, gentle as possible, leaping occasionally, as if it was its nature, for I should have thought a fish so circumstanced would have swam low; but no — all game fish are alike in that respect. Although the salmon had become used to my appearance, it still distrusted me, and started out into the current again. There he leaped a few times, and finally consented to be led back; but when it gained sight of the gaff it shot off again, though I could both see and feel that it was losing strength. After two or three more visits to the shore it became weakened, and Duncan gaffed it. The fish weighed only sixteen pounds, but it was the prettiest salmon that I had ever seen. Above the line, from gill to tail, it was a light and brilliant salmon color, and below it was like polished silver. I could not help exclaim-

ing how beautiful! There is nothing more beautiful than a
fresh-run salmon when first taken, neither is there any pencil capable of creating its apparent counterpart. To feel a
salmon fast to your fly and see its leap is alone worth a voyage to Canada to experience.

Again I swept the pool with care and got a rise. As I
could not allure the beauty to a second attempt, I concluded
to rest the pool and go to the foot of the plain water, where
I saw the salmon disporting like dolphins just above the
rapid. The bed of the river was about a quarter of a mile
wide, and shallow on my side. I therefore waded out, and
after a few casts hooked a large, vigorous salmon. After a
high leap it struck out to the middle of the river. Then it
made numerous rushes and leaps, with turns and sweeps, until finally the hook sprang back to me, and let the twenty-
pounder go on its way rejoicing. Very soon I hooked another, and it attempted to run the rapid; but I checked it a
quarter of a mile below, where it stopped to sulk behind a
rock, and before it formed another plan, my man Duncan
watched his chance and gaffed it.

Again, after half an hour's playing, I succeeded in losing a
very large fresh-run salmon. I felt mortified, and so concluded on returning to the head of the stretch to learn the
intentions of the large fish which had offered before I left,
and for which I rested the pool. I went to the head of the
pool and swept it along down until I came to where I got the
rise before I left; but it had either leaped the chute or gone
from home, and after a few rises but no strikes, I returned to
dinner. "Moving large fish, however, is held by every true
angler only second to hooking them; but many persons are
apt to despise the most skillful and patient efforts unless
crowned with immediate success." This is the experience
of John Colquhoun and every true angler.

Next morning, by dint of perseverance and continued effort, I finally hooked a salmon at the foot of the pool, and just
at that moment a loud crackling was heard in the thick un-

derwood along the shore, and Duncan called my attention to a bear that, having discovered us, was making off with all the speed possible. I could not turn to look from my salmon, for it had not yet decided upon what course of tactics to pursue. After a few minutes, when the salmon had concluded to run the hook out, I turned to see, but the bear was no longer in sight. After several runs, tacks, shifts, sweeps, and leaps, I brought the salmon home as gentle as a kitten, so that it seemed a pity to gaff it.

My friends had been fully as lucky as I had, and, as the flies were disappearing, and we had examined our plateau, walled by mountains and watered by beautiful rivers, we concluded to digest a good dinner by admiring the works of nature and enjoying the *aurora borealis* and lunar bow.

Rosy were our dreams; but, be it remembered, one of the party began to sigh for Susan Jane.

The following day, and for several days thereafter, the sport was about the same. The river soon began to shrink and clarify, and as the salmon became more scarce, the numbers of sea trout increased. Sea trout are precisely like those of Long Island. Their voyage to sea renders them as white and plump as are those of the Willows, below Oba. Snedicor's, and perhaps cleaner and whiter; but they are the same fish in ichthyological peculiarity.

The next day that I fished Rattling Run I took two salmon at its mouth, where the eddy was formed by the confluence with the St. John; and I cast again to the foot of the rapid, where my fly was usually drawn into the eddy, and before it fairly touched the water a salmon took it, and leaped some ten feet up stream, dropping it while thus leaping. As I saw the fly fall, I was in the act of retrieving my line, when another salmon was fast to the fly, and I broke the top of my rod. This proved to me that the movement of a salmon is too swift to be followed by the eye. I played and killed the salmon after the rod was broken, and my gaffer landed him.

Before I could splice another top to my Martin Kelly (a

great improvement on the Castle Connell rod) the shoal had either passed by, or otherwise had concluded to decline my flies, and I was obliged to forego the amusement of again playing a salmon that day.

As there appeared no prospect for the river rising soon, we began to think seriously of dividing the party, and two of us taking gaffers and canoes, and going to the upper falls, twenty-seven miles above. The next morning, however, was showery, and the river had risen more than a foot during the night; we therefore concluded to defer going up the river until the prospective rain should have subsided. The fitful showers of the morning increased to a steady and heavy rain in the afternoon, and both the general and banker met with fine sport, taking several salmon of fine size. This day the general evinced a commendable perseverance, for, in the heaviest shower, if a salmon parted his line and carried away his fly, he would forthwith stop where he was, and tie a fly in a drenching rain, attach it to his leader, and proceed to casting. He lost several large fish that day, and saved only three; one of these he hooked in the pectoral fin of the left side of the fish, on the opposite side from the general, as the fish started down stream, leading the general at double-quick time. I was sweeping the pool at the mouth of Rattling Run when I saw the general hastening down the St. John, along the shore. The rain was drenching. He wore rubber overalls, overcoat, and hat; the brim of his hat turned under across the forehead, giving him the air of enthusiasm so finely represented in the picture of Napoleon when he commenced crossing the Alps. Of course there was the slight difference of our general being on foot; but, with his rod stretching high in air, the storm catching his loose garment, the hat with brim turned under and giving it the military chapeau shape, the *tout ensemble* was all energy and action. Down swept the general. Rattling Run had swollen considerably, and was three feet deep and very rapid just above the mouth, into which the general dashed and waded across, holding on to his fish, which he thought a forty-pounder at least! His gaffer followed close behind, and was about to embark the general in a canoe to follow the salmon down the river; but the fish stopped in the pool where I was angling, and after a play of less than half an hour the general brought it to gaff, when it weighed 17½ lbs. This feat was the greatest of the season; and, had not the fish been hooked on the far side from the general, so that it was hard to maintain an equipoise, it would probably have torn away. I shall never forget the picture of ardor and energy which rushed down along the shore and dashed across Rattling Run, speechless with wonder and excitement. At dinner we canvassed the morning's sport, and, though the rain dripped slightly through the bark roof of our dining arbor, we began to realize that a home in the wilderness possesses an indescribable attraction, and the apparently settled rain seemed an omen for better fishing than we had yet enjoyed, and we parted that night to our several camps with a renewed stock of hope and pleasing anticipation.

SECTION NINTH.

THOUGHTS OF RETURNING HOMEWARD.

" 'Tis a midnight fair to see,
    Wondrous in sublimity.
  Lingering at our cabin door,
  Fast beside the river shore,
  Dazzled is my gazing eye
  With the grandeur of the sky.

Clouds are flying in mad chase
O'er the moon's benignant face;
  In the blue concave of air
  Stars like diamonds gleam and glare,
  While with weird, celestial glow
  Springs aloft the lunar bow.
  See! like arch triumphal, high
  How it soareth to the sky;
  See! like heavenly rainbow, bent
  O'er a showery firmament,
  How its gorgeous columns climb
  With a majesty sublime."—ISAAC M'LELLAN.

Our dreams of home were rosy. Though unlooked-for, modest flushes of the great St. John, produced by summer showers at its tributaries, caused temporary hope, yet the stream kept gradually narrowing and falling so fast that salmon refused to ascend to the fluvial part of the river. About the 20th of July the grilse began to make their appearance, and the parr rose to the fly in the most plucky manner, evincing more courage than their grandparents.

"At length the morning for our departure has arrived," said one of our party while returning from enjoying his last bath of the season in Rattling Run. Instead of learning from the

> " Tongues in trees, books in the running brooks,
>   Sermons in stones,"

we were about to exchange the scenes of nature, unadorned by art, for the crowded mart, and the hurry-scurry of aggregated humanity. The thoughts which made bearable the reflections called forth by preparing to leave our home of freedom, and felicity of angling for salmon, were the dearest of earth — home, family, and friends. For these we could endure the sights of striking tents, and loading the bark canoes for our departure to the mouth of the river.

Our tents were struck, tents, trunks, and rubber bags packed before breakfast. None but the experienced can realize how lonely appears the little spot of ground over which his tent has been stretched for several weeks, but of which nothing remains except the boughs of the fir-tree which rested him, and gave him pleasant dreams for many nights. We still heard the salmon leaping and splashing in the river, and the two lone birds piping their merry notes, though our tents were removed and packed in the canoes. But, shaking off the sense of melancholy which I felt to be gaining on me, I remembered that the lines of true anglers always fall in pleasant places, and so adjourned to breakfast.

As the general had decided to remain and see the salmon season out, 'twere wrong to deny the fact that leaving him and his lady greatly deepened the shade of our feelings at parting from the peaceful plateau. But we all put on cheerful faces and mixed our coffee with anecdotes. Our breakfast consisted of fried or broiled trout, broiled grilse, termed in Canada "*dejeuner*," signifying "breakfast." By others it is called the "white salmon." Then we had ham and eggs, hot biscuit, etc. We enjoyed our last meal as well as circumstances would admit under the conflicting feelings of a hope to soon see our families, and a regret that the lunar bow and aurora borealis, with the singing birds, would have to sing and shine without us.

As to the salmon which had played us, and at numerous times sold us, we felt as if we would have liked another contest with them; but as that was impossible then and there, as we had not the time to spare, we promised those of them which parted from us with our hooks as nose-jewels, and others that—having played us long enough—sprang the hook out of their beautiful mouths, that if we hook them again they will not get off so easily.

After breakfast, and all being ready for our departure, the stars and stripes were raised, and while the general waved his salmon-rod, we started, and a salute to our honor was fired from our only cannon as we parted from view of the plateau and disappeared from its remaining inhabitants around the foot of the mountain, at the bend of the St. John, just below the entrance of Rattling Run.

Our hearts were full as we responsively shouted hurra!

> Ye rivers, so haunted with myriads of flies,
> Whose flashes of salmon-breaks gladden the eyes;
> Scenes where the brown bear roams the thick brake;
> Scenes where the seals their gambolings make;
> When shall I tread your fair precincts again?
> When kindle my camp-fires over your plain?
> When again cast my line and my flies,
> Charming my senses—feasting my eyes?

The river was low and the reefs nearly bare, so that navigation was not so safe as when we ascended; but our guides knew how to manage bark canoes better than to speak any language, their *patois* being a medley of French, Indian, and English. But they were all trusty and industrious, as all Canadian guides are. It is best that each angler have two guides and one canoe; for, though one man only is needed to attend an angler for gaffing and rowing in the neighborhood of the encampment, yet for long journeys up rapid rivers two men are indispensable. Cabins for cooking and for lodging may also be soon erected, and they are preferable to portable tents.

The River St. John winds like a serpent between the mountains, and as the fall from our plateau to the mouth—27 miles —is more than 150 feet, the rapids are very swift; so that many times in rounding a bend we surprised a family of seals teaching their young to catch salmon, wild geese with their goslings, ducks with their broods, and expected to see Bruin, but didn't.

The row down the river was most pleasurable. The thin bark canoe responded to the lashings of the tide, and we felt as the lobster-peddler said, "All alive! all alive!" The doctor, who had taken a front seat in the canoe, with his coat on and broad-brimmed hat, had found the passage so jolly that —like Obadiah Oldbuck—he had turned over a new leaf by taking off both his hat and coat, and remarked, as we shot a rapid, "Let her went!"

The Indians were returning up the St. John to their homes in the icy regions, having disposed of their furs at the Mingan fair, and laid in a winter supply of flour and salt.

It was all vain to look kindly to these Esquimaux squaws, who are really beautiful, with their olive complexions, raven locks, and lustrous eyes. They are wedded to the forest. We met some twenty odd Indian canoes ascending the river to their homes, who knew enough of English to ask "Salmon plenty?" But very few would make so bold as to ask, "Has you nothing good for me?" Of course they do not suppose it degrading to beg from civilized men, for they consider them as appertaining to the outer world. I was greatly amused by their appearances. There were many young men among them who displayed great taste in the arrangement of their hair; and some of the squaws had heads of locks worth diamonds, and for which many of our belles would swap their eye-teeth, of best manufacture, for similar heads of natural growth.

On our arrival at the mouth of the river, the dogs came from some thirty cabins to welcome us. They were of all kinds, sizes, and colors, and their salutations were most welcome. The sight and hospitable bark of our own kind of dogs gladdened our eyes and ears, producing a charming effect. Having landed and become hospitably housed at the quarters of the government agent, while our guides attended to landing our luggage and cutting fir-boughs for our beds, we jointed our trout-rods, and walked a short distance from the cabin to the sandy shore of the river, where, within thirty minutes, we took over fifty sea trout averaging a pound each. I frequently fastened two at a time on the same cast of flies with which I had last fished on Long Island.

SECTION TENTH.

THE SILVER OR SEA TROUT.

This fish inhabits for nearly half the year the tidal waters of the streams in Canada, Nova Scotia, and Newfoundland. It is also taken in the estuaries of rivers in Maine, Massachusetts, and Long Island. Being aware of the high authorities which assert this to be a distinct family of the *Salmo genus*, I must beg humbly to dissent; and from the following description I invite anglers to decide for themselves whether the sea trout is not the *Salmo fontinalis*, or brock trout common to the streams of the northern part of North America. The sea trout is similar to the brook trout in all facial peculiarities. It is shaped like the brook trout; the vermiculate marks on the back and above the lateral line are like those of the brook trout; its vermilion, white, and amber dots are like the brook trout's; its fins are like those of the brook trout, even to the square or slightly lunate end of tail. It has the amber back and silver sides of such brook trout as have access to the estuary food of the eggs of different fishes, the young of herring, mackerel, smelt, spearing, shrimp, and even the young of its own family and those of the salmon. Owing to this food, it becomes whiter and brighter than those

THE SILVER OR SEA TROUT.—*Trutta Argentina* or *Trutta marina.*

trout which inhabit swampy waters impregnated and discolored by decayed vegetable matter, where the trout are confined without the power of visiting salt water. All the authorities agree that the sea trout spawns at the heads of fresh-water streams, ascending from the estuary in August, and not returning until the following winter and spring. All brook trout visit the heads of streams in autumn, and return to the lower waters at the close of winter. Brook trout of mountainous regions, where the streams run through rocky defiles and mountain gorges, or through a sandy soil, are always brighter than the black-mouthed trout of hemlock and tamarack swamps. I am informed that, of fifteen trout-lakes in a certain part of Scotland, there are not two lakes which contain trout entirely similar. Even the famous Gillaroo trout, which some anglers suppose to have a gizzard, has merely a lump in its stomach formed by the peculiarity of the clay and other substances on which it feeds. In the United States and the Canadas we have the salmon, the salmon-trout of the lakes, the brook trout, the silver or sea trout, which I believe to be the brook trout, the white trout, or land-locked salmon, the large brown trout (*Salmo Canadensis*), the Mackinaw trout, the winninish, and the red trout of Long Lake. All these fishes have the adipose second dorsal, are pinky-meated, and the laminary flakes are separated by a thin curd or creamy substance.

The real salmon of different waters do not differ so much in shape and surface-marks as do either the brook trout or the lake trout, though old fishermen in Canada can distinguish by the appearance of a salmon to what river it belongs; so they say, at least. Twenty-five salmon of some rivers will fill a barrel, while of those from other rivers from forty to fifty are required; but the variety in size constitutes the chief difference.

Our little party continued to take trout daily at the mouth of the St. John for nearly a week, until a schooner was prepared to convey us to Gaspe. The silver trout is indeed beautiful, being plump and round, with its polished sides glistening brightly with a satin sheen which sparkles with glowing lustre in the light. Its superior condition renders it plump, the meat very pinky, and the play very vigorous. The only drawback that I experienced in taking silver trout arose from too many offering for my flies at a time, and the little ones generally succeeding in obliging me to play and land them, when I had seen larger ones coveting my flies, and leaping at them for a taste. It was surprising to note the excitement which fly-fishing for trout produced among the cod-fishing families. Men, women, and children followed us along the river, and gladly received all the smaller trout. There was a fleet of some sixty sail of cod fishermen in the place, and their hired hands " shammed Abram to be idle" in order to see us take trout on our flies from the surface of the water. It was an easy matter to take in two hours a barrel of trout running from half a pound to four pounds. The water was so perfectly clear that we could occasionally perceive

R

a lordly salmon move majestically among the speckled beauties, no doubt waiting for a shower to swell the waters, and enable him to start on his perilous voyage to the spawning-grounds near the head of the river. As we were fishing from the beach which forms the breakwater at the mouth of the St. John, my attention was arrested by a thirty-pound salmon swimming along slowly toward the mouth, and within easy casting distance for my single-banded trout-rod. As I was admiring him, he chanced to see my motion in casting, and dashed away into the sparkling surf at the mouth of the river.

Taking trout with the fly is always more or less interesting, but, as a branch of sport, it dwindles greatly on returning from a successful trip of angling for salmon. Broadway is beautiful to those who have never visited Paris; but on returning from the *Boulevards*, the *Champs Elysées*, and the *Bois de Boulogne*, the beauties which he contemplated with admiration before he left New York lack the charm of artistic finish and the picturesque variety which youth always perceives, but which age or experience can not discover even with the aid of glasses.

THE WHITE TROUT.

While the fog is lifting from Schoodic Lake,
   And the white trout are leaping for flies,
It's exciting sport these beauties to take,
   Jogging the nerves and feasting the eyes.

This trout inhabits Schoodic and Grand Lakes in the State of Maine. Although it is eminently a lake fish, yet it is found in the tributaries and outlets near the lakes named. It is similar to the hirling in Scotland in the peculiarity of its meat varying from cream to mallow color. The average size of the white trout is from three to five pounds' weight, and in outline it is between the salmon and the brook trout, with the top of head and color of dorsal and caudal fins black and lustrous as velvet, the latter crescent-shaped, with jet spots

on the gill-covers like the salmon.   The mouth is furnished
with teeth on the palate, tongue, vomerine, palatine, and maxillary, like those of the brook trout, or as are nearly all the
young of the *Salmonidœ ;* but its head is longer than that
of the common trout, and much larger in proportion than the
salmon's.   Its scales are small, and the body is entirely white
below the lateral line, and very light gray above it, all shining with metallic lustre.   It is better game than any other
lake family of the *genus Salmo,* and will readily take the fly
on the surface of the water.   With a two-handed trout-rod,
fifteen feet long, a person unskilled in fly-fishing has taken
over a hundred in three hours of these transcendent beauties.

THE WHITE TROUT.—*Salmo albus.*

Some persons have supposed this blonde beauty "a land-
locked salmon," than which nothing can be much more absurd, for it has the common egress of a commodious river
which debouches in Passamaquoddy Bay, while those of the
lakes in the provinces have equally favorable avenues of escape.   No, it is a comparatively new luxury to the American
angler, and well worthy his attention.

Though many anglers use a two-handed fly-rod for taking
the white trout, yet it is more artistic to use a half-pound fly-
rod and single fly ; the cinnamon, Montreal with claret body
and brown mallard wing, with the yellow and blue professors, are all the flies needed for any weather, though the
coachman of white wing and peacock's herl body is a good
sunset fly, and the red ibis wing with silver body sometimes
takes very well.

The late Rev. Dr. Bethune regarded this fish and its sportive ways with enthusiasm, and the borders of Schoodic lakes

and the St. Croix River still retain many marks of his en-
campments.   The approaches to these grounds are *via* Eastport or Calais, Maine.   At either of these places the angler
will find guides to the aromatic groves which overlook the
waters where the white trout disport in shoals of thousands.

THE WINNINISH.

" At early dawn, or rather when the air,
  Glimmering with fading light, and shadowy eve
  Is busiest to confer and to bereave,
  Then, pensive votary, let thy feet repair
  To silent lakes, or gentle river fair."

This fish belongs to the *genus Salmo*, and tenants the upper waters of the Saguenay, near the outlet of Lake St. John,
in Canada.   The fish runs from three to nine pounds' weight:
and as no very young members of the family nor the spawning-beds have been seen by the *habitans* and Indians of that
region, it is reasonable to infer that they breed farther north;
and as they have a dorsal fin like that of the grayling, it is
quite probable that it is the fish written of by an officer of
the expedition in search of Sir John Franklin, whose description made " Frank Forrester" suppose it to be an American
grayling.   But it is neither the grayling nor the *omble chevalier*, but a rare delicacy of the frozen latitudes of the Canadian forests.   Professor Agassiz is said to have named it the
Northern charr.

THE WINNINISH.

The fins of the winninish, being large in proportion to its
size, render it very gamy.   It sails near the surface, with the
top of dorsal and caudal fins in view, and when it takes the

fly, leaps, runs, and plays more vigorously than a grilse. The fish is gray on its back and sides, interspersed with white scales, all of which are small, but brilliant. Epicures regard the winninish as a higher luxury than either the brook trout or salmon. Its head resembles the trout, but the mouth is larger, and equally tough for holding a hook. The meat is pink-colored. It takes either the minnow or the fly generously. Fish-culturists might with advantage turn their attention to the winninish and the white trout.

LAKE TROUT OF MOOSEHEAD LAKE.—This trout is unlike any other in the American waters. It is round in body, and resembles the winninish in large first dorsal and large tail. Its meat is straw-colored, and on each side below the gills are five or six dark spots the size of peas, and like those on the shad. It is clad in small scales, dark on the back, orange sides, and belly like the *dorée* or common river pickerel. Being so excellent a dinner-fish, it is surprising that the markets of Maine continue to monopolize it to the exclusion of epicures in other states. It is caught by the hand-line, as other lake trout.

RED TROUT OF LONG LAKE.

"I see the bright trout springing
  Where the wave is dark, yet clear,
And a myriad flies are winging,
  As if to tempt him near.
With the lucid waters blending,
  The willow shade yet floats,
From beneath whose quiet bending
  I used to launch my boats."

This is the richest and most beautiful specimen of lake trout known in the State of New York. In outline it resembles the brook trout which have access to marine feeding-grounds, except in the tail, which is forked. In color it is a reddish-brown on the back, mellowing to a pink at the sides, and a belly of white with pink tinge. The whole of its surface, except its head and belly, is thickly dotted with orange specks about the size of pigeon-shot. Like the trout of all the lakes, its scales are so small as to be scarcely perceptible, but its body is marked with fine, transverse diagonal lines, forming diamonds or canvas like the surface of fine drilling or marseilles. This is an unfailing mark of peculiarity. Its meat is pink-colored, with rich layers of cream between its flakes.

RED TROUT OF LONG LAKE.

The red trout will rise to the artificial fly, take a feathered spoon or well-dissembled minnow. Trolling is the favorite mode of fishing for this beauty, whose average weight is from five to fifteen pounds. It is very gamy, displaying much muscular force and propulsive power in its runs and leaps. To angle for the red trout is worth a voyage to the Adirondacks in June and July. It is fine sport to use salmon-tackle and take him on the fly until fatigued, when the exercise may be changed to trolling.

There is a universe of pent-up luxuries for the sportsman in that ninety-two miles square known as the Adirondacks, in the heart of the State of New York. A hundred mountains shade as many lakes, which teem with living beauties too rich in coloring and symmetrical in form to be copied by the painter's art. All the American varieties of the *Salmo genus* except the *salar* are found in these lakes and their tributaries, with the palpitations of busy life shut out, and naught but a simple tenting residence on aromatic boughs for a bed, where the timid deer comes with her spotted fawn to the margin of the lake to drink, and hesitatingly trusts the cross-paths of men. The eagles soar aloft in the heavens above the blue summits of cloud-capped mountains which seem to jostle each other. Imagination is not sufficiently vivid to realize the sense inspired in the Adirondacks by a sunrise scene. The owl has ceased to hoot, the whip-poor-will to sing, the panther to scream, and the wolves to howl; but the sun lights up each bush and spray, and the shadows and mountains form majestic basins. Now the brook trout are busy, and the day-birds are musical.

Here, in these narrow lakes of pure water, fed by trout-brooks, the gentle angler takes his morning walk, where the breaks of speckled beauties enliven the waters with hopeful expectancy, and naught disturbs the tranquillity, richness, and grandeur of primeval nature. Here the poet, painter, or philosopher may inflate the soul and invigorate the body, so that, on returning to the busy world, he may be the better able to endure its chafings and contests for another year.

TROUT OF SENECA AND CANANDAIGUA LAKES.

"The generous gushing of the springs,
    When the angler goes a-trolling;
The stir of song and summer wings,
The light which shines, and life which sings,
Make earth replete with happy things
    When the angler goes a-trolling."—STODDART.

This fish spawns in October and November, or when other families of the *genus Salmo* do; is white-mouthed and pinky-meated. Its qualities, outlines, and superficial marks are as varied as are its edible qualities. All anglers know that these depend much on the quality of water they inhabit and the food they eat. In the latter particular they resemble all animals and fishes. There are salmon-trout in nearly every lake within the State of New York; but the fish of Seneca, Canandaigua, Skaneateles, and Long Lake are infinitely superior, both as game and for the table, to those of Lake Ontario and the other great lakes.

The color of this fish is a drab, with pink tinge from the back two thirds down each side, shaded with vermiculate marks, and covered with infinitesimal scales, like the common LAKE TROUT. The fins are like those of the brook trout,

except the caudal, which is forked. The head resembles the
brook trout's, even to the teeth. By some persons this fish
is supposed to be a land-locked salmon; but it is a distinct
family of the *genus Salmo*, though in principal outward marks
of characterization it resembles the salmon-trout of Ontario
and the other great lakes, differing because of inhabiting limpid spring waters with better food.

TROUT OF SENECA AND CAYUGA LAKES.—*Salmo confinis.*

In May, after the waters become settled and clear, these
fish are taken by trolling with spinning-tackle and minnow
bait. It is necessary to sink the bait near the bottom, and,
as the trout remain near shore until June, a light sinker will
be sufficient; but when the weather becomes quite warm
they resort to a feeding-level from fifty to two hundred feet
below the surface, where they are taken by trolling with
feathered squids. The line should be two hundred yards
long, of the size used for catching cod, and from twelve feet
above the hook to twenty-five feet leads an eighth of an inch
thick are rolled at intervals on the line, sometimes to the
weight of a pound. Row slowly, and let out line until you
get a bite, and then calculate the depth to the feeding-level,
as the water in some places is a thousand feet deep.

Baiting the buoy and fishing with a drop-line is also practiced with success, though none of these methods of taking
lake trout are very attractive to the angler.

THE MACKINAW TROUT.

This trout is the largest of the *genus* in American waters,
generally running from two to five feet in length, and weighing from fifteen to fifty pounds, though Dr. Mitchill states

that it sometimes attains to the weight of 120 pounds. It is dark colored on the back, sides, dorsal and caudal fins, mellowing off from the lateral lines to a white or creamy belly. Vermiculate marks cover its back and sides. The second dorsal, like that of all the *Salmonidæ*, is adipose. Pectoral, ventral, and anal fins light cream color, as are also the irides.

The Mackinaw Trout.—*Salmo amethystus.*—Mitchill.

As this trout inhabits the deep pools in the cold lakes from Huron to the frigid zone, its meat is firm, and the fish is highly prized by epicures. It is sometimes taken as far south as the Ohio shore of Lake Erie, either by trolling with a minnow or a feathered spoon, or with cisco and young lake herrings—all captivating lures. There are many taken with gill-nets and set-lines in deep water, as also with hand-lines, by previously sinking a large stone with a rope attached, and at the other end of the rope fasten a buoy, and for several days cast in butchers' offal by the buoy until it is supposed the fish are chummed to that place as a feeding-ground, when —with large hook, heavy sinker, and codfish line—the fisher with the hand-line takes them as fast as he can bait and land them. This killing method is a favorite one with many men who fish for lake trout to sell, but it is very unsportsmanlike. In winter it is taken on hooks baited with pork through holes cut in the ice for the purpose. The best places to angle for this luxury, either with the troll or hand-line, is in Lakes Huron, Superior, the Straits of Mackinaw and Green Bay; from the latter water, Chicago, Galena, and many towns in the interior of Wisconsin are supplied. In fishing through the ice, when a fisherman gets a bite, he throws the line over his shoulder and walks away from the hole, drawing the fish rapidly up and out on the ice, where it is left to freeze. Besides the thousands of them transported every winter in a frozen state, many are salted and shipped off in the spring. This trout is the most voracious of all the species, fattening on such delicate luxuries as herrings, ciscos, and whitefish.

SECTION ELEVENTH.

AMERICAN PICKEREL, OR PIKE.

By blue lake marge, upon whose breast
The water-lilies love to rest,
Lurking beneath those leaves of green
The fierce pike seeks his covert screen,
And thence with sudden plunge and leap,
Swift as a shaft through air may sweep,
He seizes, rends, and bears away
To hidden lair his struggling prey.

This fish, like the brook trout, is almost universally known. It inhabits nearly all the waters of the north temperate zone, and varies in appearance according to its food, and the volume and quality of the water in which it is found. The large pickerel taken in the St. Lawrence River and in many Canadian waters is called by some the " great Northern pike," of the family *Esocidæ*, supposed to be unlike the common pike or pickerel, or Esox Lucius; but throughout twenty years' experience at taking pickerel, I have been unable to discover a very marked difference between the Northern pike and the pickerel south of the St. Lawrence.

AMERICAN PICKEREL, OR PIKE.

" The pike is the English name of a fish belonging to the order Malacopterygii, section Abdominales, family Esocidæ, and genus Esox."

The pickerel or pike spawns in March and April, and should not be caught between January and July. In England it sometimes attains to the weight of sixty pounds, and in Norway it occasionally rises to a hundred pounds, and more than eight feet in length, while in America it is quite rare to take one of more than twenty pounds' weight.

OF PICKEREL, AND ANGLING FOR THEM.

ISH of this family are known in the United States by the name of *pickerel*, which is the name in England for a diminutive pike. All pike, after rising above the pickerel weight, and under five pounds, in England, are known as "Jack," probably named after a poacher by the name of Jack Pike.

In the waters of the Eastern, Middle, and Western States, as also throughout the Dominion of Canada, the pickerel is found in most of the lakes, ponds, and some rivers; especially is it numerous in ponds where surface-water preponderates, and by reason of which the salmon families are excluded.

The meat of small pickerel is mealy, fresh, and without decided flavor, when—because of its yellow color—it is called *dorée*; but those from three pounds upward, taken in pure water, may be justly considered a good breakfast-fish. The pickerel of Greenwood Lake are good, because the food is abundant, and trout rills drop into the lake from every direction. As the lake is only 60 miles from New York, I used to take a seat in an evening train of the Erie Railroad, arriving in Chester at 7 P.M., and drive down ten miles to the lake in time to give Jack—the baitman—orders to have all things ready, and call me at five next morning. Tap-tap-tap at my chamber door announced that it was five, and nothing more.

Forthwith I mounted my toggery, took a cracker, and followed Jack to the boat, where all things were in readiness, and he sculled me out to a raft or float on the lake, which had been anchored at one of the best feeding-places for the long-noses. Leaving me with my half dozen poles, ten feet long each, and a pail of live minnows, Jack returned to the shore.

Among the numerous methods of still-baiting for pickerel, that from an anchored float is the most quiet and easy. As I was attaching a line to each pole, a deer, with elegant but timid tread, came to the margin of the lake and took a drink. It was September—a month for excellent venison; but then he was too pretty and innocent-looking to kill, and, though within short range, I had no rifle with me. The god of day had not yet appeared, but the merry songsters made the copse and fields joyous. To each stout pole I tied a line, three feet longer than the pole, and at the end of each I attached a gimp-snelled hook, and covered the connection of line and snell with a small strip of sheet lead. The water was from seven to nine feet deep, and for a float I tied a piece of pine shingle, which produced no resistance to a bite, but merely kept the bait a foot above the bottom. The shingle-float was ten inches long, two inches wide at the thin, feathered end, and tapered to a point, being half an inch square at the end where I made the notch and tied the line.

In still-baiting for pickerel, if the fish takes the bait, and learns that it is anchored or not at liberty, the fish at once rejects it; but by means of the sharp-ended float no perceptible resistance is offered, and the pickerel swims off toward a convenient place to gorge it. There were places arranged on the float for properly setting the poles, and arm-chairs at intervals invited to rest between bites. By the time I had baited my sixth hook and set my last pole, I saw the shingle-float to one of my lines tip up a trifle, and glide along the surface of the water, sinking gradually as it moved. I gave a sudden jerk with the pole to an opposite direction from that which the float was moving, and thus hooked and landed on the raft a four-pound pickerel. Before I had baited again, another float gave signs of agitation, and I landed another. Jack, who had observed my success, now sculled alongside, and took the two pickerel to be prepared for breakfast.

I continued fishing and admiring the scenery, with the tops of the mountains just beginning to be illuminated by the rays of a bright sunrise, and the pickerel accepted my offerings most voraciously, so that I was in the midst of a most successful contest when the horn blew for breakfast. After fastening my rods securely to the float, and seeing that each hook was well baited, I sculled ashore for breakfast.

On that lovely morning the sun seemed to have decked all nature in holiday costume. After a refreshing bath, on entering the hall leading to the dining-room, in the fragrant aroma of the coffee I scented a welcome. The pickerel, which had been first broiled or singed on the flesh side to prevent the juice from escaping, was turned, and with a renewal of hickory-wood coals was " done to a turn." Fresh butter, red pepper, and a dash of black pepper for its aroma, prepared the melting delicacy for the table. The smoke of the viands, fish, and of the tureen of mashed potatoes, with the fragrant coffee, greeted the senses like incense, and filled the measure of my hope and ambition.

After breakfast, a walk on the veranda, the discussion of a *cabana*, and a look at the morning papers, which had already been received from the city, made me again anxious to try the metal of those sly and peering long-noses. Adjourning to the hotel at eleven o'clock, forty-four pickerel included my mess, and, partaking of an attractive lunch, I returned to New York City in time to dine at seven in the evening.

SKITTERING* FOR PICKEREL AMONG THE LILY-PADS.

> "Now changed the tackle and the bait ;
> For larger prey we're all elate ;
> 'Mong lily-pads none vainly tries ;
> The line runs off—a noble prize !
> Give time to poach—now strike !

> "Now seeks his haunt the wounded prey,
> And then begins the angler's play ;
> He lengthens out, now slackens line,
> Till struggles past—a welcome sign—
> He lands a glorious pike !
> *Chorus.*—The jolly angler's is the life,
> Devoid of care, devoid of strife."

Angling for pickerel among the lily-pads and pickerel-weed is very exciting sport. The angler should use a rod from 13 to 15 feet long, flexible, but strong. For skittering a float is not used, nor is natural bait the best. Use Buel's or M'Harg's spoons, mounted with red ibis feather, and white

* Skittering is a word which belongs to an angler's vocabulary, but not found in a dictionary. It means drawing or jerking a bait along the top of the water.

feathers or hair for the under side of the spoon.   Stand near
the bow of your punt, and skitter the lure along the surface
of the water, near the margins of the lily-pads, and if you are
on Sodus Bay, or tempting the fish from almost any of the
bayous of Lake Ontario, you will find cause for surprise that
will force you to ejaculate; for it will be questionable which
will be the most astonished, the novice in the boat or that in
the water.   A most important essential is to have a man at
the stern who can use the setting-pole and sculls so as to enable you to fish the border of the lily-pads without scaring
the prey into their hiding-places.

Cuffy says, "Uf we had de gun, we might git a mess of
wood-duck." I reply, "Confound wood-duck! Don't you see
that the large pickerel is going into the weeds, and that I
can not prevent him? Turn the punt from shore."

In skittering for pickerel with live minnow, the shiner is
the best.   Use two or three hooks in a gang, as represented
for "spinning-tackle."   Keep your bait in motion, upon the
same principle that you would fish for salmon or brook trout.
It is the favorite plan of angling for pickerel in New England,
and is, moreover, essentially modern, and affords active recreation.

STILL-BAITING FOR PICKEREL.

"The angler is free
From the cares which degree
Finds itself with so often tormented;
And although we should slay
Each a hundred a day,
'Tis a slaughter needs ne'er be repented."—COTTON.

The primitive and philosophical method of angling for pickerel is with an ash or hickory pole.   The bait is a live frog.
Of course, while angling in this way, you may study nature;
but, lest you should fathom all things too soon, take books
with you, for they are frequently unfathomable.   Seek a place
on the margin of a solitary pond, shut out from the habitations of men by a dense grove.   Seat yourself on some fallen

STILL-BAITING FOR PICKEREL.

tree of ancient renown, and there beside you place your books.
Then bait your hook, and cast it off among the lily-pads or
stumps which margin the pond, and gaze away on vacancy.
There is naught set down against smoking at such a place
on such occasions.   Let the birds bill and coo in the grove
behind you, and if your mind is intent on developing a new
theory, let your bait creep up on a stump near you, to the

envy of all kingfishers who may covet it; and let it partake of your afflatus while it watches your movements, to be prepared, in case you suspect a bite, lest you should disconcert it by jerking. If you do not take a mess of fish, comprehend solitude. It has its charms, of course, for Robinson Crusoe said that sages had seen them. Disregard the Frenchman's opinion who stated that the solitude which has charms is always near cities or large towns. *Verbum sat sapienti.*

S

[*Note.*—The *larva* or grub of the dragon-fly lives in the water ten or twelve months, pursuing there its prey, until the time for its metamorphosis arrives. Then it crawls up out of the water upon the stem of some water-plant; a rent soon appears upon its shoulders, from which comes forth the dragon-fly. The "coming out" of this winged tenant of the air may be observed, around our ponds and marshes, almost any day in the months of May and June.]

CHAPTER VI.

TROLLING AMONG THE THOUSAND ISLANDS.

Here is the angler's paradise,
    A dreaming, Eden-like retreat,
With balmy perfume in the air,
    And wild-flowers springing at the feet.

ALL the charms which angling for pickerel confer are sublimated and condensed into trolling among the Thousand Islands. The pickerel of the thousand lucent streams and rapids, shaded by as many floral islands, are much better flavored than are those which dream out an indolent existence while
watching for frogs among the lily-pads, or darting, until they
wear themselves thin, after the minnows of ponds and rivers.

The Thousand Islands extend from Cape Vincent to a few
miles below Alexandria Bay, or about thirty miles, and the
average width of river is about five miles. Imagination may
better picture than I can describe the hundred and fifty miles
of trolling and casting the fly on streams dividing picturesque
islands, or islets covered with greensward and enlivened by

wild-flowers. Some of these isles are decked with large clumps of copse and grove, and others with stately trees which reach sublimely heavenward. This charming scene is enlivened by the wood-duck and other birds of gay plumage or melodious song. I venture the statement that it is unequaled any where on earth for its beauty, variety, and life of scenery. Neither the water streets of Venice with their gondolas, nor the *Bois de Boulogne* with its ornamental drives and picturesque lakes and fountains, are at all comparable with the Thousand Islands.

From Cape Vincent to within a few miles of Ogdensburg there is fishing and shooting enough to satisfy all the epicurean lovers of field-sports in America, did they but know a tithe of the riches of land and water which their excellent fish and game offer as attractions.

The Thousand Islands forms the most extensive spawning-ground between the Atlantic and the great chain of lakes; there are numerous eddies and shallow sand-bars among these islands where the wall-eyed pike and black bass spawn, but the fishermen are complaining that the annual diminution in catches calls loudly for a law of reciprocal protection between the Dominion of Canada and the United States. If the myriads of lake and river fishes which resort to the Thousand Islands to spawn were allowed to breed—unmolested by net or spear—an annual stock of pickerel, black bass, glass-eyed pike, Oswego bass, and fishes of smaller varieties would be propagated there in sufficient numbers to stock all the American waters.

All the little towns along the Thousand Islands have become attractive summer resorts. It was here that Bishop Hughes and Dr. Bethune used to recuperate body and brain, while their minds were soothed by the picturesque harmonies of nature.

On visiting the Thousand Islands for a few days' recreation, my advice is to go in pairs. A gentleman companion will answer, but a lady is better. Clayton, which is a town nearly midway of the islands, on the south side of the river, is said to be the most convenient point to select for trolling; for, in addition to the best grounds being near there, its central location enables anglers to make a trip up or down the river to the extremity of the islands and to return the same day. The hotels along the Thousand Islands are generally comfortable, and the landlords reliable. Make known your wants to the proprietor, and he will engage a man and boat for you. All the trolling-boats are superior in model for speed and comfort. The boatman furnishes rods, lines, baits, and rows his own boat. I prefer to use my own tackle, even to spoons and feathered squids. Each row-boat is furnished with two cushioned arm-chairs, in which yourself and lady are seated near the stern and facing it. The bottom of the boat is carpeted, and crimson is the favorite color. The fishing-rods are so set, by appliances in the boat and on the taff-rail, that the troll follows outside of the track, as the rods are held at right angles with the boat, like outriggers. The line is from fifteen to twenty yards long, and the troller lets it run from the reel as the gaffer rows along. The trollers soon become so enraptured with the varied beauties of the shifting scenes that they lose the consciousness of being on a fishing excursion until the oarsman calls loudly, " Bite on the lady !" which sufficiently disenchants them for the lady to reel in a pickerel or black bass, or perchance a maskinongé; when " Bite on the gentleman !" is heard, and he reels in a fish to the gaff or landing-net.

Parties leave the hotels in couples, agreeing upon a rendez-vous for lunching on some island. The boatmen take bread, ice, vegetables, and condiments, and couples sally forth upon the waters, and adjourn at the appointed time in the midst of groves of more than Oriental beauty. The fish are cooked by an artist on an extemporized fireplace, while other gaffers are spreading the cloth on the greensward, where the repast is served, and all goes on enchantingly. After luncheon they repair to their boats, when they continue trolling, or cast anchor on the shady side of a floral islet, in a narrow, rapid channel, where they cast the flies for black bass. Thus passes the day, on waters where the air is laden with perfume from wild roses and honeysuckles, and where the music of birds chimes in with the running waters as the trollers alternate between light and shade, now gliding along in gorgeous sunlight, and anon tracing narrow channels, shaded by tall forest trees, where wild ducks and other winged game are rendered almost tame by the contiguity of civilization and the frequent sight of gay and jolly fishing-parties.

SECTION SECOND.
THE MASKINONGÉ.

Where'er Ontario's waters chafe
The rocky bluffs that crown its shore,
And where Canadian banks are green,
And crystal tributaries pour,
The savage maskinongé doth roam
The tyrant of the watery plain,
No rebel to dispute his claim,
No rival in his great domain.

The maskinongé is the most beautiful specimen of the pike family. The tribe is confined to the range of large lakes and rivers of our Northern boundary, and to most of the lakes and rivers in the vast northwestern wilderness extending to the frigid zone. The Ojibwa name of this fish is "*maskanon-jä*," meaning "long-snout." When Canada was a French colony, the "*habitans*" named it *masque-longue*, signifying long visage. I submit that the Ojibwa was entitled by priority to the right of naming the fish; but as the Dominion of Canada has named it again, and in all legal enactments there in reference to it the name of the fish is written "maskinongé," I willingly accept the modification instead of either the Indian or the French name.

Thus much in explanation of naming a fish which has puzzled most ichthyologists and anglers, so that they have been uncertain and dubious on the point. The name is MASKINONGÉ.

Having heard many anglers state that they could not distinguish the maskinongé from the pickerel, I invite them to look at the diversities. The mandibles of the former are longer, the tail more forked and larger, the dark gray back and light sides are dotted in black, the outline of the fish is more delicate and elegant, presenting the appearance of greater refinement and higher breeding than the pickerel or pike. The surface differences are palpable, but they are not so marked as are the epicurean qualities. The meat of the maskinongé is compact, white, tender, and peculiarly delicate and rich in flavor, without partaking of any taint of extraneous substance such as decayed wood and bark, which so commonly affect the flavor of pickerel, and even trout. This proves that the maskinongé inhabits springs; and when taken in lakes where surface-water is supposed to preponderate, is always found at points where the fountains gush from the bottom.

THE MASKINONGÉ.

Rice Lake, twelve miles north of Coburg, in Canada, contains favorite feeding-grounds for the maskinongé. Its numerous springs, its beds of wild rice miles in length, forming a ground shade, its row of islands rising high above the level of the lake, covered with dense forests of lofty trees in whose shade the fish disport near the fountains, make this their favorite resort. These attractions, and the rivers which feed the lake and teem with shiners and other tiny baits, render Rice Lake remarkable for containing maskinongé which are equal in game qualities to any known in America; and I believe the fish has never been discovered in any water of the eastern hemisphere.

This fish often attains to nearly seven feet in length, and

to the weight of from sixty to seventy pounds in the upper lakes, as well as in Ontario and the River St. Lawrence. But when so large they are less active than when from ten to thirty pounds in weight, as in Rice Lake, and the River Oitanabee, which enters Rice Lake opposite and about four miles from Gore's Landing. The greatest number that I ever took in one day on this lake and river was sixteen, and as I took them legitimately—with rod and reel—the gentlemen at Harris's Hotel decided that I had won the spurs, and invited me to their club. I there learned that it was the greatest number ever taken from the lake in one day with a single rod and reel; and as the club was chiefly composed of retired officers of the English army and navy, with a sprinkling of civilians who own charming boxes on the margin of this beautiful lake of thirty miles in length, I regarded the compliment as a very flattering one.

Maskinongé are taken on a troll like either of those represented on another page, under the title of "Spoon Victuals for Long-snouts."

Instructions.—Troll with a striped bass rod about ten feet long, and on a reel which will carry six hundred feet of fine bass line place three hundred feet of the largest linen reel line. To the end of this line attach your feathered squid. In trolling, let your squid be about sixty feet behind the boat. The oarsman will regulate the speed. Then the first salutation that you will probably receive will be a *shock*-ing jerk, and you will see at the end of your line, and about six feet above the water, a maskinongé suspended like Mohammed's coffin, only shaking the squid so that it jingles. In that case, don't get excited, for it is the last time probably that day that you will see him. Row on; do not turn to go over the ground to retrieve your loss, but be ready for a new adventure. After he hooks himself, do not play him with too stiff a line, nor yet slack enough to let him get a bight in it. Tire him out, and bring him gently to gaff, and see that your gaff be the best of the striped bass pattern. Keep away from him after your oarsman lands him in the bottom of the boat, where he always keeps a mallet or billet of hickory wood to pound the fish on the head and prevent him from leaping out of the boat, for his saltatory powers surpass those of the salmon. It is said that a trout will rise a fall six feet high, a salmon one of eleven feet perpendicular, and a maskinongé one of nearly thirty feet.

> Far where Lake Erie's billows glance,
> An ocean-like immense expanse,
> The sharp-teeth'd maskinongé abides,
> The shark of the fresh-water tides.
> Now in the dark abyss of waves
> He glides; now where the shallow laves
> The grassy shore, and crisp waves break
> O'er the white sands that gird the lake.

SECTION THIRD.

THE BLACK BASS.

> Amid the Thousand Isles that gem
> St. Lawrence like a diadem,
> Where winds are soft, and waves are calm,
> And pine-woods steep the air with balm,
> Piscator floats the calm abyss
> 'Mid scenes of most transcendent bliss;
> Wafted across that teeming flood,
> His heart o'erflows with gratitude.

Many anglers think the black bass next to the salmon for game. It is unquestionably high game. Being numerous in many waters of the Northern States, it has come to be regarded as a commercial fish, and, through ignorance, many confound it with the Oswego bass, which is quite an inferior fish as to game and for the table. Some persons have exported the black bass both to England and France with the view of propagation, but whether they were the real black bass is questionable, as they are difficult to export after they grow to be larger than fingerlings.

The black bass is supposed to belong to the perch family, or rather *order* of fishes, because its mouth, gills, fins, and scales are similar to those of the *Percidæ;* but, in order to

distinguish it from other fishes of similar color and apparent
organization, it should be remembered that the real black
bass has a red speck in each eye like a dot of carmine. It is
also more delicate in outline, and has a smaller head than the
Oswego and the Southern bass. The black bass spawns in
the spring, and, like most fishes which spawn in that season,
is not supplied with a sac of nutriment attached to the umbilical cord.

The activity and muscular power of the black bass are sufficient to enable it to hold its own and increase its numbers
in waters inhabited by the most ferocious fresh-water fishes,
such as the maskinongé, glass-eyed pike, and the pickerel or
pike of the great lakes.

The Black Bass.—*Centrarchus fasciatus.*—De Kay.

With a view to giving the angler a list of the principal
fishes in the fresh waters of the State of New York, I append
the following extract from a letter written by an old, intelligent, and successful angler, who has resided in the central
part of the state, and fished for the most gamy part of the list
of which he writes for more than thirty years. His theory
of the black bass hibernating in clefts of rocks is corrobora-
ted by other authorities, and is doubtless true. But to the
extract.*

* " In the waters of the St. Lawrence, Ontario Lake, Seneca River, Oneida
and Cayuga Lakes, there are found the Oswego and black bass, very similar
in their shape and in some of their habits, so much so that they are often
mistaken for one and the same species. The Oswego (sometimes known as
the ' river bass') is the heavier fish, often attaining to eight pounds' weight;
are taken at all times during the year, often in winter through the ice. They
are good biters, and are game to the last.

THE OSWEGO BASS.

This fish is similar to the black bass in all outward marks, except that it has a larger head, lacks the double curve at

---

"The black bass seldom attain to more than four and a half pounds.[a] I have taken hundreds, and have never seen one weighing more. They are distinguished from the Oswego bass by a faculty of changing color in and out of water — sometimes yellow, or yellow with dark bands across, and often black as ink. All these changes I have seen in the same individual after landing him ; and they invariably emit a disagreeable musky odor. I have never known them to be taken in winter, and I think they seek a particular location and remain torpid during winter. My attention was directed to this fact about thirty years since. At that time I was in the habit of spearing fish in a mill-dam on the outlet of the Seneca Lake, at Waterloo, in Seneca County. From April to November I found numbers of bass ; from December to March I found all other varieties, but no bass.

"In the winter of 1837 the water was shut off at the lake for the purpose of deepening the channel to improve the navigation. This was considered a favorable time to quarry the limestone in the bed of the river ; and, upon removing the loose rock in the above-named mill-dam, where the ledges cropped out, there were found hundreds of bass imbedded in their slime, and positively packed together in the crevices and fissures of the rocks. My subsequent experience has done much to convince me that my theory is correct. The black bass appear in the waters of the Cayuga Lake in April. They make their beds and spawn between May 10th and June 20th, and disappear in November. The trolling commences in the early part of May, and continues until July 1st, after which time we find great annoyance from the weeds.

"In the Seneca and Canandaigua Lakes the bass make their appearance at a later date—usually about the middle of May—and spawn between June 10th and July 25th. This is the best time to take them. They locate in great numbers upon shoals and bars where there are large boulders. The Seneca Lake, unlike other lakes in this region, is very deep. It has a clean beach and bottom ; no weeds or grass except in the little coves and bays. In these places we find small patches of grass filled with all sorts of small fry, and it is about these grass patches that we have the finest sport in August and the fore part of September. By the 1st of October the bass have disappeared from their usual haunts, and the next we hear from them is at the 'Bass Grounds,' near Big Stream, where they congregate in immense numbers about the middle of October. The manner of fishing is with the hand-line and rod and line, using crawfish and minnows for bait. Hundreds are taken in a day in this place. This sport continues until the middle of November, when it ceases. The appearance of the bass in this locality I consider as another fact in corroboration of my theory. The shore is a bold, rocky cliff, and the water very deep.

---

[a] The black bass of the great chain of lakes range from three to nine pounds.—G. C. S.

the end of the lateral line at the joining of the tail, and has no red in the eye. Its flaky meat is soft and watery, and its common weight is from five to ten pounds.

Like the black bass, this fish is taken by casting the artificial fly, or by trolling with the feathered spoon, with a minnow impaled on a gang of hooks, and forming spinning tackle.

This fish inhabits most of the lakes in the interior of the State of New York, and the waters of Ohio, Kentucky, and

---

"The lakes which are tributary to the Seneca River are not all supplied alike with fish. The waters are very different. The Cayuga Lake from Aurora to the head is very similar to the Seneca Lake, and is stocked with the following varieties, to wit: Lake trout, white fish, herring-salmon, pike and pike-perch, black and rock bass, perch, suckers, eels, etc., etc.; while the lower end of the lake, very shoal and weedy, terminating in a marsh, is supplied with large catfish, small ditto, maskinongé, rock bass, pickerel, Oswego bass, black bass, pike-perch, perch, etc., etc.

"The Oneida Lake abounds in all the above-named varieties excepting the trout, whitefish, and herring-salmon.

"The Skaneateles and Owasco Lakes have very few, but excellent varieties, to wit: Lake trout, brook trout, yellow perch, and suckers. The water cold and spring-like.

"The Seneca and Canandaigua Lakes are supplied with lake trout, whitefish, herring-salmon, pike-perch, black and rock bass, yellow perch, catfish, and eels.

"The Crooked Lake has fewer varieties. We find the lake trout, whitefish, yellow perch, pickerel, catfish, and eels. About forty years since this lake was stocked with pickerel from the head-waters of the Susquehanna, and they are now very abundant.

"Our finest sport consists in trolling with the fly and minnow, the latter being preferred. In the Seneca River, at Oswego, the fly is preferred. Great numbers are taken throughout the season. Many sportsmen throw three or four flies, and often take as many bass. The manner in which this is done is to hook one fish, and, while giving him the necessary play, others take the extra flies.

"A word in regard to our method of taking the lake trout and pike-perch may interest your readers. We use one hundred and fifty yards of cod-line, with from six to ten leads—the first attached to the line about fifty feet above the hook, the others at intervals of from eight to twelve feet—weighing in the aggregate twelve to twenty ounces, regulated to suit the depth of water. Pike-perch are taken at twenty to forty feet deep; lake trout at sixty to one hundred feet deep—always at the bottom, rowing moderately. We use the silver spoon or spin the herring. In the Canandaigua Lake the minnow is considered the best bait. In the Seneca and Crooked Lakes the spoon is the most successful."

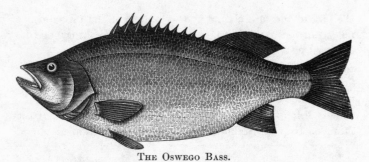

THE OSWEGO BASS.

those of many of the Western States teem with it, as do the chain of lakes on our Northern border, and the rivers and lakes in the western part of Canada, and most of the waters of the Northwestern wilderness. In some places it is known as the yellow bass, and at others as the white bass.

BLACK BASS OF THE SOUTH.

To the casual observer this fish very nearly resembles the black bass of the North. Its habits are indeed similar, and so are its fins and color; but it has a larger head, and in all points excepting contour it is like the Oswego bass. The

BLACK BASS OF THE SOUTH.

rivers in Florida are alive with this fish, and it is not difficult to take several hundred pounds of them in one day. It is taken there in winter, when the sport may be varied by shooting deer, ducks, wild geese, an occasional brown bear, and an alligator, and all from the same trolling-punt.

THE SPOTTED BASS OR SPECKLED HEN.

This is a common fish in the fresh waters of the Western States; it is also taken in the waters of the western part of the Dominion of Canada, where it is known as the speckled hen. This is one of the numerous small pan-fishes of the Western waters which naturalists have not yet classified. It ranges in weight from a quarter of a pound to two pounds, is blackish-green on the back, greenish-yellow on the sides, with a white belly, and dotted in black similar to some of the dace *genus* of Western streams. It is an excellent breakfast-fish, either rolled in flour and fried in butter, or in sparkling hot fat of salt pork. Sweet or olive oil is the best juice for frying fish in, but seldom used in America for the purpose except by Israelites.

THE SPOTTED BASS OR SPECKLED HEN.

ROCK BASS OF THE LAKES.

This is rather better game than the " speckled hen," bites freely at a feathered squid troll, or to any shiny revolving spoon bait; it also bites at the apple-worm, white grub, grasshopper, or shiner. This may also be said of the speckled hen. The Buel feathered spoon of smallest size and brightest feathers is a captivating lure for both the spotted bass and the rock bass. This fish inhabits all the lakes in the centre of the state, and is regarded as an excellent pan-fish. It is green on the back, orange at the sides, and cream-color on the abdomen; the mottled spots are black and green. This is emi-

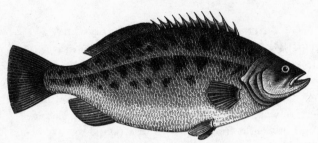

ROCK BASS OF THE LAKES.

nently a lake fish, where it is found in greatest numbers over the shallows near the shores, and contiguous to the entrance of spring streams. It ranges in weight from a quarter to a pound.

SECTION FOURTH.

THE SUNFISH.

This little fish inhabits nearly all the lakes, rivers, and ponds in the United States. Its habits are very domestic, seldom leaving its spawning-ground out of its sight, but seeks some rock or large stone where it plays about; and the remainders of shoals of a single pair may be seen disporting together, gay and lively, while watching the bottom for such ground-bait as angle-worms, and the surface for flies and grasshoppers. This tiny gormandizer is a great annoyance to fishers with the fly or worm when it becomes numerous in a trout-pond, for it will take both the worm and the fly; and, besides, it will steal the trout-eggs from the spawning-beds. But it affords ladies and children much sport, and is, withal, an excellent pan-fish; and as it affords good sport for school-boys, it should be tolerated. It never attains to more than half a pound weight; but the buffalo, a Western fish, which is similar to the spotted bass, is sometimes mistaken for this fish, and in some waters ranges from half a pound to nearly five pounds. The sunfish is dark greenish-brown on the back, greenish-yellow on the sides, lower end of gill tipped

THE SUNFISH.

with red, and the belly orange and gold. It is to be fished
for with perch tackle and very small hooks.

THE PERCH.

This fish is the head of the families of the *Percidæ* or *Per-
coïdes* of Cuvier. The preoperculum is denticulated, the oper-
culum is produced behind into a flattened spine, the infra-
orbitals are obscurely denticulated, and the tongue is smooth.
This is the common fresh-water perch—the *Perca* proper. It
is so common in American waters that a description is scarcely necessary. It is a very voracious fish, will bite to the artificial fly, and the red ibis is its weakness, while it seems
equally well pleased with any bait which the angler may
adopt or change to. Its weight is usually about half a pound,
though three-pounders are not uncommon, while it sometimes
scales as high as seven pounds, but rarely except in the large
lakes.

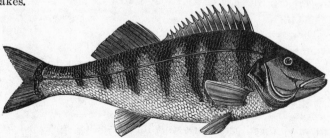

THE PERCH.—*Perca*.

In Europe it is found desirable to cultivate this fish, as it is very prolific and an excellent pan-fish; but in America, where it is no trick to take half a bushel a day on the ponds in the immediate vicinity of the city of New York, it is not deemed worth while to encourage its propagation. Indeed, so great a scourge is it regarded on Long Island, that *poachers* having a grudge against an owner of a trout-pond go in the night-time and stock it with perch.

Of the fishes belonging to this order there are over twenty families, including the numerous kinds of bass, and nearly all of those fishes of fresh waters with the first dorsal spiked or spinous rayed. Of these families there is scarcely a fresh-water river or lake on earth which does not contain a representative.

The ovarium of a perch is one fourth the weight of the fish; and a pound perch has been known to contain 992,000 eggs.

THE GLASS-EYED OR WALL-EYED PIKE.

This is one of the fishes of the Middle and Northern States. At the Southwest it is called wall-eyed, while at the North it is known as the glass-eyed pike, and by other local and unimportant names, such as the pike-perch, sand-pike, etc. But its eyes being the most distinctive mark, it is more generally known by the names given at the heading than by any other. It sometimes attains to a very great weight. Doctor Buel took one in the Kentucky River which weighed nearly fifty pounds.

They are found in all the tributaries of the Ohio River, in the range of great lakes, and most of the rivers and lakes as far east as New York, south as far as Tennessee, and west as far as Wisconsin. They also inhabit many of the waters in the western part of the Dominion of Canada. In Cayuga, Seneca, and other lakes of the western part of New York they are often taken, sometimes weighing as high as forty pounds. In Oneida Lake they are numerous; in fact, the glass-eyed pike is one of the most important commercial fishes of the lakes.

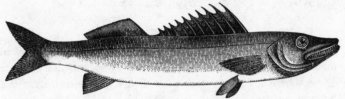

THE GLASS-EYED OR WALL-EYED PIKE.

The glass-eyed pike of the rivers in New York is very sat-isfying game to the angler.   He prefers the live shiner as a bait, and is generally found at the foot of a rapid, watching for any lame or disconcerted fish which appears not to know how to take care of itself.   The best way to angle for them, therefore, is to anchor your boat at the side or above a rapid; use shiner bait, and cast to the foot of the rapid, or let your bait run down the rapid, for they sometimes lie behind huge rocks in the rapid.   Use regular striped-bass tackle and fish with a float.   The pike of the Mohawk River are supposed to be the best for the table.   The meat is hard, and laminates in rich flakes, possessing a peculiar flavor most tempting as a breakfast dish.   Those fish which run from three to nine pounds are the best for the table; but they have been taken at the Little Falls to the weight of nearly twenty pounds, and proved to be a superior fish for stuffing and baking.

The scales of the glass-eyed pike are hard, close, and diffi-cult to detach.   The mandibles are wider and the jaws stronger than those of the pike or pickerel, while its teeth are shorter and closer set.   It is dark gray, with greenish tint on the back, gray sides with yellowish tinge, and white abdo-men.   The numerous shoals of this fish in American waters renders it common and unappreciated, but it is really one of the best table-fishes of the rivers.

There is another family of glass-eyed pike, known in Ohio and Western Virginia as the salmon.   It resembles the pike

T

of the Mohawk by being bluish-black on the back, bluish-gray sides, and white belly. It is found in the Kanawha and Miami Rivers, as also in many other streams of Ohio.

THE WHITEFISH.

This sucker-mouthed, succulent delicacy is to be found in most of the small lakes in the middle of the State of New York, where it forages near the springs which gush from the bottom, so that its meat is pure, white, juicy, and possessed of a most delicate flavor. The color of the back is gray, and the rest of the fish a clear white of most lustrous sheen. The great lakes from Ontario to Superior produce millions annually, and it is supposed the fish near the north shores are superior to those on the south side of the lakes, because a greater number of cold spring streams debouch in the lakes on the north side. The whitefish is leather-mouthed, and sometimes takes the spoon or spinning bait. In weight it runs from three to nine pounds, and there is less waste in it than in any other fish of its size. The engraving is a copy sketched from still life by Walter Bracket, Esq., a Boston artist of merit.

THE WHITEFISH.—*Corregonus alosa or albus.*

It is eminently an economical fish, requiring no butter to fry it; but, of course, those persons who unite a little knowledge of hygiene with gastronomy never fry any but the smallest kinds of pan-fishes. This is a broiler as truly as is a shad or a Spanish mackerel.

Though an abdominal, it does not belong to the *genus Salmo* any more than does the smelt, which some ichthyologists classify with that *genus*, though the smelt spawns in spring, and the whitefish late in summer or early in autumn.

Whitefish are taken with nets and placed in fish-pounds in the fall, confined by water-fencing with nets or stone, whence they are taken with large scap-nets and sent to market. The new process of dry-freezing is being resorted to at the West, so as to enable the netters to take them in the season when they are best for the table, and preserve them in a certain stage of refrigeration until it is thought desirable to market them. This is the preferable method, because, when confined in pounds, closely packed, many of them get frozen, being thus rendered unmarketable by reason of their slow death. In the winter of 1868 there were 500 lost from one pound near Detroit by freezing. The pound system should be abolished by law.

> "The fisher stakes his net and weir
> The persecuted shoals to snare;
> The seiner runs his seines around,
> Where'er their shining scales abound;
> Then, dragging to the neighboring shore,
> The white sands strew with ample store;
> Yet, spite of foe, and net, and seine,
> Unnumbered myriads yet remain."—ISAAC M'LELLAN.

THE LAKE HERRING.

The herring belongs to the *Clupeidæ* family of fishes, and is the fifth and last division of the "*Malacopterygiens abdominaux*," being the supposed link between the *Gadidæ* and the *Salmonidæ*, without second dorsal or adipose fin. The lake herring is quite similar to that of the salt waters, subsisting chiefly on animalculæ. Its back is dark gray with a greenish tinge, white sides and abdomen, and covered with large silvery scales. It is from nine to twelve inches in length, and when fresh is a good broiler; but the world knows that it is

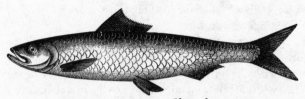

THE LAKE HERRING.—*Clupea harengus.*

cured every possible way with salt and smoke, from the delicate bloater to the shriveled, smoky-brown substance of a smoked herring-box. Nevertheless, it has been truly stated that "the ancients placed among their gods many a worse creature than a red herring." It is a great fish of commerce, and one of the indispensables to the poor in many parts of the world. Thus far, although the lakes of the United States swarm with a fresh-water herring which is not inferior to the best British, yet it has hitherto claimed little attention as a fish for exportation; but the demand for it is becoming annually greater, and the fishermen of the Western lakes are now beginning to study the best net and management for its capture. The drift-nets will probably be found the best, and the lake herrings—which are more delicate than those of salt water — will soon become an important article of commerce.

THE CISCO OR CISCOQUETTE.

The cisco is a small white fish similar to the lake herring, but differing from it by the addition of a second filmy dorsal, and in its meat being more delicate, and, when scaled, translucent as a smelt. It usually measures from six to nine inches in length, sometimes twelve inches, but rarely longer. The scales are white as polished silver except on the back, which is greenish-gray like the caplin.

The cisco is known in some places, eminently by fishermen and fish-dealers along the great lakes, as the ciscoquette, and is just beginning to be regarded as a commercial fish, great quantities being taken with the whitefish by the fishermen of

Huron and Superior. A letter from one of the principal Lake
Erie fishermen contains the statement that they entertain high
hopes of profitable enterprises in this modern luxury. The
cisco is found in all the lakes belonging to the great chain
bounding the United States on the north, and in some western lakes of the interior; but, while the lake herring—its frequent companion—is numerous in Seneca and Cayuga Lakes,
I have not seen a cisco there; but the large shiner of Canandaigua Lake may be the cisco. Both the cisco and herring
are favorite baits for lake trout, and, as food for game fishes,
the waters should be kept well stocked with them.

THE CISCO OR CISCOQUETTE.

From a recent letter to the Spirit of the Times from Camp
Sterling, on Geneva Lake, Wis., it appears that "ciscoing" is
the principal June sport for man, woman, and child in all the
area formed by a radius of twenty miles round the lake. The
cisco may be taken with bait or fly, though the latter is the
most natural food, as its small, square mouth and soft teeth
indicate that *animalculæ* or flies are its natural aliment. At
Geneva Lake there is a fly called the "cisco-fly," which appears to be its natural food; it is nearly an inch long, of gray-
ish-brown body and light gray wings, with tail and *antennæ*—
probably a *Phryganea*. The eel-fly is also said to be a favorite lure; but the cisco and cisco-fly both appear in great numbers at the same time.

The cisco is said to be excellent game of its size, and will
rise as vigorously as a brook trout, often meeting the fly before it touches the water. They should be fished for with a
single-handed fly-rod, like the trout; though a sixteen feet
perch-rod is recommended, as perch and small black bass oc-

cupy the same feeding-grounds, and often rise to the fly or take the bait. The cisco of the great lakes resembles an ale-wife, and sometimes attains the weight of three pounds.

THE SHINER.

This tiny white fish, with scales of metallic lustre, is from two to four inches long, and the best bait-fish which belongs to the fresh waters of America, where it is found in most of the brooks, rivers, and lakes of the north temperate zone. It is a greedy biter, and with a bit of angle-worm covering the point of a minnow-hook it is taken as fast as it can be drawn out with a supple willow wand. While fishing in rivers for black bass, I have moored one end of my scull-boat at the shore, and sat my waiter at catching shiners at the shore-end of the boat, while I took black bass with the shiner-bait at the other end.

THE SHINER.

As a pan-fish, it is the sweetest, most juicy, and delicate of any fish except the golden mullet; and when fried to a crisp in olive oil or fresh butter, it forms a mouthful more delicious than any other pan-fish. Many epicures in country places appreciate the delicious shiner; but as it is too insignificant in size to form an object of commerce, inhabitants of cities are innocent of any knowledge of this succulent luxury. But it is as a bait-fish that I would recommend the shiner, and a bait-can is necessary for keeping it alive.

SECTION FIFTH.

BAIT-CAN AND BAITS.

A simple tin can or pail, large enough to contain from two

to three gallons of water, with the lid perforated to let air into the bait, is generally sufficient; but some anglers prefer a double pail, the inner one perforated all over in holes the size of buckshot. In this case the pails are of equal size at the top and bottom, or cylindrical, and the inner pail may be taken out and the water changed before returning it, without the danger of losing bait. Another plan is to have a can shaped like the foregoing cut, and, instead of frequently changing the water, insert a siphon, and draw the water up and let it fall back into the can, which aerates the water and revives the bait. In carrying young trout to stock streams, the cans may be of either wood or tin, but they should be constructed with a pump to aerate the water. Clean swamp-moss, and a small piece of ice in moss, should always be placed in the water for conveying live fish several miles in warm weather.

SPINNING BAITS.

Spinning baits for trolling on all fresh waters have proved the most successful for nearly all the game fishes which inhabit them. I incline to the opinion that, if spinning minnow squids could be made strong enough for trolling with along our coasts and in our estuaries, all the surface-feeding fish of those waters might be taken in greater numbers than they are now by casting menhaden bait, and by all other fishing appliances except the set-nets and pounds, which—as they take all sizes of fishes—should be regulated by law, especially as to where they may be used, and under what conditions, etc. Of course, the rig for coast-trolling would require to be made very strong; for even the plain bluefish squid fastened to a heavy hawser-laid line is often parted by the jaws of bluefish, Spanish mackerel, bonetta, or cero. Even a fifty or seventy-five pound striped bass, or a twenty or thirty pound bluefish, would make the line hum some.   But how would it be with a hundred and twenty pound bonetta?   I have taken large striped bass by trolling for them on the Seconnet River with a bone squid covered with white linen, out of which I formed the tail.   The squid played by means of a brass swivel.   All swivels should be of brass or copper, even if silver-plated afterward.   Steel swivels rust.   The leathern satchel for carrying hooks, screw-driver, pincers, porpoise-oil, and all the appliances necessary for use in mending rod, reel, or any part of tackle, should be framed with brass.   Waterproof canvas satchels are better than the leathern, and in them hooks and other anglers' implements will take no injury.   Water-proof canvas is also preferable to leather for gaiters, and for boat-fishing they are preferable for shoes.   I prefer Russia leather boots for wear when trolling off the coast, as the spinous dorsal and pectoral fins of some fishes are sharp and strong enough to pierce any kind of cloth.

Foreigners have frequently swindled the anglers of this country by attaching hooks of inferior quality to spinning baits; but the domestic competition in the fishing-tackle business has become so strong that first-rate tackle of all kinds can be had at home; and the Buel feathered trolling-spoon, and those of M'Harg, are the best in the world for taking the principal fishes of our lakes and rivers.   The samples which I submit for the use of anglers on American waters are supposed to be the best in use.   Those just referred to I know are.   If a plain spoon is used, it should be of silver outside and copper on the concave side.

HACKETT'S SPINNING-TACKLE, CORK, IRELAND.

This piece of spinning-tackle was noticed in the London FIELD, and I think it a very good rig for trolling with a live minnow for maskinongé, glass-eyed pike, black and Oswego bass, pickerel, and the numerous lake and river fishes which delight in spoon victuals or captivating artificial lures.

In baiting, put the large hook in at the mouth, and run the

point of hook along the side, under the skin, bringing it out opposite the dorsal fin; then draw up the fish on the shank of the large hook, and insert the small hook through the upper and lower lips, thus closing the mouth; let the bait settle back so as to draw on the small hook, and you are ready for action. The hooks, screw, and swivel should be silver-plated. If the snells are of gimp, they should be made very fine; but twisted gut snells, finely made, are better. The minnow should represent a silver-side or a shiner.

This would be a killing bait to offer along the margin of a pickerel-pond while spinning it among the lily-pads with a long rod. Just cast it as far as convenient, without sinker; let it sink a trifle, and draw it along, when its spinning will soon be stopped if there is a pickerel, perch, or glass-eyed pike, or even a black bass near. Properly made and handled, it must prove a very attractive lure and successful bait.

HASKELL'S TROLLING-BAIT.—NO. 1.

The invention is patented, but may be had at most fishing-tackle stores. It is made of three sizes. The largest is $5\frac{1}{2}$ inches long; medium size, $4\frac{1}{2}$ inches; small, 3 inches. This troll must prove a successful lure if properly made. A whirling joint below the dorsal fin must require great care to render it quite free and yet sufficiently strong. I have heard good reports of the bait, and should think it would prove successful on the lakes of the Adirondacks and among the Thousand Islands.

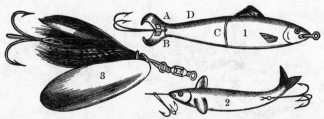

This bait is intended to represent a live fish with a screw tail. Its main feature is an ingenious combination of the *spinning* principle with that of the well-known "trolling minnow." It is constructed of thin sheet metal, beautifully and durably silver-plated. The form, as indicated by the engraving, represents a perfect fish; the main portion of the body is stationary, and keeps in a vertical position in the water, while the tail portion, D, revolves at the joint C by means of the turned ends of the tail, A and B.

It is well to have but two hooks on metal trolls, but they should be as large as allowable for the size of lure.

Needle-pointed, finely tempered steel hooks, of the Sproat bend, are as good as any.

Especial attention should always be paid to the quality of hooks for all kinds of angling, but more especially for trolling.

The brightest artificial disguises are generally the best for trolling baits.

This troll, if made strong enough, would be a very successful one for bluefish and Spanish mackerel.

THE PROPELLING MINNOW.—No. 2.

This minnow is made from gutta-percha, shaded and colored to represent a live minnow.   The pectoral fins are represented by screw propellers, which, with the curve of the tail, render the lure very attractive, as its motion in the water resembles that of a living fish.   This may be made of any size, to suit the kind of fishing for which it is required.   Andrew Clerk & Co. have them of all sizes, from those for use with a fly-rod to such as are large enough to troll with for the fishes of our great lakes.

This bait has never been tried in our waters.   It is similar to the troll for salmon in the lakes of Scotland, and, I think, will prove to be excellent for sea trout.   It received a premium at the World's Fair in Paris, and the beauty of its make surpasses any spinning bait that I have seen. A small brass swivel connects the gimp snell with the line.

BUEL'S PATENT FEATHERED TROLL.—No. 3.

Among the many efforts at making captivating metal trolls, the one with a piece of silver, in the oval or fish-form, revolving at the head of the shank of the hook, proved, from the year it was invented, the most successful; and, when the addition of feathers was introduced, I trolled with it at the Thousand Islands, Rice Lake, and on other waters, always with great satisfaction.

The hooks should be heavy and well tempered. M'Harg's troll was very popular at the Thousand Islands, chiefly because it was made with a pair of hooks; but he tells me that recently trollers prefer a cluster of three hooks. Mr. Clerk says the same. It is a great mistake, because large fish crush a cluster of hooks and disgorge them.

The feathers which I found the most taking were the red ibis. The best troll that I ever used for maskinongé is a red ibis feather for the top of the troll, and a small tuft of white hair from a deer's tail for the under side. The white hair from a deer's tail is brilliant in the water, and it disguises the point of the hook, while the attractive red feathers extend back of the bend of the hook from the top of the shank. I prefer, also, plain brass trolls, trolls of silver for one side and of copper for the other, and trolls of pure silver. The troll for maskinongé should be oval in shape, and from two and a half to three inches long, playing round from a shoulder on the shank of the hook. The hooks should be next to the largest size represented on the plate of implements for taking striped bass.

SPINNING-TACKLE FOR LIVE BAITS.

The three *desiderata* in spinning rigs for trolling with and playing live bait are, 1st, the strength and applicability of

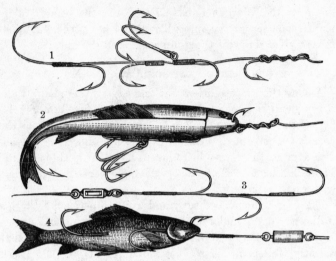

SPINNING-TACKLE FOR LIVE BAITS.

the gangs of hooks; 2d, the natural play of the bait when attached to the gang; and, 3d, the delicacy necessary to form it an attraction instead of a warning. No. 1 represents an adjustable gang, the movable upper hook sliding, and with a half-knot fastening at the bend of the hook to the correct length, to hold the fish by the lips and leave the gills free.

Always use shiners for bait when they are to be had. In impaling or affixing the minnow or shiner to the gang of hooks, first insert the bottom hook nearly an inch above the tail, and run it down and out at the tail, as represented by No. 2, so as to curve the tail; and, that the tail may have precisely the correct curve, fix the next hook, at the top of the shank of the large hook, in the skin at the side, so as to hold the tail to the curve required; then insert under the skin the two middle hooks, which fasten more firmly the bait, and confine it to the requisite curve. Then slide down the lip-hook, or upper one, and insert it through both the lips of the fish, shutting its mouth, but leaving the gills free for respiration. Take a half hitch with the snell round the shank of the hook at the curve, wind it a few times round the shank, and run it through the hole at the top of the shank of the hook. This completes baiting; and with a good swivel at the top of the snell or snood, a few inches (say six) above the upper hook, the bait will revolve in water, and remain an attractive lure for hours while trolling, unless a bite intervenes, and then the biter is quite sure to be hooked; for the triangular gang, playing to a ring on the outside of the fish, is generally sure to intercept the fish (which aims at the head of the bait) before it is taken by the tail-hook.

Francis Francis, in philosophizing upon the superiority of the spinning of artificial baits over natural ones, concludes that it is "because they are stiff throughout;" and that is one of the reasons why they do not get out of proper shape as do the living ones when not properly impaled and permanently fixed on a gang of hooks so arranged as that nothing but a bite will disturb or derange the bait. I have not the slightest hesitation in pronouncing this spinning gang the best arrangement of hooks that has thus far been presented to the American angler.

Figures 3 and 4 illustrate what is termed the "dead snap." Of course, all gangs for natural baits should either be fastened to single, double, or twisted gut snells, or to the finest possible silver gimp wire. They are generally wound to the latter with fine wire, but fresh-water trolls or spinning gangs should be fastened on silk-worm gut. Regulate the number of plies of gut to the size and power of fish to be trolled for. The present gang, No. 3, may be fastened to single gut, if the gut be round and strong.

In baiting, insert the tail hook first, then the middle hook just under the skin, and finally slide down the lip-hook and insert it through both lips. Sometimes a baiting-needle is used to insert the snell from the body out at the mouth through the upper gill-cover. The upper hook should always slide on the snell by a hole or small loop of gut at the top of the shank.

All fishes of the *genus Salmo* are more readily captured by trolling with natural baits, such as the shiner or the smelt, which is the salmon's natural food, to a troll formed of burnished silver, with the hook disguised by gay feathers, while all families of the pike and perch prefer the feathered squid. For trolling, the black bass prefers live bait; but in July he will bite at almost any gay fly, if artistically presented.

The troll is the most killing method of angling short of the net and the pound, and yet it is not nearly so popular in America as in Europe. An American gentleman would hardly consent to troll for salmon, and yet in both Scotland and Ireland they cross-fish for them by two row-boats carrying each an angler with trolling-rods, and the lines of each angler are connected at the ends, where a float marks the division. To each line numerous flies are attached, and the boats are rowed along at a convenient distance, and when a salmon bites, the angler on which side of the float the fish is fastened reels and plays the salmon, while the other angler gives line. If the oarsmen, who gaff the fish, get nervous, a snarl of lines and hooks, and a loss of the fish, are results quite naturally expected and frequently realized.

SPOON-VICTUALS FOR LONG-SNOUTS.

The larger sizes of feathered spoons are preferred in trolling for the maskinongé and the great Northern pickerel, as also for the glass-eyed pike. The difference in the two styles of troll is illustrated by A and B. Troll A revolves on a shoulder, to which two hooks are first wound with brass-wire, then soldered. On the shank, as represented, feathers are mounted. Decisive colors are to be preferred, such as red and white. Sometimes two swivels, one at the shank of the hook and the other at the end of the gimp snell, six inches above, are used to prevent the rapidity of the action of the troll from kinking the line.

Troll B is so arranged that different fly-hooks may be

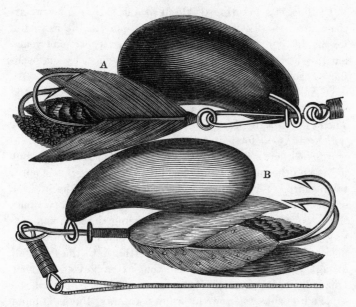

looped on by their wires at the joint, as illustrated. It is supposed by many that this rig is the best, because it permits free play to the hooks. In all other respects it is similar to A.

Feathered trolls, like A and B, made strong, with stout hooks, and heavy, strong gimp or wire snells, would be most killing among such coast fishes as the Spanish mackerel, blue-fish, and squeteague.

TROLLING WEATHER AND BAITS.

Of weather for trolling there are several opinions. Some think that the calm after a storm is the best time; others, that a windy day is best. It is good weather for all kinds of angling and trolling when the mercury is well up in the barometer and there is a gentle breeze; also when the sun looks with a modest silver face, it is much better than when the god of day is red and fiery, or glares with a golden or jaundiced stare.

Trolling is a luxurious style of fishing. It is not very artistic until the fish fastens. Then the play of the fish calls for the deftly-expert handling by an angler whose experience has taught him the strength and tricks to effect escape peculiar to each family of fishes.

Of bait-fishes, the river chub probably ranks next to the shiner. It bites eagerly to a minnow-hook baited with liver. Then there are the daces, both the horned and smooth heads, which are good for bait, and bite readily to a red fly, angle-worm, or liver. The stone-sucker is often used for bait, but it has no other merit than being firm and lasting; it is not a taking lure. I am in the habit, when angling in the interior of the country, and in want of minnow bait, to cut a two-inch thick rod, with a fork at the end, trimming the fork, and cutting it down to the length of two feet, and then fastening a piece of bobbinet lace or musquito-netting into the fork, full enough to form a bag, and with that extemporized scap-net I have always been able to scap up enough bait from the brooks or backsets from the fishing waters. But it is more desirable to carry a minnow-net on making these country excursions. The gaff-hook, landing-net, and minnow-net are essential implements toward an outfit for an expedition for general fishing.

FISH-HOOKS.

In the two rows of hooks represented opposite, the angler may see the two important *bends*, without reference to the slight bend sidewise, and called the *Kirby bend*, which may be given to either one. Some anglers prefer a Kirby bend, while others contend that it is not so good for mounting with flies for either salmon or trout; but Mr. Hyde, the best amateur expert in America, generally mounts his flies on Kirby round-bends. Of fish-hooks the shape is important, but scarcely more so than are the qualities of metal, temper, and finish. Oh, how many aching regrets and hopeless feelings of momentary desperation have been caused by a flaw in a fish-hook, or in

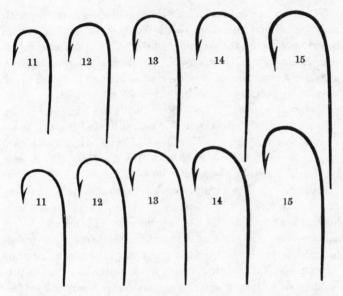

its deficiency of quality! As the quality of the hook is the foundation of the general results for the angler, it may not be a matter of surprise that I endeavor to impress the embryo philosopher with the importance of fish-hooks. I remember that, when a boy of seven summers, an extemporized bridge for carting hay was cast over a trout-brook in front of our dwelling, and that I baited a pin with a worm and lay down on the bridge, which was but a few inches above the water, and let the baited pin run under the bridge. In a moment I experienced a tremendous jerk, and pulled in my line, when the trout struggled, and finally straightened my pin-hook. Oh, what would I not have promised at that moment to give for a real fish-hook! The store was near by, where two hooks might be had for a cent, but where was the cent? I have never forgotten the feelings of that moment, and never will while life lasts. I would therefore plead for paternal generosity toward youths who early contract a penchant for angling.

U

The rows of samples include the useful sizes to mount with flies for salmon and large brook trout, or to use for bait in the river fishings for commoner fish. The upper row represent Adlington & Hutchinson's needle-pointed round-bends. This is also an excellent hook for small striped bass and black bass, and generally for fishing when a float is used.

The lower row of Sproat bend hooks are samples of the manufacture of Hutchinson & Sons, intended for the same uses as the foregoing. This bend is better than the round one for fish with a small mouth, like the kingfish. The Sproat bend appears to be the *ne plus ultra* in the form and quality of a fish-hook. The Virginia hook is quite similar in its shortness of nib and low bend, while the Kinsey or Pennsylvania hook is lower still in the nib and wider in the bend, and, being shorter from the point of the hook to the bend or centre of draught, is preferred by many; but my experience in losing large fish by their springing the hook out induces me to prefer a hook of larger wire, finer finish, and tempered better. These hooks enlarge gradually to No. 20, and in quality are truly superior.

SALMON FLIES.

The flies on the upper row are tied on the Adlington hook with *Sproat bend*, while those of the lower row are mounted on the *round bend*, of numbers from 15 to 18.

Fig. 1. Wing of diagonally barred feathers from under side of snipe's wing, in drab and black; dark blue and black pig's-wool hackle; gold tail. Fig. 2. Mottled black and white wing from a turkey's tail; body of olive-colored mohair and black hackle, with brown shoulders, and orange peacock tail. Fig. 3. Black and drab diagonally barred wing, blue and claret hackle body, with gold shoulder; tail of gold and green. Fig. 4. Brown wings and legs, drab body, all of gutta-percha; glass eyes. Fig. 5. Ribbed drab wing and antennæ; legs and body of gutta-percha; reddish-brown mohair shoulders, and black bead eyes. Fig. 6. White miller; white ribbed wings, drab body and legs, red glass eyes. Fig. 7. Brown gutta-percha wings, purple body wound with gold tinsel, reddish-brown mohair shoulders. Fig. 8. Black hackle body wound with gold; barred duck-wing tail; argo pheasant wing. Fig. 9. Purple body with gold tail; blue and purple hackle; tail of the golden pheasant top-knot; brown mallard wings. Fig. 10. Brown and white pheasant wing; gold body and tail; brown hackle shoulders, and black hackle head. Fig. 11. Golden body and tail; black hackle shoulders, with pheasant and burnt-brown wings.

Asia has contributed more material for artificial flies in her numerous families of pheasants than has any other quarter of the globe. Neither the South American fox, the barred wing

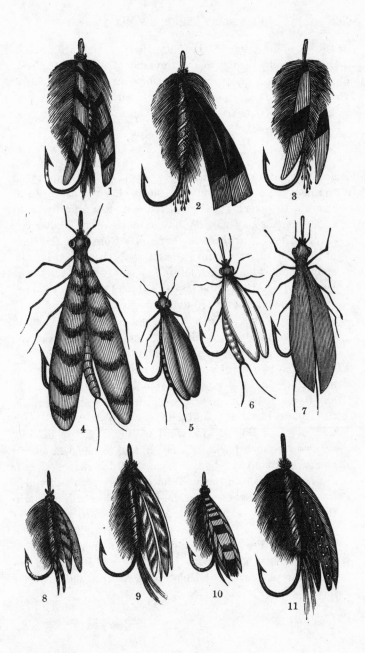

of the wood-duck, nor the brown mallard feather are equal in attraction and delicacy to the top-knot of the golden pheasant, or the feathers of the argo pheasant. The two lower rows of flies are copies of those used with success last year in Canada by Dr. Clerk, of Andrew Clerk & Co.

FLY DRESSING.

TROUT-FLIES.

Fig. 1. Preparatory to snelling your hook, which means tying the hook to a silk-worm gut snell, wind the head of the shank with several turns of waxed silk. Wax for fly-tying is the same as shoemaker's, only more clear and lighter colored. Then wind three or four times from near the bend of the hook up to the first thread at the head, and lay the end of the gut on the inside of the shank down near to the bend, and wind with the last silk thread down to the end, and fasten end as directed on the page of "loops and ties," leaving ends as 1. Fig. 3 is the same as 1, only the end of silk at the bend end of the tie is cut short, whereas the two threads of 1 are seen on 2 as follows:

Fig. 2. Place two hairs as antennæ, and the hackle that you intend for the head in the direction of the bend of hook, and fasten them by several loops; then fasten the end of the duffing like 2 or 9, and wind it round the hook to form the body, winding it afterward with a thread of gold or silver twist, or a hackle feather like 4, fastened as at 10, and wind round the body. Then add the wings like 5, finishing off like 8; or cut from a feather a pair of wings like 6, and wind them from the head so they will maintain their present spread shape. Many tyers of trout-flies tie only one wing on, but it never falls so naturally as do the two-winged flies; and, to imitate Nature perfectly, some flies require to be tied with four wings. Imitate the natural fly as shown on the plate of "natural and artificial flies."

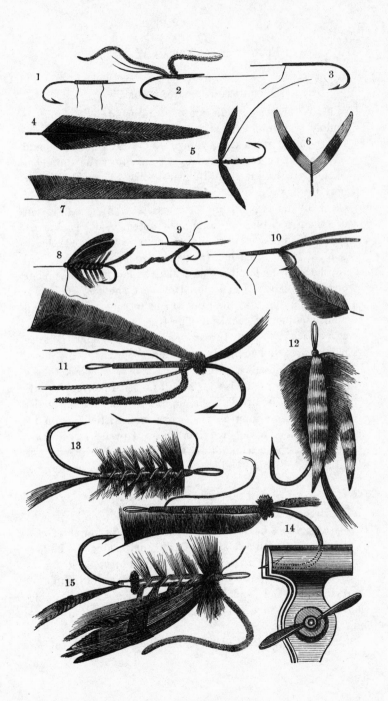

MOUNTING SALMON-HOOKS.

Fig. 11. Wind on your silk-gut loop, and wind the end of your duffing and antenna, fastening it all at the head, and forming the head of hackle as shown by 14. The hackle should be doubled, as represented by 7; and, after the duffing is wound, the hackle should cover it like 13; or the hackle may be heavy like 12. Some persons use a vice to hold the hook, as 14; but the best artists at fly-tying do not use them. After the duffing, the antennæ, and hackle are fastened, the body is usually wound with a cord of silver or gold, as 13 and 15, when the wings are fastened like 12 and 15, the head and tail finished like the latter, and the ends of threads covered and closed off with shellac. This also fastens the tinsel at the head of the antennæ; but with all your windings of hackle, duffing (the body), cord, or tinsel, carry with each your thread of silk, well waxed with transparent wax, and as nearly the color of the material you are winding as possible. First fasten well your hook to the snell, and then exercise taste and practice delicacy of manipulation. After all, an hour's instruction from an artist is worth more than all the books in Christendom on instruction for making artificial flies. I prefer to purchase flies from those who follow the art for a livelihood; but all anglers should be able to tie a fly when in a wilderness.

THE PONDERATING SINKER.

This recent invention is not in general use, or known to many anglers. I have tried it. It may do for river and freshwater fishings with a float, but for bottom fishing the hollow tracing sinker is vastly superior. The object for thus increasing the ponderosity of a sinker is to save the trouble of carrying numerous sinkers of different weights when going a-fishing, and to increase or decrease the weight without taking off the sinker.

Explanation of the Cut.—No. 1 is the smallest size of the

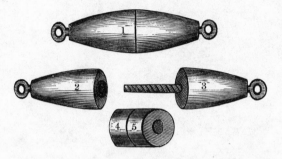

set represented. In case a heavier sinker is required, No. 1 is unscrewed, and presents the appearance of Nos. 2 and 3. The increased weight necessary is found in such wheels as 4 and 5, which are screwed on 3, and then 2 is again fastened to 3 by means of the screw. The sinkers are of lead, and the screw of 3 and the hole of 2 are brass, in order that they shall be strong and not corrode. I can not recommend them for the heavy fish of our bays and estuaries, as they are liable to unscrew on the bottom and in a strong tide; but as sinkers for float-fishing, no invention, I think, could be more opportune. They are to be found at the principal fishing-tackle stores.

Part Third.

COMMERCIAL FISHERIES.

CHAPTER I.

LAKE FISHERIES.

Statistics of a couple of Fisheries on the Western Lakes.

As I have before stated that this is not a school-book, I will add that it is not intended for the counting-room. The few statistics given are mere glimpses at a branch of industry which is a sealed book to the public. The lake fisheries of the United States are confined to the southern half of the range of lakes to which the River St. Lawrence is the outlet. Later in the history of this country important fisheries will be established on Lake Superior and at intervals far beyond. At present the few fisheries are controlled by private individuals or companies, who have not cared for the publicity which would enable reporters to make a correct estimate of this industry.

FOOD-FISHES OF LAKE SUPERIOR.

The catch of fish in Lake Superior averages about ten thousand barrels, of which nine thousand are whitefish, and the remainder ciscoquettes (ciscos); but this only applies to the fish which are salted for an Eastern market; for large quantities are shipped while fresh, of which no correct account is kept. In Detroit one firm alone ships annually some three hundred tons of whitefish, which, however, is a portion of the harvest of Lake Huron.

The largest whitefish are caught below Copper Harbor, in Lake Superior, and weigh about 8 pounds, or 60 to a barrel; those caught above Copper Harbor average 1½ to 2 pounds, and about 130 to the barrel.

From an estimate made in dollars by the dealers in Lake Superior fishes, the catch of last year, when salted, amounted to...$200,000 00
300 tons fresh whitefish, shipped by one house, at 10 cts. per lb.   60.000 00
$260,000 00

My informant—who is one of the most intelligent fishermen of the lakes—adds that "ciscoquettes" (or the ciscos) are supposed to be the finest of the fresh-water fishes taken in the lakes. "They are something like a Spanish mackerel, very fat, and becoming valuable. They are never found far away from copper-mines, and wherever copper is found most abundant there also are found the greatest number of ciscoquettes. None are caught at the lower end of the lake. Fishing is yet in its infancy, many places having never been fished before last season," *i. e.* 1867. The ciscoquette is only like the Spanish mackerel in its flavor being free from any foreign taste; but it is more juicy, and, if possible, more delicate in flavor.

FISHERY OF SANDUSKY, OHIO.

This is one of the principal fisheries on the lakes, and the following statement shows its annual catch, and the means employed:

WHITEFISH.

Taken in pounds, 1,800,000 fish; aggregate weight, 4,500,000
    lbs.; price, 10 cents the pound, or..................................$450,000 00
2000 lbs. daily, or over, for 200 days, taken in gill-nets........... 40,000 00
                                             490,000 00

GLASS-EYED OR WALL-EYED PIKE.

4,400,000 pounds, of sizes running from $1\frac{1}{2}$ to 14 lbs. each. The
    wholesale price averages 4 cents the pound....................... 176,000 00

BLACK BASS.

65,000. Average, 3 lbs. Price, $4\frac{1}{2}$ cents per lb....................   8,775 00

SAND PICKEREL OR SAND PIKE.

1,200,000. Price, 1 cent each...   12,000 00

LAKE HERRINGS.

13,500,000 fish, weight $\frac{1}{2}$ lb. each, at $\frac{1}{2}$ cent per lb................. 33,750 00

WHITE BASS.

1,200,000 fish, at a cent each...   12,000 00

MASKINONGÉ.

500 fish, 10 lbs. each, at 6 cents per lb................................   300 00

LAKE TROUT.

20,000 lbs. caught at Cape Vincent, N. Y., and 40,000 lbs. caught
    at Collingville and Greenwood, at 10 cents per lb...............   6,000 00
                    Amount total................................$738,825 00

NUMBER AND EXTENT OF NETS EMPLOYED.

The fishery has 150 pounds or stationary nets, set in waters from 20 to 42 feet deep. The length of each net is 100 rods, and the cost $1000 each. Amount total, $150,000. The cost of fish-pounds are the principal expense, though the company has in continued use 1000 gill-nets, twenty seines, and numerous small boats. The fishery is very prosperous, and owned by men of energy and business capacity.

The extensive coast and estuary fisheries of the United States, having been regularly worked ever since the eastern border was first settled by Europeans, have to such a degree absorbed the capital and enterprise of fishermen and fish-dealers that the lake and river fisheries were not thought of until within the past twenty years, with one solitary exception. Prior to that date the establishment of fisheries in the interior of the United States was not even spoken of. Now there are many, from which I have selected the foregoing exemplars to illustrate results of this growing industry.

Throughout the interior of our vast territory there is an ornamental tracery of running, sweet, and healthful waters, well supplied with food-fishes. The working of these waters is free to all fishermen, with the unimportant exception of a few depleted rivers, consequent on their having been overworked, but which are now being restocked and protected by legislative enactments during the process of recuperation. These are all near the sea-board. The lakes and lengthy rivers of the interior are still free; and where no regular fisheries are established, the inhabitants take what fresh fish they want, either with the angle, net, or spear. The poaching proclivity of some indolent persons has induced them to use the spear too freely in our small lakes during winter. In the State of New York there is a law against it, with fine and penalty attached, but it is still done in defiance of law. These poachers erect a board shanty on sleigh-runners, furnished with a foot-stove, and a hole in the ridge of the roof for the spear-handle. This shanty they draw out on the lake, cut a hole through the ice under it, lock the door, and commence spearing all the fish that come near their hole. If the constable raps at the door, no reply is meant to signify that the occupant is absent. Thus poachers squat in villages on our lakes in winter when the ice is thick, and spear the fish at a season when they are unwholesome for food. In Canada, for attracting the maskinongé to the spear, in one hand the poacher holds a line attached to an artificial minnow, which he keeps playing in the water, while with the other hand he holds the spear. The maskinongé darts to within a foot of the minnow, and, while hesitating there, the spear takes him.

The great Western rivers swarm with fish, and all the way for five hundred miles below the sources of both the Mississippi and the Missouri every tributary is a trout-stream. In addition to the pike and pickerel, the glass-eyed pike, dorée, or sand pickerel, the gray pickerel, known as the Ohio salmon, there are some half dozen varieties of bass in nearly every Western river, besides perch, sunfish, chub, bream, eels, buffalo. There are also several varieties of catfish, the most important of which are the black, yellow, and channel cats. The Missouri River is justly celebrated for the latter fish, which runs from five to fifteen pounds each, and, besides yielding excellent sport for the rod, is a choice table luxury, equaling the *salure* of the Danube, which is also a species of catfish highly prized by European epicures.

THE HAMMER-HEADED SHARK.

CHAPTER II.

COAST FISHES AND FISHERIES OF THE UNITED STATES.

THE fisheries of the Atlantic coast from Chesapeake Bay to the Gulf of St. Lawrence are so extensive as to cause regret that statistics in the catches of many important fishes are not sufficiently reliable to form the data necessary to a correct report of the numbers and weights annually caught by the thousands of fishermen who keep no account of their takes, but sell them at retail or wholesale, and live on the proceeds, without keeping an account of their expenses.

THE MACKEREL.

Coasting New England's rocky shore,
Sailing where Southern surges pour,
The daring fishers spread the sail
To Southern haze and Northern gale.
Thousands of craft the ocean speck,
Thousands of seamen pace the deck,
Eager to follow to the end,
Where'er the mackerel shoal may tend.

This is one of the most important food-fishes of the seas, as well as one of the most prolific. Nature, in the harmonious arrangement of the universe, and in turning all things toward man's good, has made the duration and existence of numerous families of fishes dependent upon their searching out brooding-places and depositing their eggs in the neighborhood of man's need. By the process of procreation, these fish form, to a certain extent, home attractions, and dally about the shoals near shore, where they are fished for with the hook, and the more sure means of a drift-net twenty feet deep by one hundred and fifty feet in length, well corked at top, but with no leads at the bottom, for when mackerel are

in a biting or a moving mood they rise to the surface.   Like
all sea fishes, the mackerel is more easily taken than fishes of
fresh waters.   He foolishly dashes at whatever he sees before
him which he thinks will not devour him.   But in this peculiarity he does not differ from the royal salmon, which will
snap at flies when out of season, and evince the most culpable
rapacity when just returned from sea, even biting at an artificial minnow, or a fly unlike any thing in existence.

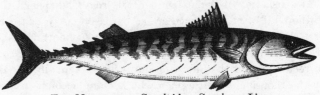

THE MACKEREL.—*Scombridœ—Scomber.*—Linn.

It would be difficult to find a fish more exquisite in form,
or more important in a commercial point of view, than the
common mackerel.   It is also capricious in its movements.
It is not always to be depended on for visiting us in great
numbers, though it has never entirely deserted us for a single season.   It is in best condition on our shores in October.
Then it is most succulent, and orders for private tables should
be made of that month's catch.   Catches early in the season
are lean.   The catch of June is scarcely worth salting; but
mackerel fatten fast, and by September are very good.   October mackerel are preferable to those of any other month in
the year, for, as a singular fact in the nature of the fish, it begins to deteriorate or lose condition in November.   In general, mackerel move away from shore gradually after the first
frost, and they finally settle off in soundings, not much influenced by the cold weather along our shores.   October is considered the closing month of the mackerel season; but about
five years since, near the 1st of December, the fishermen of
New Providence, Massachusetts, were surprised by the sight
of the saltatory exploits on the bay of myriads of mackerel
leaping, shining, and gleaming in every direction.   The boats

were supplied with bait, and manned in quick time for even Yankees, and the take that day was almost miraculous. The catch that season had been short, but that day made up the deficiency of the year. The next morning indicated that the shoal had stacked arms and was prepared to march. But few were taken that day, and less numbers each day for a week that the fleet followed them, when the shoals all sank, as by one general order, off the coast of New Jersey.

It was matter of great surprise to the fishermen that the mackerel voluntarily yielded themselves to appease the fishermen and supply the fish-casks of human need; but, having done so, the shoals seemed to have retired with a glow of satisfaction at having done their duty, even at the loss of some of their favorites.

In vain is the intimation to the pious fisherman that mackerel are as liable to mistakes in their calculations as men, and so settled, before the regular fishing season was over, in too cold a latitude, and rose during a warm term to take a lunar, and lay their course for more genial winter quarters. No! The fishermen believe that, smitten by conscience for not furnishing the usual supply, the fish voluntarily yielded themselves to the sacrifice for conscience' sake.

Mackerel, to be fully appreciated, should leap as it were from the water into the hands of the cook, and be made ready for the gridiron, broiled, and on the table in half an hour after it has left its native element. Or a salted October mackerel can not be depreciated by a person of nice taste; though, of course, a fresh fish is better than a cured one, and the sooner it is cooked after its last shuddering flutter, and its ultramarine tints die away, the better.

The mackerel frequents the Atlantic coast from Belle Isle to Long Island. It spawns in spring in the bays, bayous, and estuaries, and comes into season for the table in August.

"Whether from the abundance of suitable food found at such times, or from some other causes which influence the migrations of fish, it is hard to say, but experience shows us that on the coasts of Ireland mackerel are taken nearly all the year round. They are rarely very abundant on the coast

X

of Cornwall—although never entirely absent from it—much before March. A little later they visit the coast of Devonshire, appearing to approach the land as the season advances. At Lowestoft and Yarmouth the fishing season is still later, and is at its height during the months of May and June, whilst in the Frith of Forth June and July are the months when they usually appear. In the Orkneys few fish are taken until the last week in July or the first in August.

"The mackerel family have an extended range, and are found most abundant in warmer climes than the British Isles. The Sea of Marmora and the Bosphorus at times literally swarm with them. It is extremely picturesque and exciting to see the light and graceful 'caiques' dancing like bubbles over the clear blue sea, as, propelled by their lusty crews, they shoot here and there amongst the circling nets. Meantime the cunning old cormorants, undismayed by the bustle and splashing water, ply their occupation most diligently. As they grow audacious from long-continued impunity, they make a sudden raid over the corks into the thick of the struggling, fluttering fry. The fishermen shout, and by dint of admonitory pokes, liberally administered with the oar-blades, the greedy, long-necked throng are ignominiously expelled, and retire beyond the nets, gobbling down at leisure their ill-gotten plunder. Some idea of the abundance of fish to be found in this part of the world, and of the immunity from persecution enjoyed by these birds, may be formed by watching the countless thousands of them which at times pass, in apparently endless lines, between the Sea of Marmora and the Black Sea. I have watched them for hours without seeing any apparent diminution in their passing hosts. Vast numbers of mackerel also frequent the coasts of the island of St. Helena, where immense quantities can be captured. I have taken them with the hook and line until literally tired of hauling up and unhooking, baiting with a little strip of salt pork-rind, and throwing biscuit-dust overboard as an attraction. These fish, although of excellent flavor, are rarely more than seven or eight inches long, and are much like the *shiners*, or young mackerel, found abundantly on the English coast during the summer months; while in British waters, from fourteen to sixteen inches in length, and two pounds in weight, is not an unusual size.

"Much importance appears in past times to have been attached to the sale of mackerel in London, as we find that a law was passed in the year 1698 legalizing their being vended by a 'cry' on Sunday, which custom, as we know, still continues.

"There are several modes by which the capture of the mackerel is effected. Seines, or long nets furnished with corks at the top and leads at the bottom, are dexterously carried by fast boats round the advancing shoal of fish, which is inclosed as within a 'pound.' The ends of the net are now secured, and the fish either taken from within the inclosure with a smaller net, or drawn to the surface in the 'bunts' or bags formed in the larger seines, when the leaping, struggling fish are dipped up literally by basketfuls (by men stationed on the gunwale of the boat for the purpose) and thrown into a compartment provided for their reception. Great numbers are at times taken in ground seines or nets, which, although somewhat like those above described, are smaller, and so arranged as to be dragged to the beach with their contents. 'Trammel' and 'drift' nets may be compared to curtains suspended in mid-water, and are moored securely in the places selected for them by heavy stones fastened to their ends. In them the heedless fish, not perceiving the treacherous web, dart their heads, become hopelessly entangled, and are ultimately strangled in the meshes.

"Hook-fishing, too, lends its aid in thinning the rainbow throng. As a matter of sport and pastime, few pursuits, I think, are more thoroughly enjoyable than 'whiffing' for mackerel, and the following quotation will show that others are much of the same way of thinking:

"'It was evident the bay was full of mackerel; in every direction, as far as the eye could range, gulls and puffins of the St. Lawrence were collected, and, to judge from their activity and clamor, there appeared ample enjoyment for them amongst the fry beneath. We immediately bore away from the place where the birds were most numerously congregated, and the lines were scarcely overboard when we found ourselves in the centre of a shoal of mackerel. The hooker, however, had too much way. We lowered the foresail, double reefed the mainsail, and then went steadily to work. Directed by the movements of the birds, we followed the mackerel. Tacking and wearing the boat occasionally when we found we had overrun the shoal, for two hours we killed these beautiful fish as fast as the baits could be renewed and the lines hauled in, and when we left off fishing, actually wearied with the sport, we found we had taken above 500 pounds. There is not, on sea or river, always excepting angling for salmon, any sport comparable to this delightful amusement. Full of life and bustle, every thing about it is animated and exhilarating.'"

Hook-fishing for mackerel is very exciting sport. A brisk breeze, sky mellowed by fleecy clouds, gulls swooping and screaming, every thing apparently in excitement. Under such circumstances and surroundings, it is not strange if the troller, whiffer, or still-baiter should inflate his lungs and feast his soul until the waning sun warns him to desist and retire.

Excellent sport is sometimes to be had by rowing or sculling a boat into a thick shoal, and trolling for them with feathered squid, twirling spoon, or casting to them a white artificial fly.

Statistics of Mackerel Catches in the States of Maine and Massachusetts from 1863 to 1867, and the average wholesale Prices per barrel.

1864, Massachusetts	306,000 bbls.	$18 00	$5,508,000 00
" Maine	100,000 "	18 00	1,800,000 00
1865, Massachusetts	300,000 "	21 00	6,300,000 00
" Maine	90,000 "	21 00	1,890,000 00
1866, Massachusetts	250,000 "	17 00	4,250,000 00
" Maine	80,000 "	17 00	1,360,000 00
1867, Massachusetts	200,000 " ·	15 00	3,000,000 00
" Maine	70,000 "	15 00	1,050,000 00
	1,396,000 "		$25,158,000 00

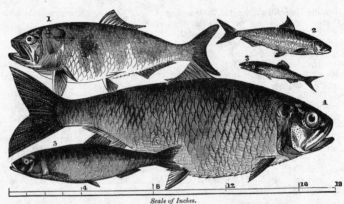

Scale of Inches.

HERRING AND PILCHARD FAMILY.—1. The Mossbonker, or Hard-head, *Alosa menhaden* (very abundant on the shores of Long Island and Mass. It is seldom eaten). 2. The Pilchard, *Clupea pilchardus.* 3. The Anchovy, *Engraulis engrasicolus.* 4. American Shad, *Alosa præstabilis.* 5. The Herring, *Clupea harengus.*

SECTION SECOND.

No. 4.—THE SHAD.

By the rice-border'd Southern coast,
  Where the Savannah River winds,
The shad shoal, an unnumber'd host,
  Its earliest feeding pasture finds.
Thence northward where the Hudson sweeps
Connecticut's transparent deeps,
Their gleaming myriads seek a home
Beyond the surges and the foam.

THE SHAD, commercially, is an important fish. It winters in the ocean, dallies among the nets in the estuaries during spring, after which it lays its *ova* in the sands above tide-water, and returns to salt water to recuperate. It is very prolific, yielding from a fourth to half a million eggs annually within the months of April, May, and June. The Connecticut River is supposed to contain the best shad, while those of the Delaware and Hudson are excellent fish—vastly superior to those of the British Isles, or to the *Alosa vulgaris*, which is numerous in the rivers of France, but so small and lean as never to be seen on the table of an epicure. The average weight of shad in Europe is less than two pounds, while in America it is double that weight. The *Alosa finta* visits some of the waters in France and Spain, and it is but recent-ly that it has been duly classified in France. The superiority of American shad in both size and quality over those of Eu-rope is probably caused by the purity of our rivers, and the greater amount of the kinds of food relished by this tooth-less spring delicacy of the breakfast-table. It feeds on ani-malculæ, and is exclusively caught with nets.

The shad season is comparatively short, but the principal Northern markets are supplied with them from Southern riv-ers in March, and sometimes as early as February. They do not enter the rivers of New York and Connecticut before the early part of April; and one of the most peculiar features in this family of fishes was discovered by Seth Green, while hatching them by artificial means at Holyoke, on the Connec-ticut River, where he hatched nearly one hundred millions of shad in less than six weeks. From the time when he strip-ped the shad, and the *ova* and milt settled in the hatching-boxes, not more than thirty-six hours elapsed before nineteen twentieths of the eggs hatched, and the remainder within twelve hours later.

THE SHAD FISHERIES.

Sixty days include the shad season in New York Bay and the Hudson River, during which time the usual catch is 1,100,000 fish,
   averaging each 25 cts. as price, or......................................$275,000
The catch in Delaware about 750,000, 25 cts........................... 187,500
      "   Connecticut, 400,000, 30 cts. 120,000
      "   Kennebec, 140,000, 15 cts.   22,500
      "   Penobscot, 20,000, 20 cts.....................................   4,000
      "   North Carolina, 500,000, 40 cts. 200,000
      "   Potomac and Chesapeake, 300,000, 20 cts...............   60,000
      "   Norfolk and vicinity, 200,000, 30 cts.....................   60,000
                                                                        \$949,000

Although the shad of Southern waters are inferior to those of the Northern, yet, as the earliest in market, they command the price of a rarity. The foregoing wholesale prices are copied from the books of the most extensive dealers in Ful-ton Market, New York.

SECTION THIRD.

No. 1.—THE MOSSBUNKER OR MENHADEN.

> On salt-sea borders, sound, and bay,
> The twinkling spring-time sunbeams play,
> And white with froth the billows shine
> Where the mossbunkers lash the brine.
> Above them flocks of sea-gulls swing,
> Beneath the hungry bluefish spring,
> And, deadlier still, the surfmen strain
> The oars, and mesh them with the seine.

The menhaden is a white fish, with large scales of metallic lustre. It disports, during spring, summer, and autumn, off the coast and in the estuaries from Delaware to the Bay of Passamaquoddy. It is from nine to twelve inches long, and in shape resembles a diminutive shad, though not so wide or thin for its length. It is a very oily fish, very bony, and therefore never eaten except by fishermen, who frequently salt it for winter use. Its flavor is like that of the shad.

The principal estimate of value put upon the menhaden is for its quality as the best bait for attracting mackerel, striped bass, bluefish, and even such of the *Gadidæ* as the haddock, and of the *Crustacea* as the lobster. It is either ground or chopped fine and cast upon the water to attract mackerel and other food-fishes to the hook, while it is the best bait for lobster-pots. The annual diminution in the numbers of mackerel taken within the past five years—as shown by the statistics—is justly attributable to the increase of the manufacture of menhaden oil. About five years since some person conceived the brilliant idea of making oil from menhaden by grinding them to a pulp, putting them under a press, and squeezing out the oil. He formed a company, which erected buildings, introduced machinery, and bought sail-boats and nets. For a couple of years, while menhaden were so abundant as to be used for manure in some places along the coast, the menhaden oil companies made generous dividends; but no sooner did this fact become known among enterprising geniuses than nearly two hundred manufactories were put in operation, and the sails of menhaden boats enlivened Long Island Sound throughout its length and breadth, their flocks of white wings extending along the Atlantic shore for five hundred miles, as if striving with the numerous shoals of porpoises to see which could do the most harm to the fishing interest by robbing the fishermen of the greatest amount of bait. But every year since the shoals of menhaden have decreased in number, so that while the fishermen begin to find the price of bait oppressive, some oil factories have been compelled to suspend operations. It may be a question worthy of attention by political economists and statesmen whether menhaden oil manufactories should not be taxed out of existence for the injury they are causing to the public; for the oil companies offer inducements which attract fishermen from their legitimate calling, enhance the prices of most kinds of food-fishes, and thus injure the public.

Laws which should adequately encourage by premiums the capture of the black porpoise and the puffer would greatly improve the coast fisheries. This course was deferred until the porpoises robbed some of the rivers of Ireland of their salmon, by watching in large shoals at the mouths of rivers when the salmon were returning to spawn. Already the black porpoise—the most injurious to food-fishes of all the mammal tribes—are becoming so numerous along the coast, and in the bays and estuaries, that the fishermen rightly consider them one of the principal causes of the annual decrease of striped bass and many other excellent fishes. The valuable oil of the porpoise would be a sufficient reward for its capture if the fishermen could be so encouraged as to induce them to decline catching menhaden for oil mills, and bring their forces to bear against the porpoise, the oil of which is the finest in the world for jewelers' use, and the lubrication of all machinery requiring a fine and pure article.

By some such means as I have hinted at the shoals of food-fishes may be checked in their eastern migrations, and induced to forage in the waters of the United States, instead of settling beyond their limits.

MENHADEN FOR BAIT.

The largest fleet engaged at catching menhaden bait along the coast is at Gloucester, Mass., where twenty fast-sailing fishing-smacks are engaged six months of the year at netting menhaden, and their annual sales of bait average in amount $75,000. Of the pilchard, No. 2, and anchovy, No. 3, they are European fishes; but the herring, No. 5, swarms along all the shores and inlets of the Atlantic during the spring and summer months; and whether it is the want of duly appreciating the fish, or because American fishermen have better employment during the season which the herring visits our shores, I know not, but it does not claim its proportionate share of interest and attention among the numerous families of American food-fishes.

FROZEN HERRINGS.

Late in autumn about fifty vessels sail annually from Massachusetts to Newfoundland for frozen herrings. Their average catch is one hundred tons each, and their wholesale price in the New York markets is three cents a pound, or $300,000.

SECTION FOURTH.

THE CODFISH—CATCHING AND CURING IT.

> Far off by stormy Labrador—
>   Far off the Banks of Newfoundland,
> Where angry seas incessant roar,
>   And foggy mists their wings expand,
> The fishing-schooners, black and low,
> For weary months sail to and fro ;
> Seeking no home, no rest the while,
> Till each is freighted full with spoil.

While visiting the mouth of the St. John River, on the north shore of the Gulf of St. Lawrence, I spent some time in examining the *modus operandi* of taking and dry-curing cod.

Fishermen from the isles of Guernsey and Jersey, with those from the British American Provinces, had come from afar, with their wives and little ones, and early in June settled in log cabins, to remain during the cod-fishing season, which, they supposed, would continue until September, when, with their freighted vessels, they would embark on their perilous voyage for home and a market.   Their fleet numbered sixty sail, with a scull-boat (in which a sail might be hoisted in case of necessity) for each vessel.   This fleet employed also two sail-boats, with nets, to catch caplin for bait.   Large shoals of caplin, smelt, and spearing foraged about the estuary and along the bay and coast, wisely intended, no doubt, as food for salmon, cod, and other members of the *Gadidæ* family, besides the more ferocious monsters of the deep, which seem to stop at nothing.   During my stay of a week among these fishermen, and from what experience I before enjoyed with the class, I am forced to conclude, with Victor Hugo and others who have studied the habits of men, and deduced therefrom theories for the influence which their avocations exert upon their dispositions, that fishermen are the most amiable, patient, and obliging class of men in the world.   They are temperate, industrious, frugal, and affectionate among themselves, and hospitable to strangers.

THE CODFISH.

The fleet sailed out of the harbor every morning, each vessel taking a supply of bait as it passed the caplin-netters, when they would come to anchor at certain distances apart along the Banks, sometimes within a mile of shore, but more generally from five to twenty miles, always following the fish

as they changed feeding-grounds. On their return in the
evening they ran alongside the planked docks, extending into
the river from the salting and packing houses, erected partly over the water. From vessels the cod were pitched up
on the docks (with forks made for the purpose), where they
were beheaded, split, drawn, and cleaned, then pitched into
the salting-room, where salt was rubbed into them for two
days, and on the third day they were spread on the flakes to
dry. The "flakes" are tables of fir-boughs, made by driving
forked stakes into the ground, then laying poles across, and
covering them with boughs of the fir-tree. These flakes were
two yards wide, three feet high, and covered several acres.
The fish, after being salted two days, on the third day are
spread singly upon the flakes to dry. Here they are left four
days, when they are grouped into small piles on the flakes
of twenty-five fish in each pile, and left in that condition two
days to sweat, when they are again spread on the flakes as at
first, and, after two days more, are piled up two days as before. Then they are gathered from the flakes and formed
into round stacks, their necks at the outer edge of the stack,
which is usually about five feet high, and contains a ton of
fish. After leaving them a week in stack, they again distribute them on the flakes to dry, and after another week they
again stack them. They are thus continued on the flakes or
in pack about a month in summer, but only half that time in
autumn, when they are considered cured. The cod cured on
the north shore of the Gulf are dried harder than those on
the south shore for the United States market. Those cured
on the north shore are generally sold in South America, the
West Indies, and to ports in the British Isles.

The question of "What luck have you had?" is more especially applicable to fishers for the market than to the disciple
of rod and reel; for, without bait, a perilous voyage and a
whole season's labor produce nothing but disappointment.
The caplin, spearing, and smelt are sometimes prevented by
rough weather from approaching waters where they may be

taken with the seine, in which case there is no use of thinking of substitutes for these baits, as the cod follow them and forage upon them far away from the ken of fishermen, or their power to follow. Thus the career of the fisherman is both hazardous and precarious.

THE JOHN DORY.

CHAPTER III.

WHALES—*Cetacea*—an order of aquatic mammals which comprises the largest animated forms in existence: some of the genera composing it are phytophagous, or plant-eaters; others are zoophagous, or animal-eaters.

WHALE FISHING.

"What though the wintry night falls dark,
And icy foes beset our bark,
And stiff our frozen rigging stands,
Enclasp'd with rigid iron bands,
While sheeted ice, like solid mail,
Thickens each spar and stiffen'd sail?
  Yet brave are whalemen's valiant hearts,
And stout are whalemen's hands;
  And strong the arm the harpoon darts,
And strong the arm that wields the lance,
When o'er the tides our whale-boats glance
    To battle with the whale.
Leviathan may lash the tide,
But soon his floating, bleeding side,
And soon the spouting streams of gore,
That o'er the ensanguin'd waters pour,
    Declare that all is o'er.
Right soon the precious oil is won,
Our dangerous labors all are done,
And homeward—homeward is the cry,
With all sails spreading to the sky."—ISAAC M'LELLAN.

WHALE FISHING.

HALING is the most adventurous occupation known within the circle of legitimate industry. It demands not only the explorations of most dangerous seas, but a residence upon them during the most inclement seasons. For many years very little whaling has been done in the Gulf of St. Lawrence and off the coast of Labrador, but the whales are again returning to their wonted feeding-grounds there, and the walruses or sea-cows nightly approach, and sometimes rest on the islands.

The Georgia shoals, and banks near Newfoundland generally, teem with nearly all the fishes of the Northern seas. Fishes from afar visit those feeding-grounds, which are formed into rich pastures by the settling of the *débris* washed down from near the frigid zone. The heavy tides whose swift currents sweep around Scotland and Ireland are met by counter tides and strong currents from Baffin's and Hudson's Bays, and these precipitate vegetable and mineral matters, including the drift of large rocks in icebergs, and, being assisted by the backing of the Gulf Stream, they have already formed the island of Newfoundland, the Fishing Banks, and the small islands which dot those waters, all of which will yet rise into an extensive territory, connecting Newfoundland with the main land south of the Gulf of St. Lawrence. The waters of the Straits of Belle Isle, which form one of the principal outlets to the gulf, are so deep, and the rise and fall of the tides so great, that they have contributed to the formation of the island of Anticosti, which is larger than Long Isl-

and, N.Y. With the great rise and fall of the tides, and the
consequent swift currents, many eddies are thus formed, and
for hundreds of miles to the south of Newfoundland, and extending to the west end of Anticosti, the feeding-grounds for
food-fishes form a larger fishing area than any other in the
world.

This meeting and mingling of the frosty Northern waters
with those more mild from the Gulf Stream are supposed to
form another attraction for fishes, and the bait-fishes are followed thither by the food-fishes, and the latter by most of the
voracious monsters of the deep, and thus procreation and
depletion keep step with supply and demand.

A voyage by schooner from the north shore of the Gulf,
and turning the west end of Anticosti while bound for Gaspé,
gave me some sights of whales in spouting groups which
would be worth a voyage from New York to those waters to
witness.   Whales generally swim in pairs, unless they have
a calf, when that swims between them for protection; but I
saw several groups at a time of more than three in each, all
spouting like politicians.   Our tub of a schooner, which kept
" bidding and bobbing" like Mrs. Toodles at an auction, reminded me of the following couplet:

> " When to the wind we spread our sails,
>   Along the pathless ocean strolling,
>   Crammed in a tub stock full of nails,
>   Like Regulus, we die by rolling."

Having thus spent a few nights and days on the turbulent
Gulf of St. Lawrence, rising one bright morning unharmed in
our tub, which seemed cast to the whales, as they surrounded
us, we were elate with joy at the brilliant display which nature afforded in the bright heavens, sparkling waves, whales
spouting in every direction, the light-house looming on the
Isle of Anticosti, and the appearance of numerous beautiful
birds swimming about our craft, which we learned were puffins, a species of duck peculiar to the Gulf of St. Lawrence
near Anticosti.   These birds are about the size of a mallard,

but robed in scintillant plumage of green tipped with purple, and farther ornamented with a beak shaped like a parrot's, of a bright vermilion color.

As the sun rose above the snowy peaks of Labrador, the sails slackened, when half a mile to westward we saw slowly rise above the waves a white triangular fin, then an enormous head which spouted a large shower of spray high above the waves, next a huge back, and finally the enormous tail of a monster double the length of our schooner.

We were shocked at the appearance of the monster, its great size, and the enormous volume of water it spouted, and the wake and roaring splash which its breaking water and diving produced. The sailors informed us that it was a sulphur whale, one of the *Mammalia*, so vicious and powerful that whalers seldom or never attack that species.

In the book on "*Salmon-fishing in Canada*," by Colonel Sir James E. Alexander, author of an important work on explorations, he devotes a considerable space to the once supposed phenomenon of mirages. Those who have sailed near the Mingan Islands have doubtless observed the singular forms assumed by objects at a distance, which is caused by a peculiar state of atmosphere, and the different degrees of temperature and qualities of the waters intervening between the beholder of the mirage and the objects seen through it. The peculiar mirage along the Mingan Islands is supposed to be caused by the number of large rivers debouching in the Gulf there, and, from their rapidity, carrying waters a great way out on the Gulf which differ in temperature and quality from that upon which they apparently float on the surface.

It is stated that "the most remarkable mirages over water have occurred in straits," as those seen by Mr. Vance at Dover, and the celebrated Fata Morgana at Messina. In the St. Lawrence they present greater and more interesting varieties of ocular deception, as at Bic, Point des Monts, Mingan, and the Straits of Belle Isle.

To return to my subject. The sight of a whale-ship round-

ing the end of Anticosti, and several game-looking boats rowing away from her, increased our anxiety, as the sailors said
that we were in the midst of numerous shoals of commercial
whales, including the "fenners" and "hump-backs." The
white pectoral fin of the sulphur was seen to rise at intervals,
receding in distance, when all at once two huge black masses
arose before us and spouted. They proved to be a mother
and her calf, of the hump-back family. Nearer and more
near approached the boats from the whaler; and, after the
whales rose to spout, as they descended the boats quickened
their speed toward where they expected the next rise. This
was repeated several times, until at last, just as one of the
monsters rose, the man at the bow of the nearest boat plunged
the harpoon deep in his body near the heart.

> "Laugh at fear!
> Plunge it deep, the barbed spear!
> Strike the lance in swift career!
> Give him line! give him line!
> Down he goes through the foaming brine."

The instant rush of the infuriated fish drew the boat hissing
through the waters at a speed which soon hid it from our
view, rendering the sight really sublime; and when adding
that the mother whale followed, lashing the waves with her
tail and leaping like a salmon, the reader may picture to his
imagination—fishing!

The mother whale swam numerous times round her calf,
trying to entice it seaward away from its pursuers; but its
strength slowly failing with fatigue and loss of blood, it rose
to spout. Then might be seen the mother's tender solicitude
for her young, as she all but caressed it and coaxed it to follow her out of harm's way, and several times persuasively
swam a little distance, and then returned to assist it.

The boatmen were meantime hauling in line and coiling
it carefully in a tub made for the purpose, when, like lightning, off the whale started again, more rapidly, apparently,
than at first. The mother cavorted and disported around

her young, as if to bid it persist and escape the wicked whalers. But the firmly-fixed harpoon held the young whale to the tether, and after several runs it rose to the surface in order to make its last fight, to which all previous efforts seemed tame. It lashed the waves with a noise like thunder, and the spray caused by it and by the leaps and writhings of the agonized mother was carried more than a mile, causing a blinding mist for many rods around. Finally, all efforts failing, the young whale gave the final shudder and was dead, lying lifeless on the surface. Then went up the shouts of the boatmen, in which we joined; but a hauser, lashed to the tail of the dead whale, enabled the crews to float it slowly toward the whale-ship, which had drawn near. But the mother whale continued to lash the waters, as with snorting and blowing she evinced signs of fury until long after the blubber-spades had dissected much of the body, and a sea of blood surrounded the ship.

I will conclude this chapter with the eloquent peroration of the gifted Burke, made in the House of Commons in 1774: "As to the wealth which the colonists have drawn from the sea by their fisheries, you had that matter fully opened at your bar. You surely thought these acquisitions of value, for they seemed to excite your envy; and yet the spirit by which that enterprising employment has been exercised ought rather, in my opinion, to have raised esteem and admiration. And pray, sir, what in the world is equal to it? Pass by the other parts, and look at the manner in which the New England people carry on the whale fishery. While we follow them among the tumbling mountains of ice, and behold them penetrating into the deepest frozen recesses of Hudson's Bay and Davis's Straits; while we are looking for them beneath the arctic circle, we hear that they have pierced into the opposite region of polar cold—that they are at the antipodes, and engaged under the frozen serpent of the south. Falkland Island, which seemed too remote and too romantic an object for the grasp of national ambition, is but a stage and

Y

resting-place for their victorious industry. Nor is the equinoctial heat more discouraging to them than the accumulated winter of both poles. We learn that while some of them draw the line or strike the harpoon on the coast of Africa, others run the longitude and pursue their gigantic game along the coast of Brazil. No sea but what is vexed with their fisheries—no climate that is not witness of their toils. Neither the perseverance of Holland, nor the activity of France, nor the dexterous and firm sagacity of English enterprise, ever carried this most perilous mode of hardy industry to the extent to which it has been pursued by this recent people—a people who are still in the gristle, and not hardened into manhood."

THE STRIPED RED MULLET.

The striped red mullet, a beautiful fish of a pale pink color, but somewhat larger than the one known to the Romans, is found in considerable numbers on the English coasts. The mullets, like the cod and some other fish which feed in deep water, are furnished with long *feelers* attached to the lower jaw, supposed to be delicate organs of touch, by which these fish are enabled to select their food on the muddy bottoms. This fish is more gamy than the golden mullet of the American borders of the Atlantic, but it is vastly inferior for the table.

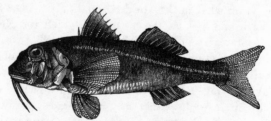

STRIPED RED MULLET.—*Mullus surmuletus.*

CHAPTER IV.

SALT-WATER FISHERIES.

COD-LIVER OIL.

MAINE and Massachusetts make annually about 5000 bbls. common oil, such as is generally used for tanning purposes, or 150,000 gals., at 80 cts. $120,000 00

200 bbls. superior oil, used for medical purposes, and made at Gloucester and Rockport, 6000 gallons, at $1 50........... $9,000 00

TONGUES AND SOUNDS.

The yearly catch of Gloucester vessels averages 1000 bbls., at $8................ $8,000 00

DRIED CODFISH.

Massachusetts. The average annual make is

350,000 quintals, at $6..$2,100,000 00

Maine. The average annual make is 200,000 quintals, at $6.. 1,200,000 00

$3,300,000 00

HALIBUT FISHERY.

Halibut caught by vessels of Gloucester, Massachusetts, average annually, for five years past, 10,000,000 lbs., at 10 cts..$1,000,000 00

Yearly catch by Boston vessels, 2,500,000 lbs., at 10 cts........ 250,000 00

$1,250,000 00

SMOKING SALMON AND HALIBUT.

One Boston house smokes 10,000 bbls. annually, at the average price per bbl. of $38. ....$380,000 00

Do., 10,000 bbls., at $10.. 100,000 00

Do., 13,000 quintals* of smoked halibut, 9 cts. per lb. 131,040 00

$611,040 00

THE EASTPORT FISHERY.

Fish caught and cured in the vicinity of Eastport, Maine :

30,000 boxes smoked herrings, 40 cts. $12,000 00

---

* A quintal is 112 lbs.

Brought forward..	$12,000 00
1500 bbls. herring oil, $30..	45,000 00
8000 quintals dried cod, $3...	24,000 00
20,000 quintals dried pollock, $2.....................................	40,000 00
10,000 " " hakes, $1 50.................................	15,000 00
500 bbls. liver oil, $30...	15,000 00
3000 bbls. pickled cod, $4..	12,000 00
5700 " " herrings, $4.......................................	22,800 00
1200 " " mackerel, $15.....................................	18,000 00
500 " " haddock, $2 50.	1,250 00
	$205,050 00

The foregoing statement is made by Captain S. Treat, of Eastport, and is an average annual catch for the past five years to 1868.

WHOLESALE FISH DEPARTMENT OF FULTON MARKET.

This includes fourteen establishments confined to the purchase and sale of food-fishes. The average annual sales by each is $150,000. Aggregate $2,100,000 00
In addition to these sales, they employ one hundred and eleven fishing-smacks, the average annual catches by each amounting to $12,000, or an aggregate of............................... 1,332,000 00

$3,432,000 00

SCOLLOPS.

The trade in scollops is annually increasing, but, like the other vast water-fields of *Crustacea*, the business is still embryotic and the trade undeveloped. East Greenwich, R. I., supplies 100 gallons daily for half the year, or 18,200 gallons at 75 cents... 13,650 00
Southport, Matatuck, Cutchogue, and Jamesport, on Long Island, supply in the aggregate six months 18,200 gallons at 75 cents.. 13,650 00

$27,300 00

SOFT-SHELL CLAMS.

Comstock & Co., of Fulton Market, sold last year 3,250,000 for $8000. It is estimated that this is about one sixth of the aggregate annual sale in the United States, which would render the sum total.............$48,000 00

I could not get an estimate on the business done in hard clams, though it is nearly or quite as large as that in soft shells.

SMELTS.

Trade in smelts is confined to six months, or to the inclement season of the year, for which time the sales in Fulton Market averaged 1,352,000 at 16 cents................................... $216,320 00

SALMON, FRESH AND SALTED.

One Boston house sells annually 10,000 bbls. salmon, the fresh
and salted fish averaging per bbl. $38............................. $380,000 00
100,000 bbls. herrings, cured and smoked in the manner of Yarmouth bloaters, $10 per bbl. 1,000,000 00

THE OYSTER INDUSTRY.

Of the delicious bivalve which "gets out of bed to be tucked in," it is impossible to arrive at an appropriate estimate of all which are canned for the
interior trade, and those sold in the shell for consumption in the Atlantic
States; but of the trade from Virginia to Massachusetts, it is computed
by the largest dealers in the industry that about 50,000,000 bushels are annually sold at 50 cents per bushel...............................$25,000,000 00

The following, copied from the Baltimore report of the industry in that single city for the past year, may give some
idea of the importance of this crustaceous bivalve:

OYSTERS AND CANNED GOODS.

This trade has been in fair activity throughout the year. The number of
houses prosecuting it now reaches about seventy-three, of which some forty
are strictly in the packing trade. The hands employed equal probably 5000
of both sexes in the various departments of shucking, packing, peeling, preserving, etc. Six to eight million bushels of oysters are consumed, one third
of which are packed raw, and the balance hermetically sealed. The cans required for these reach about 3,000,000 to 4,000,000 of half to one gallon
each, and require say 300,000 cases to pack them. The balance of the oysters, say some 4,000,000 bushels, are put up in hermetically sealed cans of 1,
2, and 3 pounds each, of which during the active season some 80 to 100,000
cans are daily packed, so that some 12 to 16,000,000 of cans are required for
this trade annually. It is estimated that some $14,000,000 to $16,000,000
are invested in this interest in and around Baltimore, and that the annual
product is worth some $6,000,000 to $7,000,000.

The number of vessels said to be engaged in that business
on the Chesapeake is over 1600, which give employment to
more than 6000 persons. Had the trade to California continued, the industry would have been greatly augmented; but
in that land of abundance fishes of nearly all kinds are more
numerous than on the Atlantic coast, so that there salmon is
too common for food, and the sardine canning industry bids
fair to supersede that of the Mediterranean.

THE CHESAPEAKE BAY FISHERY.

By the following estimate, made by Messrs. Monroe & Gemeny, of Alexandria—the largest fishery firm in the South —I am informed that 25,000,000 herrings are caught in about six weeks, and 5,000,000 shad are taken in the mean time, being in March and April. These are caught by from 20 to 25 shad fisheries, giving employment to about 1000 men and from 75 to 100 vessels. Of course, those include the fisheries along the Chesapeake, in both the states of Maryland and Virginia; yet I prefer to submit those samples of individual enterprise to the state or national reports, because they tell what may be done by showing what is being done by individual industry, instead of trying to deduce from the aggregate estimates in elaborate national or state reports what proportion of the income of all the states is derived from their fisheries; whereas these are confined to a small portion of our borders, and comparatively few men and small means are employed in them.

HADDOCKS.

The sale of "*finnan haddies*" per diem for six months of the year in
New York averages 1000 lbs., at 10 cents...............................$100 00
Boston, 2000 lbs.. 200 00
Portland, 1500 lbs... 150 00
$450 00
Thus amounting in six months for those three cities to............$81,900 00

It is stated by competent authority that 3000 lbs. of "*finnan haddies*" per day for six months in the year are cured in Portland, Maine, and that more than half of them are sold in the Dominion of Canada. It is becoming so large an industry in the United States that a brief account of its origin may prove interesting.

FINDON HADDOCKS.

The luxury known as "finnan haddies" was first cured at Findon, near Aberdeen, in Scotland. I can not learn when the industry was begun, but am informed that it was such a favorite dish with George IV. that it was constantly on his breakfast-table during the winter.

The curing of haddocks by moderately salting them and then smoking them over a smudge made of smothered peat was an invention of some pretty Scotch woman with—like most of her countrymen of both sexes—more brains and loyalty than money. She was, withal, a woman with an excellent *goût*, as her invention proved; for she had not followed the business long before many persons usurped her invention, and, instead of smoking them over the pure peat-reek fires, they used green wood of any kind that would make a smoke. Thus the Findon haddocks lost favor in some quarters; yet, poor as it was made by bad smoking, there was still left a degree of delicacy, and the flavor was still so much admired as to divide the interest with the Yarmouth bloater as a breakfast-fish. Finally, as the "schoolmaster abroad" ascertained that the waters on our Eastern coast teem with haddocks, he intimated their value as a breakfast luxury, when several members of Brother Jonathan's family were not long in seeing the point of interest in the question. The result is that, within the past five years, no industry has grown faster, according to its pasture of short capital, than has the manufacture and trade in Findon haddocks, the annual amount of which in the United States is not much short of half a million of dollars.

PRESERVING FOOD-FISHES FRESH.

The Yankee invention for refrigerating salmon in an atmosphere of such a degree of cold as is desired, and from which all dampness is excluded, has greatly increased the amount of consumption of fresh salmon in the border cities of the United States within the past three years. Already the Canadians are profiting by an invention which their proximity to salmon-waters renders of immense utility to them. This invention requires to be used when the fish are entirely fresh, and have not been much handled. It consists simply in placing the fish in the dry refrigerator the day that they are caught, and the sooner after they leave the aqueous element the better. Already the refrigerating process is in operation on railroads for the transmission of meats, fish, and fruits.

Of numerous other fishes than the salmon which are sold in a fresh condition, no reliable estimate can be made. They include thousands of tons of striped bass, cero, bonita, Spanish mackerel, sea bass, blackfish, squeteague, sheepshead, eels, flounders, flukes, crabs, lobsters, and several other kinds of coast and estuary fishes. It is, however, safe to state that they include more than half the number of pounds of fish consumed by the inhabitants of the states on the Atlantic border, and amounting annually to a value of many millions of dollars. Throughout winter the netting of striped bass is pursued along the shores of bays, sounds, and as far up the Hudson River as Peekskill, taking them at the latter place from under the ice. This practice should be inhibited by law.

Those who feel interested in the commerce of fishes will please excuse me for not condensing the statements by recapitulation. The few examples which I have submitted of the industry have been those of individual enterprise in a business which is destined soon to become one among the leading industries of the nation.

Part Fourth.

—⋈—

ANCIENT AND MODERN FISH-CULTURE.

CHAPTER I.

THE ART AMONG THE ANCIENTS.

 MONG the many arts
founded on pure phi-
losophy peculiar to
China, we find that
of propagating fishes
by artificial means to
have been practiced
there for many cen-
turies, as is proven
by their works, and
the intimate knowl-
edge of the art pos-
sessed by so many
of the inhabitants of
the Celestial Empire.

Father Duhalde, one of the earliest missionaries from
France to China, was the first to reveal to the Christian
world that the inhabitants of China might teach those of
Europe the art of water-farming. "In the great River
Yang-tse-kiang," said Father Duhalde, "not far from the
city Kieou-king-fou, of the province Kiang-si, at certain seasons of the year there assemble great numbers of vessels for
conveying away the fecundated eggs of fishes. Throughout
the month of May the river is barred at short intervals for
sixty miles with interlacings of osier and bulrushes, leaving
barely sufficient space for the passage of barks or double
chaloupes, with *lateen* sails, which are engaged in transporting ova." The reticulated weirs of osier and bulrushes are
close enough to catch and retain the ova, and the vendor

knows how to distinguish them with the naked eye when un-
practiced ones perceive nothing in the water. He therefore
dips up the water with a mixture of impregnated ova, which
many purchase in that condition, while he dips and fills vases
for others who purchase the fishes when first hatched. People are said to come from all parts of the empire for the
purchase of both eggs and fish wherewith to stock the waters
of their various districts.

Great care is bestowed on the vivified eggs placed in the
vases, and those having them in charge take turns in attending to them, so that they are never neglected either night or
day. At the end of some days, as the eggs disclose life, the
different species are removed into separate vases, and their
prices fixed and published. Father Duhalde stated that the
nett gain was often a hundred fold on the expense, and the
sale always certain, because fishes constitute a large share of
the food of the Chinese.

Many travelers from time to time referred to this practice
of the Chinese in propagating fishes, but their explanations
were always more or less vague. Father Huc, the mission-
ary, informed the French government that a great many mer-
chants of vivified fish-eggs came to the province of Canton,
and traversed the country for the sale of them to the proprietors of ponds and other preserved waters. Their merchan-
dise, being a sort of yellowish liquid, was contained in a cask.
It appeared to be oily water, similar to the color of the vase
(probably terra-cotta), in which it was impossible to distinguish with the naked eye the least animalcula or living thing.
For some *safèques*—small coin—they purchase a cup of that
turbid water, which is sufficient to stock a pond of considerable size. They pour the contents of the cup into the pond
or lake, and in a few days the eggs hatch, and by having
their preserves properly divided they keep up their stock of
fish. For the young fishes of the herbivorous families, such
as the carp, etc., they throw into the pond tender herbs for
food, augmenting the quantity as the fish enlarge. Carnivor-

ous fishes require some kind of meat, or a mixture in which meat or offal forms a part.

The fishes are fed in the morning and evening of each day, and, as they grow very fast, it becomes quite "a chore" for the boys and girls to gather them enough herbage, for they are so ravenous as to be appropriately compared to the silk-worms when forming cocoons. With generous feeding they attain to the weight of two or three pounds in fifteen days, when they cease growing, and are sold alive throughout the great centres of population.

The fish-culturists of Kiang-si raise uniquely fishes of a *goût* most exquisite. The sea-rabbit is the name given by them to a species at once the most delicate and prolific.

Fish-culture, or *pisciculture*, seems natural to the Chinese, who conduct the industry skillfully and successfully, culti-vating numerous species of herbivorous fishes, which they raise with great facility. Herbivorous fishes acclimatize much easier than the carnivorous. The French and other Europeans have commenced to import herbivorous fishes from Kiang-si; the red and gold fishes, originally imported from China, may be considered a luxury to the eye, and their sur-prisingly rapid increase in numbers without expense has in-duced the French to import such food-fishes as are prolific and of excellent flavor. The fresh-water fishes of commerce in China form much lighter and more digestible food than any fresh-water fishes of either Europe or America. They have cultivated their waters, and raised fishes for so many hundred years, and perhaps thousands, that their system is said to be much more perfect than any now practiced in Eu-rope or America; and as France has sent an agent to China to study up the subject from an Oriental point of view, it might be advisable for our government to instruct its embas-sadors to make all the discoveries possible, and report them for the benefit of fish-culture in the United States.

CHAPTER II.

FISH-CULTURE IN EUROPE IN EARLY TIMES.

THE date when fish-culture was commenced in Europe is not definitely known. Its introduction there is generally attributed to the Romans, among whom, it is stated by several writers, the art approached a remarkable degree of perfection. It is known to the student of antique inventions that, in the palmy days of ancient Rome, great attention was paid to *aquaculture*, and, by means of canals cut from the sea and the Bay of Naples to the ornamental lakes and ponds of the wealthy patricians, eminently those at Tusculum, and at other villas near Baiæ, the fishes of the sea were invited by men of taste to spawn in their preserves, which they did in great numbers, as is related by *Duval* in respect to the extensive preserves of Lucullus. But after the spawning season, and when the spent fishes sought a return to the sea, they were intercepted by wicker weirs or wire gates, and there captured and sold in the market! This last fact is sufficient evidence to prove to the modern angler or fish-culturist that the Romans knew little of the nature and habits of fish, or they would not have purchased spent fish, which is unwholesome food.

But in the evidence adduced thus far we see nothing to warrant the belief that the ancient Romans hatched fishes by the modern means of mingling the *roe* and *milt* of fishes, and placing them in a situation to be hatched. They did no more than invite or conduct fish from the sea to fresh-water feeding-grounds and spawning-beds. The Chinese had done more, for they divided rivers into spawning-beds, and before the spawn was hatched they removed it to hatching-vases.

Among the articles exhumed from Pompeii and Herculaneum, stored in the Treasury at Naples, I saw a glass vase of fish-eggs similar to those of the *genus Salmo*. Those eggs and their mode of preservation induced me to believe that a higher class of men inhabited Italy seventeen hundred years ago than do now in this iron age of intelligence. Is it not true that aggregations of high intellects—like celestial nebulæ, or the focal coruscation of rays of light and heat—cluster at different times on different parts of the earth, to reflect intellectual light to guide coming generations?

Well, it is stated that the inventions in ancient Rome, first devised to pamper the children of luxury, afterward were employed to supply subsistence to the nation. *Des viviers* having stocked their preserves with many ornamental fishes, whose graceful gambols, beautiful forms, and colors *chatoyantes* had delighted the ladies of that interesting period, did not disdain to encourage the increase of food-fishes also, with which their preserves were richly stocked.

But, if the Romans did not hatch fishes artificially, that they excelled in the cultivation of *Crustacea* can not be successfully refuted. The removal of oysters from one water and planting them in another was begun by Sergius Orata at the commencement of the Christian era, by bringing them from Brindisium and planting them in Lake Lucrin, which, according to the evidence of the *gourmêt* chief Crassus, greatly improved their flavor. Orata finally covered Lake Lucrin with reticulated paraphernalia made of wood, raised at one end on stone piers, and placed in numerous positions for the convenience of the deposit of oyster-spat. The Lake of Fusaro also, between the ruins of Cumæ and the promontory of Misenum—"the Avernus of the ancients"—being salt, was planted with oysters; and the plans for oyster culture adopted by the Romans were quite similar to those pursued in France at present.

My investigations of the rise and progress of fish-culture by the method of stripping the *ova* from the female and the milt from the male fish, and mixing them for vivification, induces me to impute its origin tò the monks—those men of genius who invented *eau da vie*—and who were ever engaged in investigations for ameliorating the wants of mankind. They found the waters idle, while the needs of the Church demanded that they should produce. They therefore applied themselves to the study of cultivating the waters, and in the fourteenth century — according to Baron Montgaudry, nephew to Buffon—*Dom Pinchion*, abbé of *Réome*, had discovered the plan of hatching fishes in boxes, the process described being quite similar to that now employed. The needs of the monastic orders for complying with the requirements imposed by their religion may be justly considered the motive cause which urged to this great discovery; and the monks not only cultivated the waters, but they left records of their progress, and gave us their opinion that the carp is the most profitable fish to propagate, and next in order is the tench. The pike is considered very useful to prevent the excessive multiplication of carps, for otherwise they soon become too numerous for their healthy condition in a pond.

At divers epochs the idea prevailed of introducing certain fishes into barren waters. The Lake Lovitel, in the department of *L'Isere*, never nourished a fish before 1670, when M. Garden placed trout in the lake, and they multiplied so that the lake has remained stocked with them ever since.

La pêcherie of Comachio, on the Adriatic, is of very ancient origin. Bonaveri, and, more recently, Spallanzani, professor in Reggio, Modena, and Pavia, have described the very extensive eel-fisheries there. In spring, when the eels ascend the rivers, the fish-farmers open communications from the basins to the lagunes of the sea, and the young eels penetrate in great masses through all the free passes. Retained in the basins, where they find nourishment abundant, they grow rapidly. At the time when their instinct teaches them to descend to the sea, the fish-farmers lead them by small artificial brooks whereby they are conducted into chambers from which they have no power to escape, and hundreds of thousands of eels are thus annually gathered and cured for market, because there is a greater number of fresh eels than is necessary to supply the markets of Italy.

At the commencement of the decade of the eighteenth century the brilliant discoveries of Spallanzani enriched the natural sciences, and proved beyond reasonable doubt the possibility of developing the mysteries which theorists had from time to time mooted, of impregnating the eggs of fishes artificially. He therefore took eggs of a frog, and impregnated them with the semen of a male frog. This he did before numerous witnesses, who saw the live frogs, and saw that from these eggs young frogs were hatched, and the triumph of the illustrious Italian naturalist was thus rendered complete.

In 1763 Lieut. Jacobi announced through a journal of Hanover the feasibility of the artificial fecundation of salmon and trout. Before, however, publishing his successful experiments, he endeavored to promulgate his discovery through the medium of celebrated naturalists, such as Buffon, De Fourcroy, and Gleditch, an eminent professor of Germany. "Les savants" of France appeared too much preoccupied to notice the Hanoverian lieutenant, especially as his writings were in German. Gleditch, who was not influenced by the same reasons, appeared impressed with the work of Jacobi, and he communicated extracts from the work to the Academy of Berlin through Baron Von Harbke.

In France the experiences relative to the artificial fecundation of fishes occurred some years later. The work of Jacobi was published in Paris in 1770. The *Marquis de Pezay*, in his *Soirées helvétiennes*, signalized the fortunate results obtained at Noterlem, including the information that England wished to recompense Jacobi by a liberal pension.

Two years thereafter, and twelve years after the successful experiments of Jacobi, Adamson, in his course at the *Jardin du Roi* in 1772, made known to his auditors the plan and practicability of artificial fecundation, stating that it was habitually practiced on the borders of the Weser, in Switzer-

Z

land, in the Palatinate of the Rhine, and in the mountains and elevated parts of Germany. For this object, he said, they take by the head a female salmon in November or December, or a trout in December or January, the times when these fishes deposit their *ova*. These fish are held over a vase with a quart of water in it, and by a light pressure on the abdomen downward, the female vents the roe. They then take a male salmon, and rub his belly down with the palm of the hand in the same manner: milt falls on the roe and mixes with it, when it is placed in a running stream and covered lightly with gravel, and after several months the fish hatch.

The Course of Natural History, by Adamson, was republished in Paris in 1845, when its information on fish-culture first attracted attention to the truths published by him seventy years previously.

The copy of the manuscript of Jacobi was sent to France by German officials, and thus became finally translated. Those who are educated to be courtiers or politicians do not always read. Apropos of this truth: the artificial fecundation of *roe* by Jacobi, imparted through his *intermediaires*, the Count de Goldstein and the naturalist Gleditch, became neglected and forgotten. During sixty years no one dreamed of reading the "*Traité des pêches de Duhamel*," the veritable work of Jacobi. The end of the eighteenth century did not retain a souvenir of the success obtained at Noterlem for the artificial multiplication " *des Truites et des Saumons.*"

If the Chevalier Bufalina, of Cesena, had succeeded in fecundating several fishes, no one saw any novel feature in the operation not developed by Spallanzani; and if Jacobi had invented a successful plan of artificial fish-culture in Germany, and if, in the region of the Rhine and in Switzerland, where fishermen were successfully practicing fish-culture and enriching their streams by it, yet the world was as ignorant of its true bearings upon the needs and prosperity of a country as if nothing had ever been said or written upon the subject; so the progress may thus far be counted as *nil*.

CHAPTER III.

FISH-CULTURE OF THIS CENTURY.

M O D E R N fish-culture is indebted to only thirty years' practice for all the wonders it has achieved. The early part of the present century was unfavorable to the development of industry. War engaged the attention of the civilized world. Many improvements known in France, Italy, Germany, and England at the commencement of their revolutions, were lost to this century; but the calm which peace restored fructified genius and utilized its discoveries.

In 1820, MM. Hivert and Pilachon, two inhabitants of the *Haute-Marne,* fecundated eggs of trout. After hatching, they took the "*alevins*" (the young, before the umbilical sac is absorbed) to the waters which they desired to stock. These facts, though confirmed by *M. de Montgaudry* and *M. Jourdier,* did not electrify the public mind, or even cause a single government to put forth an effort for restocking depleted waters to cheapen food. So the matter lay dormant again seventeen years, when John Shaw, of Scotland, fecundated the eggs of a salmon, and hatched them by artificial means, which resulted in a memoir of his experiments relative to the propagation of salmon. But this, instead of causing efforts to be-

come more numerous and of wider scope, was merged in the
side issue of the "parr question," which absorbed attention,
as indicated by an important article in BLACKWOOD of that
year upon the "Transmutations of the Salmon."

The first person in France who seriously called general attention to the study and practice of artificially stocking the
waters was *Baron de Rivière.*   He urged the peculiar advantages obtained by leading the young eels from estuaries up
artificial streams, and capturing them, to distribute in convenient proportions throughout the waters of France.

In the history of modern *pisciculture* a little event occurred
without noise in 1844, in the Department of the Vosges, which
gave rise a few years later to much excitement.

A fisherman of *La Bresse,* in the commune of Remiremont,
situated in one of the most elevated parts of the canton of
Saulxures—*Joseph Rémy* by name—having seen the trout,
at other times numerous in the streams of the mountains, diminishing so fast as to produce grave prejudice to his industry, the rivers and the brooks in the Vosges having been
dried up by a long drought in 1842, sought from Nature a
remedy.   This humble man, endowed with a spirit of observation, studied with intelligence the habits of the trout from
the moment of hatching, until he arrived at the idea of artificial fecundation, and, by numerous experiments, finally succeeded in arranging the hatching apparatus into compartments, as it is done at this day, though commencing, like
Jacobi, by placing the fecundated ova in a trough, with
wire-grating cover and ends in the trout-stream, letting the
natural running of the stream hatch the eggs, which were
slightly covered with gravel in the trough.

Rémy, chagrined at not knowing any person with means
from whom he might hope for assistance by communicating
his discoveries, became melancholy and fell sick, when he
confided his secret to the keeper of the little tavern where
he boarded, by name *Antoine Géhin.* This inn-keeper was
to him a *collaborateur,* and soon became full of zeal both as

a fisherman and *pisciculturist*. The names of *Rémy* and *Gé-hin* were destined to become indissoluble. They unveiled the advantages of the discovery to a few notable persons; but our two poor copartners met with the difficulties common to those who discover any strange improvement by means of a switch from the track of Nature. In the mean time the inspector of primary schools in the Vosges received information of the discovery, and communicated it to the Society of Emulation. This society, being of high celebrity, occupied itself at once upon the question. In a report by M. Sarrazin on the recompenses accorded to agriculture and industry by the Society of Emulation, the proceedings of *Rémy* and *Géhin* were described. M. Micard, General Guard of the Forests, had favored the early efforts of *Rémy*, and gave him in spawning-time the liberty òf the brooks of the forests.

In spite of the memoir of John Shaw—*malgré* the results which were vauntingly promised to England—*malgré* the fortunate experiments of *Rémy* and *Géhin*, encouraged by the Society of Emulation for the Vosges, all slept again.

The interest in the success of those men, whose ardor and industry greatly multiplied the number of fishes, lasted no longer than the transient sound of the murmurs of the rivers and brooks which had proved the theatre of their exploits.

But on the 23d of October, 1848, M. *de Quatrefages*, in pursuit of the development of certain animals, fished up the communication of Count Goldstein, and read at the *Academie des Sciences* a memoir demonstrative of artificial fecundation being the means for obviating the causes of destruction to the eggs of fishes.

The lecture of M. *de Quatrefages* at the Academy of Sciences was published by numerous journals, which projected the subject into the air of public favor, and the assurance of the lecturer that a pursuit of the subject would be the birth of a new industry important to the world, decided the commencement of action. All the world was at once going into the artificial fecundation project, and founded the most brilliant hopes of the new art of *pisciculture.*

The information of *Quatrefages'* lecture reached Epinal, and was seen by the Society of Emulation in the Vosges about four months after it was delivered. On the 2d of March, 1849, the secretary of the society wrote to *M. de Quatrefages* that two fishermen of *La Bresse* had been engaged since 1844 at stocking the waters of the Vosges with trout produced by artificial fecundation.

All at once, loud became the acclamation in favor of *Rémy* and *Géhin,* as if the echo had gained strength by the years in which the truth had lain dormant. Next an English engineer, M. Gottleib Boccius, announced the great advantage which the inhabitants of the Vosges had derived from re-peopling their rivers by the aid of artificial fecundation, and hatching fishes in boxes where they were secure from numerous enemies of both water and air. He had published a small treatise in 1841 with the object of benefiting landed proprietors in stocking their waters, and more especially their artificial fish-ponds. But the French philosophers regarded the discovery in a national aspect. Hence one of the *savants* most illustrious, M. Dumas, who was minister of Agriculture and Commerce, charged the most authoritative naturalist, M. Milne Edwards, to examine and give an opinion upon the divers essays published in England, Germany, and France upon the subject of stocking fluvial waters with fish.

On the 26th of August, 1850, M. Milne Edwards addressed a report to the minister, in which he reviewed the work of Jacobi, and noticed the success of *Rémy* and *Géhin* with marked commendation for their perseverance in perfecting fish-culture, whereby they had restocked the streams of the canton, besides having discovered a new industry for France. He also named a dozen important rivers and lakes which they had restocked with trout, concluding with impressively recommending them to government favor. He said they had done more than to stock the waters with trout, for they had stocked them with frogs also, because the spawn of these time-beaters is an aliment which the young trout search with avidity; and the tadpole furnishes an excellent pasture for trout more advanced in age.

For fifteen years Géhin had been working under the full knowledge of what now engaged the sages of political economy. The subject enlarged, as they thought of stocking the waters of France with all the choice fishes of the world; and, conformably with the view explained by M. Milne Edwards, a commission was named by the Minister of Agriculture and Commerce, dated September 28, 1850. The commission included MM. Milne Edwards, Valenciennes, members of the Institute; Susanne, Inspector of Forests; de Bon, Commissioner of Marine; de Franqueville, Chief of Navigation and of the Ports, and Minister of Public Works; Monny de Mornay, Chief of the Division of Agriculture, of the Department of Agriculture and Commerce; Coste, Professor of Embryogony at the College of France; Doyere, Professor of Zoology at the National *Agronomique* Institute.

The decree was signed by Dumas, and in the spring of 1851, M. Valenciennes—the ichthyologist—received a mission from the Ministry of Agriculture and Commerce to visit and procure the large fishes of the rivers in Germany wherewith to stock the lakes and ponds of France. He succeeded in obtaining several species, of which he conveyed to Paris the living individuals, including *sandre, genus Lucioperca,* Lin., the *silure,* one of the most voracious fishes in creation, the average size of which is large enough to dine eighteen persons.

The *silures* (silurus glanis), with the sandres and a dozen *lotes* (eel-pouts), were placed in the reservoirs at Marly. The selection of fishes speaks unfavorably for the taste of *M. Valenciennes.* The *sandre* grows large enough to dine eight persons, but is a dry fish; the eel-pouts are detestable, and disgusting to behold; the *glanis* is similar to a Missouri River catfish! Of this selection wherewith to stock the fresh waters of France, not one lived to leave any posterity.

M. Coste then advised that the numerous ponds of Versailles be employed as "stables" wherein to propagate fishes for the waters of France, believing that in those spacious basins fishes which inhabit alternately the fresh and salt waters, such as the salmon, shad, lamprey, and plaice, might be cultivated. The advice was followed with unsuccessful result. In the mean time, two engineers of bridges, *MM. Detzem* and *Bertol*, made large profits by peopling the *Canal du Rhône*. They had been invited by the *préfet* of Doubs to verify the method in use in the Vosges, when, with assistants, they hatched in four months 3,382,000 eggs of salmon, trout, perch, pike, etc. On May 7th, 1851, they placed in basins confided to their care 1,583,111 fishes recently hatched.

The facility for hatching fishes by millions induced them to calculate how many fishes might live in the fresh waters of France. Estimating the actual population to be twenty-five millions of fishes, they concluded that by four years' artificial hatching the number would be increased to three billions, one hundred and seventy millions, and yield a revenue of more than nine hundred millions francs.

It was evident that they had consulted but one side of the question, and that the least difficult. Myriads of fishes may easily be hatched, but the questions of greater import are, how are they to be protected, subsisted, and made to grow? These are the questions which most seriously address themselves to the student of modern fish-culture. The brains of Bertol and Detzem were made dizzy by the presence of a calculation which proved millions of revenue easily obtained, and they exclaimed, "Is it possible to endow France with such a revenue?" On the examination of results so unexpected, no member of the Fisheries' Commission evinced a sentiment of distrust, stating that they were aware the calculation produces the same impression on all those who examine the subject.

Bertol and Detzem, encouraged by the Minister of Agriculture and Commerce, followed their work with great zeal, and, established at *Loechlebrun*, near Huningue, continued the operations of hatching trout and salmon on an extensive scale. By their second report in March, 1852, they announced that since the November preceding 722,600 eggs had yielded 700,000 fishes.

From the day when M. De Quatrefages called attention to the advantages of artificial fecundation for repeopling the waters of France, M. Coste occupied himself incessantly upon fish-culture. He explained the experiments on alimentation and growth of young eels, which ascend the streams every spring. These fishes, nourished by the *débris* of the butcher-shops cemented into a sort of pie, are fattened and made to grow very fast, attaining to the weight of several pounds in a single season.

In 1853, the Minister of Agriculture and Commerce, for the object of founding an establishment of fish-culture at Huningue, accorded a credit of 30,000 francs. This credit, M. Coste stated, "is to be used in undertaking one of the most grand experiments of which the natural sciences have ever given an example." He also described the method for preparing the food for young salmon and trout with a pie formed of butchers' offal, or of horse-flesh boiled. A knowledge of the advantage of this feed was acquired by the experiments of Dr. Lamy at the artificial hatchings in the *parc du Maintenon*.

In 1856, the subject of fish-culture engaged more or less the attention of a majority of the best minds in France, whether men of state or of science, or men of wealth and enterprise. Though the felicitations and encouragement of the fishermen of the Vosges had not been cooled or diminished, yet the book-philosophers, having read up, became aware that hatching fishes by art had engaged the minds of sages in other ages; and as that was the most simple part in the train of successfully restocking waters, they were studying and experimenting to acquire a more perfect knowledge of the nature, habits, preferable haunts, and means of subsistence. M. de

Tocqueville had determined that a strong light was injurious, and that a lamp or candle should not be thrust before young fishes. This was one of the reasons for placing the government breeding apparatus at Huningue under. cover; another was to maintain in the hatching-troughs nearly an even temperature throughout the winter while hatching game fishes of the *genus Salmo*, that spawn late in autumn; for these, while young, are much more delicate than common fishes, which (spawning in spring) hatch in a few days, and require comparatively no care in the process or in the kinds of feed; for, as they come into the world without a sac of provision to last them a month suspènded to the umbilical cord, nature prepares them for fighting their way for food from the moment when they leave the shell.

Géhin had visited Paris in 1850, and was presented to Louis Napoleon, then president of the republic, as quite a personage, and received from the government, in compliance with the promise of M. Milne Edwards, the mission to stock the rivers of several departments.

There were 50,000 brook and lake trout introduced to the waters of the *Bois de Boulogne* in 1856, where they grew rapidly. At this time many of the public waters throughout France, which had rested dormant, began to astonish and delight the neighborhoods with. the leaps above water of amber beauties, which formed miniature rainbows in the gleams of the sun, and many peasants regarded this novel gift of life and beauty as a providential blessing on Napoleon's reign.

Reports of successes in *pisciculture* poured in monthly more numerously from every department. The waters were everywhere stocked with young fishes, which were doing well. The ponds, lakes, and reservoirs in public parks were each annually hatching 25,000 to 50,000 of the *genus Salmo* for the benefit of the public rivers of France.

In the departments generally, the zeal of the *préfets* kept pace with that of the government, and men of science and the *Conseils Généraux* voted the sums to successfully operate the enterprises.

Thus the great work continued to proceed with unvarying success until 1862, when the Minister of Agriculture and Commerce published a history of the perfect success of Huningue, which includes seventy acres laid out into artificial creeks, ponds, and hatching-houses. The statistics in this history were furnished by *M. Courses, Ingenieur en chef des travaux du Rhin*, to whom application should be made for vivified roe wherewith to stock waters in the United States. By my advice, Seth Green made such order in the autumn of 1865, and in the spring of 1866 the eggs came to the New York Custom-house, where official and other delays detained them until they died. The French government had generously presented Mr. Green 20,000 fecundated salmon ova, so nearly hatched as to show the eyes of the *alevins*, carefully packed them in moss, and shipped them gratuitously! And then to know that our government was so callous to the material interests of the people as not only to have neglected to make any effort toward reducing the prices of food-fishes, but to have actually rendered the revenue officers a barrier against the efforts by men of enterprise who would embark their own money in it, is humiliating!

I humbly ask, Is it not the duty of Congress to authorize the Minister of the Interior to appoint a commission for the improvement of the fisheries in the United States? Individual states can not, unaided by the federal government, import either *ova* or young fishes of choice quality from abroad. Without the seal of a United States commissioner, the collectors of revenue have no discretion but to destroy the importation by delay, exposure to heat or cold, or to the air. Any authority given to United States consuls on the other hemisphere would prove ineffectual, for there are no consuls near the great *piscicultural* establishments; and, in fact, since the fiasco of the Acclimatization Society in the preserves of Mr. Francis Francis at Twickenham, there is no establishment of fish-culture left in Europe which supplies fecundated *ova* but the national one of Huningue, and by this one all applicants are served—by order of the French government—free of expense.

The liberality of France in bestowing ova and young fishes on all applicants did not prevent her from deriving the respectable revenue in 1862 for her fresh-water fisheries of $4,000,000. In 1861 the Huningue establishment distributed about 9,000,000 ova, and in 1862 about 12,000,000.

The paramount reason for artificial culture is based on the known fact that of every thousand salmon or trout hatched in a stream in the natural way, not more than one arrives at marketable size; and as a salmon yields about one thousand ova to the pound, a pair of salmon would scarcely yield twenty-five per cent. if hatching in a stream where the eggs and alevins are unprotected, while if the 20,000 eggs were hatched artificially and the young salmon protected, the increase to marketable size would generally be two thousand per cent.

The numerous successes resulting from artificial propagation, and restocking and newly stocking waters in France, has had a favorable influence throughout the civilized world, so that within a few years Belgium, Holland, Switzerland, Germany, Italy, and Spain have establishments of fish-culture.

On the British Isles great results have been accomplished near Galway and on the River Tay, so that the rentals of some fisheries have increased fifty per cent. Through the enterprise of Mr. Francis, of the *Field*, some of the waters of Australia have been stocked by ova transported from England—fifteen thousand miles! He has also succeeded in stocking a river in New Zealand in the same manner. The River Plenty, first stocked in Tasmania, has proved a success in both trout and salmon.

That the gigantic rebellion has delayed action by the United States government is quite natural; but one of the paramount duties of government is to increase the stock of food-fishes in the waters throughout the Union. Reports from the French government have been forwarded to the President, and by him they have been laid before Congress, so that the subject will doubtless soon be acted on nationally.

Through the efforts of individual states, much has been done within the past three years. Influenced by an intelligent enterprise for which the states of New England are justly celebrated, each of those states has appointed a Fisheries Commission, and the following extract from a report of progress in one state may be accepted as a fair sample of all

" Of the 40,000 spawn recently placed for incubation in the Cold Spring trout-ponds at Charleston, New Hampshire, for the Connecticut River, the first salmon were hatched December 11th, 1865. The eyes of the embryo salmon were first clearly seen in the egg about November 25th. The eggs were taken from the parent salmon on the Miramichi October 10th, making 62 days as the period of incubation.* The first trout which broke shell at these hatching-works this season came out on November 9th, 35 days from the time when the roe and milt were shed by the parent fishes."

Fish-culture is a success. It is not only triumphant, but it is almost miraculous. Waters hitherto worse than useless may be made a hundred fold as profitable as any equal number of acres of land, and with not a tithe of the labor. But these truths, so palpably patent to many intellectual minds of the present day, are almost a sealed book to the mass of the rising generation. In view, therefore, of these facts, and the depressing truth that the fishes of the coast and inland waters are annually decreasing, while by immigration and natural causes our nation is increasing in population faster than any other on the globe, is it not advisable to make the art of fish-culture a study in the agricultural colleges?

Up to the present time the inauguration of plans for pro-

---

* Mr. Francis and other fish-culturists are not in favor of employing water so warm as to hatch in so short a time, believing that the young fish are not so hardy as those hatched in colder water.

tecting fisheries by laws, and increasing the numbers of fishes by aqua-culture and fish-culture, are due to the efforts put forth by sportsmen's clubs, scattered throughout the United States as offshoots from the parent New York Sportsmen's Club. Too much praise can not be awarded those benevolent institutions, united solely for the public good, for which they shun no duty through fear of the poacher's hatred or the malevolence of dealers in stolen goods. The poacher both hates and fears them, while they are the principal reliance for guaranteeing the public that the laws for the protection of fish and game will be sustained.

If the national and state governments will unite in stocking and protecting the fresh waters, they will soon arrive at truths sufficiently luminous from which to form data for laws adequate to govern the whole question. To the ignorance of legislators may henceforth be attributed the lack of suitable laws for the protection and stocking of water-farms of millions of acres, which might be rendered a means of recreation for the improvement of health, while offering cheap and luxurious food to the million.

CUTTLE-FISH.—*Sepia officinalis.*

CHAPTER IV.

NATURAL HISTORY OF THE SALMON.

Near head of stream, in crystal spring,
　　Or recess of the strand,
The salmon drops its precious eggs
　　Amid the pure white sand ;
And here the infant fish disport
　　Beyond the harm of tides,
Each swarming shoal resplendent
　　With dotted silvery sides.

ROM the want of data, the nature and habits of salmon were a sealed book to naturalists until, through the discovery and practice of fish-culture by artificial means, some mysteries in physiology were interpreted.

In the natural history of the salmon, two questions occur which have presented a good deal of difficulty to *pisciculturists* and naturalists in arriving at just conclusions. The first is, How long do the young salmon inhabit the fresh-water streams in which they were hatched before they migrate to the sea? The second is, How long do they inhabit the sea before they return as grilse to the rivers in which they were bred?

A salmon has properly four stages of existence. The first is when it is a parr, or a small bright fish with dark bars across the sides, which are commonly called the parr marks.

The second is when it puts on the silvery scales of the grilse, which occurs when it is about to emigrate to the sea. It appears as if the little pet, when in the parr state, required some provision against the novel effects of salt water which it is about to encounter, for nature furnishes it with a new suit of scales, bright and silvery as those of the parent salmon. These begin to develop themselves just previously to the first migration of the fish. The scales form apparently over the old skin, and in doing so they obscure the parr marks, and the fish becomes a smolt, or a miniature grilse; but that it is the same fish may easily be seen by rubbing off a few of those new scales, when the parr marks are plainly seen which were hidden beneath them. These scales are at this time very lightly attached to the skin, and can be easily detached, coming off even by the mere handling of the fish; and this insecurity of the attachment of the scales continues throughout the whole period of grilsehood, or until the fish becomes a veritable and mature salmon, when whether it develops a new suit of scales is not known, but the scales certainly become much more firmly fixed to the skin, and are far more difficult to remove. But the point in debate is how long the parr remains in the river before it becomes a smolt. Now experiment has shown us thus much, viz., that a large portion of the parr become smolts in about fifteen months, that is, supposing them to have been hatched from the egg in the fall, or say in the winter. They live in the river over the next autumn, and do not become smolts and migrate to sea until the next succeeding spring. It has been found that a very large proportion of them do not become smolts and migrate even then, but stay in the river yet another year, and so do not put on the smolt scale and migrate until the next succeeding spring. Thus some remain in the rivers altogether two years and two or three months, and others remain even for another year still, and do not migrate till the third year. These facts for a long time puzzled naturalists, and gave rise to the supposition that there was another fish of

the salmon species which *never* went to the sea, called the
"Salmo samulus," because, after the great annual migration
of the smolts, parr were yet found in the rivers, and it was
thought that as all parr became smolts in fifteen months,
those which staid behind must be of another species altogether. But science and fish-culture have dispelled this error, and it is now known that the "Salmo samulus" is a
myth.

When the smolt went down to the sea for the first time, it
was generally supposed that it returned to the river again in
a period of from two to four months, and its extraordinary
and unusal increase was always cited as one of the most valuable qualities of the salmon; for, if it could grow from the
weight of only two to three ounces to eight or ten pounds in
three months, it was almost a *lusus naturæ*. But, though
smolts do grow very remarkably under favorable circumstances, a strong doubt has been thrown upon the fact of salmon
growing quite so fast as this, *from the smolt state*, by experiment and experience; for it has been found uniformly—in
all cases where the waters were what are termed *virgin
waters*, that is, waters never before inhabited by salmon—that
when such waters were stocked with young salmon fry, or
with ova laid down for hatching, a period of fifteen instead
of three months invariably elapsed before the emigrating
smolts came back to the river as well-grown grilse of six or
seven pounds' weight; and in the instance of much larger
grilse, as those which are at times met with of even eleven
pounds' weight, that a yet longer period may have elapsed.
This, however, is merely conjecture. In the late remarkable
experiments in Australia, where no such thing as a salmon
ever was known, it was clearly proved that the smolts were
a year and some months at sea before they returned, and in
other waters never before tenanted by salmon the same result has ensued. This is very strong evidence *against* the
two or three months' theory, particularly when the evidence
supporting that theory was gathered from well-stocked rivers,

where there could not fail to arise great difficulties in identifying the fish upon which experiments had been tried; for the uncertainty and difficulty of marking a parr of two ounces, which is to grow to sixty or seventy times that weight before it can be caught again and identified, can not fail to be very great indeed. However, this is still a moot question, and it has not been as yet satisfactorily determined, though it would seem that the soundest and most reliable evidence is in favor of the fifteen months' theory rather than the other.

When the grilse returns to the river, it spawns for the first time as a grilse, in which, its third stage of existence, it is perfectly distinguishable from the salmon; for not only are the scales loose and easily detached, but the fish is more slender and delicate in shape than the adult salmon, and the tail is much more forked. Having spawned, it becomes what is called a kelt or foul fish. The flesh is white, and the fish is out of condition and unwholesome to eat. It then goes down to the sea by easy stages, and there, by the aid of the healthful salt waters and plenteous food, it soon recovers its condition and grows rapidly, often increasing four or five pounds or more in weight. In the course of a few months (and this point is clearly ascertained and settled) it returns again to the river, but in the mean time it has lost its grilse form and become a veritable salmon. The scales now are hard and firm, the fish of a hardier, rounder make, the tail has lost its forked shape, and it has reached its fourth and last stage of existence.

This change in the form of the fish actually at one time led to the belief that salmon and grilse were of a different species, and some few persons stoutly advocated this view; but the ova of salmon have been found to produce grilse, and marked grilse have been retaken as salmon, so that there are not the slightest grounds for such a wild supposition now; and, indeed, the belief always was a very partial one, and confined to one or two wrong-headed individuals, so that it is now entirely exploded. As a salmon, it continues in the same course of existence until it is cooked, or dies of old age, or of wounds and weakness from incessant fighting at the breeding-time. It seeks the river every year, as is supposed, though this is but assumption, which it is almost impossible to prove, and whether it breeds every year or only at intervals it is hard to say. The general creed, however, is, that it does breed every year, and all that it requires from man is a little reasonable forbearance, and better protection at the breeding season until it again reaches the sea; and if it is able to reach the higher ranges of spawning-beds, it will speedily crowd our rivers with delicious food, and the means of healthful and magnificent sport. In these respects the capacity of American rivers is second to that of none in the world. Our rivers ought to swarm with salmon; and when we hear of rivers in England, ridiculously small by comparison with our own, yielding their $100,000 a year, and enormous revenues besides, do we not feel it to be a sin and a shame that such splendid capabilities as ours should be suffered to be behind them, and to fall into neglect and disuse, and that such important resources should be lost to the country and to the consumers throughout the Union? If an American wants salmon-fishing, he must go either to Canada or Scotland for it, and this is disgraceful. We have many good coast and estuary fishes, but none equal to the salmon in all respects. Is there any reason why we should not have the best, and plenty of it? England and France are both putting their shoulders to the wheel. Have we less energy and determination than they?

DEVELOPMENT OF THE SALMON.

PROCESS OF INCUBATION.

The egg of any fish of the *genus Salmo*, before impregnation with the milt of the male fish, is the color of the yolk of a hen's egg, and apparently of about the same consistency, being a mixture of albumen and oil. In this particular the egg of the salmon differs from those of the families *Clupeidæ* and *Gadidæ*, which appear as infinitesimal atoms of albumen, enlarging tenfold within an hour after impregnation, turning entirely white, and the fish is hatched in a less number of hours than it takes of days for the *genus Salmo*. Incubation with all the salmon families is slow, the egg indicating no appreciable increase in size by fructification; but, being porous, with tubes and globules, scientifically termed *micropyles*, the milt fills them, and they present the appearance of white globules in the egg, as represented by Fig. 1, and enlarged like Fig. 2. After the egg has remained in running spring

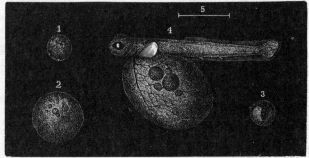

Fig. 1. Salmon egg of natural size after fecundation.   Fig. 2. Salmon egg enlarged, to show the vesicles and globules.   Fig. 3. Salmon egg in which the embryo is perceptible.   Fig. 4. Alevin just hatched, enlarged, and showing the umbilical vesicle. Fig. 5. Natural length of the alevin.

water of temperatures ranging from 40° to 50°, the egg will disclose the shape of the embryo salmon in from fifty to seventy days,* as illustrated by Fig. 3.   After the embryo becomes perceptible, and the eyes tolerably distinct, within a few days—say from five to fifteen—the salmon will hatch into the shape of Fig. 4, as enlarged from the natural size, indicated by the length of line, Fig. 5.   Suspended to the umbilical cord is a sac containing aliment for the alevin, on which it subsists by absorption from twenty-five to forty days, when the tiny creature takes its second form.   The egg,

* Salmon have been hatched in fifty-five days, and trout in thirty-five days, in water 55°; but Mr. Francis recommends spring water of from 40° to 45°, while the Cold Spring trout-ponds at Charleston, N. H., are excellent hatching-waters, and they are said to be 60° as mean temperature.

from the date of fructification to the birth of the fish, varies
from 60 to 120 days, the time required being dependent upon
the quality and temperature of the water, with the condition
of quiet and shade necessary to accelerate incubation.

While the umbilical vesicle is attached to the tiny fish it
is called an "alevin" (name borrowed from the French), but
after its absorption it is known as a "fry," or "penk." Now
it sculls along and seeks its food from imperceptible particles,
as animalculæ of the stream and the tiny fledglings falling
to the surface, or rising from the bottom to burst from their
embryotic state and take wing at the top of the stream. Like

SALMON FRY—*a, the natural length.*

the young of the finest breeds of animals on land, it appears
more delicate and less able to contend for subsistence than
do those of coarser natures. In its second form it is not
beautiful, and few would suppose it a young salmon. Its
transverse bars are plainly marked, and within three months
after its birth it assumes lighter shades, and carmine spots
begin to develop, when it becomes a parr.

This specimen is half the natural length, retaining its natural proportions. Though only between five and six inches in
length, the parr from which I made this copy was taken by me

A PARR EIGHT MONTHS OLD.

on the fly and hook with which I had that morning brought
two goodly-sized salmon to gaff. This fact proves the real

game of the pet. It was all life—a translucent thing of action—having a dark drab back, barred sides, and seven dots
of carmine on each side, which were brighter than any burnished metal or precious stone, and about the size of pigeon-
shot. It was the most anxious and voracious creature that I
had ever captured, and so sat down at once on the bank of
Rattling Run to sketch this liveliest specimen of fish kind
that I had ever seen. During the month of August parr of
the last fall and winter's hatch take their places on the reefs,
and nip the wings of flies intended for their parents; especially is this so of the part of the shoal intended to visit the sea
with the next spring freshets.

It will be perceived that while this fish has the parr rays,
or the horizontal bars peculiar to the parr, its head is taking
better form, the mouth apparently not so large, and the white
scales are almost beginning to appear; but this parr is not

A PARR FIFTEEN MONTHS OLD.
Half the natural length ; proportions natural.

to visit the sea until it arrives at two years of age or more.
Those of the shoal which do not visit the sea until after having spent two autumns in fresh water develop less rapidly
than do such as visit the sea after spending fifteen months in
the river. There being no longer a " parr controversy," the
next specimen, of the same shoal as this one, will illustrate
the difference in the development of those intended to become
voyagers on the second spring after their birth.

This fish, of the same shoal and age as the parr, is the part
of the same hatch intended for visiting the sea after remaining only one summer in the stream of its birth. Nature, more
careful than man in protecting the families of animal creation,

sends only half the shoal to sea at a time; the remaining
part of the shoal will follow next year, or perhaps a few will
remain three summers in the river before resorting to marine

A Smolt Fifteen Months Old.

feeding-grounds.   In the mean time we lose sight of the first
detachment, which falls back from pool to pool, and descends
rapids and falls tail foremost until it arrives in the estuary,
where it faces to the right about and prepares to protect
itself from the monsters of the deep.   For some days, and
perhaps weeks, it dallies in the lower reaches and estuary,
feeding on small caplin, shrimp, and the roe of coarser fish until its burnished sides form an armor to protect it against the
briny deep.   Where the marine feeding-grounds of the salmon are it is impossible to state from indubitable data.   Salmon are sometimes found in soundings off the Isle of Jersey,
several hundred miles from any salmon river, and yet in Canada the netters capture all their fishes approaching their rivers on the north shore of the St. Lawrence from the west,
when the sea is at the east.   That this *genre* of fishes, like all
others habitually visiting fresh-water streams to spawn, return and enter the rivers of their birth, is well authenticated,
while it has been satisfactorily proven that if scared away
from the estuary by nets or other unnatural fixtures they
will enter other rivers.

   In the physical transmutations of the salmon, from the time
it breaks the egg and hides about in crevices with a part of
the egg attached to its abdomen, to the time when it fully
matures into an adult salmon, there is no form it takes which
is so graceful and beautiful as that of the grilse, the last stage

short of the mature salmon. A shoal of them is like a joyous ball-party in full costume. It lacks the *embonpoint* of the salmon as much as the young people of a gay ball-party do that of their parents. The grilse—when attached to a hook—plays more gayly and with less judgment than does the full-grown salmon, skipping about and playing with great energy, and never stopping to sulk, or, more properly, to study the cause of its grief, until it gayly darts up to the gaffer and falls an easy prey, as does the coquette to the practiced skill of a heart-thief.

THE GRILSE.

The grilse is the same fish which left its river as a smolt. In its ocean pastures, where it has spent one or two winters, it has doffed the clumsy guise of puppyhood, and the top of its head, dorsal, and caudal have become velvety, while the black beads on its gills and upper mandible begin to appear. It lacks the jetty intensity which the top of the head and some of the fins of the adult salmon disclose, but its white is equal in satiny sheen to the salmon of best condition. Its weight is from five to eight pounds, and, having never spawned, it follows the salmon up toward the spawning-pools at the head of the stream, reaching them toward the end of the spawning season; and after spawning, the next spring, during its early rains, or in winter before, it falls back again over cataract and rapid until it gains the estuary, to return to sea, and fatten, and enlarge to a veritable salmon.

Thus the reader may have seen that the fingerling becomes the parr, the parr develops scales to cover the bars on its sides and becomes a smolt, goes to sea and returns a grilse, then returns to sea and comes back a salmon.

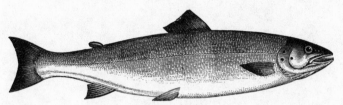

THE SALMON.

I have endeavored to illustrate the marks and forms of the
salmon in its different stages, concluding that pictorial illustrations from life are more comprehensible than explanations
in letter-press, especially to the student at angling, who has
not enjoyed many summers since he first wet a line for salmon, and heard the beautiful music of the reel, so charmingly
described by Stoddart:

> "A whirr! a whirr! the salmon's out
>   Far on the rushing river ;
> He storms the stream with edge of might,
> And, like a brandished sword of light,
> Rolls plashing o'er the surges white,
>   A desperate endeavor!
> Hark to the music of the reel!
>   The fitful and the grating ;
> It pants along the breathless wheel,
>   Now hurried, now abating."

THE SWORD-FISH.

CHAPTER V.

FISH PROPAGATION ASSISTED BY ART.

As fish-culture assisted by art has become a business of magnitude in France, and in England increased the revenue from salmon-waters over a hundred per cent.,* and as the Northern and Eastern rivers and lakes of the United States are well adapted to the rapid increase of the *genus Salmo*, being wooded, shaded, and fed by living springs,† what excuse is there for longer delay in restocking the rivers which used to teem with salmon and trout, and stocking anew those many waters wherein fishes of the *genus Salmo* would thrive? It is true, the inhabitants of the New England States are hopefully in earnest, and anxious to stock and protect their salmon and trout waters, and have appointed a competent Fisheries' Commission, including the following gentlemen:

Maine—Charles G. Atkins, Augusta; N. W. Foster, East Machias.

New Hampshire—Hon. II. A. Bellows (chairman), Concord; W. A. Sanborn, Weir's.

Vermont—Prof. A. D. Hagar, Proctorsville; Hon. Charles Barrett, Grafton.

Massachusetts—Alfred K. Field, Greenfield; Theodore Lyman (secretary), Brookline.

Connecticut—H. Woodward, Middletown; James Rankin, Old Saybrook.

But this question is equally applicable to the State of New

---

* The fishing rental of the Tay in 1852 was less than $40,000; in 1864 it had risen to $75,000, and this year it is over $100,000.

† "Let any one look at the map of New England, with its thousands lakes and rivers, and imagine what riches ought to dwell in those waters."—N. E. Fisheries' Report.

York and the vast West, especially those waters 'running northward and eastward, all of which may, with a trifling expense, be made alive with shining shoals of the mighty salmon and the beautiful speckled trout.

It is also important to assist the propagation of other food-fishes by artificial means. Legislatures should appropriate sums for these pressing objects, which not only cheapen meats, but add to the variety of food a source of health as well as luxury, and so cheapen it as to bring it within the means of all.

Next in importance to artificial propagation is the purifying of rivers from the numerous pollutions incident to a careless procedure in manufacturing, where poisonous minerals, tan-bark, sawdust, etc., drain into the streams, instead of being conducted away from them or consumed. Commensurate in importance with the purification of the rivers are properly-constructed fish-passes, to enable a salmon to surmount dams and falls to reach their spawning-pools at the heads of streams, for without such means procreation can not go forward, and of the first stock few may be taken in the same river, but the greater number will seek more accessible spawning-beds at the heads of other rivers.

Of the numerous reasons in favor of artificial propagation, the following are not the least important:

It has been proven by experiment that of salmon not more than one in a thousand hatched naturally arrive at maturity. Of trout, it is probable that double that proportion mature, for the present experiment of propagating trout and salmon side by side in Australia proves that trout thrive best, and are what Lord Dundreary would call "the most wobust." But the ranks of the speckled beauties in our trout-streams and ponds have been eliminated, and require filling up. This can not be done without the assistance of art. Let us suppose that a pond which is supplied by streams suitable for spawning is stocked with five hundred trout, each of which weighs a pound. In the course of one season they will de-

posit 250,000 ova. Granting that a considerable portion of
these are hatched, is it ever found that a fiftieth or a hun-
dredth part of the whole arrive at maturity? Far from this
being the case, the number of trout will continue almost the
same for years, without any perceptible increase. The reason is plain. So soon as the fry are hatched, they are exposed
to the attacks of the parent trout. Within the limits of the
reservoir there is not the remotest chance of their ultimate
escape. It is true, if the fingerlings knew enough, they might
ascend the tributaries of the preserve to shoals where the
parent trout could not follow; but they do not know, and
man, being placed over the kingdoms of inferior animals,
should preserve them for his own good. Salmon which
spawn in the natural waters generally go to the heads of
the streams during the fall floods and deposit their spawn;
when the waters subside, the ova is sometimes destroyed by
being left on dry land. Other fish deposit their spawn and
cover it on prior beds of spawn. Others spawn in the current of the stream, and a freshet carries it down the current
as food for all the inhabitants below. In other cases the female salmon makes her spawning-bed, and deposits and covers up the ova, while the male fish is down at the foot of the
pool guarding it from the incursions of an army of water-
guerrillas. Sometimes the place in the stream selected for
the spawning-bed is very good while preparing the trenches
for the spawn, but by the time the spawn is deposited the
stream has become a torrent, and washes away the ova; and
yet—just like a headstrong specimen of humanity—if the female makes up her mind that she will spawn at a place, the
rapidity of the flood of water never daunts her, though the
swiftness of the current prevents the roe from ever touching
bottom. Long Island is formed of a net-work tracery of trout-
streams, and yet there are but ten establishments for the artificial propagation of trout. Some proprietors and the poachers of the island capture trout in winter to stock ponds which
are kept for the commercial advantages of letting them to be

fished by amateurs with the fly, or the trout are fed, and then netted and taken to market. There is no general attention paid to the procreation of the speckled beauties. Many of the best preserves on the island are depleted of trout by sheer neglect. They should divide their ponds, and catch their large trout and use them for stocking subsidiary waters. In a word, they should tap their dams with pipes, and conduct water into spawning-boxes. Where their dams are near a road or turnpike, they should run the pipes underneath, or place their boxes along the embankment of the dam in such position as to form a rather swift flow of water throughout the line of boxes. Nothing can be more simple or safe. The trout hatched in that way should be placed in small ponds, each brood by itself, thus necessitating three of these small ponds. As each brood arrives at two years of age, it should be turned into the main preserve, and that preserve should be swept annually with a large-meshed net, and all the large trout so taken should be transferred to the pond of propagation, which should be watched during spawning-time—in September, October, and November—and when found ripe for spawning they should be netted, and the roe and milt taken from them and laid in the breeding-boxes.

Before proceeding farther, let me say here that what I may state about propagating salmon is equally applicable to brook trout; for the only difference in the treatment of salmon and brook trout is found in the fact that trout will always prey upon roe and young fish—even its own—while only the salmon *kelt* is so unnatural; but this maternal obtuseness is supposed to be acquired from not returning to sea with her brood, and, thus left to the mercy of fresh-water insects and the scanty food of the river, she becomes what the habitans of Canada call a "*meagre*," with no more soul than a miser.

BEST WATER FOR HATCHING SALMON.

Spring water from 45° to 55° is probably the best. Spring water is preferable, as being more pure than river water even after being filtered, while its temperature is more equable, being nearer the same throughout the year. Too much surface or rain water is injurious, containing less vitality for game fish, but more predaceous insects, so that their larvæ may be mixed with the eggs in the hatching-boxes, and prey on the spawn before it is hatched.

In situations where spring water can not be obtained in sufficient quantities, the river water should pass through a filter of sand and gravel. If the spring is large enough and the ground suitable, it may be divided into artificial rills, with a pipe of two inches run of water to each. Under all circumstances, a gentle, equable, and pure current is indispensable.

HATCHING-BOXES FOR THE INCUBATION OF THE EGGS OF SALMON OR TROUT, AS ADOPTED BY THE COLLEGE OF FRANCE.

These boxes are fed from a horizontal pipe two inches in diameter, by faucets tapping it at every tier of five boxes; and to break the force of the jet so that it will not derange the ova in the first box, and to assist in aeration, a perforated zinc cap is sometimes placed before it, as the object is to maintain a regular movement of the current throughout the tier of boxes, which are about six feet long and two and a half wide. A constant flow of water, of nearly equal temperature, through the boxes is a necessity. At Huningue, in France, all the hatching-boxes are in a well-ventilated building; and as hatching-time continues from October until February, a cover to the hatching-boxes is essential; and in England, to protect the ova from thieves, Mr. Francis recommended a cover of perforated zinc, with the ends which are above the water of zinc also; and in order to regulate the temperature of the water, the horizontal pipe should be sup-

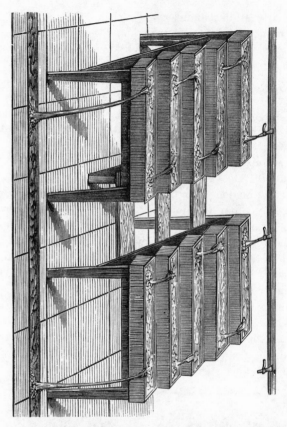

plied from a reservoir by a pipe running through a dry-air refrigerator (or through a chest filled with ice), by which modern American invention the temperature may be regulated at any degree required between freezing and ten degrees below zero. The pipe should be coiled in the refrigerator.

The aquarium presented above is the one selected by the College of France from numerous samples, and it has proved a success; but the object of it is more especially for studying the eggs during the time of incubation. The water is there-

fore nearly all husbanded after it passes through the boxes
by catching it in a marble trough and sending it back to the
supply reservoir by a pipe from a hydraulic ram, or a turbine
like that by which many reservoirs are supplied from rivers
or springs.   These plans of aeration enable fish-culturists to
run the same water several times over the hatching-boxes;
but it is thought by some professors that—for perfect safety
to the ova—the water should be continually renewed, and not
flow over them a second time.

In establishments of fish-culture like the government one
at Huningue, they endeavor to imitate nature more perfectly
than it can be done by a tier of boxes.   They therefore build
a race-way thirty feet long, a yard wide, and eight inches
deep, as the trout-brook, and the fountain of equal temperature feeding it by pipes is the spring.   In this race-way are
placed crosswise numerous trays of terra-cotta, glazed inside
to prevent contact of confervæ with the ova, and in which, to
a frame of wood, glass tubes are fitted, and called a *gril*, the
French name for gridiron.   The tray is six inches wide, four
inches deep, and as long as the race-way is wide.   Both the
tray and the grille may be moved with ease to another race-
way, or the grille may be moved to clean the bottom of the
tray or for other purpose.   The following cut may help illustrate.

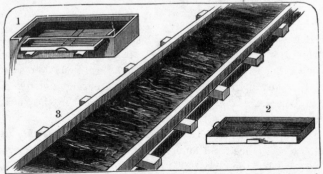

Fig. 1. Terra-cotta Tray, to fit crosswise in race-way.   Fig. 2. Grille of glass tubes,
made to fit in the tray.   Fig. 3. Race-way, as wide inside as the length of the tray.

After the roe becomes fructified by the milt, the case of grilles, Fig. 2, is placed in the tray, and then deposited cross-wise in the race-way, where the tray is mechanically confined, when the ova is emptied on the glass grille, and left for nature to do the rest, only seeing that the water continues to form a stream like a natural brook through the race-way, and that the light be never glaring or the temperature of the water too high, bearing in mind that there will be several degrees of difference between the water at the head and foot of the way.

The grilles should be examined daily, and any addled or dead eggs removed from contact with others. This should be done so as not to disturb the other eggs, as great quiet during the months of incubation is necessary.

The following cut represents the implements for removing dead eggs.

Fig. 1. The Siphon, used for examining the eggs.   2. Pincers for picking out dead eggs.
3. Fine brass wire for taking up dead eggs.

The siphon is used in France to draw up the dead eggs; but, as it generally disturbs so many of the live ones, its general use in fish-culture is now confined to examining the eggs, while pincers with sharp-pointed nibs are often used for picking out the dead eggs; but Mr. Francis states in his "Fish Culture"—a small but very useful volume—"Some use a

B B

small needle tied to a stick; but the toughness of the ova resists the prod of the needle, and goes on slipping about. * * *
The best plan, by very far, is to twist up a piece of fine brass
wire into an eye just big enough to take the ova, tie it to a
fine-pointed handle, bend it to the most convenient angle for
lifting, softly introduce it between the ova and under the one
you·wish to withdraw, and fetch it out swiftly, but steadily."

SPECIAL DIRECTIONS ABOUT PREPARING SPAWNING-BOXES.

The following explanations were made by one of the fish-
culturists engaged on the Tay, in Scotland:

The boxes for containing the ova were twenty-four in number, each being six feet long, eighteen inches wide, nine inches
deep, and open at the top. The whole were disposed in a
double row, parallel with the original course of the rill. Each
row consisted of twelve boxes, placed end to end, the beds of
the foremost commencing shortly below the lower end of the
dam. A piece of three inches in depth and nine in width was
cut from each log, in order to allow a free passage for the
stream through the whole series. At the junction of each
box was nailed a sheet of tin, with turned-up sides, to prevent the escape of the water. A couple of pipes, a yard in
length and two inches in diameter, conveyed the stream to
the foremost box in each row, the end of the pipes inserted in
the dam being covered with fine wire gauze to prevent the
entrance of trout and insects. The whole were arranged on
a gentle slope, so as to avoid stagnation, and insure a tolerably rapid flow of water.

The boxes being arranged, a strata on which to place the
ova was then formed. It consisted of a mixture of sand and
gravel, of the depth of several inches, upon which were deposited pebbles of the ordinary size of road metal. When
properly prepared for the reception of the ova, the stream averaged two inches in depth above the pavement.

At a short distance below the dam two ponds were constructed to contain the fry, the one receiving the stream from

the double row of boxes, and the other from the bed of the rill. The superficial area of each was two hundred and forty yards, being much too small, as finally ascertained, for the hosts of fry with which they were ultimately tenanted.

SECURING THE OVA OF A SALMON.

The process by which a salmon is made to exude its roe or milt is illustrated by the engraving; but the abdomen of the fish should be kept under water, and a napkin is better than the naked hand wherewith to hold the tail. It being difficult to hold a salmon, three persons are frequently required. But what says our authority?

In order to obtain the spawn in a perfectly mature state, the fish were taken from the spawning-bed in the very act of its deposition. They were caught with nets at night. When taken they were instantly, and without injury, put into an oval tub one fourth full of water. So soon as a pair of suitable fish were captured, the ova from the female was immediately discharged into the tub by a gentle pressure of the hands from the thorax downward. The milt of the male was

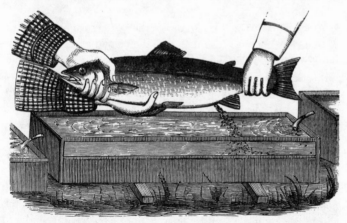

ejected in a similar manner, and the contents of the tub gently stirred with the hand. After the lapse of a minute the

water was poured off, with the exception of sufficient to keep
the ova submerged, and fresh supplied in its place. This also
was poured off, and fresh substituted previously to removing
the impregnated spawn to the boxes prepared for its reception.

In discharging the ova from the abdomen of the female all
violence was carefully avoided. If, on examination, the ova
were found to be immature, the fish was immediately returned to the river, and others in a more advanced stage taken.
When a sufficient quantity of spawn was collected, it was at
once removed to the hatching-ground. An amount propor-
tioned to the size of the boxes was carefully poured in at the
head of each, the action of the water scattering it pretty
equally among the crevices of the stones. A temporary increased flow of the stream easily distributed it wherever it
might happen to be too closely crowded together. Out of
24,000 roe deposited in the spawning-boxes, 20,000 were successfully hatched.

MR. JOHN GILLONE'S PROCESS OF PROPAGATING TROUT AND SALMON.

As owner of the "Longland Fishery," the opinion of Mr.
Gillone is received with much confidence and respect throughout England. "In the first place," he states, "we have one
mill-dam hecked at top and bottom." (As the word *heck*
means "an engine or instrument for catching fish," we suppose that he means a peculiar net or singularly constructed
weir for preventing trout or salmon from passing it, and rendering them liable to capture in the attempt.) The upper
part of the dam was laid with gravel suitable for salmon or
trout to spawn in naturally. There is also a very suitable
stream for trout or salmon to deposit their spawn, and, so
soon as our fishing season is about to close, we take the number of fish required to fill our breeding-boxes with fecundated
ova, and put them into the dam, and keep them there until
we see them beginning to spawn. (Spawning is sometimes

continued for several days, and sometimes weeks, by a single pair of fish. The male trout or male salmon sometimes forces the female to the spawning-bed before all the ova is sufficiently matured for deposition.) We then shut down our upper sluice, catch and examine all the fish, and keep in a large wooden box all the fish ready for manipulation, returning the rest to the dam till we see them beginning to spawn a second time, and so on till we get them all spawned.

We spawn them in a box three feet six inches long, seven inches wide, and nine inches deep, with as much water as will cover the fish. We first take the female fish from a large box filled with water close at hand, lay her in the little box as she swims (that is, her back up), taking her by the tail with the right hand, and with the left hand gently press from the neck to the vent until you get all the roe exuded. We then pour off about half the water, and use the male fish the same way, mixing the milt with the water by the hand. After mixing the ova, we have a large filter that fits the neck of a bottle, water-tight, with a rim of wire gauze two inches deep. We then fill the bottle and filter with water; then, pouring off the greater part of the water in the spawn-box, we empty the roe and water into the filter. The roe, of course, sinks into the bottle; the water runs off through the wire gauze, and prevents any of the ova from being spilled. The bottle is marked off in divisions, each division holding 800 eggs of an average size. By this way we count our roe with little trouble that we deposit in our breeding-boxes. In putting the ova into the breeding-boxes, I have a tin tube that fills the neck of the bottle, tapering to about a half-inch circle at the top. This tube I place below the water in the breeding-box, and gradually empty the roe into glass jars. Our breeding-boxes are two in number, or rather a continuation of one. They are laid quite level, so that the water circulates down the one and up the other. The boxes are made of wood, four inches deep, one foot wide, and the length of the two boxes combined is 135 feet. These boxes are supplied with frames inside each three feet long, filled with narrow strips of glass, with the sharp edges ground off to prevent cutting the young fish. The glass is laid across the stream, forming gutters, in which the ova is placed in rows across the run of the water; the glass is supported in the frames three quarters of an inch from the bottom of the box, the water flowing freely both above and below the ova. These boxes are capable of hatching at a time 15,000 salmon or trout. This season we have 24,000 salmon eggs deposited in them, and the eggs are becoming quite visible. In depositing the ova in the several boxes, I keep each fish's eggs separate, and marked on the boxes 1, 2, 3, etc. I keep corresponding numbers in a book, with a remark on each fish's roe at the time of spawning; and during the time of incubation, if I see any thing worthy of notice, I take a note of the number and what has happened. I pick out all the dead ova once or twice a week, and keep an account of the number, and when the hatching is finished I subtract the number of the dead from the number deposited, which will show about the quantity we have hatched.

CARE IN OBTAINING FECUNDATED SPAWN.

Whenever practicable, it is desirable to take the trout from the spawning-beds by means of nets, so as to insure the maturity of the ova. It can best be done in the night. So soon as caught, the fish should be placed in a large tub, or other vessel, partially filled with water, till a milter and spawner are taken. In ejecting the ova, the female should first be held over a bucket or large tin can half full of water, the lower end of the abdomen being inserted in the water, in order to prevent the exposure of the ova to the air. A gentle pressure of the hand from the thorax down each side of the abdomen will discharge the ova, if mature, without the least injury to the fish. The water in the bucket should then be reduced to three or four quarts previously to ejecting the milt of the male. In expelling the milt the course pursued is precisely the same as that just described, the lower end of

Stripping a Trout.

the abdomen being in this case also inserted in the water. After stirring the contents of the bucket with the hand, the water should be poured off and fresh supplied several times in succession, until no trace of the milt can be seen, always taking care to keep the ova submerged. The spawn may then be moved to the hatching-ground or boxes; for the artificial spawning-bed may be made in a ditch, dug for the purpose, and paved, and supplied through pipes with water, as well as in boxes; but experiments have given the preference to boxes, as susceptible of forming thereby a stream more equal in flood, volume, and temperature. In the removal of the ova for a short distance, it is unimportant in what manner they are conveyed, so long as they are not much shaken. In transporting ova a great distance, it should be done in the winter or spring, placed in tanks lined with sponge and swamp-moss, with an aerating pump placed in it for frequently moving the water, changing it, and exposing it to the air. Fecundated ova have been packed in moss by Seth Green and sent by mail a thousand miles, and then hatched with very small loss.

A SIMPLE PROCESS FOR PREPARING A SPAWNING-BED.

If you have a trout-pond, tap it at the sluice in the dam with several pipes of two inches diameter, covering the ends in the pond with fine wire gauze to exclude young fish, or the eggs of such fish or reptiles as are enemies to trout. Conduct the water through these pipes to rows of boxes about two feet wide and six feet long, the boxes from the head one nearest the dam resting two inches lower than the one which immediately precedes it, so as to produce a current sufficiently swift in this artificial stream formed of a row, or several rows of boxes, and each row formed of half a dozen boxes. One pipe to supply each row of boxes, and then you may have as many rows of boxes as you have water to supply, always bearing in mind that the water must run continually. The waste water, after it leaves the boxes, may be conducted by a ditch into the brook below the dam, or into a pond prepared to receive the young trout. The bottoms of the boxes are next covered to the depth of a couple of inches with sand and small pebbles, upon which is laid a pavement of stones from three to six inches in diameter. The water should be as much as two inches deep above this pavement, and fill the boxes two thirds full. The boxes are open at the top. Then pour the fecundated roe equally over the paved bottom of each box, and it will soon find its way into the crevices of the stony bottom, and within from sixty to seventy-five days the trout will be hatched, and a bag connected to the abdomen by an umbilical cord contains sustenance sufficient for forty days, after which the tiny creature begins to seek food, and should be removed to its pond.

FEEDING YOUNG TROUT OR SALMON.

After the absorption of the abdominal vesicle, the fry require food of a fine and nourishing kind—crumbs of boiled liver in small particles, minced meat or fish of any kind, or a paté of the intestines of any animal or fowl; horse-flesh is

very good; cheese-curd, farinaceous food, may be mixed and all put in solution, and fed to the tiny things through a syringe; maggots—called gentles—a bait for sale at all the rod-fishing places in Europe, and the larvæ and flies of the season, form good food after the fish are two months old.

STOCKING OLD PONDS WITH TROUT.

Old ponds, even if inhabited by trout, are apt to fill with weeds, which grow from all parts of the bottom except the channel cut by the creek flowing through it; and if the stream be too small compared with the size of the pond, so that the water is not renewed sufficiently often, then the eels, sunfish, perch, and pike are apt to accumulate, to the ultimate extermination of the trout. It becomes necessary, therefore, before stocking an old pond, that the water be drawn off and the bottom of the pond thoroughly cleaned. The expense of cleaning a pond is partially paid by the manure thus obtained. Some persons, after cleaning a pond, sow the bottom with lime and salt. The creek should also be cleaned up to its source by sweeping it with small-meshed nets; but all its shades on the margin of the stream, and its hiding-places of rocks and stones in the stream, should be left, and pegs or

piles driven into the bottom, leaving the tops of them a foot
or so above the bottom, to prevent poachers from netting the
pond or stream.   The dam may or may not be constructed
so as to permit the trout to follow down the stream to its
estuary and return at will.   This would depend upon agree-
ment between the different owners of the stream.   But when
the stream debouches into a bay or river of salt-water, a tumbling dam offers an inducement to smelt, herring, etc., to
spawn in the pond, and thus stock it with the best feed possible for trout, for those trout which feed on shrimp, smelt,
spearing, young herring, and the roe of fishes are always superior to such as feed on worms brought down the stream by
a freshet.   Although one of the principal charms of the trout
is that he feeds on the flies which swarm on the surface of
the water, thus enlivening and beautifying the water by
breaking to the surface and forming numerous wakes of large
circles, and sometimes rising above the surface and disclosing
miniature rainbows of amber and gold, yet there are times
when he prefers something more substantial, and will not
touch a fly.   In this he imitates humanity, which requires
roast beef, as well as plum-pudding and *omelette soufflèe*.   So
the trout requires his *piece de resistance* of something more
substantial than flies.

Dubravius, Dr. Lebault, and many piscatorial professors,
dwell at great length upon preparing fish-ponds and taking
care of them.   We therefore extract the gist of their advice,
intermingled with our own, as follows: A pond intended for
either profit or pleasure should be cleansed once every three
or four years, especially if large compared with the stream
by which it is fed, or if sustained by more surface-water than
of spring-water.   It should be drained and lie dry six or
twelve months, both to kill the water-weeds and the animals
which feed on trout and its roe.   The letting your pond dry
and sowing oats in the bottom is also good, for it purifies the
bottom of the pond.

In reconstructing your pond after draining it, and having

made the earth firm where the head of the pond must be, Lebault advises that you drive in two or three rows of oak or
elm piles, which should be scorched in the fire or half burned
before they be driven in the earth, for being thus used it preserves them much longer from rotting; and having done so,
lay fagots or bavins of smaller wood between them, and
then earth between and above them; and then, having first
very well rammed them and the earth, use another pile in
like manner as the first were, and note that the second pile
is to be of or about the same height that you intend to make
your sluice or flood-gate, or the vent that you intend shall
convey the overflowings of your pond, or any flood that shall
threaten to break the pond dam. Then he advises the planting of willows and osiers about the dam, and cast in charred
logs not far from the side, as also upon the sandy places, in
order to protect spawning-beds and form hiding-places for
the small fry. All ponds should contain places of gravel bottom, and places sandy and shallow, where trout may disport
themselves and burnish their sides. Fish should also have
retiring-places, such as hollow banks, or shelves, or roots of
trees, to keep them from danger, and to shade them at times
during the day in the extreme heat of summer, also from the
extremity of cold in winter. If too many trees grow about
your pond, the leaves, falling into the water, will impreg-
nate it and injure the flavor of the fish. Although towering
trees form too dense a shade, and the foliage is bad for the
stream, while they yield cover to invite winged game and
the consequent gunner, yet shooting much about a fish-preserve is injurious, and I would advise the planting of willow
and alder to partially shade the stream or pond, and render
firm the shores.

Two trout-ponds are more profitable than one of the same
area as the two, because they may be cleaned alternately,
and the trout turned into one while the other is under cleaning process.

In small ponds, or ponds where the small fry of common

fish often form food for trout, Lebault advises the feeding of
trout by throwing into the pond chippings of bread, curds,
grains, or the entrails of chickens, or of any bird or beast you
kill to feed yourselves. On the score of feeding trout in preserves, our experience is that they are generally fed too much.
In ponds where feed is scarce, living bait should be thrown
in, such as minnows, mummies, shrimp, and all kinds of fish
which nature intended for bait by forbidding them ever to
become more than three inches in length. But even this
should be done sparingly. We have known several ponds on
Long Island where the fish died while they were fed sump-
tuously, and when dead were found to be in excellent condition. We regret to state that some animals endowed with
the exterior semblance of humanity keep trout-ponds, and pre-
tend that they are waters intended for the propagation of
trout, when, in reality, they are pounds, or liquid bastiles,
wherein to imprison trout until they command a high price
in Fulton Market. When they get orders for them, they at
once feed them with a huge meal of mummies (small fish),
and when the trout have gorged themselves so that, in some
instances, the tails of the fish which the trout vainly endeavored to swallow are seen protruding from their mouths, these
Peter Funks then sweep the pond with a net, and send the
trout thus stuffed to market, and receive therefor the price
which healthy trout command. During the past season one
dollar and a half a pound has frequently been paid for trout
bought at wholesale. It is said that these Peter Funks rob
the trout-streams of their neighborhoods by means of nets
during the close season—between the first of September and
the first of March—and deposit their stolen gains in liquid
pounds, where they feed them until the market opens, for it
is unlawful to catch or sell trout during the close season, except for the purpose of science or the object of propagation.

SECTION SECOND.

AINSWORTH'S RACE AND SCREENS.

A. Top of Race.   B. Water Level.   C. Upper Screen, or Sieve.   D. Under Screen.   E. Bottom of Race.   G. Supply Pond.   H. Filtering Gate.

The Upper Screen is represented from the ground-plan, in order to show the form of the perforated bottom, and the same after paving it with pebbles. The bottom of the Race is also represented from the same view; but the side only of the Under Screen is represented. The whole is suggestive, calling for judgment and science in construction.

The object of this invention is to induce trout to spawn where the fish-culturist may gather the eggs and protect them until he can transfer them to the hatching-boxes once or twice a week, and it is a valuable step on the road of *aquaculture* toward husbanding all the resources of a stream. The object is to form a race-way of water in a stream of moderate flow, and divide this race into three compartments. Those are the bottom of the race paved with cobble-stones, E; a few inches above it, and of the same width, is the lower screen or sieve, D; a few inches above which is the upper screen, C. Trout have access to screen C for spawning, and as the bottom of it is perforated with holes twice as large as a trout's egg, of course the eggs laid on it will run through the bottom of the screen and lodge on the under one, which is perforated with very small holes to drain it, but not pass the eggs. Screen C is divided into trays, with handles at the sides for removing them by the hand; the bottom is then covered with pebbles, as indicated by the upper half of the screen; the lower, or left half, merely represents the perforated bottom of zinc. Screen D, for catching the fecundated eggs, is the same width and length as C, divided into trays also for removing their contents conveniently.

The engraving represents the race from the supply pond half way to the outlet of the race into the creek or lower pond. Screen C is open at each end, so that trout from the creek below or the pond above may enter freely, it being an artificial imitation of a natural spawning-bed. The following is the inventor's description:

"This race may be built like the races made for the artificial impregnation of spawn used by nearly all trout-breeders to entice the trout up from the pond to spawn. It can be made of any length from 10 to 50 feet, and from 2 to 6 feet wide, according to the number of trout which are to use it, and the amount of water for the supply of the pond. It should be made with plank sides and bottom, so tight as to keep out all sediment. Paving the bottom nicely with small stones will answer. The bottom, whether of plank or stone, must then be covered with a half-inch layer of fine, well-washed gravel.

"When one has large trout to spawn in the race the water should be 2 inches deep at the upper or supply end, and 15 inches deep at the lower end where it empties into the pond, with a gentle current throughout its whole length. This will give good spawning depth to the water for trout of all sizes from 6 to 24 inches long. Usually a race 3 feet wide, and from 15 to 20 feet long, will be quite sufficient for a pond of 1000 or 1800 trout.

"The bottom of this race must be covered with fine wire-cloth screens, of about 10 meshes to the inch, made of zinc or galvanized wire, so as not to corrode, and thus injure the spawn. Iron wire, *if painted*, will answer where zinc can not be obtained. These wire screens must be nailed to wooden frames, made of inch-square stuff, the frames to correspond in length with the width of the race, and to be as wide as the cloth will permit—say 2 feet. Strips of three-quarter-inch stuff must be nailed to the bottom of the race for the screens to rest on, in such a manner that they will be raised one quarter of an inch above the gravel on the bottom. This is done to give good circulation to the water under the spawn as they fall on to these wire screens. These screens must be laid the whole length of the race, side by side, to catch the spawn as it is deposited by the parent trout.

"Now place over these another set of screens made of coarse wire-cloth, of about two or three meshes to the inch, so that the spawn will drop through easily. These screens must be nailed on frames of the same length as the others, but of two-inch stuff, and as wide as the cloth will permit. These screens must be strong enough to hold 2 inches of well-washed coarse gravel from three quarters of an inch to 2 inches in diameter. They should be so large that there will be interstices between the gravel large enough to let the spawn pass down, if necessary, to the lower screen. The upper screens should have handles on each end to lift them by, as they will have to be taken out and replaced every few days during the spawning season.

"When these two sets of screens are placed the whole length of the race, and all is complete, the water will pass over all, 2 inches deep at the supply end, and 15 inches deep at the lower end, with a moderate current through the whole race. The reader will perceive by the description and diagram that there is one inch of space between the two screens to hold the spawn as they are deposited by the parent trout, with a gentle current passing over and under them, and that the upper screen prevents the spawn from being destroyed by trout and insects, so that they are perfectly safe until removed to the hatching-box.

"When the trout is ready to spawn she will enter the race from the pond and prepare her nest. This she does by whipping all the sediment from the gravel with her tail, and then she whips or digs a hole in the cleansed gravel about 2 inches deep, or down to the upper screen, and about 4 inches in diameter. She then bends herself down in this hole and presses her abdomen on the gravel, and forces out from 100 to 500 spawn, which fall to the bottom of the hole, and down through the upper screen to the lower one. She then passes up the race, and the male trout attending her comes over the nest and spawns, and ejects his milt on the ova; he then whips the water in the hole with his tail, sending the water and milt in all directions, so that the milt reaches all the spawn on the screen or in the gravel, and, as they are ripe and ready for the milt, impregnates every one of them. As soon as this is done the mother trout returns and covers up the spawn and fills the hole, and soon digs another in like manner, and so on till she has deposited all her ova, which sometimes takes two weeks.

"There may be from 20 to 50 trout in the race spawning at one time, and all, or nearly all, of the spawn will be found perfectly impregnated and fully matured, so that they will all hatch if taken out every three days or once a week, and placed in hatching-boxes.

"To take the spawn from the lower screens, first take out two of the upper screens, with what gravel is upon them; then remove the lower ones, and wash the spawn off into a large pan of water carefully, and replace one set behind you, and then take up one set at a time and place back until all are returned. Should any spawn remain in the gravel, by raising the screen up and down a few times they will drop down through the interstices. The race must be kept well covered during the time of spawning, all persons must be kept away, and the fish disturbed as little as possible.

"By this method the spawn are all saved, are perfectly matured, are all impregnated, and will all hatch; the young will be perfect, few or none will die, as their sack-food is complete, and they will be strong and healthy when they commence seeking food for themselves. It is much less work to take the spawn than by handling, and no parent trout are lost."

As salmon and trout spawn along at intervals of several

weeks, it is natural to infer that all the eggs do not mature at one time. That this is the case has been proven by the officers of French fisheries. About the time when France endowed the Institution of Huningue, and when the waters, which had for many years remained still and dead, all at once became enlivened by the leaps of trout and the splashings of salmon, the "habitans" regarded the sight as supernatural, and an evidence that Heaven was pleased with Napoleon's reign. About this time, when France had first voted 30,000 francs for the advancement of fish-culture, and then increased the sum to 80,000, the study of all residents along salmon-rivers and trout-streams was how to procure the eggs of trout and fecundate them. They read all about Joseph Rémy's plan, and the result was that all the streams were robbed of game fishes for procuring eggs to sell to the establishment at Huningue. Of course the poor fishes were squeezed to death in forcing them to exude immature ova, and the streams becoming thereby depeopled, induced the unbelievers in fish-culture to set their faces against the wanton destruction. The French government then advertised that it would purchase no more fecundated ova unless the roe and milt were exuded by employés of government. Government agents thereafter were notified by those who had trout ready to spawn, and the agents visited the place, and took the ova only which was exuded without pressure, leaving the rest to restock their streams. Since then, water-farming has been an uninterrupted success.

FURMAN'S NATURAL HATCHING-RACE.

At Maspeth, in Kings County, which is within or joins the metropolitan district of which New York City is the centre, Mr. William Furman has been propagating brook trout artificially for the past ten years; and as he is a gentleman of genius, energy, and means, and, withal, an excellent fly-fisher, his devotion to the art of fish-culture has been rather for love than profit. In his hatching-race there are millions of fecun-

C c

dated ova far enough advanced to render their eyes distinguishable, and they are hatching daily, thus proving its perfect adaptability to the objects intended of hatching and protecting the eggs. It differs from that of Mr. Ainsworth in having but one race, with perforated bottom of zinc, with three holes to the inch. The bottom is covered with pebbles, and accessible to the trout from his pond during the spawning season, when may be frequently seen a dozen pairs of spawners at a time. The water flows gently down the race, and the spawners keep it constantly agitated throughout the spawning season, so that the fecundated ova falls through the perforated zinc bottom to the bottom of the stream, which is made of sand and gravel, on which the eggs hatch.

It will be perceived that this race differs from the Ainsworth one, which has two perforated races or troughs above the bottom, from the lower one of which the fecundated eggs are removed to hatching-boxes, while the Furman race consists of but one perforated race or trough, from which the eggs fall to the bottom, and remain during the period of incubation, or until hatched.

I have not deemed it necessary to illustrate the form of the Furman race, as it is similar to the Ainsworth one, only it has but one screen, and the bottom is not formed of movable trays, but the eggs drop to the bottom of the stream, where they hatch as in a natural stream, only that they are protected from destruction by their parents or other families of the finny race, which have no access to the compartment of the stream.

These imitations of the natural stream and spawning-beds are the latest invention in American fish-culture. Thus far they have proved successful, and promise to render unnecessary the artificial fecundation by handling the spawner and milter for forcing exudation of the seed. These plans simplify artificial fish-breeding, and promise to prove a greater improvement on the French grilles and hatching-trays than were the latter upon the troughs with wire-cloth ends placed in streams to hatch the fecundated ova by Lieut. Jacobi or Joseph Remy. Messrs. Furman and Ainsworth being both gentlemen of leisure, who devote their time to fish-culture *pro bono publico* and for their love of the subject, much benefit may therefore be reasonably expected from their experiments in water-farming.

"GENERAL DIRECTIONS," BY SETH GREEN.

For the general management in propagating salmon and trout, and the transportation of fecundated ova and the alevins, the following advice, founded upon successful experiment and entirely reliable, may be read with interest by those who are about to commence fish-culture by artificial assistance:

"Build your ponds according to the amount of water you have. If you have but little, build small. The water should be changed every 24 or 48 hours, and the oftener it changes the better. The trout can be very plenty if they have sufficient fresh water and food.

"I can send ova a fifty days' journey packed in a box with moss. I place the moss in a tin pail, filled with sawdust, so that the spawn will not feel the changes of heat and cold.

"*Directions for handling the Spawn.*—Pick the moss carefully off from the top of the spawn. Then put the box in a pan of water and turn it nearly bottom-side up, and pick the moss out very carefully. The spawn will sink to the bottom, and you can pick the moss out of the pan. If there is a little left it will do no harm. Then pour the spawn in your hatching-trough by holding the edge of your pan under water, and 'place' them, without touching the spawn, by agitating the water with the bearded end of a feather. The dead spawn will turn a milk-white color, and should be picked out. Your trough should be so arranged that the water will run in it about twelve feet per minute. The water should be filtered by running through gravel or cloth screens, to prevent the sediment from reaching the spawn. I run about one inch of water over my spawn, and if any sediment gets on them and is allowed to remain there long, it will surely kill them. Remove all sediment with the bearded end of a quill by agitating the water, without touching the spawn.

"Large ponds with but little water get too warm in summer and too cold in winter for trout to do well. It is detrimental to have any other fish with trout. Any kind of fish or fish-spawn is good for feed. The young should be fed twice per day, very slowly; if fed fast, the feed sinks and befouls the trough, and the trout will sicken and die. If fed regularly, and the trough kept clean, with a good change of water, and not kept too thick, they will live and do well. If neglected, they will surely die.

"*What is Death to Spawn.*—The sun, sediment, rats, mice, snails, crawfish, and many water insects.

"My troughs are 25 feet long and 15 inches wide. The water that feeds each trough would go through a half-inch hole with a three-inch head. Use fine gravel that has no iron rust in it. My troughs are three inches higher at the head. The average temperature of the water is 45°, and the fish hatch in 70 days. Every degree colder or warmer will make about six days difference in hatching. Trout hatch the soonest in warm water. The sack on their bellies sustains them for 40 or 45 days after hatching; then they need food.

"When the fish are hatched, raise the water in the troughs about four or five inches by putting on a piece of board of that width on every cross-piece, thus keeping the fish separate—about an equal number in each square. If you have small streams of shallow water near the head of your pond, put a few in a place in the stream and pond, and they will take care of themselves better than you can. The object of distributing them is that they will get more food. All old streams and ponds have plenty of food for small trout and large, which you will find by examining the moss, sticks, and stones in your ponds and streams, as they are full of water-insects.

" The fish, after hatching, should be fed twice daily for two or three months, then once a day—the grown fish once a day or oftener. For the young fish, liver should be scraped and chopped very fine, and mixed with water, to give it about the consistency of clotted blood. Toss this to the fish a little at a time, so that they can catch and devour it before it reaches the bottom of the trough; no more should be given than the fish will eat, because if any is left it will settle on the bottom and foul the water, and the fish will sicken and die. The fish may be fed on curds, fish offal, or other animal matter, provided it be small enough for them to swallow."

EVERY FARMER SHOULD HAVE A TROUT PRESERVE.

From a perusal of the foregoing descriptions for breeding salmon and trout by the most celebrated and successful fish-culturists, it will be perceived that they do not differ much in the *modus operandi*. Nearly every farmer has a spring on his place yielding surplus water sufficient to hatch trout in boxes. If he does not wish to go to much expense in erecting a dam to form a preserve, he might at least hatch the trout in boxes and sell them, for they are as ready sale as any product of a farm. Mr. Ainsworth, of Bloomfield, N. Y., said: " The original stock (of trout) was put in my pond, containing 61 square rods of ground, 14 feet deep, supplied with springs, three years ago, 1400 in number, age from 1 to 4 years. They weigh now from 1 to 3 pounds each. They are about as tame as kittens—come at call, and show themselves clear out of water in their haste for food by the five hundred at a time, and some take it out of a spoon six inches above the water. Think of seeing five hundred trout all at the same instant, weighing from 1 to 3 pounds, and from 12 to 18 inches long !"

A two-pound trout will furnish about 8000 spawn, smaller ones less in proportion. They commence spawning when one year old.

In this way they can be increased and grown to any extent, and all the ponds and streams in the country stocked to overflowing.

We conclude with the statement of both hope and confidence that the reader will find fish-breeding in boxes so simple and sure that he will at once prepare to engage in the interesting and profitable occupation.

GENERAL OBSERVATIONS.

Upon the breeding-times of different fishes, and their resorts at certain seasons in the year to hibernate, there is no fixed data. We know that eels spawn in salt waters if they have access to them, and visit fresh waters to recuperate and fatten. On the other hand, salmon seek the heads of rivers to spawn, and resort to unknown marine pastures to gain strength and fatten.

Most white-meated fishes spawn in the spring, yet the fish known as the *whitefish* spawns in early autumn. All members of the *genus Salmo* spawn in autumn.

The striped bass, with which our anglers on the rivers entering the coast are as familiar as with any other game fish, spawns at indefinite periods. It is known that in the Chesapeake Bay it spawns in spring; that in the estuaries and bays near New York and along the coast of Long Island it begins spawning in April and continues until July. The late Judge Morris and myself were once trolling in Hell Gate in September, and suspecting that a striped bass which we had taken contained ova in an advanced stage, we had the fish eviscerated, when the ova was discovered to be nearly mature. Striped bass taken in the Vineyard Sound in autumn are frequently found to be big with roe nearly ready to drop. These facts present questions for solution by ichthyologists. Do striped bass—like the hens—continue laying for several months? Or do they lay twice a year—spring and fall?

Both the flounder and plaice, or fluke, spawn in winter. Smelt spawn at intervals from February until April.

CHAPTER VI.

SALMON-PASSES, LADDERS, ETC.

HAVING studied ancient aquaculture and fish-culture, and examined the *modus operandi* for water-farming, with its profits a thousand-fold greater than those from cultivating the soil, the reader will have arrived at the threshold of an improvement as necessary as are all the previously-named operations.

One of the most important questions of the day in reference to the fresh-water fisheries of the United States—especially to those devoted to the propagation of salmon and trout—is how to expand and develop them to the greatest extent, so as to interfere as little as possible with existing arrangements as to mills and proprietary rights. That the salmon should breed, it is absolutely indispensable that it should be able to reach the heights and shallow portions of rivers, which alone afford suitable gravel-beds for the operation of depositing the ova and rearing the young. If it can not get to these, the breed of salmon is soon extinguished, and this has been the cause of its extinction in ninety-nine rivers out of every hundred. Mill-dams, those terrible enemies to the salmon, are the principal offenders in this respect. Commercial and manufacturing interests being almost too strong for the salmon, the question which has been agitating the minds of the most enlightened *pisciculturists* of the age for years has been, How we can best contrive that the fish shall have a free passage up the rivers, in order to continue its species without any loss of water-power or profits on the part of the mill-owners? If we can show them that this is possible, we have a natural right to compel those who have blocked up our rivers for their own profit to give the fish a free passage as a public benefit. The very best passage through a dam is an open run by means of a good wide pass in the centre of the dam, or, at any rate, in such part of it as will easily be found by the salmon, in showers, when the water-power is generally more than enough for the requirements of the mill and factory. There can be no great difficulty about this (proper regard, of course, being paid to the stability of the dam), except on rivers where the power is at all deficient, when contrivances, such as ladders, etc., etc., are needed to prevent the waste of any of the water-power. It is true that salmon can jump up a fall of considerable height. Indeed, salmon have been known to partly jump and partly swim up falls of ten or twelve feet in height, and even much more; but the capability requires certain conditions for its performance, and chief of all these is a good deep pool at the foot of the fall or dam as a starting-place, and the more arched or slanting out of the perpendicular the fall is, the easier the salmon will surmount it. It used formerly to be supposed that a salmon jumped out of the water in the way that mites are seen to jump in a rotten cheese, viz., by putting the tail to the mouth, and then, by the exertion of a sudden effort of muscular expansion, forcing its broad tail to act upon the water so as to shoot the fish ahead. This is now known to be fallacious, as it is seen that the salmon is quite powerless to leap any dam when the waters at the foot of the dam are shallow; and it is known that salmon leap like all other animals (except cheese-mites), viz., by acquiring the utmost attainable velocity by means of a run, and then, by a sudden and powerful spring, giving the impetus. This spring must be made, of course, by the assistance of every fin that can aid it, but chiefly by a strong stroke of the tail. Unfortunately, however, the majority of mill-dams are so spread out across rivers that the water runs over them in the thinnest possible sheet, and the soundness of the dam requires a foundation on the lower face. This foundation is assisted and protected by a wooden sheathing called the apron, and this is placed as near the surface of the water as possible, and extends down stream for fifteen or twenty feet below the dam, so that the *understanding* of the dam may not be undermined ; and thus it constantly occurs that while the pool below the dam is of great depth and capacity, yet it only forms a sort of reservoir for the fish, which the owner of the dam catches at his leisure, the fish being unable to approach the dam even so as to swim or pass over it ; and a dam of this sort, if only three or four feet high, would be as impassable to salmon as if it were four times that height. A salmon will scull up a pretty swift stream that does not perhaps cover his back, so long as his tail and pectoral fins, which are the propelling power, are immersed,* provided in such waters he is not called upon to make a perpendicular jump. This he can not do without a run to start him. In considerable depths, for a short space, a salmon can force his way through extremely rapid and heavy waters, but there are limits to this capability ; and *the difficulty which pisciculturists labor under is the ascertaining what weight or rapidity of water a salmon can stem.* Some salmon, of course, can stem a stronger torrent than others, but the problem must be taken as applicable to the weakest fish, not the strongest, inasmuch as the object is chiefly to permit the passage of female fish very heavily laden with ova. A female fish, full of eggs, carries something like a fourth of its own entire weight in that commodity, and *unless such fish*

---

* The tail is the most important organ in this proceeding, the fins being used chiefly for balancing and steering the fish, though they all aid propulsion on unusual occasions calling for great and sudden effort.

are let up, there is little use in letting the others up. Therefore the easier these passages (of whatever kind they may be) are made for the salmon, the better it will be for the fishery.

Now it has been ascertained that a slope of one in seven or eight is very near the extreme of steepness which a strong salmon can make his way through—that is, for any distance. It may be that by a sudden effort of the tail, *for a yard or two*, he can shoot almost any thing, but when he has been a dozen yards or more of such gradient, unless he can somehow obtain a fresh starting-point, the effort fails, and the fish is driven back by the weight of the stream.

Therefore it is desirable, in all passes which are long or full-steep, to have a resting-place, or a quiet pool whence the salmon can take wind and make a fresh start. It is impossible to lay down any definite rule for the construction of all fish-passes, since the architect must be governed by the facilities or difficulties presented by the dam or fall, and probably few dams should be treated precisely the same. Various methods have been employed where the water at the pool below the dam is too shallow to offer the fish a good start to leap the obstruction. One of the first and most simple plans constructed on the New England and Canadian rivers was a series of leaps from pool to pool, with a small dam thrown across the stream below in order to raise the water enough to give the salmon a start.

A stone pier is erected above the fall to break the ice in spring, and to check the force of the timbers and the heavy *débris* of the stream during spring freshets.

On small streams, a rough dam of big boulders, logs, etc., has been made a few yards below the existing one; this will probably be almost half the height of the other, and is comparatively easy to get over. It returns the water against the lower face of the original dam, and so makes that much easier, and by making a pool between them of some depth, it gives the fish the start it requires. This, on small streams, has been found very effective, and can not in the least affect

SALMON LEAPS.

the mill-power; but upon large rivers the plan is impracticable. The same principle can be applied to a pass which is imperfect, and it has been found to answer. A curving pier has been built out from the dam below, so that the water falling over the dam is thrown back by it, and though it is open at one end, yet it passes far enough across the bed of the river just below the fall to so raise the water that fish get a start to leap the dam. To increase the depth of water between this pier and the dam, a large beam of wood, in slanting direction from the top of the dam to the pier, conducts a wide sheet of water from the top of the dam to between the dam and the pier. This method for a salmon-leap can not injure the water-power. In all cases, the importance of such vital means of assistance to the salmon requires that the architect should be a man of natural genius as well as learning in his profession, and be, withal, a good angler, or know the habits of his client.

When the mill-power is of so much consequence that no water can be wasted, and if the fall be great, a fish-ladder is indispensable. Fish-ladders were first invented by Mr. Smith, of Deanston, in England, and were employed by him very successfully, and the great secret of his success was in the easy gradient which he gave them. His original plan was something like a fall of one foot in twenty; but so easy a gradient as this greatly lengthens the ladder, and adds very largely to the expense. The chief object of all ladders should be to deliver the water they carry to the spot where the fish are most likely to find it and to use it. This is, in all dams, close to the foot of the dam, and as near as may be conven-ient to the strong main stream. If the foot of the ladder should be carried too far down the stream below the dam, the fish which are at the foot of the dam will be so far above the entrance to the ladder that they will not find it; and if it be in some wide eddy or part of the stream *where it might be more easy to construct the ladder*, the fish will not go to that part, out of the main stream, to seek it. When it is necessary, by reason of the height of the dam, to have a long ladder, it should be turned in the middle like a double pair of stairs, with a landing or pool half way, so as to deliver the water close to the foot of the dam. The far-famed fish-lad-der at Ballysadare, in Ireland, is made upon this principle, and by the aid of it salmon manage to surmount a fall above thir-ty feet in height. The opposite engraving will show the principle.

A stone pier above the entrance of the water to the ladder, as at D, is essential in American waters to protect the ladder from the ice and the terrific *débris* of spring floods. The sal-mon are all turning their pretty noses toward the ladder, and many of them are ascending. They must think the Irish a kind people to have erected such a convenience for them.

BALLYSADARE SALMON-PASS.

A. Face of Dam.   B. Entrance to the Ladder, easily found.   C. Resting-pool, of from one to two feet depth.   D. Exit from Ladder above the fall.

The steps in the ladder extend three fourths its width, leaving the stream and eddies represented.   This sketch illustrates a very important principle, which can be varied at pleasure.   The gradient of a salmon-ladder should really not be less than 1 in 9 or 10, and 1 in 12 is better still.   The chambers between the steps are greatly improved if the bottom—instead of being all upon the same slopé as the general gradient of the ladder—is broken into steps, so that the water is deeper immediately behind the steps, or little steps or falls formed at the passage past the steps. Indeed, if it be practicable, the more the chambers are hollowed out, so as to deepen the water as much as possible in places, and thus to break and deaden the force of the stream, the better. Excellent results have been obtained by this arrangement. Of course this adds somewhat to the expense, but people should consider rent when they are making a salmon-fishery, which, if it is made, may in all probability be worth a very large sum of money annually, to risk the loss of which for the want of any little precaution, which may cost but a very trifling sum comparatively, is very bad economy, and hence every possible chance should be given to the fish.

Salmon-ladders can be made of wood, but they are far better of stone, being less liable to destruction or damage. It is a question, however, whether a salmon-ladder could not be better and more cheaply made and put together of iron. Such a structure might be supported very easily and firmly by means of light iron piles driven into the head of the river below the dam, and made in lengths which could be bolted on to the dam and riveted together, much easier than stone or mason's work can be secured.

Among other passes, there is one which is perhaps better suited to a natural fall, though it was in use formerly upon navigable rivers, where locks and dams were placed to suit the navigator. This was an artificial cut, coming into the river at the foot of the dam, but let out of the river some distance above it, so as to make the ascent, which is broken by the dam, gradual and easy. There are many contrivances for helping fish surmount falls and dams, and they vary considerably, according to the nature and position of the obstruction; so that, while it is impossible to lay down any general rule of construction for all, yet the principle that a certain depth and head of water is reserved for the passage of the fish, and that no fall of water up which a salmon has to pass should have a greater incline than 1 in 9 or 10, are those by which alone the construction can be guided.

THE SLIGO SALMON-STAIRS.

These stairs, of heavy timbers and mason-work, are intended to assist salmon and trout up small natural falls or dams,
and for such object are highly successful. A dam may be
necessary across the stream a few rods below, so as to deepen
the water below the fall, and give the fish a swimming start.
The height of this sub-dam should be three feet, and the
whole work well considered, and designed with much attention to the gradient, depth of water, and place for the foot of
the ladder.

The most important American ladder is the one adopted
by the Dominion of Canada, a sketch of which will be found
on the following page.

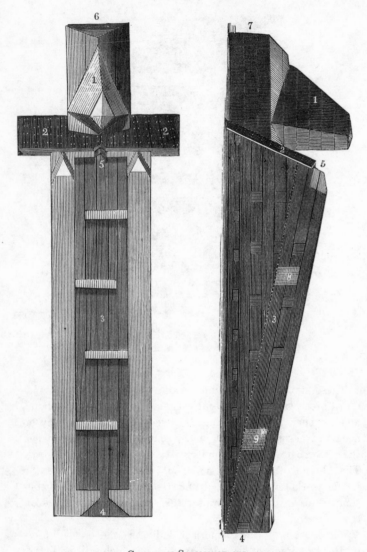

CANADIAN SALMON-STAIRS.

Fig. 1. Stone Pier to protect the Dam.   2. Plank and spike Dam, stone foundation.
3. Bed of the Pass or Stairs.   4. Entrance to the Pass.   5. Egress from the Pass.

This pass is built into the dam, and constructed of heavy timbers filled in with stone, or all of solid masonry. ' It is intended to be strong enough to resist and break up the acres of thick ice, and to prevent the huge trees swept down the stream by the spring freshets from injuring any material part of the structure, which is so strongly erected, and of such heavy material, and imbedded so firmly, as to strengthen the dam of which it forms so important a part.

Fig. 6 is the ground plan, and 7 the side elevation, with dotted line showing the bed of the pass, and with the ends of the steps indicated by 8 and 9.

The whole subject of passes and ladders is of extreme importance to our fisheries, and it is one which calls for the closest, most patient, and most scientific investigation; for if fish are not allowed to reach their breeding-places, it is useless to look for salmon; and the difficulty is how to deal with the vested rights of mill-dams, etc., so as not to arouse the opposition of the manufacturing sections.

The following account of foreign experience tells with equal force in America:

"I watched the fish with a race-glass for some ten minutes before disturbing them, anxious to observe what Nature was teaching me. There is a very deep pool at the point where the waterfall joins the lower level of the water. The fish came out of this pool into the air with the velocity of an arrow; they gave no warning or notice of their intentions, but up they came, and darted out of the surface of the water with a sudden rush, like rockets let loose from the darkness of the night into the space above. When they first appeared in the air their tails were going with the velocity of a watch-spring just broken, and the whole body, sparkling as though they had been enameled, was quivering with the exertion. They looked as much like flying-fish as ever I saw any thing in my life. As they ascended their tails left off quivering, for these tails were machines made to act on water, and not wings to act on air. Their course was somewhat trajectory in form,

D d

but not so much as I should have expected.   Not one single
fish, alas! did I see get over; some of them jumped into the
body of the waterfall, and were hurled violently back into the
pool, like the pictures we see of soldiers of old thrown down
headlong from the ramparts of a besieged city.   Other fish
would put on more steam, and were in consequence carried
by their own impetus right through the sheet of water, dashing themselves with the force of a cricket-ball against the
solid wall which formed the weir.   These also, poor things!
fell back into the pool half stunned, and with cut and bruised
noses.   While the bigger fish were making these strenuous
efforts to ascend, their smaller companions were jumping distances more or less high up into the falling water.   Many
had evidently given it up for a bad job, and were swimming
about with their little black noses projecting out of the white
boiling water, doubtless crying out, 'We can't get up, we
can't get up.   Cruel miller to put the weir.   Do what you
can for us.'   'Wait a bit, my dear fish,' I said; 'the Duke
of Northumberland is a kind man, and he is going to make a
ladder for you; the plans are nearly settled, and you shall
then jump for joy, and not for pain.   In the mean time read
this.'   So I pinned a large piece of paper on the weir, which
read thus: 'Notice to salmon and bull-trout—no road at
present over this weir.   Go down stream, take the first turn
to the right, and you will find good traveling water up stream,
and no jumping required.'"

Passes for trout over common dams may be accomplished
by building a tumbling dam, so that the fish may surmount
it by small leaps.   That common fish should ascend dams is
as important as that trout and salmon should, for the common fish and their roe form food for the game fish.   Smelts,
herrings, moss-bunkers, chub, dace, spearing, caplin, sardines,
launces, etc., are made as subsistence for salmon and trout,
and the stairs and passes should be so graduated as to enable
them to pass up and procreate their generations.

In propagating trout, it is frequently necessary that they

should be prevented from running up a stream beyond a certain point; hence the following screen is intended to prevent them from leaping a small cascade.

THE HORIZONTAL SCREEN.

This may be constructed of horizontal bars placed three inches apart, instead of lattice-work; or it may be of copper wire.

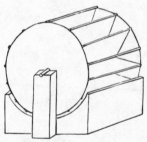

THE CURRENT WHEEL.

This wheel will prevent fish from passing up stream, while the horizontal screen allows the passage of floating food.

Concluding that enough information has been laid before the student for enabling him to begin fish-farming and pursue it with success, I will therefore proceed to another topic.

Part Fifth.

—⋈—

A GLIMPSE OF ICHTHYOLOGY.

CHAPTER I.

A GLIMPSE OF ICHTHYOLOGY.

GLIMPSES at the sciences are generally worse than superfluous, and to "drink deep or taste not" is the true advice; but the angler and the general fisherman may find it an advantage to know enough of ichthyology to qualify them for correctly describing the fish they catch, and it is for this object that the following "glimpse" is submitted. The specimen of the pike-perch, being the fish known in Ohio and some other states of the West as the salmon, is presented for teaching the names of fins.

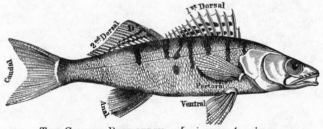

THE COMMON PIKE-PERCH.—*Lucioperca Americana.*

In describing a fish, the size, form, and color are given— the number, character, and position of the fins—and fre-

quently the shape and character of the scales, the character
of the gills, and the number of the gill-openings.

The most important and easily recognized of these features
are the *fins ;* and in describing them the *names* are given,
and the number of *spines* or *rays* in each.

FIRST CLASS OF FISHES.

SPINE-RAYED BONY FISHES. (*Acanthopterygii.*)

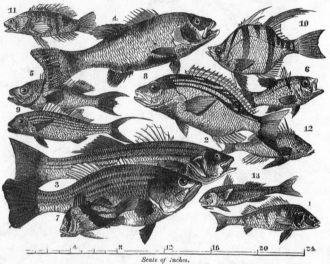

Scale of inches.

THE PERCH FAMILY.—1. American Yellow Perch, *Perca flavescens.* 2. Striped Sea Bass,
Labrax lineatus. 3. Black Bass, or Black Perch of Lake Huron, *Huro nigricans.* 4.
Growler, or White Salmon of Virginia, *Grystes salmoides.* 5. Black Sea Bass, *Cen-
tropistes nigricans.* 6. Mediterranean Apogon, *Apogon trimaculatus.* 7. Two-band-
ed Diploprion, *Diploprion bifaciatum.* 8. One-spotted Mesoprion, *Mesoprion unino-
tatus.* 9. Ruby-colored Etelis, *Etelis carbunculus.* 10. Armed Enoplossus, *Enoplossus armatus.* 11. Lettered Serranus, *Serranus scriba.* 12. Spined Serranus, *Serranus
anthias.* 13. Red Surmullet, *Mullus barbatus.*

THE PERCH FAMILY. (*Ctenoids.*)

The spine-rayed bony fishes comprise more than three
fourths of all the various kinds that are known.   From fourteen to seventeen different families, some of them embracing
several hundred species each, have been included in this division.   At the head of the whole stands the Perch family,
the most numerous of all.   Most of them are salt-water fish,

but about one fifth of the whole number inhabit fresh-water streams, or occasionally ascend them from the sea.

Scale of Inches.

1. Mailed Gurnard, *Peristedion malarmat.* 2. Big Porgee, *Pagrus argyrops.* 3. Banded Ephippus, or Three-tailed Porgee, *Ephippus faber.* 4. The Sheepshead (famed for its exquisite flesh), *Sargus ovis.* 5. Streaked or Rock Gurnard, *Trigla lineata.* 6. Axillary Sea Bream, *Pagellus acarne.* 7. Bearded Umbrina, *Umbrina vulgaris.* (The Umbrina is given as the representative of the family of the *Maigres,* which includes our Weakfish, Corvinas, the Chub, Kingfish, and the *Drum,* the latter noted for the loud drumming noise which it makes, and the cause of which is still a mystery.) 8. Common Mackerel, *Scomber scomber.*

The several species of the Pilot-fish, of which so many curious stories have been told, also belong to the Mackerel family. The ancient naturalists asserted that the common pilot-fish, which is a pretty little fish about a foot in length, joins company with the tempest-tossed bark of the anxious mariner, indicates to him his nearest course to land, and leaves him as soon as it has fulfilled this kind office.

Others, with much reason, deny this assertion, and allege that the pilot, like the shark, follows vessels for the purpose of obtaining a share of the garbage which may be thrown overboard. Certain, however, it is, that their perseverance in this respect is very singular, as is narrated in the case of an English vessel which was accompanied by two pilot-fish

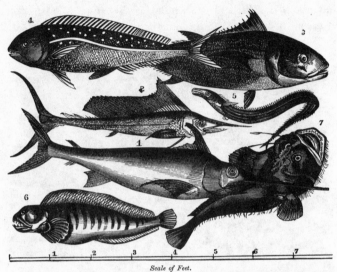

Scale of Feet.

1. Common Swordfish, *Xiphias gladius.* 2. Indian Swordfish, *Histiophorus Indicus.*
3. Common Tunny, *Thynnis vulgaris.* 4. Dolphin of the Ancients, *Coryphœna hip-*
puris. 5. Scabbard-fish, *Lepidopus argyreus.* 6. Wolf-fish (a fighting character, belonging to the family of the Gobies), *Anarrhichus lupus.* 7. Fishing Frog, *Lophius*
piscatorius.

during its entire voyage of eighty days from Alexandria, in
the Mediterranean, to Plymouth.

It is a current opinion among sailors that this fish acts a
pilot's part to the shark, and accompanies and befriends it as

THE PILOT-FISH.—*Naucrates ductor.*

opportunity offers; and certainly there is a great amount of
evidence which goes to show that there is something very
much like a confiding familiarity between these two companions of the weary mariner. Numerous well-authenticated

cases like that which we quote from Cuvier, respecting the habits of this fish, might be given.

With the ancients, however, as described by their poets, this little fish was the faithful companion of the *whale* instead of the shark; and Oppian thus alludes to the services which these pigmy pilots render to their unwieldy associates:

> " Bold in the front the little pilot glides,
> Averts each danger, every motion guides;
> With grateful joy the willing whales attend,
> Observe the leader, and revere the friend.
> Where'er the little guardian leads the way,
> The bulky tyrants doubt not to obey,
> Implicit trust repose in him alone,
> And hear and see with senses not their own."

When, and on what grounds, the misunderstanding of the pilot with his "fat friend" took place, history fails to inform us; but that he is now the ally of the dreaded shark, which he escorts in safety through every sea, is matter of general notoriety and almost daily observation.

In addition to the foregoing spike or spine rayed fishes, many others of them among the food-fishes and those for the angle will be found described in another part of the book, under the names of the fishes.

THE ROACH AND THE DACE.

SECOND CLASS OF FISHES.

SOFT-RAYED BONY FISES. *(Malacopterygii.)*

Scale of Inches.

THE CARP FAMILY.—1. Golden Carp, or Goldfish, *Cyprinus auratus.* 2. The Roach, *Leuciscus rutilus.* 3. The Loach, or Beardie, *Cobitis barbatula.* 4. The Tench, *Tinca vulgaris.* 5. The Barbel, *Barbus vulgaris.* 6. New York Shiner, *Cyprinus crysoleucas.* 7. Common Carp, *Cyprinus carpis.* 8. Common New York Sucker, *Catostomus communis.*

FISHES WITH ABDOMINAL VENTRAL FINS.

The carps may be placed at the head of the soft-rayed division. They are the least carnivorous of all fishes, and embrace, besides the common carp and its kindred, the several species of the barbel, the gudgeon, the tench, the roach, the dace and shiners, the minnows, the loach, and the American suckers. They are the most abundant fish in the fresh-water streams of Europe and America.

The carp, tench, roach, and kindred fishes are said by the Abbé Dom Pinchon—the original fecundator and hatcher of fishes by artificial means—to be the most profitable to stock ponds with; and unless they should become so numerous as not to find sufficient feed, introduce a few pickerel or perch.

THE PIKE FAMILY.—1. Saury Pike, *Scomber-esox saurus*. 2. Common Pike, *Esox lucius*.
3. Common Garfish, *Belone vulgaris*. 4. Guiana Garfish, *Belone Guianensis*. 5. Common Flying-fish, *Exocilus volitans*.

SALMON AND TROUT FAMILY.—1. Whitefish of the Lakes, *Coregonus albus*. 2. Common
Sea Salmon, *Salmo salar*. 3. New York Brook Trout, *Salmo fontinalis*. 4. Troutlet.
5. Great Lake Trout of Europe, *Salmo ferox*.

Descriptions under each fish will be found in another part of the book, including those of the SHAD and other members of the Herring and Pilchard family.

THE GADIDÆ FAMILY, OR FISHES WITH THE VENTRAL FINS BENEATH THE PECTORALS, CALLED *Sub-brachials.*

Scale of Inches.

THE COD FAMILY.—1. Three-bearded Rockling, or Sea Loche, *Motella tricirrata.* 2. The Torsk, *Brosmius vulgaris.* 3. The Haddock, *Morrhua æglefinus.* 4. Coalfish, *Merlangus carbonarius.* 5. The Ling, *Lota molva.* 6. Five-bearded Rockling, *Motella quinquecirrata.* 7. The Whiting, *Merlangus vulgaris.* 8. Great Forked Hake, *Phycis furcatus.* 9 Common Cod, *Morrhua vulgaris.*

The cod and haddock are among the most important food-fishes in the world. They are caught with the hand-line on the edges of soundings, and visit the bays along the Atlantic coast to spawn. The Georgia Banks and the Gulf of St. Lawrence form pastures for millions of them, where they feed on launces (small eels), caplin, and young menhaden. The haddock is said to refuse all kinds of bait in stormy weather.

The cod and haddock, as important commercial fishes, are treated of in another part of the work.

THE FLATFISH FAMILY. (*Pleuronectidœ.*)

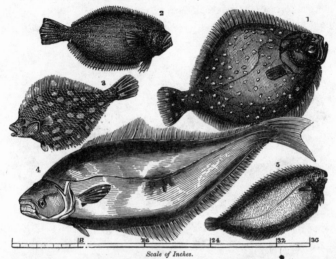

Scale of Inches.

FLATFISH FAMILY.—1. The Turbot, *Rhombus maximus.* 2. Oblong Flounder, *Platessa oblonga.* 3. The Plaice, *Platessa vulgaris* (similar in form to the *Rusty Dab* of our coasts). 4. The Halibut, *Hippoglossus vulgaris.* 5. Common Sole, *Solea vulgaris.*

The turbot of Europe is regarded as the aldermanic fish, answering to our sheepshead. Both the sole and turbot are great delicacies, and even luxuries. Boiled sole, served in a napkin on a hot plate, with cauliflower as a vegetable, and fresh drawn-butter, is not easily refused by the most pampered epicure. These fishes are generally taken with the hand-line and with the deep-sea casting-net. The meat of the sole is very white, and the taste pure and of delicate flavor. It is said to feed in deep waters along chalk cliffs.

Fishes 2 and 3 are the common flounder and the fluke. The lower jaw of the flounder is on the right side of the head, and that of the fluke on the left side. These are among the first biting fishes of the early spring season in most of the estuaries on the Atlantic coast. They are excellent fishes, but not sufficiently known or appreciated by epicures.

Until within the past ten years, it was supposed that neither the turbot nor the sole inhabited waters along the Atlan-

tic coast of North America; but recently a few turbot have
been taken off the coast of New Brunswick, and it is thought
their feeding-grounds will yet be found along our shores.

THIRD CLASS OF FISHES.

CARTILAGINOUS FISHES.   (*Chondropterygii.*)

SHARKS.—1. Large-spotted Dog-fish, *Scyllium catulus.* 2. Tope, or Penny-dog, *Galeus vulgaris.* 3. Blue Shark (the most common shark on our coasts), *Carcharius glaucus.* 4. Porbeagle, *Lamna cornubica.* 5. Small-spotted Dog-fish, *Scyllium canicula.* 6. Picked (or Piked) Dog-fish, *Acanthias vulgaris.* 7. Smooth Hound, *Mustelus lœvis.*

STURGEON AND CHIMÆRA FAMILIES.—1. Common Sturgeon of the Atlantic, *Acipenser sturio.* 2. Northern Chimera, *Chimæra monstrosa.* 3. American Lake Sturgeon, *Acipenser rubicundus.*

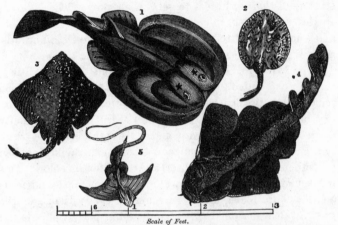

THE RAY FAMILY.—1. Common Torpedo, *Torpedo vulgaris*. 2. Many-spined Trygon, *Trygon histrix*. 3. Thornback Ray, *Raia clavata*. 4. Angel-fish, or Monk-fish, *Aquatina angelus*. 5. Eagle Ray, or Whip Ray, *Myliobatis aquila*.

THE CATFISH FAMILY.—1. Brown Catfish, *Pimelodus pullus*. 2. Common Catfish, or Horned Pout, *Pimelodus catus*.

The Catfish family embraces the numerous fresh-water fish which are known in this country by the common names of catfish, horned pouts, and bullheads. They mostly inhabit muddy streams and lakes, are destitute of scales, sluggish in their movements, and, like the famous fishing-frog or angler, to which they bear some resemblance, depend more upon

E e

stratagem than swiftness to seize their prey. The different species vary in length from three or four inches to four feet; and some are said to have been caught in the Ohio and Mississippi Rivers measuring eight feet in length.

In addition to the brown or black and common catfish, there is one called the "lady-cat," or channel catfish, which tenants the Missouri River, and is not only a great table luxury, but one of the most gamy fishes of the West. It usually ranges from five to fifteen pounds in weight, is symmetrically formed, with smaller head, and finer in general outline than the others, and is also lighter and brighter in color. This fish remains in the swiftest waters of the channel, and feeds on the chub, roach, and other small fry. It is one of the greatest delicacies of the fish kind, and in play it affords the disciple of rod and reel a treat long to be remembered. It is fished for with minnow for bait, using heavy bass tackle with a tracing sinker. When hooked, its run is very swift, and it is hard to turn and coax out of the channel, or to the gaff or landing-net.

The following singular circumstance, going to prove the affinity between the common horned pout and the bullfrog, may interest the naturalist:

n a recent occasion, while with Matteson, the artist, he informed me of the experience of Dr. White—one of the principal physicians in the central part of New York State — in fishing for horned pout, known throughout the country as bullheads.

The doctor, having a taste for angling, which he indulged whenever the condition of his patients permitted, was on his return homeward from visiting a patient, when a summer shower reminded him that it would sharpen the appetite of the bullheads in the river which he was approaching, and he therefore reined up under a shed near the river, hitched his horse, cut an ash pole, found a line armed with a hook and sinker in his pocket, dug some angle-worms, and forthwith went a-fishing.

There was a punt moored at the shore, and, leaving it anchored to the side of the stream, he stepped into it and began to fish. The bullheads put in an appearance immediately, so that within half an hour he had taken some two dozen fish, and as fast as he took them he cast them on the grassy bank of the shore. Having a pretty good mess, he cut a switch and went to string them, when not one was to be found. This surprised the doctor, and he at once concluded to solve the mystery, and so commenced fishing again, and throwing the fish on the shore as he had before done, but keeping a sly watch of them. After he cast the fourth one, a large bullfrog leaped from the water, took hold of a bullhead, and rolled into the water with it; leaping out immediately, and taking another fish, he rolled in as before, and so continued until he had returned the four to the water. The doctor continued fishing, and as fast as he had cast three or four fish on shore, the bullfrog returned and helped them back into the river.

As Dr. White is an educated gentleman who enjoys the confidence of a very wide professional and intellectual connexion, I feel assured of the truth of the foregoing incident, and therefore report the case for Professor Agassiz or some other naturalist, with the view to a learned decision on the nature of the link which connects the bullhead and frog.

The bullfrog could not have helped the bullheads back to the stream to feed on them, for the spiked dorsal and pectorals of the latter forbid it. Even the pike—the most voracious fresh-water fish in the world, excepting the *siluræ,* which is a species of catfish—is deterred from the attempt.

The important question for the naturalist is, Why did the
bullfrog help the bullhead? Does the celestial quality of
charity influence the lower strata of vertebrates?

SECTION SECOND.

THE COMMON EEL.

This *apode* is too common in both the salt-water estuaries,
and in the fresh waters throughout America, to require a minute description. Though many fishes come into fresh waters to spawn, the eel spawns in salt water when it can get
to it, going down stream in autumn, and returning in spring.
It is a bottom fish, and winters in the mud at the bottom of
eddies or shallow still waters in streams, where the fisher poles
his boat along with the handle of an eel-spear, and jabs right

THE COMMON EEL.—*Anguilla.*

and left in the mud, frequently impaling the writhing fish.
The silver eel at the mouths of the trout-brooks on Long Isl-
and is a great luxury when either fried hard or made into a
stew. It is regarded as so great a dish at Vandewater's, at
South Oyster Bay, as to be preferred to a trout in the trouting
season. In skinning the eel and drawing it, cut deeply each
side of the backbone, and from the vent, several inches downward, cut off all the part which appears to be a receptacle of

clotted blood. Yarrel informs us that "the London market is principally supplied from Holland by Dutch fishermen." The cultivation of eels and lampreys is now rendered very remunerative in Italy and in some parts of Germany. The average weight of each is from one to three pounds, but they have been known to attain to fifteen pounds' weight.

THE LAMPREY.

A member of the *Petromyzidæ* family, constituting the section cyclostomi of the "Règne Animal," distinguished by an imperfectly developed skeleton and want of pectoral and ventral fins, combined with an eel-like form of body. The mouth is circular, consisting of a cartilaginous ring formed by soldering together the palatine and mandibular bones. The branchiæ, instead of being pectinated, are purse-shaped, and open externally by several apertures.

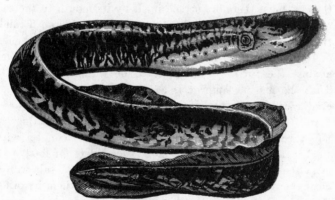

THE LAMPREY.—*Petromyzon marinus.*

The lamprey is supposed to be the lowest of the vertebrate animals. They are usually two feet in length, and the engraving is a fac-simile of them. Having no swimming-bladder, and being also without pectoral fins, they usually swim near the bottom; and, to save themselves from the constant muscular exertion which is necessary to prevent them from

being carried along with the current, they attach themselves
by the mouth to stones or rocks, and were, in consequence,
called "Petromyzon," or stone-suckers; while the circular,
purse-shaped form of the mouth induced the name "Cyclo-
stomes," or round-mouthed fishes.

The lamprey is highly esteemed for the table, and is therefore much sought after in the rivers where it is found. Like
the eel, it ascends rivers in the spring, and returns to salt
water in the fall. Sir W. Jardine supposes they spawn in
fresh water, but he probably confounds them with the river
lamprey, which is a more common fish, and less sought after
by the epicure. It is known that the marine lamprey attaches itself to vessels for traversing the coasts, rivers, and
canals; and some Continental naturalists argue that, as the
lamprey is much slower than the eel, but visits the upper
parts of rivers about the time when salmon and shad appear
there, it must therefore attach itself by its mouth to the salmon and shad, and is by them towed up the rivers. I think
the idea absurd, though it has the sort of sanctional belief
of Doctor Gunther, and that which Professor Agassiz gives
against the turtle's willingness to be turned on its back.
That the marine lamprey is a more active fish than it has
credit for being is probably nearer the truth.

Both eels and lampreys may be cultivated by cutting canals through soft marsh and swamp lands to connect with
tidal waters, as they redaily enter such inlets for food, and,
after they grow large and fat, and turn toward salt water,
close the copper-wire gates on them, and lead them by other
sluices to chambers from which there is no egress.

The eel fishery at Comacchio nets annually $70,000. The
Po is a shallow, sluggish river, which debouches into the
Adriatic by its legs of the Reno and Volano, between which
is a large swamp and numerous lagoons. Here eels, which
enter in the spring and fatten through the summer, are intercepted on their way back to sea in the fall by closing
the main outlets, and leading them by devious channels to

pounds prepared for their reception. They are then salted, some smoked, some roasted and salted, while the markets of Milan, Verona, Padua, Venice, and other cities are supplied with fresh ones. The same could be done along a hundred rivers on the Atlantic coast; but we do not yet realize the scarcity of fish.

QUEER FISHES.

The estuary catfish is an oviparous abdominal, and one of the recent visitants to our coasts and estuaries from the Bahama Banks. The first rays of the dorsal and pectoral fins are rigid; second dorsal adipose; head broad, and depressed on the top, with small catfish eyes placed far apart; long antennæ; two distinct nostrils at end of nose, with ear-vents at the side, below the eyes. It is without scales, and its blue back mellows to pink sides and white abdomen. Its colors and brilliant sheen are like the Spanish mackerel's, without its spots. It is leather-mouthed, and the mouth small, armed with a cushion of fine, needle-pointed teeth round the borders of both jaws, showing that it may forage on *crustacea* and the inhabitants of the waters generally. An individual 20 inches long weighed scant two pounds, and it seldom attains to a greater weight than ten pounds; and, from its great delicacy, it resembles both the lady-cat of the Missouri River and the Spanish mackerel of the Atlantic coast. Though generally captured in fykes, it is a bottom-biter to the angle, with menhaden or shedder-crab baits.

The *silure* is a native of the River Danube, and, from the high esteem in which it is held throughout Europe as a table luxury, acclimatizers and *pisciculturists* have introduced it into most of the waters of Germany, some of France, and a few of England. Bertram, in his "Treasures of the Sea," says of the *Silurus glanis* that its character is rather under a cloud, as its capacious maw has been said to contain the arm and shoulder of a man; and from the immense weight to which it attains, of from 200 lbs. to 300 lbs., and the knowledge that it is the most voracious of all fresh-water fishes, the story gains credence.

It is a bottom-feeding fish, like the catfish, and, like that, it

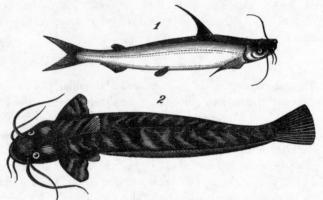

No. 1. Estuary Catfish.   No. 2. The Silure, or *Silurus glanis* of the Danube.

is a great gormandizer, thinning off the frogs, and proving a perfect terror to all young fishes of the ordinary families. As fattening this fish for market is very expensive, it would scarcely pay to import it for stocking any of the American waters but the Mississippi and Missouri, where it would form one more family of the catfish species, and make up their sum to six varieties of this ugly-looking delicacy.   The London *Times* states that the *Silurus glanis* rises to the ponderosity of over 300 lbs., and " has been known to reach the enormous weight of 54 lbs. in four years; that its flesh somewhat resembles veal in appearance, and partakes of the rich flavor of the eel."

SECTION THIRD.

FISHES FOR ACCLIMATIZING IN AMERICAN RIVERS.

The INDE, a fish somewhat resembling the shad, grows to the weight of nine pounds; subsists on aquatic plants and insects; affords good sport to the angler.   It is found in Scandinavian waters.

The SALMO HUCHO, or the *huchen*, is a very voracious fish, and would do well in our Western rivers. It can be imported from Huningue. It affords good sport to the angler.

The MOUNTAIN MULLET is said by Mr. Francis to be "one of the most delicious edibles to be found among fish." It inhabits rapid streams, grows to the weight of two or three pounds, is fished for with light tackle, and is rapturous sport for the angler. It is abundant in Jamaica, and the streams of the Southern States may easily be stocked with it.

The SCANDINAVIAN CHARR is a delicious fish of from three to five pounds' weight, is fine game for the fly, and might be successfully introduced into the waters of the Northern and Eastern States.

OMBRE CHEVALIER.—This is regarded as the most rare European fish delicacy. It is found in the Lake of Geneva and many other waters of Switzerland, its eggs commanding a cent each at the fish-cultural establishment of Huningue, in France. This fish, of the *genus Salmo*, and running from eight to twelve pounds in weight, may be acclimatized, and all the Northern waters in America readily stocked with it. So with the *Salmo umbla* and the *salvalinus*. They are rather more nearly related to the families of salmon and trout than are the *charr*, and from what I have heard of the Moosehead Lake trout, I should not be surprised to learn that it is an *ombre chevalier*.

The GRAYLING.—This fish affords the fly-fisher as great a treat as any fish belonging to the family of the *genus Salmo*, provided it be fished for with delicate fly-tackle. It usually ranges from fifteen to twenty-five inches in length, and from two to four pounds in weight. The rivers of New England and New York might be readily stocked with this white-meated luxury.

A few rivers and lakes south of the St. Lawrence—eminently those inhabited by pike, pickerel, perch, and the fresh-water families of bass—might be economically stocked with MASKINONGÉ, which is the head of the *genus Esox* as well in edible qualities as in size, and in saltatory powers and gamy habits while playing on the angler's hook.

The WINNINISH, of the upper waters of the Saguenay River, in Canada, should by all means be introduced to the rivers of Maine and New Hampshire. It is the richest game for its size of any belonging to the *genus Salmo*, and a higher luxury for the table than any other of the numerous salmon families.

"But, after all," to use an American phrase of emphatic significance, the brook trout and salmon of our Northern waters are among the best fresh-water fishes in the world for both the epicure and the angler. Add to these the numerous delicacies of whitefish, cisco, black bass, and the farther armies of our lakes and rivers, with the teeming millions of our coasts and estuaries, and we should be satisfied if we can continue our present ample store until we can conveniently add a few kinds more.

THE SHORT SUNFISH.

Part Sixth.

---◇◇---

SOUTHERN FISHES,

AND

HOW ANGLED FOR.

CHAPTER I.

FLORIDA FISHES AND FISHING.

SECTION FIRST.

" Oh how blest to dwell forever,
　'Mid these scenes of placid peace!
If some power the past could sever,
　If the tones of mem'ry cease,
Ah! not Faith herself dare cherish
　Hopes unstain'd by 'wild'ring fears;
Could we dream the *past* might perish,
　What shall quench our *future* tears?
　　Vale of bliss? what joy to wander
　　Where thy glittering waters flow!
　　Here, e'en Guilt in peace may ponder;
　　Here, Despair forget her woe!"

To favor the angler with at once a succinct and comprehensive view of Florida water sports, I premise with the following communication by the pen of Mr. C——, an accomplished sportsman and learned ichthyologist, who has devoted several winters to the field-sports of this genial climate.

"Mr. G. C. Scott, in his 'Fishing in American Waters,' says, 'It would be well worth while to make an angling tour southward in autumn.' I have been making such a tour this winter, the results of which I will give you: my first fishing was at New Smyrna, near Musquito Inlet, in East Florida. Here I found an excellent boarding-house, kept by Mr. E. K. Lowd, which is truly the sportsman's home. The sheepshead is here the principal fish, and its numbers may be judged by an extract from my journal:

"*March* 15. Fished one hour on flood tide, with hand-line and clam bait, from boat anchored to mangrove bushes—fifteen fish, weight sixty pounds.

"*March* 16. Fished two hours, same bait — seventeen fish, weight seventy-one pounds.

"*March* 18. Fished one hour, high-water to ebb — twelve fish, weight fifty pounds.

"*March* 21. Fished two hours, half flood — fourteen fish, weight sixty-one pounds.

"*March* 22. Fished one hour and a half, young flood— twenty - seven fish, weight one hundred and ten pounds. Largest sheepshead, seven pounds.

"I might have caught many more, but it would have been a waste of the good gifts, for we could not have used them; what I did catch being ample for the use of the house. Besides these, we catch the *whiting,* a small but excellent fish, shaped like the white perch,* double dorsal fin, with strong spines in front; color, gray on the back; belly, yellowish white; mouth small, teeth do.; weighs from one to two pounds. Also the *sea trout,* which is well described on page 82 of Mr. Scott's book, with the exception that I found the inside of the mouth yellow, teeth few, but strong. In general appearance it much resembles the lake trout of the Adirondacks, and is a very handsome, game fish, of good edible quality; weighs from one to twenty pounds. But the best and most sporting fish I found here is the *redfish,* or *channel bass,†* which bears a general likeness to the striped bass (*Labrax lineatus*) in its excellence on the table, and its game qualities when hooked; fighting to the last, and showing much sagacity, as well as great activity and vigor. First dorsal fin, eight rays, with sharp spines; second dorsal, twenty-four soft rays; pectoral, six rays, soft; ventral, five rays, soft; anal, eight rays, soft; tail, square. Color: back, steel-blue; sides, copper-red; belly, white—a black spot, half an inch in diameter, at the base of the tail on both sides; from

---

* Probably the real white perch, which are much larger than at the North.—G. C. S.

† Local names for the spot-tail bass.—G. C. S.

which mark, if the fish has not already been named, I would call it *Labrax bimaculatus*—the two-spotted bass. In size I found it here from three to ten pounds, but am told that it frequently is taken weighing from forty to fifty pounds, and has been seen of nearly one hundred pounds. We also found the *scup** and the sea *catfish* at Musquito Inlet; the latter like the fresh-water catfish of the great lakes, but a handsomer fish in shape and color — weight, from two to ten pounds.† There are also plenty of sharks, rays, and the sawfish, sometimes ten or twelve feet long, with a saw of four feet in length. We find here the green turtle very common, and oysters of the best quality every where for the picking up.

"At Musquito Inlet the redfish were generally about from three to six pounds in weight; but we were told that in Indian River we should find them of great size, and that there was in that river quite a variety of sporting fishes. So, being rather weary of catching the sheepshead, my friend and I hired a sail-boat and boatman, put on board a tent, blankets, and camp equipage, with some provisions, and started for Indian River. These rivers, as they are called in Florida, are like the bays on Long Island; wide, shallow reaches of salt water, separated from the ocean by a narrow sea-beach.‡ We sailed one hundred and twenty-five miles south to the inlet, where we camped, and fished for some days. We found here the redfish and channel bass in great numbers, and took them with mullet bait, cut up as you cut menhaden for the striped bass. They were from five to thirty pounds, and full of fight and vigor, so that we lost a great many large ones from the parting of our lines, which were the best hand-lines used by the Newport fishermen. Our hooks were broken, our hands were cut to pieces, and we frequently came off second best in our battles with these copper-colored kings of the river. With rod and reel of the right sort, the sport

---

* Porgee.   † See *Estuary Catfish*, p. 440.   ‡ Like Fire Island.

would be glorious, and several New York anglers so equipped have enjoyed it this winter.

"Besides the bass, we caught at the Indian River Inlet the *black snapper*. Resembles in form the tautog, and belongs, I think, to the *Wrasse* family; large mouth, strong teeth, bites eagerly at mullet, and pulls hard; is silvery in color when first taken, then turns red, and afterward black: a rich and savory fish—four to sixteen pounds.

"*Cavallo.*—This fish is in form between a dolphin and a mackerel; has the brilliant hues of the former; very active; a surface fish, going in schools; takes a red rag or spoon as well as mullet bait—from two to fifteen pounds; in taste like the mackerel.

"*Sargent Fish.*—A rapacious fish, in form like the pike-perch, with underhung jaw like the pickerel; silvery sides, with a black stripe from gill to tail, whence its local name; lies under the mangrove bushes for prey—weight, from two to twenty pounds.

"*Croaker.*—In form like sheepshead, but not so thick; color, silvery; bites eagerly, and pulls hard. A good fish for the table.

"Of the following we heard, but did not catch them: *drum, hogfish, bluefish,* from six to fifteen pounds—same as the Northern fish of the name; *Spanish mackerel,* two to sixteen pounds; *Jewfish,* twenty to one hundred pounds; *bezuga,* said to be the best fish in these waters except the pompano—weight, one-half to one pound.

"*Pompano* resembles the cavallo in form; does not take the hook; is always taken in a net by night; best fish in Southern waters; bones boil soft.

"We found in the St. Johns River the 'black trout,' as they call it, but which is almost identical with the black bass of the North-west. It grows to the weight of twelve pounds, and is very plenty in that river, so that we caught numbers of them by trolling with a spoon from a small steamer, with one hundred yards of line. Game in this region is very plenty; such as bears, deer, panther, wild cat, raccoon, opossum, gray squirrel, wild turkey, quail, many kinds of ducks in vast quantities, curlew, plover, herons, bitterns, and cranes. The climate is mild, so that you can live in a tent all winter, and there is very little rain except in summer."

Several gentlemen of my acquaintance — men who have seen the world, and either cast a line or carried a gun over the most celebrated sporting grounds of the eastern hemisphere — have for several years past, spent their winters in Florida; and they unite in recommending it for the geniality of its climate, the great abundance of sport for rod and gun, and for the purity and floral aroma with which the atmosphere is laden, thus rendering the air throughout winter like the bland and balmy season at the North when the gardens are in full bloom. The magnolia, and many flowers which vie with the camellia-japonica, the rose, and honeysuckle, lend a fragrance every where, while lemons and oranges are green, ripe, and ripening, and the flowering almond and fig trees in blossom remind the sportsman of the Garden of Eden. Even Italy, with its Cornice Road and cactus hedges, is not so fertile of winter flowers and fruits as are the American Floridas, which promise in course of time, and that not very remote, to become the winter residence of an intelligent population and present the most elegant specimens of architecture; and besides the railroads in every direction, there will be drives more beautiful than the Pradas of Vienna and Florence, with labyrinthine walks and paths for horseback riders, by which the peninsula will cast into the shade all other countries in Christendom, for its beauty of scenery, its mild climate, its fragrance and floral beauty, with its incomparable out-of-door recreations.

Florida is pre-eminently the place to sojourn in winter. Not only does it contain sports for the angler and gunner throughout the inclement season of the North, but to the aged and infirm it offers restoration, and brings back the vigor and elasticity of youth.

F F

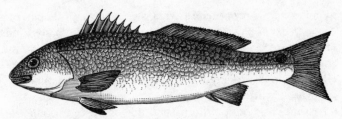

SPOT-TAIL BASS.—*Corvina ocelata*, or "*Labrax bimaculatus*," the two-spotted bass.

CHAPTER II.

SECTION FIRST.

THIS fish is particularly described by our learned corre-spondent, C——; therefore I have only to state that the en-graver cut out one of the spiked dorsals, as there should be eight; though the fish after which I made the drawing from still-life had a lunated instead of a square tail. Otherwise, it was in all particulars like the bass described by C——.

Dorsal fins and caudal, black; all other fins red; dark gray back and sides; white abdomen; steel-blue head and jaws, covered with scales, and armed with sharp teeth; scales rath-er large, and the ends dark-colored.

It will be observed that the head and mouth resemble our kingfish, except wanting the barb under the lower mandi-ble; it is therefore necessary to fish with a striped bass hook, about No. 7, made of heavy steel wire and well tempered. Those of the Virginia shape, with short bend, or like the Isl-and Club hooks, would be preferred. Fish with strong bass tackle, the rod about nine feet long, two joints beside a stiff lancewood top, with agate or bell-metal tip. A reel large enough to carry two hundred yards of thirteen-strands linen line. A bright bait—the side of a scup or shedder-crab are the most attractive. The habits of the two-spotted bass, or spot-tail, are quite similar to those of the striped bass of Northern waters, seeking at the first turn of flood-tide along the shallows and weedy shores for *crustacea* and the small fishes which delay too long their weedy shelters by the hope of picking up fresh delicacies in approximate danger.

By the following extracts from a letter by Isaac M'Lellan, the poet, written at Smyrna, on Halifax River, inviting me to Florida, the reader will find further items of interest. The rivers along the coast are like the bays of New Jersey, separated from the sea by a sandy beach, or like the Great South Bay, protected from the heavy waves of the Atlantic by Fire Island. To quote: "In these rivers are found sheepshead and many other kinds of fish in great plenty. A Mr. B——, from Brooklyn, who is a great angler, has been staying here for some time, and says the fishing is 'too good.' He gets from fifty to one hundred sheepshead every time he goes out, besides many channel bass, of from four to twelve pounds' weight each. This is the spot-tail bass." * * * "As to shooting," he states, "there is no end to the feathered and fur game." * * * "*To get here:* Take steamer from New York for Savannah, or take a through ticket to Jacksonville, by which you will save several dollars, and you may remain in Savannah, if wishing to stop, and thence you may either go by railroad or steamer on the through ticket. Heavy fishing-tackle, heavy spoons, such as are used on the great lakes, and such as are used in trolling for bluefish and Spanish mackerel." [Also take the smaller feathered spoons, to troll on the rivers of the interior for the black bass, which is similar to the Oswego bass.]

"Bring a double duck-gun, and a lighter one for the woods, and a rifle—breech-loader, if possible. Bring your ammunition, especially if you use fixed. You will want a row-boat and a cat-rigged sail-boat, with flat floor and a centre-board. The boats you can procure here.

"If, at this place, you could be at a central point whence to sail up and down the rivers of bays, you would find it a real paradise for sportsmen."

The spot-tail bass is said to be numerous in the Gulf of

Mexico, the Caribbean Sea, and all over the Bahama Banks, along the coast of Florida, and as far north as South Carolina.   As a dinner fish, it is generally regarded by the epicures of New York as superior to the sheepshead—the hitherto aldermanic dinner fish *par excellence.*

This beautiful, gamy, and excellent fish is coming northward.   It is now more numerous annually off the Carolina shores; and, like the sierro (cero), cavallo, and bonetta (*bonito*), may soon become another valuable gem to our coast fishermen, if perchance the menhaden is spared, as the most attractive bait-fish in the world, to allure the rich fishes of that vast area known as the Bahama Banks.

It is interesting to notice that the débris from the currents around the north of Ireland and the east of Baffin's and Hudson's bays are forming the prospective new continent included in the area of Newfoundland, Anticosti, and the Georgia Shoals, and that the subsidence of the tides about the Bahama Banks and Florida Reef are enlarging the islands.   These phenomena neutralize the temperature of the Gulf Stream between the Northern and Southern great banks, so as to form the Atlantic shore between them into the most extensive feeding-ground in the world.

Fishings for the rod and reel on the bays and estuaries along the Atlantic coast south of New Jersey, having hitherto been approximately neglected by lovers of field sports, we hope soon to learn that these Elysian fields and waters for the disciples of Fishrod and Nimrod are being enjoyed in proportion to their attractions.   Our wealthy gentlemen who like angling, trolling, and shooting, should erect winter dwellings in Florida, and maintain boats and shooting-boxes there.

"Oh! dulcet is the poet's rhyme,
  When the angler goes a-trolling;
Dulcet and glad the river's chime,
  A pæan in the march of Time!
  When the angler goes a-trolling."

SECTION SECOND.

"Would you Sbeak mit Me?"

OUR initial letter friend having had an intimation that good angling could be had in Florida, concluded to purchase an Izaak Walton, and peruse it so as to learn how to tie flies and take trout, with other game fish, according to the highest style of art. He is pleased to think that he can study and angle at the same time. While at this double occupation, he is called upon by the "hydragos," to learn whether the angler wished to speak with him; he probably wanted to bargain for larger bait.

The red snapper is rather more chubby in shape than the striped bass, being between that and the tautog, or black-

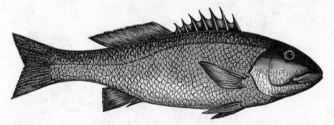

THE RED SNAPPER.—*Lutjanus aya.*

fish, of the coasts of New Jersey and New England. It is clothed with very large scales, covering the body and the lower half of the head. The first dorsal is spiked, as is also the anal, with one sharp and strong spike at front of the fin. It has a rather large mouth, armed with sharp and powerful teeth, but not so closely set as are those of the bluefish or the Spanish mackerel of our waters. It is therefore good sport to rod and reel, or with the troll, biting readily at a silver or pearl squid, or to a hook baited with a piece of mullet or porgee.

The color of this fish is vermilion on the back and a lighter tint of red as it approaches the abdomen, which is a light pink. The eyes are red, with black pupil. Its average weight is about twelve pounds, though it attains to very great weight—some say one hundred pounds. Its meat is creamy white, flaky, and juicy; and by many is supposed to be the best dinner fish of the coast.

The red snapper is found in greatest numbers in the bays of the Bahama Banks and the Gulf of Mexico and the Floridas; but it is taken throughout the western archipelago. It spawns in the spring season, and, like the striped bass and others of that *genus*, it requires from one to two months to lay its eggs.

This fish belongs to the same *genus* as the black snapper, which my learned friend C—— thinks may belong to the Wrasse family, though I believe it is one of the bass or mackerel tribes. It is quite certain that it is an excellent commercial and game fish, affording capital sport, and I leave the rest to the "scientists."

LONG-BARRED MULLET.

The long-barred mullet is an excellent trolling bait for these waters, and the manner of mounting it upon hooks tied on wire-gimp snells, with a loop to attach to a swivel and gimp leader, forms the best spinning tackle wherewith to troll with rod and reel, or to angle in a swift current on the bay-rivers of Florida; but the hooks should be of heavier wire than those represented.

The kingfish of the West Indies is numerous along the southern shores of the Caribbean Sea, around the islands of steep shores and deep waters of the West Indies, and in the

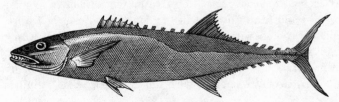

THE KINGFISH.—*Cybium regale.*

Gulf of Mexico. It is also found in the bays off the Florida shores. It is one of the swiftest fishes, more active than the dolphin, and does not wait for the flying-fish to alight on the wave, but leaps high above it and takes his prey on the wing. He is a terror to young Indians, who dare not bathe when naked, for fear of losing a finger or toe, while occasionally one *perdres son vie* by those steel jaws and teeth, which are as sharp as a surgeon's knife, and clip off a digit quicker than a flash.

The color of the kingfish is dark blue above the lateral line, and lightens toward the belly, where it is a light gray. The first dorsal is spike-rayed, while the first ray of the second dorsal and top of pectoral fin are each guarded by a spinous ray. Like the Spanish mackerel and bonetta, the tail is framed at top and bottom by a rigid bone frame, so that it never falls together, but, to make up for the otherwise want of balance support, there is a short row of fins on each side, extending from the root of the tail three to four inches up the side. The back fins and upper part of caudal are black, and the others gray. Covered throughout, except the top of its head, with infinitesimal scales on a tough skin, it presents the appearance, when first captured, of burnished steel. It ranges in weight from eight to forty pounds, and its sweet and juicy meat renders it a great delicacy, whether boiled, broiled, or formed into chowder.

This fish will take a hook disguised by white or red cloth,

or a bone or metal squid, and when hooked in trolling will leap ten feet above water several times, and show the most vigorous play of any fish belonging to the mackerel tribes. It is said that small ones, of from ten to fifteen pounds weight and from thirty inches to four feet in length, are frequently taken with rod and reel, gimp snells, and strong hooks, in the bay rivers along the southern shores of Florida. A fish of such rare edible qualities and great sport is worthy a long journey to capture with rod and reel. Small mullets

CROSS-BARRED MULLET.

form a favorite bait for both trolling and still-baiting for any of the surface-biting game fishes of the Atlantic coast. A mullet rigged by pinning his jaws together with a hook, as here shown, breathes freely through the undisturbed gills, and will live several hours, whether trolling or still-fishing.

SECTION THIRD.

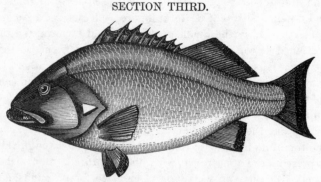

THE GROUPER.—*Epinephalus*, St.

This fish weighs from fifteen to seventy-five pounds; or those which are sold in the Southern markets range between those weights. I should suppose it belongs to the *genus Tunny*, were it not for its short, square-ended fins, its large scales and chubbed form, being both wide and thick, with a huge head and large mouth, armed with numerous short and sharp teeth, in several rows on each mandible; it is, therefore, unlike any other fish of our bays, being much more powerful than the drum, and several fold larger than the sheepshead or sea bass, these being the fishes which it most nearly resembles in outline. The top of its head is black, and the ends of all the fins but the pectoral are edged with an inch-wide band of jet black; the rest of the fins being neutral-tinted, the back, a dark brownish gray, fading regularly toward a white abdomen. This is eminently a South American fish, which forages north as far as extend the Bahama Banks. It feeds on such *crustacea* as crabs, mussels, soft-shell clams, shrimp, and does not refuse eels, butter-fish, mullets, and porgees. Besides its large jaws and numerous teeth, its first dorsal is strongly spiked, as is also the top ray of its pectoral fin; and it is further armed with a short and strong spear on the outer gill-cover each side of the head, as represented by the white triangular figure on the gill; and the grouper has the power to turn its point at right-angle with the body, or to lay it down flat in its sheath on its huge and powerful gill-cover. The grouper is an excellent dinner fish, and when boiled and served with drawn butter and shrimp or lobster sauce, is said to fully equal the turbot.

It is taken in nets and on the troll. It plays very vigorously, alternately leaping and plunging, contending for some half an hour on the strongest-armed metal squids, and which he often crushes and escapes, though the hand-line to the troll be manned by an experienced and expert fisherman.

It frequently gives trollers in the Gulf of Mexico and in the bays around Florida a test of its qualities for game. The following sketch is intended to represent a student belonging to the Hand-line Committee, who concluded not to be troubled with holding his line, so fastened it to his leg; and when reading up to the most interesting part of an eventful story, succeeds in getting the bite of a grouper!

Both the red and black drums afford the angler great sport; but for the table the red drum is infinitely the superior of the two fishes, which are the most numerous in the estuaries and bayous of Florida; also very plenty along the coast of Virginia during the month of May. They are occasionally taken in the bays of New York in August and September. They range in weight from ten to eighty pounds;

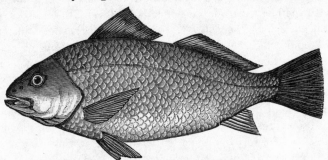

THE RED DRUM.—*Pogonias chromis.*

and though a bottom-biting fish, when hooked they make long runs, and show most generous play. They are fond of mussels, clams, and oysters, while they fairly revel on soft-shell and shedder crabs; and it is usually on this latter bait that anglers take them in New York waters.

Mr. N. Saltus, a coast angler, who usually spends his winters in Florida for the sake of its excellent fishing, thus writes me: "The drum fishes are found in the month of February in Indian River, Florida, and about this time they commence their northward trip for summering. About the first week in March they enter the Matanzas and the St. Augustine inlets, where for the next three weeks they may be heard drumming, as they feed on oysters and have in their throat a crushing mill, where they grind the oyster-shell, extracting the oyster [equal to a lawyer] and rejecting the shell, the crushing of which makes the drumming sound, after which the fish is named. Early in April they appear in the rivers about Beaufort, South Carolina, and about June 1st are discovered at Cape May, which is near the limit of their northern trip. A few stragglers extend to the waters about Staten Island. They run in shoals, and weigh from eight to a hundred pounds; but forty to sixty is the run of large ones. When caught with a bass rod and reel they make fine sport, but they play low. A 'baby drum' of from five to ten pounds is as fine eating as any fish; but larger than ten pounds they increase in coarseness, though a good table fish as a boiler from twenty to thirty pounds."

The drum is in New York considered a game fish, and Mr. Brown, of the Latourette Club, won "high-hook" at a contest in Newark Bay, in August, 1872, by capturing a forty-pound red drum.

The red drum is red on back, fins, head, tail, and white abdomen. Its mouth is armed with a forest of fine teeth, covering the border of the mouth for a half inch all round; and in its throat it has an upper and lower millstone, by which it crushes oysters, clams, and mussels, and producing a sound like the beating of a muffled drum. Its fins are formed of soft rays, as represented by the engraving, which is a very exact likeness, even to the square tail and large tongue.

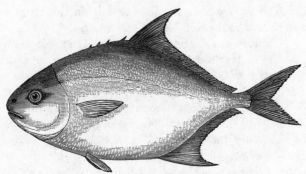

THE POMPANO. — *Trachynotus Carolinus.*

CHAPTER III.

SECTION FIRST.

THIS excellent broiler is an equally good boiler; for, according to Mr. C——, "its bones boil soft." It is a delicious, creamy luxury, melting in the mouth, and without any foreign taste, it being the best possible in itself. It is mullet-mouthed; never takes a bait except by mistake. It is caught by nets set in the night-time. It is supposed to spawn in spring-time, each pair of fishes producing a shoal of fifty thousand or more; but as it does not become abundant, not a market ever having been known to be glutted with it, tithes of each shoal must go to satisfy the capacious maws of the dolphin and numerous shoals of rapacious food-fishes, which get partly paid for it when they undertake to swallow a squid or bait with a hook in it.

The weight of the pompano is from half to a pound and a half. There are three movable spikes at front of the dorsal, being its only protection, except that it is a swift swimmer, and can lie closely hidden against the rocky bottom. Its infinitesimal scales radiate the light, and when alive it is a sparkling gem. In tints the pompano is decked with all the colors of the rainbow, blended so as to sparkle, and form of it a gem of superior brilliancy and beauty.

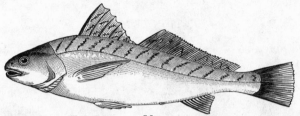

THE CROCUS.—*Micropogon costatus.*

This is the best pan-fish or broiler, not excepting the pompano or Spanish mackerel. It is a mullet, of course, and even better for the table than the black mullet. It is a small drab fish, with soft-rayed fins and square tail. The small corrugated rayures on the fins and above the lateral line form a lively relief. The fish runs from a quarter to a half pound, and is eminently a string pan-fish. Mr. Terry, the principal fish-dealer in Charleston, South Carolina, recently sent me a string of fish, including the crocus and pompano, when I found the crocus superior to all the others as a breakfast dish.

It is taken in fykes of very small meshes, or by fishing for it in the manner of taking smelt, as described elsewhere.

> "A merry fish on a stallion hair,
>   'Tis a pleasant thing to lead
> On May-days, when the cowslip fair
>   Is yellowing on the mead."

This tiny fish, of from one-fourth to a half-pound, is found near the banks along shore from Virginia to Florida, foraging in shoals, and keeping close to overhanging shores shaded with low brambles. It bites readily to a small clam 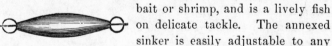 bait or shrimp, and is a lively fish on delicate tackle. The annexed sinker is easily adjustable to any depth of water, by a wire at each end extending beyond the ring.

SECTION SECOND.

THE CAVALLO.—*Species of Carangus.*

This is a beautiful and excellent fish of the Florida waters. It is beginning to visit our bays and inlets, the first having appeared along the New Jersey coast, and between the Narrows and Fire Island, in 1871, and every summer since; but, like the advent of the bonetta, which has now become too numerous, it advances in small shoals, like scouts sent out to find foraging-ground. Without doubt, the menhaden (vulgarly called moss-bunker) is the chief bait-fish which has attracted the half-dozen families of excellent food-fishes from the Bahamas and the Southern coasts within the past ten years, headed by the Spanish mackerel, and the cavallo and pompano bringing up the rear.

The pompano having a wide reputation for being one of the best breakfast fishes in the world, and the cavallo resembling it in shape and beauty of tints, sparkling with small scales, the fish-dealers at once called it the pompano, and it commanded over a dollar a pound; but as it became more abundant, and the real pompano appeared, it fell below the Spanish mackerel in price.

The weight of this fish is from three to fifteen pounds; and it will be seen by comparing the engravings from the drawings made of the fishes when present, that the cavallo is a much more beautiful fish in outline than the pompano.

The dorsal and anal fins are rigid, and there is a sharp spike just forward of the anal.   The curved lateral line from the gill to the centre of the body is continued to the caudal by a line of prickly bones, which form its chief protection. The color of the upper fins is neutral, with a reddish tint; the lower ones a light ash color.   The back of the head is nearly black, the back being dark purple of brownish shade, lighting to the lateral line, below which it is a light rose and azure blended on a most brilliant sheen, descending to a satin-white abdomen.

The cavallo is very numerous in the saline rivers of Florida, and along the coast to the Carolinas.   It is a surface-biting fish, forages in shoals, and may be taken on an attractive troll, either metal, pearl, bone, or with red cloth; but it is well to ornament a bone or metal squid with red silk.   It also affords excellent sport when taken on the usual rod and reel bass tackle.   Its fine teeth seldom part tackle, and as it is one of the most active of all food-fishes, it may be properly regarded as one of the angler's luxuries.   Mr. C—— very properly states that its form is between the dolphin and mackerel, and in taste it resembles the latter.

LAFAYETTE: THE SPOT.—*Leiostomus obliquus.*

This fish is a luxury for both the angler and epicure.   It is nearly or quite identical with the little luxury taken in October in our waters, and known as the Lafayette, because it made its first appearance in waters about New York the same year that General Lafayette visited America the last time. Its shape is like the porgee, and ornamented with diagonal dark bars on each side, and a black spot just back of the gills on each side of the body.

The natural feeding-ground of this excellent pan-fish is the waters which wash the shores of bays and estuaries on the coasts of Virginia and the Carolinas. Its weight is from one-fourth to a pound and a half; but generally about a half-pound. The edge of the small mouth is thickly covered with very fine short pin-teeth, merely forming a rough edge to the jaws.

The colors of the spot are a blackish green on the back, fading to a yellowish drab at the sides, and white abdomen. The dorsal fins are separated, though both soft-rayed and nearly black, as is also the caudal fin; but the pectoral fin is light yellow, and the belly fins are white. The top of the head is black; eye yellow, with black pupil. The meat is white and succulent; will fry in its own fat. It is taken on light bass tackle, with trout hooks and fine linen line. All lines for use in salt water should be of linen, for silk is too elastic to respond, and it wears out sooner than linen. Besides, the perfection in the make of linen lines renders them fine enough for almost any kind of fishing. The favorite baits are soft and hard clams; but it will take shedder-crab and small bits of any shiny parts of the white mullet, or scup. The Virginians call this fish the "spot, or salt-water roach." Its scales are very small, and the fish is beautiful when first taken from the water; and its meat being compact and rather solid, it does not soon deteriorate. It is taken from the first of June to the middle of October.

Few anglers about New York properly appreciate the Lafayette; they confound it with the sand-porgee, which is one of the smallest and most worthless of the bait-thieves that infest the waters in October about the metropolis; whereas it is the most delicate pan-fish that rubs its scintillant sides on the rocky shoals above Fort Wadsworth and off Rabineau's Point, at the confluence of Kill-Van-Kull and Newark Bay.

The spot taken in Northern waters are so small—seldom weighing over a quarter of a pound—that it is best to fish with small brook-trout hooks, single gut leader and snells, and bait with small pieces of clam or shrimp. If anglers will rig for them about the 20th of October, and bait and fish carefully with a pair of small trout-hooks, they will be rewarded with messes of pan-fish superior to any which the New York markets afford at that time of year.

SECTION THIRD.

THE VIRGINIA HOGFISH.—*Lachnolœmus caninus.*

This fish differs greatly from the hogfish of the Bahamas of page 98. While it offers good sport to the angler, it is a superior table luxury, being so oily as to fry itself; and its white and juicy meat is sweet and of excellent relish. The dorsals and caudal fins, with the top of the head, are black; black back, and fading to a light-gray abdomen, with pectoral, anal, and ventral fins a gray, with yellowish tinge. The irregular marks with which the fish is ornamented are a gold color. This fish is toothless, except very fine pin-teeth in the edge of the jaws and on the palate. Its weight is from a half to two pounds; bites at clam, shedder, and small bright bits of the scup. It is taken on light bass tackle, bites readily, and gives good play.

The shadine belongs to a family of the mullet tribes; is

G G

from the size of a minnow, or shiner, to the length of nearly a foot. It is a very active and vigorous bait-fish, as scintil-

The Shadine.

lant as a diamond. It is taken in great numbers in the bay-ous of New Jersey, where it is preserved in olive-oil, and put up like. sardines. It is a new luxury; but it is here intro-duced as the best bait-fish, for either trolling or still-baiting in a swift tideway, of any on the Atlantic coast.

The Silver, or Gray Mullet.

This is a beautiful fish, white and scintillant below the lateral line, with infinitesimal scales. Its favorite feeding-ground is along the coasts of Maryland, Virginia, and the Carolinas; its weight is from a quarter to two pounds; very tender, toothless mouth; to be fished for with fly-hooks, like the smelt, baited with a bit of fish or clam. Back of head, black; dorsal and caudal fins, dark-gray; lower fins, very light.

The white mullet is taken in the bays and saline estuaries of the Carolinas and Virginia, in night-time, by rigging a punt with boards painted white and attached to boat at each side, and lighted by a pine-knot fire on the bow of the boat, when one person rows gently, and a second person raps with his hands each side of the boat. Attracted by the light, the white boards at the sides, and the thumping noise

made by the caller, the fish leap into the boat by hundreds;
and it is said that if the light is not extinguished, the white
mullet will leap into the boat in such numbers as to swamp
it. It seems almost a fish story, but the retailers of the story
are so numerous and respectable that I believe it implicitly.

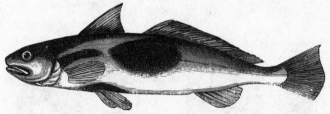

THE BLACK MULLET.

This fish is regarded along the coasts of Virginia and
North Carolina as the best pan-fish of Southern waters. Its
marks of black on a light gray and shining white body render it singularly picturesque. It is captured by thousands
daily throughout the summer and up to November in nets;
while anglers, with light tackle and very small hooks, find it
interesting sport, as it is a ready biter, and evinces such surprise at hooking itself that it darts about spasmodically,
shakes its head, and never yields to be taken into the boat
until it swoons. It is taken on very light tackle, single-gut
leader, and fine round gut snells, with small trout-hooks.
Bait with small bits of fish or clam, and fish with the adjustable float, as represented below. The float is adjusted
to the depth of water by an end of wire extending from
each end of the float beyond the ring. By this method the
float may be more easily attached to the line, and changed
to suit different depths of water, than the old style of trout-
float. A copy of the float is given below.

CHAPTER IV.
FRESH-WATER FISHES OF THE SOUTH.
SECTION FIRST.

WHITE PERCH, OF MISSISSIPPI.

This fish was taken at the head waters of the Chickasaw River, Mississippi, by Mr. B. F. Moore, Jun., of Meridian, Mississippi, who has done me the favor to furnish the Southern trout (channel cat); and at his instance Colonel James F. Taylor, of Raleigh, North Carolina, furnished me with the excellent drawing and description of the chub-robin, one of the gamiest small fishes of any water.

The white perch of the South is the most beautiful fish of the numerous *Percidæ* tribes. It inhabits ponds and running streams; loves eddies and deep holes, schooling in fall near a shaded bank or brush in the stream. It bites almost exclusively the minnow, preferring a live one, but was never known to bite a worm. It bites throughout spring and summer, and is the latest biting fish in autumn. Its best months for biting are October and November, though it is a very wary biter, seldom sinking the float—*a decided nibbler;* bites like a minnow, while swimming, and tows the cork along on the surface of the water. Its mouth is very tender, and it is difficult to land, for the hook often parts from its paper

mouth. It deposits its eggs in July and August. The flesh
of the white perch is white, no small forked bones, having
a delicate flavor, but not equal, perhaps, to the best of the
genus Percidæ.

The united dorsals comprise six spinal and fourteen soft
rays; caudal, seventeen soft rays; anal, six spinal and seventeen soft rays; ventral fin, one spinal and five soft rays; pectoral, thirteen soft rays; eyes large and bluish, with black
pupil; length of head, compared with body, as three and a
half to eleven; mouth large, and armed round the edge with
two or three serrated rows of small teeth, with teeth also on
the palate; seven gill rays. Though white and sparkling, it
is ornamented with bluish rays on the body and fins, with
medallions on the caudal. The color is white below the lateral line, and pale blue above. The white perch is not migratory, and it attains to the weight of five pounds or more.

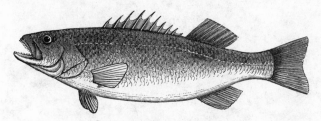

SOUTHERN CHUB, OR TROUT.

Six branchiostegous rays; first dorsal, nine spinal rays;
second dorsal, one spinal and twelve soft rays; caudal, eighteen soft rays, slightly lunated; anal, three spinal and ten soft;
ventral, one spinal and five soft; pectoral, thirteen soft rays.

This fish is evidently a perch-chub. It has teeth on the
edge of both mandibles, like a perch, and on the palate like
the chub and other leather-mouthed fishes. This fish is not
known in Northern waters. The fish from which this drawing was made was taken in a stream near Meridian, Mississippi. For the table it is considered the best fresh-water
fish of the Southern States. It weighs up to ten pounds;

have heard of larger ones, but its usual weight is about three pounds. It inhabits both ponds and streams; is non-migratory. Bites at feathered squids, flies, minnows, but seldom at worms. The color above lateral line is blue, fading to creamy white below middle of side. Mouth large, and lower jaw projecting; has card-like teeth on the upper and lower edges of the jaw; eye large; throat and breast always white. Very active and strong; spawns during all the summer months; bites best in fall and spring. The perch-chub should be angled for with regular black-bass tackle, the rod being pliable, but with snap enough in the lance-wood top to respond and hook the fish at first intention.—B. F. Moore, Jun.

SECTION SECOND.

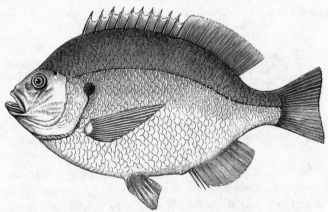

Chub-Robin.—*Pomobis rubellus.*

This gamy little pan-fish inhabits many streams and lakes of the South and South-west, but its natural latitude is from Virginia and the Carolinas, westward. My brother having taken it in Western Missouri, induced me to procure a drawing and description of it, which has been done by a true angler and ichthyologist, Font Taylor, Esq., of Raleigh, North Carolina.

This fish differs in weight, like most other fishes, from its food and its habitat. In lakes it is larger than in streams. It is eminently a fresh-water fish, and not at all allied to the sea-robin (*Prinotus lineatus*).

The chub-robin ascends the Neuse River about the last of February, same time with the robin-red-breast thrush (*Turdus migratorius*). The bird winters in the Eastern Carolinas, and so does the chub-robin fish; both red-breasted, and appearing at same time of year, there was thought a resemblance, and named alike the *Pomobis erythonoventralis*, " red-throat;" and this fish is more widely disseminated in the up country, and is a finer flavored pan-fish than the calico bass (which is similar to the " speckled hen" on page 285, only the spots are larger and more irregular).

The chub-robin averages from a half to a pound in weight, and is the gamest fish on the rod of all the minor fauna of the *Percidœ* tribes.

First dorsal, ten spinal rays; second, eleven soft; anal, three spinal and ten soft; ventral, one spinal and five soft; pectoral, twelve soft; caudal, sixteen soft rays; scales rather large; black spot at the upper end of gill, on body; dark-gray back and fins, yellow sides, and red breast and abdomen, with the lower fins reddish and yellow; eyes rather large, and little pin-teeth on rim of jaws.

This ravenous little fish bites at worm or fly, and never backward, but wondrously astonished and angry when hooked, showing fight until exhausted.

Angling for the chub-robin is fine sport on delicate tackle, and the fish will sometimes take very small minnows; but the white grub-worm is its delight.

Of breams in American waters the *Cyprinus* (carp-bream) is the largest, and both families are found in our lakes; while in some small lakes in South Carolina the *Abramis* is numerous, and excellent sport. It is one of the most wary fishes, and old anglers state that it keeps sentinels stationed over its feeding-ground during the feeding-times, from five to nine in the morning, and from four in the afternoon until dark.   To take this cunning fish, it is necessary to use great circum-

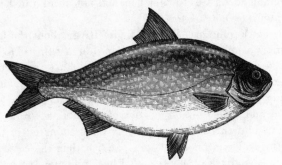

The Bream.—*Cyprinus brama*, and *Abramis chrysoptera*.

spection and fish with the most delicate hair or silk line, with the finest silk-worm gut for leader.

> "Where'er you ply, your labor will be vain,
>   If you the rules of art do not attain;
>   For diff'rent waters diff'rent species yield,
>   The angler's art commands the widest field."

> "The trout prefers a very rapid stream,
>   While the placid lake pleases best the bream."

The *Abramis brama*, or common bream, attains to the weight of ten pounds, and is very prolific.   It used to be regarded in Europe as worthy of stately dinners; but since the *Salmonidæ* have become more common, this fish is chiefly cultivated in Germany for profit, and generally caught in nets; but in France it is still appreciated.

It is covered with scales of medium size.   In coloring, its back is a gray *bleuetre*, fading to light bluish gray at the lateral line, with a white abdomen; the superior fins dark, and lower ones very light gray.   It has a forest of little teeth in its small mouth, and a hard throatal cartilaginous bone in the throat which helps mastication.

The milter has two bags of milt, and the spawner two bags of spawn.   Like other members of the family *Pleuro-*

nectidœ, it is remarkably prolific; and as it is really a game fish which affords excellent sport with very delicate tackle, it would be well to stock the lakes in the Middle States with it, where it is much less numerous than in Southern waters.

For baits, it will take gentles, angle-worms well bleached in moss—and fennel is said to be good to mix with moss; grasshoppers with the legs taken off; a paste made of brown bread and honey.

Use fine horse-hair and silk lines with quill-float, and fish near the bottom. There is a pond near the junction of the railroads from Augusta and Columbia toward Charleston, which has become celebrated for bream of best quality, and it used to be a great resort.

SECTION THIRD.

THE CHANNEL CATFISH.

OF protectionists, the strongest and most unselfish member of the *amphibia* is the bull-frog. Thus far his protection has not been proven to extend to other inhabitants of the waters than the bullhead, and of course its congener, the catfish; and the bullhead may perhaps be — by some inscrutable distribution of nature — a congener of both; for he is generally found in the same fishing - holes. —*Vide* Dr. White's opinion, as given on page 434.

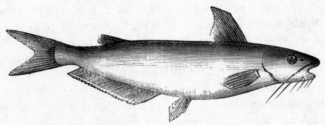

CHANNEL CAT.—*Abdominal.*—*Malacoperygii.*

This fish is equally good for game and the table. The fish
from which we made the above copy of a drawing was taken
in the Chickasaw River near Meridian, Mississippi, by B. F.
Moore, Jun. It is also known there as the croaker and blue-
cat.

There is a scarcely perceptible lateral line running from
gills down the centre of each side to tail, above which the
color is blue, as are also the superior fins, the lower ones being nearly white, and the sides are light bluish-gray to an
inch below the lateral line, the abdomen being satiny white.

Pectoral fins, one spinal and eight soft rays; ventral, sev-
en soft rays; anal, thirty soft rays, rooted in an adipose
membrane; caudal, eighteen soft rays, very forked; first
dorsal spinal, and six soft rays; second dorsal, adipose; two
barbels or feelers, one each side of upper lip, length of tail
about one-fifth of the fish; two very short barbels on the top
of the head; four barbels on the chin, two each side; branchiostegous rays, three; head one-sixth of the whole length.
Mouth very small for a catfish; with brush-like teeth on upper and lower lips, and card-like teeth on the upper and lower sides of throat near the maw; four gill-rays, and a semblance of a tongue filling the entire lower jaw; eyes large;
throat and breast always white. Runs in small streams from
one to five pounds in weight; but in the Upper Missouri
River, where they are regarded as superior to any other fish,
the trout included, they attain to fifteen pounds, and even
more. It is there called by some the lady-cat, because of its

great beauty and symmetry, while it is as active as any fish
known; and, on landing it, the fish croaks: hence it is known
by some as the croaker.

It never inhabits lakes, but its habitat is the channel of
clear streams. This fish bites every month in the year, but
best in February, March, and April. Its favorite bait is
crawfish, but it seldom refuses a live minnow.

The channel cat offers as good play as the trout, and when
angled for with fine tackle the sport is unsurpassed. He
makes the reel hum; and if the line is not kept clear on the
reel and the fish played gingerly, so as to make him contend
for every foot of line, he is quite sure to part tackle.

Very interesting sport in fishing for the channel cat is indulged on the Upper Missouri River, by both ladies and gentlemen. The following is the *modus operandi:* A party with
several scull boats rendezvous above a rapid in the river,
and to the handles of several dozens of empty jugs, well
corked, they attach to each a line about four feet in length,
rigged with a strong hook, well baited, when they throw
over the jugs, and let them drift down stream. Then the
party usually regales itself with a luncheon, after which the
rowers start to pick up the floating jugs. Presently several
of the jugs are seen to dive here and there, and the rowers
follow them up until the fish become fatigued, and, prone on
their sides, they float on the surface of the stream, and are
easily lifted into the boats. A catfish dinner and a hop
usually winds up the day's recreation.

Part Seventh.

---—⟨✕⟩—---

MISCELLANEOUS FISHES,

AND

HOW TO TAKE THEM.

CHAPTER I.

MISCELLANEOUS FISHES.

SECTION FIRST.

LAKE TROUTS.

THE non-migratory lake trouts of North America, as far as has been yet ascertained, comprehend three forms, to which the following specific names have been given: the NAMAYCUSH, or GREAT TROUT OF THE LAKES; the TOGUE, or GRAY-SPOTTED LAKE TROUT; and the SISCOWET. The first was described by Pennant at the close of the last century, the second by Dekay in 1842, and the third by Agassiz in 1850. According to the present state of our knowledge of their haunts, it appears that the namaycush inhabits the great lakes extending from the Northern United States to the Arctic Sea. The togue is said by some writers to fre-

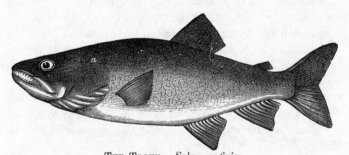

THE TOGUE.—*Salmo confinies.*

quent only the New England, Nova Scotian, and New Brunswick lakes, including the State of Maine; while the siscowet is seemingly restricted to Lake Superior, where Agassiz also recognized the namaycush. But little is known of their habits; moreover, several instances have occurred lately of one or other of these trouts turning up in lakes where their presence was unsuspected.   It is, therefore, not unlikely, when their geographical distributions are better worked out, that this seeming partiality to certain waters may, after all, be more apparent than real.   Further, it appears that their claims to be considered distinct species, rest altogether on certain minor details of structure and coloring in each, which, however, have been further abridged by late researches.

I therefore—and for other reasons—believe all lake trouts to be non-migratory, and to partake of peculiarities produced by habitat.   For example, the Seneca and Canandaigua lake trouts are far more beautiful and finer flavored than the Cayuga Lake trout.   The reason may be that the two former lakes are more profound and of mineral bottom, while the latter is shallow, with vegetable bottom.   These lake trouts are gray-bodied, more or less clouded according to age (the young only being clouded), and they are further marked with vermicular tracery, and have fins placed like those of the salmon, but not the same shape.   They are fork-tailed, but not so finely lined in all their proportions.   The trout of Moosehead Lake and of a few lakes in New Brunswick are said to be the best for the table.   They are scarce, and are never found south of the Boston fish markets.

The namaycush is one exception to all other lake trouts, being what is termed, on page 265, the Mackinaw trout, its habitat being Lake Superior.   This fish is supposed by naturalists to be a distinct family of lake trout.   It is larger than any other lake trout, and a more delicate and succulent fish than any other *confinies*, except the siscowet and those of Maine and New Brunswick.

The namaycush is generally taken in winter through the ice by hand-lines; for it would be superfluous to troll for him in summer in fifteen hundred feet depth of water, as there is no summer market for him, and the angler can find abundant sport more attractive.

"A distinction between the Mackinaw salmon (namaycush)

and the other two, togue and siscowet, consists in the ventral fin being placed farther back on the former, and the tail being more forked. They have also a double row of teeth, extending a half inch backward on the vomer. The teeth, gums, and roof of mouth have a tinge of purple, hence Mitchell's name, 'amethystine salmon.'"—A. Leith Adams, M.A., M.B., F.R.S., F.G.S.

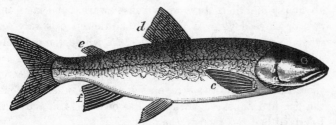

The Siscowet.—*Salmo siscowet*, Agassiz.

The siscowet is known by this native name, apparently in contradistinction to the namaycush, both being found in Lake Superior. This fish is said to be plentiful about Isle Royal — a large island near the north-west shore of Lake Superior. Agassiz gives this fish the following distinctive characters: The lower branch of the pre-operculum, *a*, is more extended than the upper, *b*. The pectoral fin, *c*, is longer, and farther from the gill opening than in either the other trouts; and the dorsal, *d*, is said to be larger, with a more slender and less club-shaped adipose fin, *e*. The anal, *f*, is as long as the dorsal, but not so wide.

The cisco, or ciscoquette, of page 293, as a congener of the lake herring, is a mere *clupea*, while the siscowet is the nearest approach to the real salmon of any lake trout. The following extracts by our learned friend C——— (who favored me with notes on Florida fishes), will be found interesting to disciples of the gentle wand, and I give them as follows:

"You mention the cisco, and it appears that you may have confounded it with the siscowet, which is a good salmon, having all the marks of that family, while the cisco is a

H h

small fish of the herring family; it seems to be the connecting link between the families of *corregonus* and *clupea*. It is found in all the great lakes, and in some of those of the second class, such as Geneva, or Big Foot Lake, in Wisconsin, where the annual catch of ciscos takes place on the 15th of June. They feed upon the eel, or shad-fly, a species of ephemera which makes its appearance in the lake region about the middle of June in immense swarms, and lasts only two or three days. At Geneva Lake the cisco is only seen when this fly is on the water; then the whole, ten or twelve miles long, is covered with fish breaking the surface, and all the anglers in the country are there at work. I went there once from Milwaukee, on the 16th of June, and found the fish had appeared with the flies on the 14th, and when I arrived had returned to the depths.

"I think if you were to pass a summer among the lakes of Wisconsin and Minnesota, and the trout streams about Lake Superior, you would collect material for a capital book. Lake Superior is the great home of the salmons, and would itself occupy the naturalist for months to study its fishes thoroughly. There is a river on the north shore, very little visited, called the Nepegan, which is, I suppose, the best trout stream in America. I have the outline of a brook trout, twenty-one and a half inches long, and five deep, which weighed four pounds when cleaned and smoked. This I received from a party of anglers of St. Louis, on their homeward trip. They had a barrel of these smoked trout, with many as large as the one I outlined, which must have weighed six pounds when caught. They had none less than two pounds, and the average weight of their takes daily was over two pounds each fish, and a fish at every cast on a single fly. These gentlemen, who were persons of education and general intelligence, assured me that they had found a land-locked salmon on the north shore of Lake Superior, besides the *Salmo namaycush* and *Salmo siscowet*, and that they twice took the whitefish with the fly on the lake."

The siscowet is eminently an angler's fish; rising generously to the fly, and like the winninish, or great northern
char, it averages in weight from three to nine pounds.   It
will also take a feathered squid, and vies with the large
brook trout in the northern part of Lake Superior, for both
its offer of sport, and its superior edible qualities.

SECTION SECOND.

THE CALIFORNIA SALMON.—*Salmo quinnat.*

My initial friend having learned that the son of an English
diplomat advised his father to "give the Yankees 54° 40', for
the salmon out here (Oregon) won't rise to a fly," concluded
to try them with a cast of Irish flies, and found the salmon
as eager to taste them as he could wish.

At our present writing, perhaps there is no better salmon-
fishing in the world than is to be found on many rivers in
Oregon; and as to artificial flies, they are as well mounted
and tied in New York as in any city in the world.   There
is a marked difference between the salmon in the Northern
Oregon rivers and those of California.   The former are simi-

lar to the salmon of the rivers, emptying into the River and
Gulf of St. Lawrence, the real salmon and worthy head of
the *Salmonidæ*.

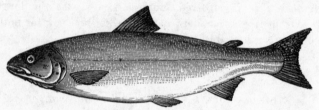

CALIFORNIA SALMON.

This fish differs from the Eastern salmon in being much
wider according to its length, the flesh red instead of pink,
and not so firm as the *Salmo salar*.   In other particulars it
is like the *salar*.   It thrives in warmer waters and in streams
of vegetable bottom; spawns in less time than the Eastern
fish, and is scarcely so good a fish for the table.   On another
hand, it is a more profitable fish than the Eastern salmon,
for it grows faster, and in waters of not so frigid a temperature; hence it is well adapted to the waters of Pennsylvania,
and perhaps to those of Maryland and Virginia.

In 1872, the subject of importing fecundated salmon *ova*
from California to the States on the eastern slope was suggested, and in that year Mr. Livingston Stone—under the
auspices of the Federal Government, through Spencer F.
Baird as its commissioner—went to California in August;
and, by the aid of the California Fish-Culturist's Association,
received the right to erect hatching-houses on the M'Cloud
River, three hundred miles north from San Francisco.   Having succeeded in importing to Troutdale, New Jersey, several
thousands of fecundated *ova*, they were there hatched and
placed in the Delaware River, where a number of grilse from
that planting have since been taken; some, it is said, of
from eight to ten pounds' weight.   Since 1872 many Eastern rivers have been stocked with California salmon, and
it is confidently anticipated that the Delaware and Sus-

quehanna rivers will soon teem with a salmon as beautiful, and affording as good sport as does the salmon of the North-east.

Although I am credibly informed that salmon will not rise to a fly in the Sacramento River, yet they rise generously on its tributaries. Of course they will rise in the upper waters of the Delaware and Susquehanna, for its eastern congener of the artificial stock has been found to rise for flies in the Connecticut River, and the California branch is said to be the most rapacious, and more willing to risk all for a fly, of any of the salmon families.

> "A birr! a whirr! a salmon's on,
>   A goodly fish, a thumper!
> Bring up, bring up the ready gaff,
> And when we land him we shall quaff
>   Another glorious bumper!
> Hark! 'tis the music of the reel,
>   The strong, the quick, the steady:
> The line darts from the circling wheel;
>   Have all things right and ready."—STODDART.

SECTION THIRD.

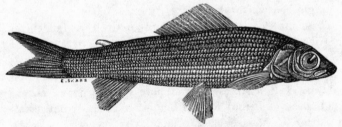

THE GRAYLING.—*Thymallus signifer.*

This fish is a member of the family or tribe *Salmonidæ*, and is termed by Linnæus *Salmo thymallus;* by Cuvier, *Thymallus vulgaris;* by Agassiz, Heckel, Kner, and other naturalists, as *Thymallus vexillifer.*

Although anglers meet the grayling in a few of the trout

streams in England, and on the continent as far north as
Russia, and south as far as Italy in very many of the salmon
rivers and trout streams, yet it is by no means a common fish
in Europe; while in America it is found in but a few rivers
in a small part of the Canadian dominion, and in the United
States only in a few streams in Michigan, as between Grand
Traverse Bay on the west, the Straits of Mackinaw on the
north, and Thunder Bay on the east. It has been discovered
in Au Sable River at the south; so that it probably inhabits
many of the waters of Northern Michigan, and in the great
North-western territory it will probably be found in many
rivers. The grayling is also said to be numerous in Montana in the streams entering the Missouri River above the
falls. W. V. Spencer, late of the United States Army, is supposed to have given the fish its proper name in Montana, in
1867. The discovery of the grayling in Montana was highly appreciated, both because it is a superior game fish, and it
is in season in the late autumn, when trout are spawning and
unfit for food.

For the benefit, therefore, of anglers and epicures to whom
the grayling is an entire stranger, I will jot down his principal marks and characteristics, so that the fish may be easily
distinguished when taken.

The name "*Thymallus*" is probably derived from its smelling like wild thyme; and in some places where it is called
"*umber*," it is because of its color and its fleetness—*umbra*,
"like a shadow."

Izaak Walton states: "First, note that he grows not to
the bigness of a trout, for the biggest of them do not usually exceed eighteen inches. He lives in such rivers as the
trout does, and is usually taken with the same baits as the
trout is, and after the same manner; for he will bite at both
the minnow, or worm, or fly, though he bites not often at the
minnow, and is very gamesome at the fly, and much simpler,
and therefore bolder than a trout; for he will rise twenty
times to a fly if you miss him, and yet rise again. He has

been taken with a fly made of red feathers; and he will rise at a fly not unlike a gnat or a small moth, or indeed at most flies that are not too big. He is a fish that lurks close all winter, but is very pleasant and jolly after mid-April, and in May, and in the hot months. He is of a very fine shape; his flesh is white; his teeth, those little ones that he has, are in his throat; yet he has so tender a mouth that he is oftener lost after an angler has hooked him than any other fish. Though there be many of these fishes in the delicate River Dove, and in Trent, and some of the smaller rivers, as that which runs by Salisbury, yet he is not so general a fish as the trout, nor to me so good to eat or to angle for, and so I shall take leave of him."

"*Genus Thymallus*, Cuvier.—Of this genus the grayling (*Thymallus vulgaris*) is the type. The fish is common in some of our streams, but is a local species. It differs chiefly from the trouts or salmons in having the mouth less deeply cleft, the orifice square, the anterior dorsal very high, and the scales larger."—*Penny Cyclopædia.*

In France the grayling is classified with the *genus Ombre* (umber), of which there are several families in the streams of Europe; and the *Ombre commune*, or grayling, is characterized by a very small, square mouth, like that of the smelt or the mullet, but provided with numerous infinitesimal teeth far back in the mouth, on the roof or palate; by scales, rather large and very exactly placed, one lapping another; by a high and wide first dorsal fin, which commences much farther forward than others of fishes belonging to the *genus Salmo*, and by its close resemblance to the trout in internal conformation.

"The grayling, though sufficiently common in divers points of France, is rarely seen in the markets of Paris. It is one of those beautiful fishes of the fresh waters. Nothing so graceful as its gradual elongated form from the front of its high dorsal to its tail. Nothing is more elegant than its *nageoire* dorsal, a magnificent sail, very long, and of a remarka-

ble height.   It is only necessary to compare him with other
fishes for judging why he is so fortunately conformed for
easy and rapid swimming.   Fishermen are often ready at
seeing the fishes traverse the limpid stream, but the grayling renders unavailing the exercise of the eyes.   It has
passed like a shadow—*comme une ombre.*"—EMILE BLANCH-
ARD, *Member of the Institute, Professor of Natural History,
etc., Paris.*

The dress of the grayling, though extremely modest in
tone, being a shining steel-color, and its polished scales with
borders of yellowish tinge, are so exactly placed as to appear like mosaic; and the yellowish ends and black base,
with the top of head black, and the dorsal fin divided by
small transversal stripes of black, with its abdomen like
white satin, and white inferior fins shaded with yellow at
their base, renders this fish so peculiar that no one could
mistake it.   The number of scales in a line from head to tail
vary from eighty-five to ninety along the lateral line, and
there are from seven to eight rows each side of said line.
The scales are detached with the utmost ease, when each
one is a gem of beauty.   They are a trifle wider than long,
with angular borders gracefully festooned and regularly
concentrated.   The number of rays of the dorsal fin exceeds
those of any other of the *Salmonidæ* tribe, there being from
sixteen to eighteen.   The tail is forked, long, and narrow.
The second dorsal is adipose, and the pectoral, anal, and ventral fins are large for the size of the fish, and as transparent
as gauze.

The grayling remains on its reddes, or spawning-beds,
during winter, and lays its eggs during the latter half of
February and the first half of March.   The eggs are very
numerous, and they hatch in about a fortnight, being a shorter time than is consumed by any other of the *Salmonidæ.*

The grayling is eminently a summer and autumn fish.   It
is generally regarded as a good table fish, and " Father
Izaak " says that it should be scaled with the hands, without

applying a knife, the flesh is so tender. It is of delicate flavor, some persons considering it the queen of delicacies, while others term it the flower of fishes.

It is but natural that the discovery of grayling in America should have been made by anglers. My attention was called to the fish about seven years ago by Mr. Samuel C. Clark, I think, as the first. Since then I have heard annually of the Michigan grayling, and of the poachers harvesting them with nets and spears while the fish were on their spawning-beds; but I concluded that the sportsmens' clubs of the State would apply for legislative aid to protect so rare a fish for the rod and the table; but it appears from a letter by D. H. Fitzhugh, Jun., that the race is being depleted as fast as the indolence and cupidity of the poacher will permit.

In angling for grayling, use small flies. Mr. Fitzhugh, who appears to be the discoverer of the grayling in Ausable River, Michigan, purchases his flies from Andrew Clerk & Co.; and he has probably instructed them as to the most taking fly. Mr. Mather, the fish-culturist of Honeoye Falls, New York, regards the grayling as superior game to the trout, and fly-fishing on the River Ausable, in Michigan, and taking grayling from a half to two pounds each, as equal sport to the best trout-fishing in America. He also states that the grayling is easier cultivated than the trout, eating far less to keep in good condition. Seth Green thinks to the contrary; that grayling will not live in the same stream with trout, because the trout will feed on them. This can scarcely be the case, as the grayling is the swiftest fish of fresh waters. There may be other conditions to render the grayling difficult to propagate; but it should be tried, and it might be important to consult Mr. Mather as to the conditions necessary for stocking streams with this rare and delicate luxury to both the angler and epicure.

CHAPTER II.

SECTION FIRST.

THE RED BASS OF CANADA.

WHO WOULD 'AVE THUNK IT!

THIS fish is taken in the waters which empty into the Georgian Bay and Lake Huron. Its weight ranges from three to fifteen pounds, and is very high game, while it is an excellent dinner fish. It affords rare sport for farmers' boys on rainy days, when they can not work out-of-doors. They use the red angle-worm, and the white grub taken out of old

CANADIAN RED BASS.

soft maple and cherry logs; or they bait with minnow or
crawfish. The red bass is a good biter, and a wondrous
saucy fish on the hook, leaping, running, and jerking as if
greatly astonished.

The first dorsal includes seven spiked rays, the anal one.
The soft-rayed fins are distinctly illustrated. The tail is
square, or, rather, rounded a trifle at the end, the reverse of
lunated. It is armed with a forest of small teeth, as an inside border of the mouth, a half-inch wide or more, and there
are teeth in the throat. I am not aware that the fish has
been classified; but as an angler's fish it is a luxury. It
takes the troll readily, especially the feathered spoon of
McHarg.

The back of the fish is a dark-brownish purple, fading to a
pink at the lateral line, with a white abdomen. The dorsals
and upper part of the caudal are the same color as the back,
while the pectoral, ventral, and anal are a light pink. The
top of the head is black, with a tinge of red; large eyes.
The meat is entirely white, juicy, and flaky; more rich,
sweet, and juicy than any other fresh-water bass.

OTSEGO LAKE BASS.—*Corregonus alosa.*

This is a very delicious whitefish. Once in a great while
it is taken on a feathered or small silver spoon, by trollers;
but its mullet mouth is too tender to hold a hook, and it is
eminently intended to be caught in nets.

This whitefish has been called the Otsego Lake bass for a
hundred years, and it is only within the past ten years that
the propriety of this appellation was questioned; but with
the inauguration of fish-culture in this country, the stock of

domestic fishes was canvassed, and fish nomenclature has
undergone some change. This fish is more like a cross between the whitefish of the great lakes and the families *Clupeidæ*. It is neither so white or oily as the whitefish of
Lake Ontario, nor has it the large scales and thin shape of
the herring or shad. The body is nearly as wide as it is
deep; the meat is white, sweet, and rich, but not so adipose
as the common whitefish. I believe Seth Green is endeavoring to disseminate this great table luxury by artificial propagation. The whitefishes of Seneca and Canandaigua lakes
are nearly or quite as good a fish as is that of Otsego Lake,
misnamed a bass.

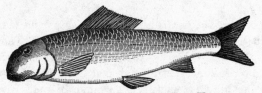

GENESEE RIVER MULLET, OR RED HORSE.

This is a sucker-mouthed carp (*Cyprinus*), being the probable link between the sucker and the carp. It ranges in
weight from one pound to forty, and the scales are very
large. The fish is a light orange and gray on the back, orange fins, and approximately orange head below the top,
which is dark gray. It inhabits many streams of soft surface waters. Youth think fishing for red horse in Genesee
River very great sport; for when it occasionally sucks in
the bait of angle-worm, grub, or crawfish, it plays very vigorously. It has teeth on the tongue and palate, and enjoys a
wonderful conceit of itself, sometimes trying to imitate the
trout and black bass in rising to a fly; but it is naturally
a bottom feeder, to be angled for with a small and strong
hook, baited with the red earth-worm, after the bait has
been scoured in moss several days, so as to be tough and
transparent. The meat is about as savory as a sucker, but
not so bony.

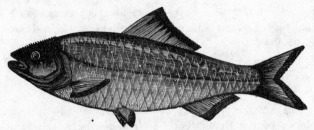

THE HORNED DACE.

This is eminently the school-boy's fish of the Middle States. Its burnished steel scales and fins, the latter edged with bright pink—like ribbon trimmings—and with its dark steel top of head armed all over with little points, render it, next to the brook trout, the prettiest fish of our small streams.

It rises generously to the fly, preferring the red ibis, and when I have been wading a trout stream and fishing with the fly, this pretty rogue has annoyed me frequently by taking the fly before the more wily trout had made up its mind to. It is an excellent pan-fish, and will take angle-worm eagerly; thus conferring great recreation to recuperate studious school-boys on Saturdays and during vacations. It is to be fished for with light perch rod, trout-hooks, light sinker, and quill-float. The size of the horned dace runs from one to three-eighths of a pound.

The smooth-headed dace is a congener of the horned dace, and by many supposed to be the female. It is a fish of about the same size and appetite, though more plain in appearance, being a light gray with white abdomen.

The brook chub also disports in the same waters with these dace. It is a fish of about the same size, gray on back and sides, drab fins, and white belly. It is sprinkled all over with jet-black dots, no larger than a dot in writing. It is also a greedy fish for angle-worm; and in large creeks it rises to the *plumptitude* of a quarter of a pound. It is not at all like the river and lake chub, which sometimes scales three pounds; and though they will also take the fly—great-

ly to the annoyance of fly-fishers for trout at sundown—yet
they affect liver.   Liver is an excellent bait for almost any
brook fish.

SECTION SECOND.

THE WHITING.—*Merlangus vulgaris.*

The whiting is a delicious table-fish, found in comparative
plenty on the British coasts.   This fish is by some thought
superior to all the other *Gadidæ.*   Very little is known of
its natural history.   It deposits its spawn in March, and the
eggs are not long in hatching — about forty days, I think,
varying, however, with the temperature of the season.   Before and after shedding its milt or roe, the whiting is out of
condition, and should not be taken for a couple of months.
The whiting prefers a sandy bottom, and is usually found a
few miles from shore, its food being much the same as that
of other fishes of the family to which it belongs.   It is a
smallish fish, usually about twelve inches long, and, on the
average, two pounds in weight.—J. G. BERTRAM.

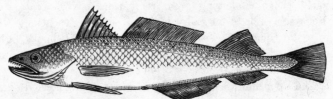

WHITING, OF NEWPORT, RHODE ISLAND.

This fish is of very recent discovery on the American
coast; and as usual, in reference to rare fishes, I first saw it
at Sutherland's restaurant, in Liberty Street.   It is very delicate, precisely like the whiting of England, and generally
taken with a deep-sea trawl about six miles seaward from the
Newport shores.   It is to be hoped that so great a luxury
will be more generally sought for, and soon be so cheapened
by abundance as to become a commercial fish.   The fish is
white-meated, and silver-white below the lateral line, and

light gray above it.   Light gray fins, with which it is admirably furnished for great fleetness.   The scales are infinitesimal.   The flavor of the fish is remarkably delicate, tender, and sweet, without bones to trouble the epicure.

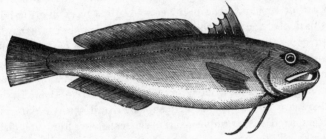

THE LING.

This is a congener of the cod and haddock, belonging also to the *Gadidæ* family.   It is a commercial fish, and taken on the hand-line when fishing for cods, with menhaden, capelin, spearing, or smelt as baits.   It is a common coast fish, all the way from Nantucket to the Georgian Bay.

GURNARD.—*Genus Trigla*, Yarrell.

This is a harbor channel fish, vulgarly known as the sea-robin, because it croaks like a tree-toad.   It is without scales, but the top of its head and gill-edges are armed with prickly bones, besides its spiked dorsals.   Its long pectoral fins are like wings; and when lifted from the water, in lieu of a beautiful kingfish or sea bass, the angler can hardly repress a hard word for the bait-thief, which costs the anglers about New York several thousand dollars annually for the bait it consumes. The gurnard and channel-crabs are the greatest annoyances to anglers on Jamaica Bay or the Great South Bay; for when paying three dollars a dozen for shedder-crab, to have them destroy a couple of dozens in a day, and oblige the angler to retire from the contest minus a mess of fish, it is rather trying to the patience. Anglers have many trials of patience, and they sometimes serve as lessons. Gurnards are generally bottom-biting, and their thefts of bait teach the angler to fish with a moving bait. The angler with rod and reel, if he fishes with still-bait on the bottom, is no more an angler than is a member of the Hand-line Committee. There are some very game fish which are always bottom-biters, such, for example, as the sheepshead. For such fish you should let your sinker feel along over the feeding-ground, not letting it rest more than a half-minute in a place. Still-baiting from a boat in bays and estuaries is beautiful sport; for, being away from shore on the water, there are no confused noises to disturb meditation, and the sights of the shores and waters are more enchanting than when viewed from any other position.

> "Now fleecy clouds, and gently warming beams,
> Alternate, overshade and gild the streams:
> And, like the wicked, fish unalarm'd view
> Their fellows perish, and their path pursue.
> Fish have their various characters, defin'd
> Not more by form or color than by mind;
> We cheat the finny fools, ourselves as blind,
> Fools, in our turn, are cheated by our kind!"

APPENDIX.

APPENDIX.

COOKERY ADAPTED TO THE RESOURCES OF SPORTSMEN IN THE WILDERNESS OR ON THE WAVE.

OOKING in the wilderness is a high art. It is not supposed that these simple directions will be of service to that class of sportsmen who take to the woods or water a retinue of cooks and attendants, but they may be of use to those who have a keen appetite for the more rugged features of such a life.

An officer of the American Army, who made me several valuable contributions to this department, states: "A sportsman ignorant of these matters is an entire stranger to that which constituted in my day one of the most agreeable phases of fishing and hunting life. With some knowledge of the subject, he can at least instruct others if he dislikes the practice himself; otherwise he becomes a mere dependent on those who may be more ignorant than himself. On the plains of the West, in the lake region of Canada, in the lower provinces, and on the waters of Maine, he might, and would, of course, subsist, and so would the Indian and the Esquimaux, but with this difference, that while the latter are ignorant of any better or more agreeable food, the modern sportsman would be half his time hankering after his flesh-pots at home."

BOILING POTATOES.

Wash them, cut off each end, put them in a pot of cold water, with a tea-spoonful of salt for every quart, cover them with a lid, and let the water merely cover them; place them over a good fire, and boil so fast that the water tumbles, until you can stick a dining-fork easily through them; then pour all the water off, and take the lid off, placing the pot on some embers beside the fire. Do not leave the least water in the pot, or it will steam them, and prevent them from drying mealy.

ROASTING POTATOES.

Wash and cut off the ends of the potatoes (especially the seed-end) and, when dry, draw the coals of the fire forward and place the potatoes on the embers, cover them with hot ashes, then with embers, topping off with coals, and after they have been roasting half an hour, try them.

QUICK-MADE YEAST.

Take a pint of new milk, a tea-spoonful of salt, and table-spoonful of flour, and stir well together; set it by the fire and keep it lukewarm, and it will be ready for use in an hour. It is necessary to use twice the ordinary quantity of this yeast, and it must be soon used or it is good for nothing. It is suited to make biscuits in a hurry, but bread made of it dries soon.

QUICK-MADE ROLLS.

Mix well together one quart of flour, two small tea-spoonfuls of cream of tartar, one tea-spoonful of soda, and one pint of milk, and bake *immediately*.

FRENCH ROLLS.

Take one egg, one cup of milk (or water in lieu of it), three spoonfuls of leaven, one spoonful of butter, a little salt, and as much flour as will make it a thick paste; then make it into rolls, and when well risen bake them in an oven, covered dish, or fry-pan.

A PERFECT OMELET.

Take six eggs, leaving out the whites of two; beat them till they are very light, and add pepper and salt to your taste; divide two ounces of butter into small pieces and put them into the eggs.

Put a quarter of a pound of beef or veal drippings into a fry-pan, and when they boil put in the eggs; fry gently till of a light brown on the under side; add parsley if you wish it plain, and then double it over and serve.

If you wish it of cheese, beat it in with the eggs in an earthen dish if you have one. For veal, ham, kidney, or oysters, they must be first cooked, and then put in just before the omelet is doubled over.

SCRAMBLED EGGS.

Beat six eggs enough to mix white and yolk together; put two ounces of butter in a pan set on the fire, and when melted, take off the pan, and add salt, pepper, and, if you like, a pinch of nutmeg; mix it in; then add the eggs, with a tablespoonful of gravy or essence of beef; put the pan again over a slow fire, stir constantly till cooked to suit, and serve warm.

TO FRY SALT PORK NICELY.

Cut it in thin slices, and put it in a fry-pan covered with hot water; let it boil up once, and then pour it off; shake a little pepper over it; let it fry on both sides in its own fat, then take out the pieces and add to the gravy a large teaspoon of flour; stir it till smooth and free of lumps; then add a cup of milk; stir over the fire a few minutes; shake more pepper over it; then pour it over the pork, and serve; or thin-sliced boiled potatoes, or fried or boiled cold parsnips, may be fried in the gravy when the pork is taken out.

CLAM OR OYSTER FRITTERS.

Open and dry them with a towel; mix two well-beaten eggs, somewhat less than half a pint of thin liquor and half a pint of milk (or the same quantity of liquor in addition if you have no milk), with a pint of flour; beat it thoroughly together till it is free from lumps; then stir in the clams or oysters; cut up some salt pork in small pieces, and try it out in a fry-pan, and remove the pieces of pork. When the fat is boiling hot, put in your clams or oysters with a large spoon, with one or two clams, etc., and batter in each spoonful. Let them brown, and then turn them over; as soon as done, remove them from the pan, and lay them on a gridiron with a dish under it to catch the drippings. There should always be enough fat in the pan to cover, or nearly cover the fritters.

SMOKED BEEF AND EGGS.

Shave half a pound of beef thin, and if very salt put it in a fry-pan and cover it with boiling water; set it on the fire and let the water come to a boil, then pour off the water; put in a piece of lard, beef drippings, or suet cut fine, about the size of two hens' eggs; shake pepper over it to taste, and fry for a few minutes over a quick fire; then pour over it as many well-beaten eggs as you please; stir up all together till the eggs are cooked to taste, and serve. In lieu of eggs, dredge the beef over with flour, or add a tablespoon or two of canned tomato, if you have it.

HAM GRAVY AND TOAST.

Take the remains of a ham; break or saw the bones small; put them in a sauce-pan with hot water enough to cover them; let them simmer slowly over the fire till the marrow is extracted from the bones, then take the pan off the fire and strain the contents; add a little pepper, fine sage; dredge in a table-spoon of flour previously browned in a fry-pan, and a tea-spoon of butter; set it over the fire again and stir for a few moments; lay your toast in a dish, and pour the gravy over it, and serve hot.

CORN-MEAL FRITTERS.

Beat three eggs very light; then mix them with a pint of milk, a tea-spoon of salt, and enough yellow meal to make a thin batter; have lard, beef drippings, or pork in a fry-pan boiling hot, and then put in the batter with a large spoon, and fry each side brown; when done, put them in some dish where the fat on them can drip off.

FRIED POTATOES.

Peel and cut raw potatoes, thick or thin; let them lie in salt water as long as convenient; have your fat very hot; put in your potatoes, and as soon as brown remove them with a skimmer into some perforated dish, or on a cloth where the fat can drip from them and leave them dry and crisp. The fat must be as hot as possible.

VENISON SAUSAGES.

Take equal quantities of the odds and ends of *raw* venison (or other fresh meat) and old salt pork; chop fine; add pepper and sage, or other herbs to taste; make them into small cakes, and fry in a pan without any fat, that in the sausage being enough. Venison is best; the meat from the neck and fore-quarters is as good as any other part for this purpose; three tea-spoonfuls of sage, one and a half of salt, and one of pepper to a pound of meat is a good proportion.

VENISON SAUCE.

Half a pint of port or other wine made hot, a table-spoonful of pulverized white sugar, currant jelly, and a piece of butter the size of an egg, will make an excellent sauce.

LIVER AND KIDNEY BROCHET.

Split the kidney (if of beef) lengthways in four equal parts; then cut them crossways into pieces about half an inch thick. If they are of smaller animals, cut them crossways only, and in all cases remove the fat and the stringy parts; then cut your liver and salt pork as near as may be of a size and thickness of the pieces of kidney; put a piece of kidney on a skewer or stiff piece of wire, then a piece of pork, then a piece of liver, then a piece of pork, then a piece of kidney, and so on till the skewer or wire is full; press them well together; drive two small crotched sticks into the ground before the fire, and rest the ends of the skewer on each crotch; put a dish under it to catch the drippings; turn and baste from time to time till the pork looks dried; or bake them in an oven with the ends of the skewers resting on the edge of a tin dish. Either kidney or liver alone *with pork* is just as good.

SCALLOPED OYSTERS.

Drain a quart of oysters from their liquor; butter the sides and bottom of a deep tin dish, and put in the bottom a layer of bread-crumbs or grated biscuit; season the oysters with pepper, salt, and a little mace or nutmeg; cover the crumbs with a layer of oysters, and spread over them several small lumps of butter; then add another layer of crumbs, and again a layer of oysters, and so on till the dish is nearly full; let the last or top layer be of crumbs, and fill up with the oyster juice; cover the pan with a tin plate (if you have no bake-oven); then put live coals on and under it, and bake brown.

FRESH MACKEREL À LA MAÎTRE D'HÔTEL.

Split the fish along the back; wipe it clean and dry; pour over it oil, with pepper and salt, and let it soak in this as long as convenient—the longer the better; then boil it first on the inside (as all fish should be boiled); then turn it over, basting it from time to time with the oil, etc.; mix thoroughly a piece of butter, some chopped parsley, salt, and pepper together, and put it in a dish; when the fish is done, put it on the mixture and serve hot.

DANIEL WEBSTER'S CHOWDER.

4 table-spoonfuls of onions, fried with pork.
1 quart of boiled potatoes, well mashed.
1½ lbs. sea-biscuit, broken.
1 tea-spoonful of thyme, mixed with one of summer savory.
½ bottle mushroom catsup.
1 bottle of port or claret.
½ nutmeg, grated.
A few cloves, mace, and alspice.
6 lbs. fish, sea bass or cod, cut in slices.
25 oysters, a little black pepper, and a few slices of lemon.
The whole put in a pot and covered with an inch of water, boiled for an hour and gently stirred.

MAJOR HENSHAW'S CHOWDER.

Cut up a pound and a half or two pounds of *old* salt pork into small pieces, and put it in a pot that has a close cover. Put in four table-spoonfuls of sliced onions when the pork is nearly tried out, and when the pork is entirely tried out remove the pieces with a skimmer or large spoon.

Then take six pounds of sea or striped bass, cod, or any other firm fish, and cut it in slices; a pound and a half of broken biscuit; twenty-five large or fifty small oysters (these may be omitted if out of season); one quart of boiled potatoes well mashed; half a dozen large, or eight or ten small tomatoes sliced (or half a bottle tomato catsup instead); one bottle port or claret, or other wine (the two former are best); half a nutmeg grated, a tea-spoonful each of fine summer savory and thyme, and a few cloves, mace, allspice, black pepper, and slices of lemon. Put the first five articles in the pot in layers, and alternately, in the order above stated; sprinkle over each layer a portion of each of the other ingredients, then put in water enough to cover all. Cover close, and let it simmer, and stir occasionally till done. It should not boil, but simmer slowly, and the cover should be taken off as seldom as possible; on this the flavor depends. When the fish on top is done, serve up the chowder.

CLAM CHOWDER.

Butter the bottom and sides of a deep tin or earthen dish; strew the bottom thickly with bread crumbs or rolled cracker (soaked); sprinkle over it pepper and pieces of butter the size of a hickory-nut, and parsley chopped fine; then put in a double layer of clams. Sprinkle also over them pepper and pieces of butter, then another layer of soaked crumbs or cracker, and again a double layer of clams, pepper, butter, and so on, the last layer being of crumbs; add, finally, a cup of milk, or, in lieu of it, water. Put a plate over the top, with coals above and below, or bake in an oven three quarters of an hour. If too dry, before it is done add enough milk or water to moisten it.

Fifty clams, half a pound of soda biscuit or bread crumbs, and a quarter of a pound of butter, is the quantity necessary for this receipt.

FISH EN GRILLE OU EN PAPILLOTE.

Scale and draw your fish, wipe it dry, but use no water. Cut off the head, tail, and fins. Take dry, mealy potatoes boiled and mashed, and mix plenty of butter with them; when thoroughly mixed into paste or dough, envelop each fish in a coating of them, and broil it on a gridiron till done, or wrap it in oiled or greased *white* paper, and bake in hot ashes. Small fish are best by this process.

FISH SAUCE.

Take half a pound of anchovies, half a pint of port or other wine, a gill of strong vinegar, a small onion, a few cloves, a little allspice and whole pepper, a few blades of mace, half a handful of green or dried thyme, and a small lemon with the peel sliced. Put all in a saucepan, cover it close, and stew gently until the anchovies are dissolved; then strain off, and bottle the liquor for use when wanted.

WHITE SAUCE FOR FISH.

Mix well together a lump of butter, a little warm water, and a table-spoonful of flour, and add, if you have it, a little fine-chopped parsley; let it simmer slowly a few minutes, and pour over or serve with the fish.

SAUCE À LA MAÎTRE D'HÔTEL.

Mix and knead well together in a bowl two ounces of butter, a table-spoonful of chopped parsley, and the juice of half a lemon; add salt to your taste. Vinegar may be substituted for lemon, but it is not so good. Pepper, chopped chives, and some grated nutmeg may be added, if liked.

STEWED FISH.

Clean and wipe the fish; heat from two to six ounces of butter in a pan (according to the size of the fish); heat hot; then put in your fish, and let it remain over the fire five minutes; turn it over, and let it remain five minutes more, and be careful not to let it burn. Take the fish out, and put it in another stew-pan with a cover; dredge some flour into the juice and butter, let it remain over the fire three minutes, and pour it over the fish. Then take a quarter of a pound of butter, roll it well in flour, and put it in with the fish also; add two blades of mace, ten cloves, a little cinnamon, red pepper, and salt, with just enough water to keep it from burning; cover close, and let it stew slowly. When half done, add a pint of port or other wine; when done, put the fish in a dish, pour the sauce over it, and garnish with lemon or horseradish.

BECHAMEL SAUCE.

Mix dry in a tin saucepan two ounces of butter.and a table-spoonful of flour; when well mixed, add a pint of milk, and dissolve the butter and flour paste in it; set it on the fire, and stir constantly. When it gets rather thick, take it off and pour into it the yolk of an egg (previously well beaten in a cup), and add a tea-spoonful of water; salt and white pepper to taste. Mix it all well again, and it is ready for use.

TO MAKE DELICIOUS BUTTER EASILY.

Spread out three clean coarse towels one over the other, and lay a pint of thick cream on the top; tie up all the tow-els as close as possible, and bury them eighteen inches deep in dry earth for twenty-four hours; then take them up, put the cream in a cool earthen basin, and stir it for five minutes in summer or fifteen minutes in winter, and you will have a lump of as cool, fresh, delicious butter as you could desire.

A ROYAL SALAD.

Let your lettuce be perfectly dry. First boil an egg fully fifteen minutes; then take the *yolk*, a tea-spoonful of salt, three tea-spoonfuls of pure, dry mustard, a little Cayenne pepper, half a dozen very young green onions *chopped very fine:* this must not be omitted; if not to be got, *a due proportion* of the youngest onions must be used. Mix all the above, except the onions, well together; then add and mix in well a table-spoonful of vinegar; then add two table-spoonfuls of oil, and mix it in thoroughly; then mix in thoroughly half a tea-spoonful of first-rate brown sugar; then cut up your lettuce of a size to taste, and the white of the egg small, and mix them with the onions, turning them over carefully till well incorporated; after which mix all the ingredients together, taking care not to bruise the leaves of the lettuce, and serve immediately.

When celery is used instead of lettuce, double or treble the quantity of mustard is necessary. It can not be excelled if the different mixtures are thoroughly done.

AMELIA SALAD.

Beat the *yolk* of a raw egg with two table-spoonfuls of oil; mash two moderate-sized boiled potatoes thoroughly; add (according to taste) salt, mustard, and vinegar to the oil and egg (and add more oil if preferred); then incorporate the whole well together, after which cut your lettuce to taste, and mix it in carefully, so as not to bruise the leaves.

In using celery, a larger quantity of all the ingredients is necessary.

POTATO SALAD.

Take cold boiled potatoes and slice them; rub the dish intended for them with garlic; make a dressing of oil, vinegar, pepper, salt, and parsley, if you have it, or lettuce, cut very fine, and mix all together. To the above may be added any odds and ends of meat, fowl, or fish you have, cut into pieces of the size of dice. Ham, cold veal, anchovies freshened, or herrings are excellent with it; also any cold fish that is coarse-grained and firm, such as porgee, sea bass, salmon, and salmon-trout.

FRENCH PILAU.

Boil your fowls or other birds in enough water to cover them, and when done, take them out. Take out also a portion of the liquor; then put into the rest of the liquor enough rice (previously well washed) to cover the birds. When it is done, take it out and butter it well; put half of it in a dish; lay the birds on it; add the liquor; then cover the birds with the rest of the rice; make it smooth, and spread over it the *yolk* of two well-beaten eggs. Cover the dish with a tin plate, and coals above and under, or bake in an oven, with a moderate fire.

QUAIL, RAIL, PLOVER, AND OTHER SMALL BIRDS,

are prepared and cooked as directed for snipe and wood-cock, except that you cut off the head, and remove the crop and trail before cooking. Some remove only the crop from the very small birds.

CRANES AND HERONS,

when young, are often stewed and broiled like chickens, and are considered very good, but I prefer to make a soup of them, with gumbo.

Pick and dress them like any fowl; cut them up with a piece of fresh beef, or a gill of the essence of beef to two or three birds, and put all in a pot, with a table-spoonful of lard or pork, an onion, sliced or not, as preferred, and water enough to cook the meat. After they have become soft, if you have them, add 100 or less oysters, with their liquor, or soft or hard crabs previously cleaned and cut in quarters. Let it simmer a couple of minutes or so, if oysters are used with crabs, till they are done. Just before serving, stir in, till the soup becomes mucilaginous, one or two table-spoonfuls of gumbo. Okra is commonly called gumbo; their properties are similar, but one is a vegetable pod, the other a leaf. The only place it can probably be found at in this city is Coolidge & Adams's, John Street. It is cheap.

POTTED PIGEONS, CURLEW, OR OTHER DRY BIRDS.

Thoroughly pick and clean them; make a stuffing of one egg, one cracker, and an equal quantity of suet or butter, and sweet marjoram or sage; make small balls of the stuffing, and put one of them, with a small slice of salt pork, into each bird; dredge the birds well with flour, and lay them close to-

gether in the bottom of a pot; cover them with water; throw
in a piece of butter; cover the pot, and let them stew slowly
for an hour and a quarter; if they are old birds, an hour and
three quarters.

ENGLISH OR JACK SNIPE, AND WOODCOCK.

These birds live by suction, and have no crop, the stomach
being somewhat pear-shaped, and about the size of a bullet.
They should be cooked without being drawn, either by broiling, or skewered, with the ends resting on crotched sticks or
on the sides of a small tin pan. A small, thin slice of pork,
covering the breast, should be tied round the bird, with a
slice or two of toast laid under it to receive the drippings.
Cook fifteen or twenty minutes, according to size, before or
over a lively fire. Those who do not like the trail should
nevertheless cook the bird whole, and remove the trail after
it is served up, otherwise the flavor of the bird is nearly
lost. The trail, head, and neck are worth all the rest to epicures.

TO SELECT MUSHROOMS.

They grow in open pasture; those near or under trees are
poisonous; they first appear very small, round in shape, and
on a small stalk; the upper part and stalk are white; as they
increase in size, the under part gradually expands, and shows
a fringe fir of a fine salmon color, and so continues until the
increase in size is considerable, when it changes to a dark
brown. The poisonous kind have a yellowish skin, and the
under part is not *a clear* salmon color, while the fringe or fir
is white or yellow. The good smells pleasantly, the other
rank.

GENERAL RULES FOR COOKING.

SOUPS.

Let them simmer rather than boil. Put cold water in the pot, and let it heat gradually; only uncover the pot to skim the soup. A tea-spoonful of salt and a quart of water to each pound of beef is a fair average. Remove every particle of scum before you put in the vegetables. If soup is too thick, always thin it with *boiling* water. Never put in green vegetables till the water boils. Hard or fast boiling makes meat tough and hard. Put your herbs in when nearly done. All soups require simmering from four to five hours.

BOILING VEGETABLES.

Cabbage should boil an hour; beets, an hour and a half; parsnips, an hour or an hour and a quarter, according to size; squashes, the larger end should boil half an hour, the neck pieces fifteen or twenty minutes longer; new potatoes, fifteen or twenty minutes; old ones, from half an hour to an hour, according to size: never let them stop boiling (if you wish them mealy) till they are done; then turn off the water and let them dry.

BOILING MEATS.

Hard or fast boiling makes all meat dry, tough, and hard. Corned beef should, after being cooked, be left in the liquid till it is perfectly cold, or it will be dry. Fifteen minutes to each pound of ham is a fair average. Hams and meat should be put in hot, but not boiling water; cold water draws out the juices. Beef tongues of a fair size require full three hours' boiling.

BOILING FISH.

Ten minutes to every pound of fish is a fair average; if large and thick, a few minutes longer; cover close; simmer rather than boil; take out *immediately* when done. A fresh cod of four or five pounds takes about twenty minutes to boil. Never put the fish in till the water is boiling hot. Salt fish should never boil for a moment, as it makes it hard; it should lie in scalding water two or three hours, and then be allowed to simmer, and the less water you use and the longer it simmers the better it will be. The fish is done when the meat is easily detached from the bones.

FRYING FISH.

Never put your fish in the pan till the fat is boiling hot. Always cut your pork small, and don't try it out or otherwise cook it too fast, as it will lose much of its sweetness. Score the fish and roll them in flour before laying them in the sparkling fat. In using lard, a table-spoonful of salt to a pound is a fair average.

BROILING FISH.

Wipe your fish, and use as little water in cleaning it as possible. Put the inside of the fish to the fire first. Mix thoroughly in a dish a tea-spoonful of salt and pepper with about four ounces of butter, and melt it. When your fish is done, turn each piece over and over in the butter; cover the dish, and keep it hot till ready to serve.

BROILING STEAKS.

Put the steak on the gridiron for a few moments, and scorch both sides; then take it off, and when perfectly cold proceed to broil it to your taste; this mode preserves the juices of the meat.

No sportsman's larder can be complete now without a few cans of the essence of beef, for making gravies and enriching a soup, together with a few herbs and spices for flavoring.

K K

COMPOUNDING FANCY DRINKS.

EGG NOGG.

Take six eggs, a quart of milk, half a pint of brandy (or a gill each of brandy and rum), or use any other liquor, and six table-spoonfuls of sugar. Beat the yolks of the eggs and the sugar well together, and the whites very hard. Mix in the brandy with the yolks, then boil the milk, and add it to the mixture. When well stirred up, crown the whole with the whites of the eggs.

SHERRY-COBBLER.

Put in a tumbler a table-spoonful and a half of powdered sugar and a slice or two of lemon; then fill it half full of crushed ice; then pour on it a wine-glassful or more of sherry. Pour the whole from tumbler to tumbler till well mixed, and drink through a straw, if you have it.

MULLED CIDER.

Take a pint of sweet cider; reserve a tea-cupful of it, and add to the remainder an equal quantity of water. Set it to boil, with a tea-spoonful of whole allspice added to it; then beat three eggs very light, and stir gradually the reserved cup of cider into them; then stir this mixture gradually into the boiling cider and water, and continue stirring till the whole is smooth; sweeten to taste; grate a little nutmeg over it, and serve hot in tumblers.

MULLED WINE

is made in the same way as mulled cider.

ARRACK PUNCH.

Mix four tumblers of Jamaica rum (Antigua is best), three quarters of a tumbler of arrack, half a tumbler of lemon-juice, and the rind of a lemon and a half; add sugar and water equal

to twice the quantity of liquor. Before adding the sugar and
water, let the mixture stand some ten minutes or so.

CLARET PUNCH.

Take one bottle of claret or Burgundy, one bottle of plain
soda (some prefer two), one lemon, one glass of sherry, and
sugar to taste. Mix all well and ice it thoroughly, and at
the *moment of serving* add another bottle of soda. This
punch is excellent in hot weather.

COMMON PUNCH.

Mix well together one tumbler of crushed sugar, half a
tumbler of any liquor, six tumblers of water, the rind of two
lemons and the juice of one, or half a tumbler of lemon sirup,
and ice if to be had.

AGRAZ.

Pound some unripe white grapes, and add some white sugar and water. Strain till it acquires a very pale amber or
straw color; then, if possible, freeze it in ice, and use. This
is a Spanish receipt, and is considered by many of that nation the most delicious and refeshing hot-weather drink ever
devised.

REGAL PUNCH.

Peel twenty-four lemons; steep the rinds for twelve hours
in two quarts of Jamaica rum; squeeze the lemons on three
pounds and a half of loaf sugar; add two quarts of dark
brandy and six quarts of water. Mix all together; add two
quarts of boiled milk; stir until the mixture curdles; strain
it through a jelly-bag until clear; bottle and cork.

FLIP.

Put the quantity of ale, porter, or beer you wish in a tin
cup, and add sugar to taste; heat the end of a *thick* piece of
iron red hot, plunge it in the liquor, and stir round till the

liquor ceases to bubble, and drink hot. This is the most refreshing and strengthening drink either before or after a
hard day's hunt that I know of. A piece of iron of the shape
and size of a large soldering-iron is the best.

GENERAL REMARKS.

Although sportsmen and mariners do not seek either the
wilds or the waves for the luxuries of the table, yet they set
a higher estimate on heaven's bounties than to suppose meat
and drink given to sustain life only. They consider them
rather as bestowals for strength and enjoyment to man, and
as such they are to be used intellectually and in moderation.

In the foregoing list of edibles, there is not a rare article
named, or one which is cumbrous to convey on fishing excursions. Meats, sauces, and vegetables of nearly all kinds are
now canned or desiccated, and put up in convenient packages
to carry, so that for a camp life of only a fortnight on the aromatic boughs of fir or hemlock it will pay to provide them.

Persons who have never enjoyed camp life out of the reach
of primary elections are not expected to realize the great luxury of satisfying the cravings of real hunger caused by sportive exercise in the forest, and especially are those creature
comforts double blessings when storm-bound and confined
to the camp.

Thus much I have considered necessary to state as an excuse for adding the culinary and bibulous part as an appen-
dix, for there are not wanting those who consider eating and
drinking undignified duties.

Bermuda onions, potatoes, and salted side-pork are necessaries in the wilderness; these, with eggs and flour, are about
the only articles to be sent in bulk. Trout are cooked only
four ways in the wilderness: the large ones are boiled, or
rolled in a sheet of paper which has been well buttered, then
protected farther by four or five thicknesses of brown paper,
when it is placed on hot ashes, and covered with hot ashes

topped off with live coals, and thus left twenty minutes for every pound weight. When taken from the fire the wrappers are removed, including the skin, which will adhere to the paper, and it is placed on a hot plate and seasoned to the taste. The third way is to draw the trout, clip off the fins, score it across on each side, roll it in flour, and place it in a pan of sparkling hot butter, or fat tried from salt pork; dredge with flour, and turn it several times for a thick crust. The fourth way is to spit it, with a thin slice of salt pork along one side, on a birch fork, turning it by hand over a camp-fire until done. Lemon-juice is a refreshing luxury on salmon or trout. In using sea-biscuits, soak them previously in cold water; they are then good when fried in the gravy left from frying ham and eggs.

To those who can explain the recondite harmonies which subsist between the velvet calipash and the verdant calipee, nothing farther need be added; and for those who do not comprehend them, words would prove superfluous.

NOTEWORTHY ITEMS.

Drying Lines.—Fishing clubs provide posts and hooks at headquarters for drying lines, but in wet or foggy weather they are useless. Experienced anglers therefore generally carry a small reel with them, for linen bass-lines, when in use, should be dried every evening.

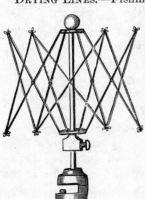

This reel, which is formed of 24 narrow slats, tied at the ends in threes, and moving by a double button or screw in the centre, closes like an umbrella, being light, and occupying very little room in a trunk. For using it, fasten the

REEL FOR DRYING LINES.

foot by a screw to a board or table-leaf; open it by sliding up on the staff the lower base to which the slats are fastened, and fasten it, by the screw represented, to the centre-shaft or staff. Hold the line with one hand and turn the reel with the other. The reel may be bought at most of the fishing-tackle stores, such as Clerk's, Conroy's, Bates's, Pritchard's, in New York, or at Bradford's, in Boston.

COPAL VARNISH.—This is the best varnish for tackle, hook-dressings, etc.

WHITE WAX.—This is made like cobbler's wax, and stretched until it becomes nearly white, dry, and brittle; or mix beeswax, resin, and tallow; pour into water, and stretch and work it with the hands.

SPERMACETI.—Good to dress lines. To take the kink out of linen lines, darken their color, and not weaken them by preparation, dip them into tanner's or lamp oil, and, when saturated, hang them up until they dry, when pack them in mahogany dust, and leave them several days, or until the dust has absorbed the oil.

INDIA-RUBBER DRESSING.—This is recommended both for dressing lines and for patching India-rubber boots. For lines, cut into small pieces some white rubber and dissolve it in turpentine—about $\frac{25}{100}$ rubber and $\frac{75}{100}$ turpentine. Set the vessel containing them in hot water, as you would glue; or rubber may be dissolved in chloroform. Rubber dressing for lines is not liable to crack, and is therefore preferred to varnish; but spermaceti is preferred by our best fishing-tackle manufacturers. Boiled linseed oil with a lump of resin, or a little gold size, is preferred by some.

TO DRESS LEATHER WADING-BOOTS.—Cut into shavings some black India-rubber (the vulcanized is not good for these preparations), and place them in a vessel containing double the amount of spirits of turpentine; place the vessel in hot water until the rubber dissolves, when mix, and let it cool so as not to burn the leather, and rub the uppers and creases above the sole, and they will be water-proof.

Some sportsmen cut black rubber into shreds and mix it with hot tallow until dissolved, when the mixture is supposed to keep the boots both dry and soft.

To dress wading-boots in summer, rub them over every morning while they are in use with a piece of bullock's scrotum. It will prevent them from leaking, and render them as soft as chamois-skin.

To keep Moth from Feathers.—Place them in a close case with the gum of camphor, or, what is better, with vanilla beans; what is still better is scrapings of Russia leather. Boxes made of cedar or sandal-wood are the best. Tobacco, and both black and red peppers, are good to sprinkle the feathers with, or to place in large amounts in the boxes of feathers.

To preserve Silk-worm Gut.—Keep it neither wet nor dry. A dry cellar forms the best store-room for it. Keep it packed and out of the air.

Oil for Hooks and Reels.—That from the head or jaw of the porpoise is the best.

Clearing Ring should be about two inches in diameter, and half a pound weight for coast-fishing; one fourth pound for fresh-water fishing. The line attached to it should be wound on a spool or reel, as shown on the cut in the title-page, or that in salmon-fishing. In case the hook gets fast, let the ring run down to dislodge it; or if a salmon or striped bass sulks, let the ring glide down on the line to his nose, and he will generally change quarters.

To Stain Gimp.—Mr. Francis quotes "Book of the Pike" in stating: "Bright brass gimp is easily seen by the fish. To discolor it, soak it in a solution of bichlorate of platinum mixed with water—one of platinum to eight or ten parts of water; then dry before the fire."

Marine Glue is recommended for covering splices and securing ties.

Silk, Tinsel, etc.—To preserve them, keep them dry, and away from the fire and air.

PRESERVING WATER-PROOFS.—Do not hang them on a nail or peg; either hang them over a chair-back, or spread them out on the tent floor. Do not dry either boots or coats near a fireplace or a stove. At our principal club-houses there is a drying-room; but on fishing excursions it were better not to dry boots and coats than to injure them.

FEET DRESS FOR FIELD-SPORTS.

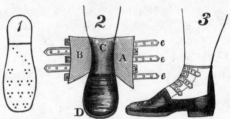

Figures 1, 2, 3, represent the sole, front, and side views. A and B show the laced lapping at the ankle, C the wide tongue, and D the sole.

I copy these designs from a communication to the *Field* by "The Forester," who is one of the leading sportsmen in England and Scotland. By the wear of these boots it is intended that the ankle shall not be easily sprained, and that the alternate lacings on each side of the instep keep the shoe more natural and firm than if laced on one side only; and, besides, the lacing is less liable to gape.

In the first place, the last on which the boots are made should be a shaving all round wider than the naked foot, and then the sole should be a trifle larger than the bottom of the last. The heel should be low, and extend forward in line with the front of the ankle-bone. The straps should be made of soft leather, and, being broad and flat, they gather the heel portion of the boot well up, and support the ankle and instep. The boots should be large, to admit a heavy ribbed stocking of wool, rather loose, for a weft too close causes the feet to be too warm. This writer objects to water-tight boots, and at night, after a day's sport, he drains his boots, wipes them out, greases them to keep them soft, sets them in a dry place very remote from the fire, and the next morning he dons them over a pair of heavy, ribbed, dry stockings, and is again ready for the fray. Use small tacks, placed in threes on the soles, and as they lose, replace at evening.

"The Forester" is doubtless right for a shooting-boot, or for a boot to fish along the stream for trout, or from the rocks for striped bass; but for wading, in summer weather, the pegged shoe of the American army regulation is the best covering for the feet.

Stiff leathern leggins, like those worn by the Zouaves, are useful to protect the shins when threading rough undergrowth of thorns and briers along a trout stream. For wading-boots I have found alligator-skin the best uppers for the feet, and Russia leather the best for the legs.

Getchell's rubber boots, lined with cloth, and with silk extensions above the knees, are the most perfect articles of the rubber kind.

AMERICAN GAME-LAWS.

AMERICAN LAWS FOR THE PROTECTION OF FISH, GAME, AND INSECTIVOROUS BIRDS.

The leading features of these laws are included in those for the State of New York and the Dominion of Canada, and I therefore give them for the benefit of the remaining part of North America, as the laws for regulating the protection and capture of game and fresh-water fishes should be similar throughout the United States and their borders.

GAME-LAWS OF THE STATE OF NEW YORK.

An Act to amend and consolidate the several acts relating to the Preservation of Moose, Wild Deer, Birds, and Fresh-water Fish, passed May 13, 1867.

The People of the State of New York, represented in Senate and Assembly, do enact as follows:

MOOSE AND DEER.

SEC. 1. No person shall kill, or pursue with intent to kill, any moose or wild deer save only during the months of August, September, October, November, and up to and inclusive of the 10th day of December, or shall expose for sale, or have in his or her possession, any green moose or deer skin, or fresh venison, save only in the months aforesaid, and up to and inclusive of the 10th of December.

WILD FAWN AND GRAY RABBITS.

SEC. 2. No person shall at any time kill any wild fawn during the periods when such fawn is in its spotted coat, or expose for sale, or have at any time in his or her possession, any spotted wild·fawn skin, or any gray rabbit, from the 1st of February to the 1st of November.

WILD PIGEONS.

SEC. 3. No person shall kill, or catch, or discharge any fire-arm at any wild pigeon while in any nesting-ground, or break up or in any manner disturb such nesting-ground, or the nests or birds therein, or discharge any fire-arm at any distance within a quarter of a mile of such nesting-place at such pigeon.

WILD-FOWL.

SEC. 4. No person shall kill, or expose for sale, or have in his possession after the same is killed, any wood duck (commonly called black duck), gray duck (commonly called summer duck), mallard, or teal duck, between the 1st day of February and the 15th day of August in each year. No person shall at any time kill any wild duck, goose, or other wild-fowl, with or by means of the device or instrument known as swivel or punt gun, or with or by means of any gun other than such guns as are habitually raised at arm's length and fired from the shoulder, or shall use any such device, or instrument, or gun other than such gun as aforesaid, with intent to kill any such duck, goose, or other wild-fowl. No person shall in any manner kill, or molest with intent to kill, any wild ducks, geese, or other wild-fowl, while the same are sitting at night upon their resting-places. But this section shall not apply to waters of Long Island Sound or the Atlantic Ocean.

PENALTY FOR VIOLATION.

SEC. 5. Any person violating the foregoing provisions of this act shall be deemed guilty of a misdemeanor, and shall likewise be liable to a penalty of fifty dollars for each offense.

INSECTIVOROUS BIRDS.

SEC. 6. No person shall at any time, within this state, kill, or trap, or expose for sale, or have in his possession after the same is killed, any eagle, fish-hawk, night-hawk, whippoorwill, finch, thrush, lark, sparrow, yellow-bird, brown thresher, wren, martin, swallow, tonager, oriole, woodpecker, bobolink, or any other harmless bird, or any song-bird ; or kill, trap, or expose for sale any robin, blackbird, meadow-lark, or starling, save during the months of August, September, October, November, and December ; nor destroy or rob the nests of any wild birds whatever, under a penalty of five dollars for each bird so killed, trapped, or exposed for sale, and for each nest destroyed or robbed.

This section shall not apply to any person who shall kill or trap any bird for the purpose of studying its habits or history, or having the same stuffed and set up as a specimen; nor to any person who shall kill on his own premises any robin during the period when summer fruits or grapes are ripening, provided such robin is killed in the act of destroying such fruits or grapes.

PINNATED GROUSE.

SEC. 7. No person shall, at any time within ten years from the passage of this act, kill any pinnated grouse, commonly called the prairie-fowl, unless upon grounds owned by them, and grouse placed thereon by said owners, under a penalty of ten dollars for each bird so killed.

WOODCOCK, RUFFED GROUSE, QUAIL, RAIL, AND PARTRIDGE.

SEC. 8. No person shall kill, or have in his or her possession, except alive, for the purpose of preserving the same alive through the winter, or expose for sale any woodcock or ruffed grouse, commonly called partridge, between the 1st day of January and the 1st day of September, or kill any quail, sometimes called Virginia partridge, between the 1st day of January and the 20th day of October, or have the same in possession, or expose the same for sale between the 1st day of February and the 20th day of October, or have in his possession any pinnated grouse, commonly called prairie-chicken, or expose the same for sale between the 1st day of February and the 1st day of July, under a penalty of five dollars for each bird so killed, or had in possession, or exposed for sale. Provided, however, that in the counties lying along the Hudson River, and Susquehanna River and its branches, and in the counties lying south of the north line of the county of Greene, and the county of Columbia, and in the counties bordering upon the waters where the tide ebbs and flows, it shall be lawful to kill, or possess, or expose for sale any woodcock, or rail, or ruffed grouse, commonly called partridge, between the 3d day of July and the 1st day of January.

TRAPPING PROHIBITED.

SEC. 9. No person shall, at any time, or in any place within this state, with any trap or snare, take any quail or ruffed grouse, under a penalty of five dollars for each quail or grouse so trapped or snared.

VIOLATING THE SABBATH.

SEC. 10. There shall be no shooting, hunting, or trapping on the first day of the week, called Sunday, and any person offending against the provisions of this section shall, on conviction, forfeit and pay a sum not exceeding twenty-five dollars, or be imprisoned in the county jail of the county where the offense was committed not less than ten days nor more than twenty-five days for each offense.

TRESPASS.

SEC. 11. Any person who shall at any time enter upon the lawn, garden, orchard, or pleasure-grounds immediately surrounding a dwelling-house, with any fire-arm, for the purpose of shooting, contrary to the provisions of this act, or shall shoot at any bird or animal thereon, shall be deemed guilty of trespass, and, in addition to the damages, shall be liable to a penalty of ten dollars.

POISONING FRESH-WATER STREAMS.

SEC. 12. No person shall place in any fresh-water stream, lake, or pond, without the consent of the owner, any lime or other deleterious substance, with intent to injure fish; nor any drug or medicated bait, with intent thereby to poison or catch fish; nor place in any pond or lake stocked with or inhabited by trout, black bass, pike, pickerel, or sunfish, any drug or other deleterious substance, with intent to destroy such trout or other fish. Any person violating the provisions of this section shall be deemed guilty of a misdemeanor, and shall, in addition thereto, and in addition to any damage he may have done, be liable to a penalty of one hundred dollars.

BUILDING AND MAINTAINING DAMS.

SEC. 13. Every person building or maintaining a dam upon the rivers emptying into Lake Ontario, the River St. Lawrence, or Lake Champlain, which dam is higher than two feet, shall likewise build and maintain, during the months of March, April, May, September, October, and November, for the purpose of the passage of fish, a sluice-way in the mid-channel at least one foot in depth at the edge of the dam, and of proper width, and placed at an angle of not more than thirty degrees, and extending entirely to the running water below the dam, which sluice-way shall be protected on each side by an apron at least one foot in height, to confine the water therein.

SPECKLED BROOK TROUT.

SEC. 14. No person shall at any time, with intent so to do, catch any speckled brook trout or speckled river trout with any device save only with a hook and line; and no person shall catch any such trout, or have any such trout in his or her possession, save only during the months of April, May, June, July, August, and September, under a penalty of five dollars for each trout so caught or had in his possession; but this section shall not prevent any person or corporation from catching trout in waters owned by them to stock other waters belonging to them. But the counties of Kings, Queens, and Suffolk shall be exempted from the provisions of the above section so far as to allow the taking or catching of trout in the counties last named during the month of March.

SALMON-TROUT.

SEC. 15. No person shall take or have in possession any salmon-trout between the 15th day of October and the 1st day of February in each year, under a penalty of five dollars for each fish so taken and had in possession. But this section shall not apply to the waters of Otsego Lake.

BLACK BASS OR MASKALONGE.

SEC. 16. No person shall take or have in possession any black bass or maskalongé between the 1st day of January and the 1st day of May, under a penalty of five dollars for each fish so taken or had in possession.

NETS, TRAPS, ETC.

SEC. 17. No person shall at any time take any fish with a net, spear, or trap of any kind, or set any trap, net, weir, or pot, with intent to catch fish, in any of the fresh waters of this state, nor in any of its tidal waters inhabited by brook trout, except as hereinafter provided ; and any person violating the provisions of this section shall be deemed guilty of a misdemeanor, and shall likewise be liable to a penalty of twenty-five dollars for each offense; but suckers, catfish, eels, whitefish, shad, and minnows are exempted from the operation of this section; *Provided, however,* That nothing in this section shall be so construed as to legalize the use of gill-nets in any of the fresh waters of this state. But in the waters of Otsego Lake, seines may be used from the first day of March to the last day of August, and gill-nets may be used during the months of July and August; but no such seine or net shall have meshes less than one inch and three-quarters in size.

VIOLATION.

SEC. 18. No person shall sell, expose for sale or purchase, or have in his or her possession, any fish taken contrary to the provisions of this act, under a penalty of five dollars for each fish so sold, exposed for sale, purchased, or had in possession, with intent to violate the provisions of this act.

TRESPASSING.

SEC. 19. Any person trespassing on any lands for the purpose of taking fish from any private pond, stream, or spring, after public notice on the part of the owner or occupant thereof, or of said lands, not to so trespass, shall be deemed guilty of trespass, and in addition to any damages recoverable by law, shall be liable to the owner, lessee, or occupant in a penalty of twenty-five dollars for each offense.

HOW PENALTIES ARE RECOVERED.

SEC. 20. All penalties imposed under the provisions of this act may be recovered, with cost of suit, by any person or persons in his or their own names, before any justice of the peace in the county where the offense was committed or where the defendant resides ; or when such suit shall be brought in the City of New York, before any justice of any of the District Courts or of the Marine Court of said city ; or such penalties may be recovered in an action in the Supreme Court of this state, by any person or persons, in his or their own names ; which action shall be governed by the same rules as other actions in said Supreme Court, except that in a recovery by the plaintiff or plaintiffs in such suit in said court, costs shall be allowed to such plaintiff or plaintiffs, without regard to the amount of such recovery; and any District Court judge, justice of the peace, police, or other magistrate, is authorized, upon receiving sufficient security for costs on the part of the complainant, and sufficient proof by affidavit of the violation of the provisions of this act, by any person being temporarily within his jurisdiction, but not residing therein, or by any person whose name and residence are unknown, to issue his warrant, and have such offender committed or held to bail to answer the charge against him ; and any District Court judge, justice of the peace, police, or other magistrate, may, upon proof of probable cause to believe in the concealment of any game or fish mentioned in this act, during any of the prohibited periods, issue his search warrant and cause search to be made in any house, market-boat, car, or other building, and for that end may cause any apartment, chest, box, locker, or crate to be broken open and the contents examined. Any penalties, when collected, shall be paid by the court before which conviction shall be had, one half to the overseers of the poor, for the use of the poor of the town in which conviction is had, and the remainder to the prosecutor. On the non-payment of the penalty, the defendant shall be committed to the common jail of the county for a period of not less than five days, and at the rate of one day for each dollar of the amount of the judgment, where the sum is over five dollars in amount. Any court of special sessions in this state shall have jurisdiction to try and dispose of all and any of the offenses arising in the same county against the provisions of this act ; and every justice of the peace shall have jurisdiction within his county of actions to recover any penalty hereby given or created.

POSSESSION OF GAME PRIOR TO PROHIBITED PERIOD.

SEC. 21. Any person proving that the birds, fish, skins, or animals found in his or her possession during the prohibited periods were killed prior to such periods, or were killed in any place outside of the limits of this state, and that the law of such place did not prohibit such killing, shall be exempted from the penalties of this act.

COMMON CARRIERS AND EXPRESS COMPANIES.

SEC. 22. In all prosecutions under this act, it shall be competent for common carriers or express companies to show that the inhibited article in his or their possession came into such possession in another state, in which state the law did not prohibit such possession, and such showing shall be deemed a defense in such prosecution. No action for a penalty under the provisions of this act shall be settled or compromised, except upon the payment into court of the full amount of such penalty, unless upon such terms and conditions as may be imposed by the district attorney of the county in which such action shall have been brought.

LAKE ONTARIO.

SEC. 23. Nothing in this act contained shall apply to fish caught or to the taking of fish in the waters of Lake Ontario, or any of its bays or estuaries within the counties of Oswego, Jefferson, and St. Lawrence, nor to the catching of fish in any way in the St. Lawrence River.

ONEIDA LAKE.

SEC. 24. The provisions of this act shall not be deemed to apply to or affect the taking of fish in Oneida Lake, at a distance of one mile beyond the shores thereof.

KENNYETTO CREEK AND SACANDAGA VLAIE.

SEC. 25. It shall be unlawful to use or draw, for the taking of fish of any kind whatever, any seine or net in Kennyetto or Fondasbush Creek, in the county of Fulton, or in the Sacandaga Vlaie, or in any part thereof in said county, above the covered bridge, near the village of Fish House, commonly known as the "Vlaie Creek Bridge," or in any of the streams emptying into the said Vlaie.

VIOLATING THE PROVISIONS OF THE PRECEDING SECTION.

SEC. 26. Any person violating the provisions of the preceding section shall, upon conviction thereof, be deemed guilty of a misdemeanor, and also liable to a penalty of twenty-five dollars, which may be recovered in the manner prescribed in section twenty of said chapter eight hundred and ninety-eight, hereby amended.

REPEAL OF PREVIOUS ACTS.

SEC. 27. All acts and parts of acts inconsistent with the provisions of this act are hereby repealed, except chapter one hundred and seventy-three of laws of eighteen hundred and sixty-one, which is hereby continued in full force and effect.

SEC. 28. This act shall take effect immediately.

Passed May 9, 1868.

State of New York, } ss:
Office of the Secretary of State, } ss:

I have compared the preceding with the original law on file in this office, and do hereby certify that the same is a correct transcript therefrom and of the whole of said original law. HOMER A. NELSON, Secretary of State.

The following is the act of 1861, referred to in section 27:

An act for the Preservation of Fish in Canandaigua Lake and the outlet thereof, lying in the Counties of Ontario and Yates.

The People of the State of New York, represented in Senate and Assembly, do enact as follows:

SEC. 1. It shall not be lawful for any person or persons to take, catch, or procure, in or from Canandaigua Lake, or the inlet thereof, lying within the Counties of Ontario and Yates, any fish, with or by means of any seine, gill-net, or other net.

SEC. 2. No person shall knowingly sell, or offer for sale, any fish caught in or from said lake, or inlet thereof, contrary to the provisions of the first section of this act, and it shall be unlawful for any person knowingly to purchase any fish so taken in or from said lake or inlet.

SEC. 3. Whoever shall violate any or either of the provisions of this act shall be deemed guilty of a misdemeanor, and shall also be subject to a penalty for each offense of not less than ten nor more than twenty-five dollars, to be recovered in a civil action, with costs, as hereinafter provided.

SEC. 4. Any person may bring or prosecute an action in his own name for the recovery of the fines or penalties imposed by this act, before any justice of the peace of either of said counties, upon first giving to such justice of the peace security for costs, satisfactory to such justice, in case he shall fail to recover ; and in case of a recovery, the amount thereof, when collected, shall be paid to the court before which such an action shall be prosecuted, together with costs of such suit. The court before which such action shall be brought shall certify the reasonable costs and expenses thereof, and pay the same out of the moneys so received, and shall pay the residue thereof, if any, to the treasurer of the county in which such action is brought, for the support of the poor of said county.

SEC. 5. All laws inconsistent with this act are hereby repealed.

SEC. 6. This act shall take effect immediately.

Passed April 12, 1861.

THE GAME AND FISHERY LAWS OF THE DOMINION OF CANADA FOR EIGHTEEN HUNDRED AND SIXTY-NINE.

(By EDWARD C. BARBER, Esq., Ottawa, Author of "The Crack Shot," etc., etc.)

ONTARIO AND QUEBEC.

Since the last issue of the *Year-Book*, very considerable changes have been made in the game-laws of the Provinces of Ontario and Quebec. The fishery-laws of the Dominion have also been revised to some extent, and it is now believed that if sportsmen will respect the provisions of the acts, and aid in enforcing the penalty against the poacher for infractions thereof, game and fish will again become plentiful.

It is greatly to be regretted that the Legislatures of the different provinces have not provided the means for carrying out their various enactments on the subject of the protection of game, and herein is felt the inconvenience of these matters being dealt with in detail by the various provinces instead of by the Dominion. Had the Dominion Legislature been vested with the power of legislating upon the subject of game as well as upon the fisheries, the fishery overseers might have been made efficient aids to the different game-clubs throughout the country. To those of Quebec and Montreal much praise is due for their efforts to protect game ; but it is absurd to suppose that individual effort can stay the devastating hand of the pot-hunter. Much good would be accomplished if the municipalities could be induced to afford their aid.

In Ontario, the close season for deer or fawn, elk, moose or cariboo, extends from the 1st of December to the succeeding 1st of September, not to be trapped ; the close season for wild turkey, grouse, pheasant, and partridge is between the 1st of January and the 1st of September ; for quail between the 1st of January and the 1st of October ; and for woodcock and snipe from the 1st of March to the 12th of August ; and no wild swan, goose, or *any* description of duck is allowed to be killed between the 15th day of April and the 10th day of August ; neither is it to be trapped, or taken by means of traps, snares, or springs, or killed by any other method than by shooting. It is also unlawful to use sunken punts or batteries, or night lights.   No eggs of any kind of the birds above enumerated are allowed to be taken or destroyed at any time. No beaver, muskrat, mink, sable, otter or fisher, is to be taken or trapped between the 1st of May and the 15th of November.*   There is also a clause protecting any particular kind of game that may be imported by parties desirous of breeding the same.   The fine varies from $2 to $25 for each head of game illegally killed, and in default of payment offenders are imprisoned in a common jail for a term not exceeding thirty days.

Speckled trout can be taken between the 1st of January and the 1st of October, but only by angling by hand with hook and line.   Whitefish or salmon-trout are not to be taken by *any* means between the 19th of November and the 1st of December, nor by means of any kind of seine between the 30th of May and the 1st of August.   The close seasons for bass, pickerel, maskinongé, and other fish are to be fixed by the governor in Council, to suit different localities.

In Quebec, the close season for elk, moose, cariboo, deer, fawn, or hare, is from the 1st of February to the 1st of September ; for grouse, ptarmigan, partridge, woodcock, or snipe, between the 1st of March and the 1st of September. No wild swan, wild goose, or *any* kind of wild duck is allowed to be shot at, trapped, or killed between the 20th of May and the 1st of September, except in that part of the province east of the Brandy Pots, where the inhabitants are allowed, for *food only*, to kill the same between the 1st of September and the 1st of June.   Neither is it lawful to kill any of the above between sunset and sunrise.   All the game animals and birds mentioned in the act *except* hares and partridges are protected from trapping.   No eggs of any of the kinds of birds mentioned, or any species of wild-fowl, are allowed to be disturbed, injured, or taken.

No lynx, wild cat, mink, or marten to be taken or killed between the 15th of April and the 1st of November ; no otter between the 1st of May and the 1st of November ; no beaver between the 30th of April and the 1st of September ; no muskrat between the 1st of June and the 21st of October.   Nor shall any person buy, sell, or have in his or her possession any unseasonable skin of any of the said animals.

Fines vary from $1 to $50, and in default of *immediate* payment the penalty is imprisonment in the common jail for a term not exceeding three months. No proceeding under this act can be set aside by *certiorari*, an appeal only lying to the Circuit Court of the chief place of the district wherein the offense was committed.   The jurisdiction is very summary, and the general provisions very stringent.   No kind of trout (or lunge) can be taken between the 1st of October and the 1st of January ; whitefish and salmon-trout are not to be taken in any way between the 19th of November and the 1st of December, nor by means of any kind of seine between the 31st of July and the 1st of December ; between the 31st of October and the 31st of December it is unlawful to kill shad or whitefish in Missisquoi Bay, Lake Champlain ; salmon can not be fished for in Ontario and Quebec, or the River Restigouche (N. B.), between the 31st of July and the 1st of May, except by fly surface-

* The close season for hare is from the 1st of March to the 1st of September.

L L

fishing, which extends in Ontario and Quebec from the 30th of April to the 31st of August.

It is believed that much good has already been accomplished by the recent act for the protection of insectivorous birds. By its provisions it is made unlawful to kill or snare, between the 1st of March and the 1st of August, any kind of bird whatsoever except eagles, falcons, hawks, wild pigeons, kingfishers, crows, and ravens. This act applies to both Ontario and Quebec.

NEW BRUNSWICK.

The law in this province is very strict as regards moose, the only game-laws of the province being those relating to the protection of moose and partridge. The close season only extends from the 1st of February to the 1st of May: fine $40; and any one is empowered to kill any dog found hunting within the prohibited time. No one is allowed to kill more than two moose within a period of twelve months: $12 for each offense. The killing, except for food, is prohibited; and leaving the carcass in the woods subjects the offender to a fine of $20. Partridges are not to be killed between the 1st of March and the 1st of September. There was an act making it unlawful to kill deer on the island of Grand Menan for a period of three years, but it expired June 8, 1868. The fishery regulations are the same as those of Quebec and Ontario, except that the close season for salmon is, for net-fishing, from the 15th of August to the 1st of March, and fly surface-fishing from the 15th of September to the 1st of March.

NOVA SCOTIA.

Chapter 92 of the Revised Statutes of Nova Scotia has also been amended, and now reads that no moose shall be killed between the 1st of January and the 1st of September; no cariboo between the 1st of March and the 1st of September. The close time for partridge is from the 1st of January to the 1st of September; and for woodcock and snipe, from the 1st of March to the 1st of September. The prohibitions respecting the killing of cow moose, and the limitation of the number allowed to be killed, have been removed. Pheasants are not allowed to be killed. The export of moose and cariboo hides is prohibited: fine from $20 to $50, and forfeiture of the game or hides. Otters, minks, and muskrats are not allowed to be killed between the 1st of May and the 1st of November, under a penalty of $8. It is absolutely forbidden to kill robins, swallows, sparrows, etc., and birds of song. Penalty $1 for each bird so killed.

The anomaly of the game-laws being dealt with by the various provinces in detail is strikingly apparent when the close seasons are considered, e. g. : In Ontario the legal time for killing deer ends on the 1st of December; but in Quebec it is lawful to kill until the 1st of February. The same with regard to ducks : In Ontario the sportsman is debarred from knocking them over after the 1st of March, but his Quebec brother can pop away at them until the 20th of May ; and so in other instances. This causes, and will continue to cause, a great deal of trouble to secure convictions against parties for illegally killing game. These provinces being only separated by the River

Ottawa makes it difficult to establish the fact of the illegal killing. Would it not be well to have a convention of sportsmen agree on close seasons that would answer for all the provinces, and press the adoption of them in their respective Legislatures? Of course there are difficulties in the way, but these could easily be got over if sportsmen would only approach them in a candid and conciliatory spirit.

PRINCE EDWARD ISLAND.

The game-laws of Prince Edward Island prohibit the killing of partridges between the 1st of March and the 1st of October, and salmon in the fall.

NEWFOUNDLAND.

There is only one game-law in this island, entitled "An act for the Protection and Breeding of Wild-fowl and Game." It prohibits the killing, taking, purchasing, selling, or possessing of partridges from the 20th of February to the 25th of August, and applies a similar prohibition in the case of snipe, or any other wild or migratory birds frequenting for the purpose of incubation (except wild geese), from the 1st of April to the 20th of August.

BRITISH COLUMBIA.

It is unlawful to buy, or sell, or exhibit for sale, any deer or elk between the 1st of March and the 1st of August; or any grouse, prairie-fowl, or partridge, or to destroy or collect their eggs, between the 1st of March and the 10th of August. Fine $50, or three months' imprisonment.

A WORD IN CONCLUSION.

And now, brethren of the angle—students in fish-culture—men anxious to develop American fisheries and establish effective game-laws—farewell. If true anglers, you are sure to be gentle; and as the truly gentle are always virtuous, you must be happy. But the best friends must part.

I have endeavored to throw together some pleas in favor of the "gentle craft," and to hint at the importance of water-farming. If my mite, contributed to the general stock for the promotion of rational enjoyment and useful occupation, shall be found worthy of those readers whom it is my pleasure to honor, it will be a source of gratification to know that my labors have not been in vain.

Let neither prosperity nor adversity deaden "the fresh feeling after Nature" which the use of the rod and reel always heightens or confers. Whether overladen with good fortune or suffering under the shocks of adversity, forget not to take the magic wand and repair to the murmuring waters. "The music of those gentle moralists will steal into your heart;" and, while invigorating physical energy, your souls will be charmed, and your minds soothed and tempered by the music of birds, the sights of nature, and the sounds of inferior animals above, around, and beneath the enlivening waters.

With rosy dreams and bright streams, breezy morns and mellow skies, a light heart and a clear conscience, may "God speed ye well."

INDEX.